Jessica Dimmock

ARI BERMAN is a political correspondent for *The Nation* and an Investigative Journalism Fellow at the Nation Institute. His writing has appeared in *The New York Times*, *Rolling Stone*, and *The Guardian*, and he is a frequent commentator on MSNBC and NPR. He lives in New York City.

www.herdingdonkeys.com

Additional Praise for *Herding Donkeys*

"A telling look at the grassroots organizing base of the Democratic Party . . . While a scoop-rich tome like John Heilemann and Mark Halperin's *Game Change* can tell us a lot about how campaigns are won and lost from the top down, Berman's more thoughtful book is equally good fun in telling the story of the election from the bottom up."   —Dana Goldstein, *The American Prospect*

"Berman's voluminous reporting . . . chronicles how the Democrats' harnessing of grassroots activism ultimately propelled Barack Obama to the White House in 2008."
     —Chuck Leddy, *The Boston Globe*

"Berman approaches his subject with a measured objectivity, digging into local political divides and peculiarities with a gumshoe's just-the-facts approach."   —*Baltimore City Paper*

"Berman . . . knows his politics, and it shows."
     —*Washington Monthly*

"Berman's book is a worthwhile document of an American political revolution."   —*The Christian Science Monitor*

"Superb . . . draws back the curtain on what has *actually* been happening in the door-knocking, home-entering, meaningful-conversation-having politics of the last five years."
     —*Newcity* (Chicago)

"A timely reminder that the fortunes of both the Democratic and Republican parties have historically been cyclical."
     —*The Advocate* (Baton Rouge)

"Ari Berman tells the rollicking and rousing story of the fight for the soul of the Democratic Party that has reshaped American politics. Full of riveting revelations, vivid reporting, and a cast of colorful characters, *Herding Donkeys* captures the exhilaration of the grassroots insurgency that Howard Dean launched—and Obama seized—to realign our political map. At a time of disillusionment with establishment politics, this book is solace for the soul. It is a timely reminder that the grit of tenacious organizers and anti-establishment politicians in red, blue, and purple states alike offers Hope 2.0."

—Katrina vanden Heuvel, editor and publisher, *The Nation*

"Political reporting at its finest. In his spirited debut, Ari Berman takes readers inside the back rooms and living rooms where politics actually happens, but his novel vantage point doesn't prevent him from rendering the tough but fair judgments every great political reporter needs to make. This is a ripping account of the Democratic Party through an intense period of historic transformation."

—Michael Tomasky, author of
Hillary's Turn: Inside Her Improbable, Victorious Senate Campaign

"With a keen appreciation of political strategy as well as an eye for telling anecdote and amusing detail, Ari Berman tells the amazing story of the Democratic Party's revival. Berman's reporting vindicates the fifty-state strategy of Howard Dean and the determined organizing of Barack Obama—and shows why grassroots activism is still the most potent force for change in America."

—Joe Conason, author of
*Big Lies: The Right-Wing Propaganda Machine
and How It Distorts the Truth*

"Engaging and balanced—a stand-out book."

—*Kirkus Reviews* (starred review)

ARI BERMAN

PICADOR

———

FARRAR, STRAUS AND GIROUX
NEW YORK

www.picadorusa.com

www.twitter.com/picadorusa • www.facebook.com/picadorusa

Picador® is a U.S. registered trademark and is used by
Farrar, Straus and Giroux under license from Pan Books Limited.

For book club information, please visit www.facebook.com/picadorbookclub
or e-mail marketing@picadorusa.com

Designed by Abby Kagan

Library of Congress Cataloging-in-Publication Data

Berman, Ari.
   Herding donkeys : the fight to rebuild the Democratic Party and reshape
American politics / Ari Berman.—1st Picador ed.
      p. cm.
   With a new afterword.
   Includes bibliographical references and index.
   ISBN 978-0-312-61062-3
   1. Democratic Party (U.S.)   2. United States—Politics and
government.   I. Title.
   JK2316.B47 2012
   324.2736

                                                        2011035087

First published in the United States by Farrar, Straus and Giroux

First Picador Edition: February 2012

10 9 8 7 6 5 4 3 2 1

IN MEMORY OF JOHN ALEXANDER

This party has come from the grass roots. It has grown from the soil of the people's hard necessities.

—Senator Albert Jeremiah Beveridge of Indiana,
Progressive Party convention, August 1912

CONTENTS

HERDING DONKEYS

PROLOGUE

They said this country was too divided, too disillusioned, to ever come together around a common purpose. —Barack Obama

The news has just come through: CNN projects that Barack Hussein Obama will be the next president of the United States. Two massive video screens transmit the announcement to the hundreds of thousands of Obama supporters crammed into Grant Park, known colloquially as the Windy City's front yard, where forty years earlier Mayor Daley's cops brutally clubbed antiwar protesters at a disastrous Democratic convention. Downtown Chicago breathes deeply and lets out a collective cry of euphoria tinged with disbelief. There is yelling, dancing, weeping, hugging, stomping. At 11:00 p.m., on the dot, out strides the new first family—Barack, Michelle, Malia, and Sasha. The president-elect stands in the center of a huge stage, surrounded by two dozen perfectly arranged American flags. The crowd goes silent. All eyes are on him. "It's been a long time coming," Obama tells them, and the hundreds of millions of people watching around the world, "but tonight, because of what we did on this day, in this election, at this defining moment, change has come to America." The TV cameras scan the crowd for indelible reaction shots, none more instantly iconic than Jesse Jackson Sr. weeping tears of joy.

You won't see him on TV and you can barely spot him in the

crowd, but standing directly in front of the stage, roughly one hundred feet away, is Howard Dean, chairman of the Democratic Party. Though you'd hardly know it from following the campaign, watching the election night celebration, or reading the newspapers the next day, Dean deserves a great measure of credit for paving the way for Obama's unlikely ascent. The two men couldn't be more different. Obama is serene, elegant, and poetic—the quintessential celebrity politician, this century's John F. Kennedy. Dean is brash, rumpled, and gaffe prone. He throws his $125 JC Penney suits in the washing machine, carries reusable L.L.Bean shirts while traveling, and wouldn't be caught dead on the cover of *Us Weekly*. On election night, Dean wears a black suit, starched white shirt, and black tie—attire more appropriate for an undertaker—but there's a look of total calm and a wide smile across his face.

Dean has just come from campaigning in Arizona, John McCain's home state, and North Dakota, two places nobody thought would be remotely competitive but where Obama ran surprisingly strong. He stands next to his chief of staff, Leah Daughtry, a forty-four-year-old black woman, Pentecostal preacher, and CEO of the Democratic convention in Denver. Dean takes in the enormity of the moment—a Democratic president, a Democratic Congress, a 375-electoral-vote landslide. "In one night," he told me later, "we, the American people, managed to undo a significant portion of the damage imposed on this country over the last eight years. We still have these huge problems—the deficit, the war, income inequality, and so on—but we sent a message to the world that America was still the America that people believe in." He pauses, reflects for a moment, and then repeats himself in a hushed tone. "In one night."

Following his election night speech, Obama strolls to a nearby white tent where fifty of his top political backers have gathered. Dean and Daughtry nestle near the end of the rope line, in between Iowa governor Chet Culver and Massachusetts governor Deval Patrick. Obama walks down the line and graciously shakes hands with each one of his marquee supporters. "You did a great job at the convention," Obama tells Daughtry. "Thanks, Reverend." Then he gets to Dean, stops, and clasps his hand. "I want everyone to hear this," Obama says to those gathered nearby. "I wouldn't have won without you," he tells Dean. "Your fifty-state strategy laid the groundwork for my campaign and I will always be grateful. I thank you from the bottom of my heart." Daughtry is so touched she fights back tears. "It was a moving moment for Dean," she says. "To have the candidate say that to you is an important thing."

"That was nice," Dean says to Daughtry as they walk back to their hotel.

"Yes, it was nice," she responds. "And well deserved."

"He didn't have to say that," Dean replies.

"It's good that he did," Daughtry says, knowing full well all the criticism and mockery Dean has endured as presidential candidate and head of the party. Such recognition would've been inconceivable four years earlier. Back then, the Democratic Party possessed no discernible strategy, and Dean had been relegated to the dustbin of history. The battles he subsequently waged culminated in the triumph of that night in Chicago.

Yet the celebration proved to be a fleeting one. The fight to remake the Democratic Party and reshape American politics, which Dean kick-started, would continue long after Obama's election.

Four years earlier, on the eve of the Iowa caucus, books like Al Franken's *Lies and the Lying Liars Who Tell Them* and Michael Moore's *Dude, Where's My Country?* topped the bestseller list. After watching the Supreme Court hand the election to George W. Bush and their party capitulate in support of the Iraq war, the Patriot Act, John Ashcroft, tax cuts for the rich, and countless other sins, many Democrats had reached a *Network* moment. Like another Howard, Peter Finch's Howard Beale, they were "mad as hell and not going to take it anymore!" Precisely because of the tepidness and calculation of his challengers, Howard Brush Dean III—a Park Avenue kid from a long lineage of bond traders who ditched a life of privilege to become a no-frills doctor in Vermont—became an unlikely and often ill-fitting leader of the country's newfound liberal opposition, his plainspoken denunciations of the Bush administration and its Democratic accomplices rallying this spontaneous insurgency.

Dean ran for president, as the five-term governor of one of the country's tiniest states (Vermont's capital, Montpelier, has a population of 8,035), because he wanted to talk about a balanced budget and health-care reform. After all, he'd been a practicing physician for twenty-five years. But his campaign, quickly and unexpectedly, became much bigger than that—an experiment with a new kind of politics aimed at revitalizing American democracy, reviving the Democratic Party, and ending the Republican Party's electoral dominance. Dean's run for the presidency embraced and amplified a few unique notions that profoundly altered modern American politics, namely, that committed volunteers are cheaper and more effective than the same old crew of professional campaign consultants; that small donations in large numbers can do more than large donations in small numbers; that the Internet and new social-networking tools could level the playing field for seemingly quixotic candidacies and attract hordes of new people into politics for the first time; and that Democrats needed to compete everywhere, including in the hinterlands of long-forgotten red America, stand up for some core principles, and stick with them. The cause was as much about the means of doing politics as the ends. Dean and his followers fervently believed that the Democratic Party could still be fundamentally reformed and focused their activism toward that end. It wasn't about left versus right as much as outside versus in—the soul of the party and the future of politics were suddenly up for grabs. Dean certainly did not intend to become a catalyst for these changes, but that's where his campaign ended up.

It was a thrilling ride, at least until Iowans had their say. In the days before the caucus, three thousand Deaniacs from across the country streamed into the Hawkeye State in the numbing cold, donning bright orange wool caps of the variety usually reserved for hunting deer. They were known as the Perfect Storm. In case you've forgotten, the waves crashed the other way.

Dean plummeted even faster than he rose. His distant-third-place finish was humiliating enough, but nearly everyone who tuned in for his infamous "scream" on caucus night—listening aghast while the candidate emphatically listed state after state that had yet to vote, as if he were teaching a hyperkinetic geography course on cocaine— viewed the speech as a meltdown for the ages. The verdict among political insiders came swiftly: Dean was done. Predicted one Republican media strategist, echoing the views of many, "He'll melt and melt and melt until there is no more Howard Dean."

Who could predict that Dean's wild rant would become an unexpected blueprint for his party's revival? His campaign effectively ended after Iowa, but a year later, when Dean became chair of the Democratic Party in a stunning turn of events, he really did go to all those states he shouted out on that chaotic January night. So did Barack Obama four years later, in the midst of an endless primary that everyone originally expected would end with Hillary Clinton's nomination. So many of those places, red states thought to be enemy territory for Democrats, ended up holding the key to the party's electoral resurrection. Dean saw this trend before nearly anybody and got a second chance to do something about it. The Dean campaign provided the manual—albeit a messy, imperfect one—for a bottom-up mass movement in politics, and his fifty-state strategy provided the foundation for electing Democrats across the map. The Obama campaign proved it was willing and able to perfect both of these transformational ideas. In the wake of John the Baptist, Jesus came forth.

"They said this day would never come," Obama remarked as he stepped to the podium on January 3, 2008—the night of a very different Iowa caucus—his crowd deeply ebullient but the man deadly serious. "They said our sights were set too high. They said this country was too divided, too disillusioned, to ever come together around a common purpose." He was speaking not only to millions of Americans but also to many of the leaders in his own party, establishment mainstays who stereotyped his supporters as doe-eyed college students, antiwar leftists, and politically marginalized African-Americans. That's no coalition to build a winning presidential campaign around, they said, snickering. He'd be another McGovern or McCarthy or Dean, an insurgent flavor of the month.

The Obama campaign rode into Iowa talking about unity, transformation, and renewal, with signs that read, simply, HOPE. What kind of new age mumbo jumbo was that? Obama was mocked and underestimated by his opponents. Many in his own party celebrated his speech at the Democratic convention in 2004—when the Illinois state senator briefly electrified the country with an inclusive, poetic vision of a more perfect union—but dismissed his presidential bid. His campaign was a cult of personality and the candidate a false messiah, if not a crypto-Muslim socialist. The country wasn't ready to elect a black man named Barack Hussein Obama president, and certainly not in places like Indiana and North Carolina, dominated by old-fashioned, conservative, God-fearing Bible-thumpers. Even some of the most celebrated and towering figures in America failed to appreciate the redefinition of politics at the beginning of the twenty-first century. They couldn't sense the possibility of a new mood in the country, a reaction against the divisiveness of 9/11, Iraq, and the culture wars.

Obama could never slay Goliath. And then he did, because he understood what those who doubted his campaign didn't. The bottom could prevail over the top. This book will tell the frequently overlooked and untold stories of the organizers and activists who labored in obscurity to make his victory a reality. There will be dozens of books written about Obama and his historic election in the coming years, but most will focus obsessively on the candidates and their glitzy inner circles, devoting far less attention—if any—to the political upheavals, at the grassroots level and on up, that propelled the Democrats into power, created the conditions for Obama's election, and now hold the key to the success of his presidency and party in the coming years.

It's easy to forget that Obama's election was hardly inevitable, especially given the presumed and overwhelming strengths of the Clinton campaign. Nor was a Democratic landslide assured in 2008. Forty years after Johnson trounced Goldwater, the Republicans had assembled what Karl Rove hoped would be the "permanent Republican majority." The subsequent catastrophes of the Bush administration—though a major contributing factor—couldn't alone explain the Democrats' resurgence. After all, the arrogance and incompetence of Bush were all too glaring in 2004, and still John Kerry and Democratic candidates across the country lost. A new politics would emerge only if Democrats brought in new people in new places in new ways.

That's what Dean realized when he came back from the dead to lead the Democrats in 2005. At a time when leaders of his own party ran away from him and pundits scoffed at the impossibility of his platform, Dean had a simple message: there were Democrats everywhere—and soon to be a whole lot of disaffected Independents and Republicans—and under his leadership the party would travel to all fifty states to find them. No longer would Democrats be a party of eighteen states dominated by a small circle of well-endowed political consultants. This message proved surprisingly controversial for a business-as-usual party that had become accustomed to losing election after election. Many battles were fought along the way, but Dean's idea endured and eventually caught fire. Democrats in states like Colorado, Indiana, and North Carolina eagerly responded to the call, planting the seeds of a potentially massive political realignment. Along the ride, the fifty-state strategy became the fifty-state campaign.

In the early days of Obama's presidency, it really did feel as if a new day were upon us: he passed a $787 billion stimulus bill with ease, presented an entirely different America to the world, and effortlessly swatted flies in the middle of TV interviews. These glimmers of hope, however, soon gave way to the harsh realities of governing. During the fight over health-care reform in the sweltering summer months of 2009, the same old intransigences came back into play. It didn't feel at all like a fresh start in politics. In fact, things seemed as dysfunctional as they ever were in Washington, with Republicans smelling blood, the ascendant "Tea Party" movement demanding scalps, and Democrats unable to stop squabbling.

The longtime divisions inside the Democratic coalition that Obama tenuously held together during his general election campaign—between old and new, liberals and conservatives, establishment and grass roots—once again came spilling out into the open. Conservative Democrats in Congress used their red-state roots as an excuse to oppose key elements of the president's agenda, while liberal blue-state Democrats howled that their majority had been hijacked by a rogue group of predominantly white men from small rural states. Obama seemed caught in the middle of this fracas, unable to satisfy the many parts of his big-tent party. Welcome to the unintended consequences of the fifty-state strategy. What was the point of having a Democratic congressman in Idaho or Western North Carolina, Dean- and Obama-inspired activists asked themselves, if that person simply opposed whatever the most popular Democratic president in a generation proposed? Did all those unlikely victories in unexpected places render the party unable to govern? Even with the eventual passage of a number of historic pieces of legislation in 2010, such as health care and financial reform, and the repeal of Don't Ask, Don't Tell, the politicians elected to usher in a new era seemed incapable of solving the great many problems the country faced.

Dean soon found himself on the outs in Obama's Washington, unwelcome in the administration he helped elect. His old nemesis, Rahm Emanuel, a consummate Washington insider, took the reins of the White House at its pivotal beginning, before skipping out just before his party's disastrous midterm election. Even Obama's most loyal supporters began questioning the priorities of the president. These doubts were only magnified after the Democrats' electoral "shellacking" in November 2010. Was Obama still a champion of the grass roots? Or had Obama been co-opted by the very forces he promised to fight during his campaign? Did his tenure in the White House represent a profound shift among the American public or a mere electoral anomaly? Amid deep turmoil at home and abroad, what did the president and his party now stand for?

1 ★ INSURGENT VS. ESTABLISHMENT

I was the biggest insult you could have—an outside-the-Beltway guy who didn't want to play by the Washington rules. —Howard Dean

It was one of those expansively clear summer days in the Mountain West. On August 23, 2003, Howard Dean's campaign had just embarked on the frenetic Sleepless Summer Tour—ten cities in four days across 6,147 miles, raising a quick million via its campaign blog in the process. You could watch the dollar amount inch upward in real time on a giant baseball bat posted on the website. Dean had kicked the tour off in Falls Church, Virginia, then flew to Milwaukee. That morning he was headed to Portland, followed by Seattle, Spokane, San Antonio, Austin, Chicago, and ultimately concluding in New York City's Bryant Park. In between Milwaukee and Seattle, the campaign added an unannounced stop in the most seemingly impractical of places—Boise, Idaho.

Idaho didn't get a whole lot of visitors from national Democrats, except maybe for trips to their ski chalets and summer homes (John Kerry had one in Ketchum). "Let It Be Perpetual"—the state's motto—might as well have described the Republican control of government there. So when a few local Democrats in Boise requested some face time with the former Vermont governor, they didn't expect to get an affirmative reply. But Dean unexpectedly said yes, as he was prone to do with these types of requests. After much internal wrangling among his staff, the campaign figured it needed a refueling stop anyway, so what the hell? Let's go to Boise!

As Dean's chartered Boeing 737, otherwise known as the Grassroots Express, took off from Milwaukee, his press aide, Matt Vogel, announced the stop. The campaign was going to deplane for an hour in Boise and was expecting "fifty people or so," Vogel said. When Dean landed on the tarmac, 450 people were waiting to greet him, holding blue DEAN FOR AMERICA signs. A social worker named Delmar Stone could barely contain his exuberance. "The last time I was this excited about someone who could change the world," Stone said, "was when I heard about Jesus!"

Dean was not quite the Messiah, but he had been on quite a roll. He'd just graced the covers of *Time* and *Newsweek* and would soon shatter Bill Clinton's three-month fund-raising record by amassing an army of small donors over the Internet, using that money to air TV ads in six states a full five months before voters in Iowa went to their first-in-the-nation caucus. He now led in polls in Iowa and New Hampshire and had staff on the ground in twelve states and volunteers in all fifty. Assembling this kind of organization by August, said Dean's media consultant Steve McMahon, was "unprecedented. It's never even been contemplated." Dean's mad-scientist campaign guru, Joe Trippi, dubbed it "a frickin' revolution." Boise was living proof. If the campaign could draw hundreds of people for an unannounced stop in the Republican hinterlands, the possibilities were endless. By discarding the old playbook, Dean had become a new type of candidate, running a different kind of campaign.

Dean stood onstage behind a large American flag perched on a hangar. The five-foot-eight, 180-pound Vermonter, who was often described as "sartorially challenged," wore a blue and white seersucker shirt with the sleeves rolled up (it gave him a salt-of-the-earth look), dotted red tie, and black chino pants, held tight by his late brother Charlie's black and silver rivet belt, which he wore every day. (In 1973, twenty-four-year-old Charlie, the most likely politician in the Dean family, traveled to war-torn Southeast Asia and never came back, killed by guerrilla captors in Laos.) Next to Dean onstage rested another flag. "You see this flag?" he asked, grabbing it for emphasis. "This flag does not belong to John Ashcroft and the right wing of the Republican Party! This flag belongs to the people of the United States of America," he said sternly, with more than a tinge of anger in his gravelly voice, "and we're gonna take it back!" As it happened, Attorney General Ashcroft was scheduled to be in Boise the very next day, defending the controversial Patriot Act, which nearly every Democrat in Congress blindly went along with in the aftermath of 9/11, one of a series of capitulations to President Bush that Dean and his followers deemed unforgivable. The crowd loved Dean's fiery rhetoric and plainspoken populism, especially when he asked, "When are Democrats going to stand up and be Democrats again?"

At the end of the impromptu rally, Dean promised to return to Idaho as soon as he could. Indeed, he went back two months later during another swing through the West, prompting a local columnist to joke that he must have a girlfriend in town, he visited so much. There was some logic to the Boise visit—Idaho would hold its caucus between the Wisconsin primary on February 17 and a glut of nine primaries on March 2, and Dean was already preparing for a lengthy primary. But the larger meaning was symbolic, a message to fellow Democrats not to take anything for granted, for Dean's campaign—thanks to its grassroots support—could go anywhere, at any time, and leave its imprint.

A Democrat hadn't held a major statewide office in Idaho since 1994, the year Republicans took over everything. The last man to do so, former governor Cecil Andrus, happened to be in the crowd that day. "I've never seen this kind of energy in Boise," the seventy-two-year-old Andrus told Dean's adman, Mark Squier. A careful student of political imagery, Squier watched the scene with amazement. "There's a bunch of old-timers in the crowd," Squier reported to Trippi, "and they're going, Finally!" Squier punched his fist in the air to capture the intensity of the moment. "A Democrat who's not afraid to grab the flag and stick it in the ground . . . It's like they've been dying twenty years in the desert looking for someone that they can beat back with." Such experiences drove home Dean's conviction that there were Democrats everywhere, in the reddest of so-called red America, and that it was time for the national party to stop pretending they didn't exist.

Twice a year, the various members of the Democratic Party—state party leaders, representatives from the different interest groups, elder statesmen—gather for the biannual meeting of the Democratic National Committee (DNC) in Washington. During the election season, the Democratic candidates for president are invited to speak. These functions tend to be polite, sterile, scripted, backslapping affairs. That wasn't what Dean had in mind when he arrived at the podium on the afternoon of February 21, 2003.

Just a few weeks earlier, Colin Powell had gone before the UN and made what many pundits and politicians deemed to be an unassailable case that Saddam Hussein possessed weapons of mass destruction and needed to be forcibly disarmed. But Dean still wasn't convinced, and he was increasingly agitated by the unwillingness of Democratic leaders in Congress and on the campaign trail to question the Bush administration's march to war—and the broader failure of Democrats to challenge Bush on the domestic front. "The Democrats were shell-shocked, they were behaving like Republicans, they were afraid of their own shadow," Dean said of the mood at the time. "And the Democratic public really wanted something different." But he hadn't yet articulated precisely those sentiments, and no one really knew who he was. In January 2003, Dean still had only $157,000 in the bank and seven staffers crammed into a tiny office (the kitchen doubled as a conference room) above a pub in Burlington. Al Sharpton was leading him in the polls, to say nothing of John Kerry, John Edwards, Dick Gephardt, and Joe Lieberman.

At 10:45 a.m., Dean sat in his hotel room at the Hyatt Regency on Capitol Hill. He'd just gotten off a red-eye (his preferred mode of travel) from California and was operating on two hours of sleep, which even for a doctor/politician was pushing it. He was due to speak at 11:15 and hadn't yet prepared a speech. "So what do I have to say?" he asked his small group of advisers—media consultant Steve McMahon, then-campaign manager Rick Ridder, longtime aide Kate O'Connor. McMahon brought along his business partner, Joe Trippi, to feel out the candidate that day. Dean had met Trippi only a handful of times but knew of his reputation as a bit of a loose cannon, wildly inventive but deeply insecure and difficult to control. Trippi urged the candidate to pose a series of rhetorical questions about the decaying state of the Democratic Party. "Let's take it to them," Trippi said.

"This is a little incendiary for Capitol Hill," Ridder said worriedly.

"We need to push the button now to create the movement," Trippi responded.

"Movements don't win elections," Ridder said, "candidates do."

"This will create a buzz," McMahon chimed in, "but is it the buzz we need now?"

Dean, ever the pugilist, liked Trippi's idea. "Let's just draw the contrast," he said.

Trippi wanted him to say "What the fuck happened to the Democratic Party?"

Dean knew he couldn't be quite so explicit. "How about if I say, 'What I want to know is'?" Dean pulled an envelope out of his pocket, kneeled down in front of a coffee table, and scribbled a litany of one-word indictments. The entire speech, if you could call it that, was hatched in ten minutes. "There was a dynamic tension in the room," said Dean's campaign chairman, Steve Grossman, "that led me to believe that Howard had something he needed to say to the DNC, to the American people, to the media, and he knew this was the moment." But as was so often the case, nobody quite knew exactly what shoot-from-the-hip-Howard would say once he took the stage.

His staff had passed out little packages of Vermont maple syrup and cheddar cheese as goody baskets, so Dean started the speech with a line thanking his campaign team for its hard work. Then he paused, licked his upper lip, and got right to the point.

"What I want to know," he said in a deadly serious monotone, "is why in the world the Democratic Party leadership is supporting the president's unilateral attack on Iraq." So much for a formal introduction. Scattered cheers came from a group of supporters holding white Dean signs in the back of the room.

Usually, political speeches take a while to get going, but Dean chose not to bury the lede, as they say in the news business, and continued his refrain. "What I want to know is why are Democratic Party leaders supporting tax cuts? The question is not how big the tax cut should be, the question should be can we afford a tax cut at all with the largest deficit in the history of this country?" A few more isolated cheers. Most members of the audience sat uncomfortably in their seats.

"What I want to know is why we're fighting in Congress about the Patient's Bill of Rights when the Democratic Party ought to be standing up for health care for every single American man, woman, and child in this country." More nervous clapping and scattered cheers.

"What I want to know is why our folks are voting for the president's No Child Left Behind bill that leaves every child behind, every teacher behind, every school board behind, and every property tax payer behind." Dean was picking up steam, and amid a few more hoots and hollers people were starting to stand up and get in on the act. He waited for a moment, then delivered the punch line he'd unknowingly borrowed from the late senator Paul Wellstone, who was killed in a plane crash days before the election in October 2002.

"I'm Howard Dean," he told the room, "and I'm here to represent the *Democratic* wing of the Democratic Party!" The room finally exploded, with more than one person asking themselves, "Who is this guy?!"

Steve Grossman led the DNC from 1997 to 1999 and had sat through more than a few of these gatherings. He'd never seen one like this before. "The response to all of the candidates was rather tepid, but people flew out of their seats for Howard," he said. "The applause was thunderous." Grossman sensed immediately the larger significance of the speech. "He challenged the Democratic Party right to its core," Grossman said. "To some extent he was challenging the people in the room, but they didn't see it that way, because they were always chafing under party orthodoxy and many of them were grassroots activists and they were looking for somebody to galvanize them and pull them out of that morass." Dean emerged the clear winner of the early cattle call. "He just blew those people away," said Joe Klein of *Time* magazine. "It was one of the most effective speeches I've ever seen a candidate give." The question was, would it be a temporary blip or the beginning of something bigger?

The Dean offensive had begun. For Trippi, "it was sort of like love at first sight," he recalled. Soon after, he went up to Burlington to run the campaign full-time. He and Dean proved a combustible mix, like throwing vinegar on baking soda in chemistry class. "There's an unpredictability about Howard Dean that's mirrored by the unpredictability of Joe Trippi," Grossman said. "You never knew on any given day exactly how it was going to turn out." Dean's speech on February 21 marked the beginning of that wild ride, which would continue long after his presidential campaign came crashing apart.

"My goal was not to be the best friend of all the people I was running against," Dean said. "My goal was to win. And I thought the party wasn't going to win unless we underwent fundamental change." His DNC speech, more than any other single event, set the tone for the rest of the campaign and shifted the arc of the Democratic Party for years to come. What direction the party would take, however, was hardly a settled question. Could Democrats once again become a party of the people, motivated by core principles and powered by grassroots activists out in the states? Or would the party remain a Washington-centric institution, plagued by caution and calculation and dominated by a privileged group of mega-donors and political operatives? In the weeks and months and years that followed, Dean would become a folk hero to insurgent Democrats across the country, but also a marked man among a circle of increasingly discredited yet stubbornly unyielding power brokers eager to hold on to their turf. The fight was much bigger than one person; Dean was only the match that lit the fire.

A year and a half earlier, Dean strolled into the office of his top aide, Kate O'Connor, a thin, wiry, meticulous thirty-seven-year-old native Vermonter, and casually told her he was planning to run for president. She barely blinked. "If George Bush can do it," O'Connor told her boss, "then why can't you?"

In presidential politics, there are really only two types of characters worth paying attention to: the establishment candidates and the insurgents. Those in the former club rely on their lifetime of experience, well-to-do friends, media connections, and influential circle of advisers to bulldoze over their lesser opponents. The British writer Henry Fairlie, in 1955, famously described "the Establishment" as "the whole matrix of official and social relations within which power is exercised." Despite claims to the contrary, such an establishment most certainly still exists.

Insurgents, by contrast, possess none of these claims to power and usually start off broke and unknown. They must create buzz—usually by saying something unusually substantive for a politician that is counter to the position of the establishment candidate(s)—to get in the papers, which they hope will help them raise money. From the very beginning Dean was, by default, an insurgent. He hardly visited Washington, spent little if any time socializing with the political and media in crowd, and had never raised more than $1 million for any of his campaigns. "I'm going to be dead last in fund-raising," Dean predicted early on. He liked to be home on weeknights and in Burlington on weekends. Though he was happily married, his wife, Judy, a practicing physician, hardly ever campaigned with him, which had to be a first for any presidential candidate. Nor did she upgrade to cable television in order to follow the campaign from afar. Dean's own mother, an art appraiser in Manhattan, described his campaign effort as "preposterous, and besides, it's very expensive."

True, Howard Brush Dean III wasn't exactly a stranger to high society. His relatives came over on the *Mayflower* and hunted whales off of eastern Long Island. He'd grown up on Park Avenue in Manhattan, descended from a long lineage of Republican bond traders (his great-grandfather was a managing partner at Smith Barney), spent summers in the Hamptons (where his dominating father, Big Howard, played golf at the exclusive Maidstone Club), and attended a Waspy boarding school in Rhode Island and then Yale. Dean's grandmother asked Dorothy Wear Walker Bush, future grandmother to George W., to be a bridesmaid at her wedding. But after an uninspired stint at the white-shoe trading house Clark Dodge, Dean eschewed the stuffy corporate existence by moving to Vermont for his medical residency in 1978, taking up stock in the Green Mountain State. His neighbor Esther Sorrell happened to be the grande dame of the Vermont Democratic Party, which is how Dean got his start in the business, serving as a local precinct captain and rising through the ranks. A friend described him as "a member of the club with a strong fuck-you mentality."

Temperamentally, Dean was certainly more suited to the insurgent variety—frank, flinty, allergic to staying on script. He was the kind of guy who, though he could afford far better, drove a blue Chevy Malibu, rode a thirty-year-old mountain bike that his wife joked he'd bought for $10 at a garage sale, and painted his own house for relaxation, sometimes mixing paints to save money. His political consultant Steve McMahon recalled, upon first meeting him in 1992, that Dean was "remarkably and refreshingly honest and candid, and not a very snappy dresser. He didn't really fit the stereotype of a politician as much as he fit the stereotype of a doctor."

Dean knew he'd be an underdog if he ran, and circumstances gave him little choice in the matter. He'd thought about running for president in 2000, but Al Gore put the kibosh on that one. Since then, he'd had some time to think about the matter, and knew full well the odds were steep and slanted. Only one insurgent candidate · had captured his party's nomination and gone on to win the presidency in the past quarter century, and that was Jimmy Carter in 1976. As it happened, Dean had volunteered for Carter's campaigns in 1976 and 1980, and knew a thing or two about the man. He flew down to Georgia and consulted the former peanut farmer turned president, receiving what, by this time, could be considered predictable advice: go to Iowa.

It was Carter who put the Iowa caucus on the map, and that initial victory gave his campaign the instant credibility, money, and staff it so desperately needed. Dean knew that if he just did well enough in Iowa, he'd be in good shape in New Hampshire, where voters next door knew him. From then on, he reasoned, he could win a war of attrition against his opponents, competing in every state and going all the way to the convention if need be. He'd drive to every state himself if it came to that or fly cheaply on his favorite airline, Southwest, whose travel schedule he'd memorized.

Dean began the journey by following Carter's trail to the Hawkeye State. His closest confidante, Kate O'Connor, would also make the trip. They'd attend fund-raisers for local candidates, drop by a dinner for a county Democratic Party, meet with farmers and businessmen, try to do an interview or two with a small newspaper or radio host. "Who are you and why are you here?" would be the most common responses. To say they were winging it would've been an understatement. "We would go to Iowa and we wouldn't know anybody," O'Connor said. "People really did think we were insane."

Dean's travel habits were suited to life on the road; he packed sparsely, with a small carry-on bag, and, like Carter, stayed in supporters' houses, both to get to know the locals and to save money. If he had supporters in a given town, that is. At the time a lifelong technophobe, Dean eschewed a laptop or BlackBerry for a clunky cell phone, whose voice mail he sometimes had trouble accessing. Just like Carter, Dean stressed his distance from Washington and his record as governor—he'd balanced budgets in Vermont, given kids health care, and shifted the tax burden from poorer towns to wealthier ones in order to build better schools. What had his opponents done while Rome burned? Unlike his inside-the-Beltway competitors, Dean was sensible, honest, pragmatic. He wanted, he said, to be the candidate for "moderate Democrats, moderate Republicans and Independents," like John McCain in 2000.

In those early days, Dean was entirely unprepared for what would come next. Everybody was.

Everybody, perhaps, except for Trippi. He'd been dreaming up a radical campaign like this for a million years and was compelled to spread the news to anyone who would listen. Most chose to ignore him, as you would a crazy man on the corner ranting about the endtime. In a world of dapper political consultants, Trippi styled himself as a hopelessly shabby Don Quixote. Vermont congressman Peter Welch, who hosted the first strategy session for Dean at his apartment in Burlington, described Trippi as "the weirdest guy I've ever met in my life." While everyone else drank coffee and orange juice that morning, Trippi dipped on a can of Skoal and consumed what must have been a case of Diet Pepsi—a staple of any workday for him, Dean staffers soon learned.

Trippi loved romantic losers, quoted films about hapless underdogs, and, every four years, caught presidential fever like few in the business. He was there for Ted Kennedy in 1980 and Walter Mondale in 1984 and Gary Hart and Dick Gephardt in 1988 and Jerry Brown in 1992, when Governor Moonbeam raised $5 million in three weeks in $100 increments via an 800 number in a last-ditch effort to stop Bill Clinton. *Time* called it "the Touch-Tone Rebellion," led by "Public Enemy No. 1 for Establishment Democrats."

In the 1990s, Trippi decamped to Silicon Valley and advised start-up tech companies, which opened his eyes to the possibility of using the Internet and technology to democratize politics. Meanwhile, back in Washington, Newt Gingrich and his band of suburban culture warriors grabbed the insurgent mantle, and Clinton spent the bulk of his eight years in office fighting for survival. The 1990s were not a good time for anti-establishment Democrats. In order to stay afloat and moderate the Democratic brand, Clinton cut deals with the Republican opposition on issues like taxes and welfare reform—a hallmark of his "Third Way" strategy of triangulation—invited wealthy businessmen to sleepovers in the Lincoln Bedroom to raise money, and brought in the widely reviled hatchet man Dick Morris to direct his reelection campaign. Clinton proved that he was a "different kind of Democrat," not like those tax-and-spend New Deal liberals—but at what cost? Clinton skillfully won two presidential elections, largely due to his own personal charisma, but his party shrank during his tenure in office, losing congressional seats, governors' offices, and state legislatures. After Clinton's election, Democrats controlled 57 seats in the Senate, 258 seats in the House, and 30 governorships. When he left office in January 2001, Democrats found themselves a lonely minority, holding 50 seats in the Senate, 212 in the House, and only 19 governorships.

Politics had become an unseemly business in both parties. Decade after decade, campaigns grew more and more expensive, while fewer and fewer people voted. Civic engagement was at an all-time low, a disturbing trend captured in works like Robert Putnam's *Bowling Alone*. "Our politics has been trivial and even stupid," E. J. Dionne Jr. wrote in his excoriating book *Why Americans Hate Politics* in 1991. "For most of us, politics is increasingly abstract, a spectator sport barely worth watching." The soap operas of the Clinton years did little to refute that notion. With their majorities relinquished and their hold on power increasingly tenuous, a growing number of Democrats felt that their party had lost its compass (and just maybe its soul). Those sentiments only grew bleaker after Democrats suffered an electoral massacre in 2002, and Democratic leaders in Congress lined up in support of George W. Bush's invasion of Iraq and post-9/11 policies. As Dean would later say, "Democrats are almost as angry at their own party in Washington as they are at George Bush."

Dean was hardly the first person you'd nominate to lead a political rebellion. During his twelve-year tenure as governor, he studiously read *Foreign Affairs*—the holy grail of elite foreign policy wisdom—and for most of his life he'd considered himself more of a hawk than a dove; sure, he'd protested the war in Vietnam like many of his peers and flirted with voting for Eldridge Cleaver, but he supported the first Gulf War and Clinton's interventions in Bosnia and Kosovo. And he was often the target of progressives in Vermont, who found him to be too stingy with the budget and unwilling to spend money on ambitious social programs. "The left was always mad at me for something," he said. Dean got his start in politics agitating for a bike path rather than protesting the spread of nuclear weapons or U.S. aggression in the Cold War. He became governor only when, as lieutenant governor, his Republican boss died of a heart attack in office. Dean was performing a physical when he heard the news, and calmly continued the procedure before rushing to the state capital of Montpelier. But perhaps because he became governor by accident, Dean wasn't congenitally afraid—as most politicians are—of taking a potentially unpopular position. After he signed a bill in 2000 establishing civil unions for gay couples in Vermont, he received death threats and was forced to wear a bulletproof vest that fall and summer as he traveled the state. At one stop near St. Albans, an elderly woman called him a "fucking queer-loving son of a bitch." Such taunts were good preparation for a presidential campaign.

After 9/11, Dean had taken to reading the *Financial Times* and *The Guardian* and noticed that the European press was far more skeptical of the Bush administration's case for war—particularly the president's claims about Saddam Hussein's supposed weapons of mass destruction—than their American counterparts. Like a typical doctor, Dean did an examination and reached his diagnosis. If the evidence was, at best, mixed about Saddam's weapons program and ties to terrorists, then why was it so vital to unilaterally invade and occupy Iraq? Dean began to question whether Saddam indeed presented an imminent threat to America. "We cannot be successful in the long run by being unilateralist," he told the *Concord Monitor* editorial page as far back as December 2001, "and I think there's very little support among our allies for bombing Iraq."

As he kept speaking his mind, Dean marked a sharp break not just from his Democratic counterparts but also from the stage-managed and overproduced politics of the 1990s. As a governor, Dean had been a devoted Clintonite, but the times now called for a different approach. "What a lot of people learned from Bill Clinton is that if you accommodate and you co-opt, you can be successful," Dean said in the winter of 2003. "And Bill Clinton was very successful. But that role doesn't work for everybody, and it's not the right time for it anymore. It's a new time to be blunt, to be direct, and to stand up for what you believe. That's really the fault line—and the war is a piece of that."

His stance on the war suddenly made Dean relevant. And the Internet would soon grant him an audience and a platform the candidate could never have imagined. A new movement was about to emerge, but it was difficult to see it coming. The chaotic, unpredictable next year, full of exuberance and anguish, would have been impossible to script.

The all-powerful x factor for any would-be insurgent—a rush of positive publicity—swelled quickly after Dean's DNC speech, even though this was still well before the advent of YouTube. People began visiting the campaign's website in larger and larger numbers and asking to get involved in the campaign. Bands of committed supporters did one better and began organizing their own gatherings. If one had to put a date on when, precisely, Dean realized that the campaign was suddenly a whole lot bigger than he had ever anticipated, it was a couple of weeks after the DNC speech, on March 5, 2003.

That night, he looked down from the balcony of the Essex lounge in lower Manhattan and couldn't believe how many people were packed into the rectangular-shaped bar. Nor could he believe that a few hundred more had been denied entry outside, lingering in a block-and-a-half line on the streets of the Lower East Side. Dean was expecting sixty people, and more than eight hundred showed. "All of a sudden the lightbulb went off in my head that this was a real campaign," Dean said, "and my days of wandering aimlessly in living rooms were over." More amazingly, his campaign hadn't even put the gathering together. It was done by a group of volunteers through a then-obscure website called Meetup.com.

"You're number two in meetups," Kate O'Connor informed Dean one day.

"What's meetups?" Dean asked blankly.

O'Connor explained. A group of people signed up on a website based on their interests and then got together to discuss them. The site's cofounder Scott Heiferman first had the idea after watching *The Lord of the Rings* and realizing that fellow Tolkienites around the country had no way to discuss the travails of the Hobbit kingdom in person. The campaign figured Meetup could become a great way to identify a network of supporters, a good many of whom probably also happened to be *Rings* fans.

"Who's number one?" Dean asked.

"Witches," O'Connor responded. It had been a source of much consternation among Dean's Web team that the Wiccan coven still bested them.

News of the site spread like a game of telephone. O'Connor heard about Meetup from Trippi, who heard about it from a blogger named Jerome Armstrong, who heard about it from another blogger, Aziz

Poonawalla, a twenty-nine-year-old medical student in Texas who founded the first unofficial Dean blog and one day in January received an e-mail from a Meetup salesman. Trippi, who by March was up in Burlington running things, began pushing for the candidate to attend a big meetup in New York City, which would in turn inspire supporters in other cities and states to hold their own, generating press attention, money, and new recruits. He initially met resistance from some inside the campaign, who worried about holding a large event in the wake of the fire that killed ninety-six people at a Rhode Island nightclub, or preferred that Dean do a fundraiser instead. There was also the question of how many people would show. A meetup in Manhattan the month before, wrote the organizer David Nir, an associate at a hedge fund, had drawn a "very good turnout" of "around fifteen people." Nir was planning another event for early March. Trippi figured that in the wake of the DNC speech, the crowds would grow exponentially. After the number of RSVPs passed three hundred, Dean's scheduler, Sarah Buxton, gave the okay. They planned it for a Wednesday, in the hopes of making *The New York Times*'s influential Circuits column the next day.

That same week, the Bush administration continued to try to rustle up the votes for a second UN resolution to authorize an invasion of Iraq. General Richard Myers announced plans to "shock" Saddam Hussein into an early defeat. War seemed all but certain. "It is time for regime change," Dean told the boisterous crowd. "We need regime change in Washington!" No other major candidate at the time dared challenge the popular war president in such a confrontational manner. A week later, Trippi got his Circuits column, splashed across the front page of the *Times*'s technology section. "Like Online Dating, with a Political Spin," the headline read. "We had intended to run this as a traditional campaign—an underdog campaign, but a traditional campaign," Dean later said. "But then the Internet exploded and became this enormous, growing phenomenon."

Soon after, Trippi made the Internet the centerpiece of the campaign, which had not exactly been tech savvy up to that point. The server was based out of Colorado, and you had to call one of two people in Denver to make any changes to the website, no matter how minuscule. Staffers called it "fishing in mud." There were separate unofficial Dean blogs but no central one. Everyone worked on clunky old PCs. All of this soon changed. Around Trippi sprung a legion of tech-savvy underlings who came to define the campaign, for better or worse. They all had stories of how they ended up in Burlington, as if it were akin to a pilgrimage to Mecca.

Matt Gross drove all the way from Utah, told Trippi he blogged for MyDD.com, and was hired as the campaign's blogger. Gray Brooks, a tall, blond Alabamian, deferred his sophomore year at Presbyterian College in South Carolina and became a programmer for the website. Nicco Mele tried and failed to get into the March meetup in New York, quit his job at Common Cause anyway, and became the campaign's Webmaster. Joe Rospars left a job and a girlfriend in Sweden to write e-mails and blog for the campaign. Zephyr Teachout, an iconoclastically named Utilitarian from Norwich, Vermont, made a flowchart one day of all the different ways she could change the world. She figured the Dean campaign was her best route, so she took a leave from work as a death penalty lawyer in Durham, North Carolina, and became the campaign's director of online organizing. On the outside, soon-to-be-influential young bloggers like Ezra Klein, Matt Yglesias, and Nico Pitney talked up and defended the candidate on a proliferation of blogs and websites.

All this technological innovation struck those who knew Dean as more than a little ironic. At the beginning of the campaign—before Trippi arrived—the candidate and his top advisers, de facto Luddites, didn't even know what a blog was.

One day in mid-February, Teachout, one of the campaign's first staffers, rushed excitedly into the office of Rick Ridder, Dean's campaign manager pre-Trippi. "Rick," she said, "Howard just blogged!" For the first time, Dean had posted a message to his supporters on the campaign's website.

"You mean clogged?" Ridder replied, thinking of an old-fashioned folk dance still practiced in Vermont. "I didn't know Howard knew how to dance."

"No," Teachout responded incredulously. "Blogged. As in *Web log*."

Dean walked into Ridder's tiny closet office a few minutes later. "I understand you're the first presidential candidate ever to blog," Ridder told his boss.

"Is that what I did?" Dean cluelessly responded.

Such was the birth of the Internet Campaign.

In early May, the campaign moved into a spacious new office in a nondescript section of suburban Burlington. The Internet was now the only thing Trippi wanted to talk about. He'd sit slouched in his office, behind a desk strewn with mounds of empty Diet Pepsi and Skoal cans, hunched over a laptop, scanning blogs and chatting with Dean supporters all day and night. In those days each department of the campaign wanted to control the website and nobody knew who was in charge. A heated turf war was about to ensue. On May 13, Trippi called a staff meeting for 10:00 p.m., a seemingly late hour for a crucial business meeting but standard fare on the sleep-deprived Dean campaign.

A dozen top staffers gathered in the sparsely decorated conference room, sitting on folding metal chairs around a cheap wood table. Trippi stood in front of a giant preinstalled whiteboard and for the first time mapped out a legitimate path to victory. He detailed how the campaign was going to use the Internet to raise unprecedented sums of money, attract an untold number of supporters, and win the primary by bypassing traditional political channels in the media and fund-raising world. "We're gonna make history," Trippi said. "People might laugh at us now, but we're gonna build something bigger than ourselves." His scribbling—lines and lines that arched into the distance—looked like incoherent scrawl to a casual observer, but everyone in the drab conference room got the message. "That was a critical moment," Mele said, "because everyone got on the same page." After the meeting, Trippi created a PowerPoint presentation based on the talk, traveling around the country trying to spread the gospel of a new political model to skeptical political insiders. "Everybody I gave the presentation to looked at me like I was from Mars and probably on massive quantities of hallucinogenic drugs," he told *The New Republic*.

Trippi was particularly obsessed with MoveOn.org as a guiding light. MoveOn launched during the Clinton impeachment hearings but came of age and grew rapidly because of its organized opposition to the war in Iraq. "There is no way to understate the importance of what MoveOn and its members proved—that the net can be used to mobilize huge numbers of grassroots to take local action beyond their monitors," Trippi wrote in a campaign blog. They'd also raised $4 million for political candidates during the 2002 campaign, an impressive sum at a time when the Internet was just emerging as a fund-raising source. "They raised a lot of fucking money on the Internet and nobody else had," Mele said. Trippi called MoveOn's San Francisco–based founder, Wes Boyd, and twenty-two-year-old campaigns director, Eli Pariser, constantly for advice. Technically, MoveOn offered to help all the Democratic candidates, but only Trippi took them up on the offer. Soon enough, MoveOn's organizing director, Zack Exley, was dispatched to Burlington. The emergence of a new liberal power center, galvanized by the likes of MoveOn, both complemented and enabled the rise of the Dean campaign.

Thus began a remarkable spring and summer, when the campaign built a plethora of new tools that would fundamentally change political campaigns and the nature of public communication. "It was the most amazingly inventive, creative, intense, stressful, but exciting period during the campaign," Teachout said. "I'd argue that in those four months, all the seeds of what then became the Obama campaign were created." Soon enough, Dean supporters could plan events online and invite other Dean supporters in their area (a precursor to Obama's my.barackobama.com), create their own profile page on a website and network with other activists (a precursor to Facebook), follow speeches by the candidate and upload their own content to the campaign's website (a precursor to YouTube), call a list of targeted voters anywhere in the country from their own homes (technology that would become standard fare four years later), and receive campaign information via cell phone text messages (ditto). Never before had ordinary campaign supporters had so much power. Suddenly they went from passive consumers to active organizers. A grassroots army could be fielded in ways previously unimaginable. Building a "party of the people" was no longer a theoretical or purely aspirational undertaking. "Trippi knew that he had unleashed something potentially dramatic and unpredictable," Steve Grossman said. "It's like if you're in a chemistry laboratory and you're fooling around with unstable compounds. You know that you could blow up the lab, you know that somewhere in the back of your mind you are playing with fire, but you're driven to do it because you're pushing the frontiers of chemistry and science." A volatile experiment was under way.

When Colorado senator Gary Hart ran for president in 1984, nearly upsetting former vice president Walter Mondale in the Democratic primary, he talked about what he termed the "politics of concentric circles." Hart would drop a pebble in a certain place—finding a dynamic organizer in a given town or state—and watch the movement ripple out in waves. Hart's dictum made a lasting impression on Trippi, even though he worked for Mondale at the time. It seemed a perfect way to run a successful insurgency—"you could spread a candidate or a cause or an issue like a virus—starting with a small, key group of people and let them run wild," he wrote. "Unfortunately, back then there was no tool that would help you create the momentum." Thanks to the growth of the Internet, the Dean campaign was able to undertake what Trippi called "concentric circles on steroids."

To be sure, there had been plenty of innovation in political campaigns—particularly on the presidential level—before the Dean campaign. JFK conquered the television era in 1960, and Richard Nixon struck back eight years later by hiring slick Madison Avenue admen to produce his campaign commercials and rebrand him as the "New Nixon." George McGovern's campaign discovered in 1972 that a direct-mail solicitation could yield hundreds of thousands of dollars in small donations, a trend the Republicans soon took advantage of and surpassed Democrats at. Twenty years later, Bill Clinton's brash, jean-jacket-wearing young advisers pioneered the hard-hitting style of "war room" rapid-response communication in the age of cable news. A WWF wrestler named Jesse Ventura got himself elected governor of Minnesota in 1998 by almost exclusively using e-mail to attract supporters to his unorthodox campaign. John McCain raised $2 million in two days over the Internet after winning the New Hampshire primary in 2000. All of these were thought of as major developments at the time. Yet at the beginning of the new millennium, the Internet remained a primitive medium, and TV consultants and megadonors still prevailed.

On June 17, 2003, George W. Bush kicked off his reelection campaign with a $2,000-a-head cocktail reception at the Washington Hilton featuring the city's top corporate lobbyists and Republican fund-raisers, whom Bush, in a classic Freudian slip, once referred to as "my base." Each "Ranger" pledged to raise $200,000 for the campaign, toward an end goal of a $200 million war chest. That night alone, Bush netted $3.5 million, and his two-week fund-raising tour had just begun. That money gave the Republicans a marked advantage. Even before Bush's fund-raising spree, Republicans out-raised Democrats in every dollar amount except donations of $1 million and above. Thanks to the McCain-Feingold campaign finance reform bill of 2002, which outlawed unlimited "soft money" contributions, Democrats lost that lone advantage too. Republican election lawyers referred to McCain-Feingold as "the Democratic

Party suicide bill" and predicted they'd out-raise and outspend Democrats for decades to come.

Back in Burlington, Trippi calculated how many rubber-chicken dinners the Dean campaign would have to hold in order to even come close to matching Bush. Suffice it to say, the poultry industry would've made a fortune. If the campaign did things the way they'd always been done, Bush would make a laughingstock of whoever became the Democratic nominee. Trippi reasoned, from a purely tactical perspective, that the campaign had no choice but to go an unconventional route.

On June 23, 2003, Dean stood before a sea of five thousand supporters in downtown Burlington and officially announced his candidacy, unveiling a new campaign slogan, "You Have the Power," as in, "*you* have the power to take our country back." What seemed like feel-good hippie talk to his opponents resonated among Dean supporters, who liked the fact that he was challenging the powers that be in both parties. "Our founders have implored that we were not to be the new Rome," Dean said in his announcement speech. "We are not to conquer and suppress other nations to submit to our will. We are to inspire them."

That Tuesday, following the speech, $300,000 came in over the Internet. The same thing happened Wednesday and Thursday. On Friday, the campaign put up a picture of a baseball bat—a soon-to-be-familiar motif—to measure the progress, with a goal of $4.5 million for the end of the month. When the take jumped to $6.5 million over the weekend, Dean thought the website had been hacked. On the last night of the fund-raising quarter—numbers closely monitored by political operatives and campaign reporters, dollars being the only language Washington really understands—$828,000 poured in, with an average donation of $112. "End of Story, Howard Dean Is the Story," *National Journal*'s insider rag, *The Hotline*, declared. He was now irrefutably a contender, and quite possibly his party's nominee. It sent "shockwaves through the entire Democratic Party in June when that money all came in," Trippi said. If two million people each gave $100, the campaign could match Bush. That idea—stunningly simple yet profoundly ambitious—became the mantra for the Dean campaign and the small-donor revolution that would follow.

Over the Fourth of July weekend, Dean's pollster, Paul Maslin, a thirty-year veteran of the business, called up Trippi. "Joe, you know what this is, don't you?" Maslin told him. "This isn't Jimmy Carter or George McGovern or Jerry Brown or Ross Perot or any of the analogies people are making. You know who this is?"

"Yeah, I know exactly who," Trippi responded. "It's Andrew Jackson."

"If we really pulled this off," Maslin said, "you'd have the equivalent of that scene where Andrew Jackson becomes president and the people just break down the fence at the White House and say, 'This is our place.'"

Of course, Dean repelled as many people as he excited, most notably those Democrats accustomed to running the show inside Washington. Talk of a populist revolt sent shivers down the spine of Al From and Bruce Reed, leaders of the Democratic Leadership Council (DLC). "What activists like Dean call the Democratic wing of the Democratic Party is an aberration: the McGovern-Mondale wing, defined principally by weakness abroad and elitist, interest-group liberalism at home," From and Reed wrote in a fiery memo titled "The Real Soul of the Democratic Party" on May 15, 2003. Four days later, after Dean won the endorsement of the 1.5-million-member public employees union AFSCME, the DLC denounced the union as "fringe activists."

Since its founding in 1985, the DLC existed to break the power of liberal interest groups inside the Democratic Party and attract support from the business community. Former congressional aide Al From aggressively expanded what had been an informal caucus of southern and western congressmen into a $7-million-a-year operation at its peak in 2000. By that time it had five thousand members, and politicians, policy wonks, and lobbyists flocked to its annual summit. The DLC's support for free-market policies (and the money that brought in from major corporations) and its early media savvy enticed an ambitious young Arkansas governor into becoming its chair in 1990. After Bill Clinton's election, DLC strategists Bill Galston, Elaine Kamarck, and Bruce Reed became top domestic policy aides in the White House. When Newt Gingrich took over the House in 1994, From instructed Democrats to move to the right and "get with the [DLC] program." The DLC quickly became the new Washington establishment, launching state chapters, creating the New Democratic Coalition in Congress, and expanding its Progressive Policy Institute think tank. A top aide to Jesse Jackson groused of Clinton's Democratic Party, "The DLC has taken it over."

The DLC's accommodationist instincts—Clinton's strategy of triangulation was all about peeling off core Republican positions—led them years later to emerge as a key supporter of the war in Iraq. At a ceremony at the Rose Garden announcing the war resolution, current and former DLC chairmen Evan Bayh, Joe Lieberman, and Dick Gephardt flanked President Bush. No candidate embodied the DLC's ethos better than the hawkish Lieberman, who shared a pollster—the cantankerous Mark Penn—with the organization. During the campaign, the DLC, Lieberman, and Penn became Dean's sharpest and most vocal critics. "A Dean nomination could again mean Democrats lose 49 out of 50 states," Penn told *Newsweek*, without acknowledging why his own candidate was floundering in the polls. Indiana senator Evan Bayh echoed this broader ideological attack, proclaiming: "The Democratic Party is at risk of being taken over from the far left."

Ironically, in 1996 the DLC had praised the reelection of "the centrist Gov. Howard Dean" as indicative of blossoming "New Democratic leadership." Indeed, Dean didn't fit neatly into any prearranged ideological boxes, which helped explain why he was becoming so popular. He was socially liberal, fiscally conservative, opposed to the war in Iraq but generally hawkish on foreign policy, and had been endorsed in Vermont by the National Rifle Association and the National Association for the Repeal of Abortion Laws (NARAL). *Slate* noted that during the campaign he'd drawn comparisons to just about every possible candidate, including Bill Clinton, John McCain, Jimmy Carter, George McGovern, Harry Truman, and even Ronald Reagan. When Dean talked about representing the "Democratic wing of the Democratic Party," he meant standing up for some basic principles rather than pushing the party far to the left. The criticism of Dean by DLC types led some political analysts to wonder whether the DLC's animosity was more about power than ideology. "Mr. From fancies himself a kingmaker," wrote *Wall Street Journal* columnist Al Hunt, "and Dr. Dean hasn't supped sufficiently at his table."

Dean had become the messenger for a much bigger battle. "I knew very well that if I was going to be the front-runner, everybody was going to do everything they could to get rid of me," Dean said. "I had no connection to Washington, and I was the biggest insult you could have—an outside-the-Beltway guy who didn't want to play by the Washington rules."

The staggering amount of money that poured in over the Internet after his official announcement speech—in three months Dean raised more cash than he expected to amass during his entire run—allowed the campaign to do things that heretofore seemed both illogical and impossible. From the very beginning of his bid, Dean wanted to build an organization in all fifty states. "I didn't need fifteen or twenty percent in the polls," he said. "All I needed was twenty-five people in each state who would organize, and that would be enough." Vermont can be a pretty isolating place, but as far back as 1997 Dean traveled frequently to far-flung red states as chairman of the Democratic Governors Association. "We've got to go to the places where nobody else goes," he told O'Connor. He figured these appearances would boost local Democratic parties and candidates, give him a foothold in states no other presidential aspirant bothered to visit, and help his campaign once the race got past Iowa and New Hampshire and became a battle for delegates. Certainly no other presidential hopeful was crazy enough in May 2002 to attend the Wyoming Democratic Party's annual convention at the Outlaw Inn in Rock Springs. Dean returned to the Cowboy State two months later as part of another tour through the West, also hitting Colorado, Idaho, and Nebraska.

At the start of the campaign, crisscrossing the country didn't strike Dean's advisers as a very practical idea. "We literally had like $100,000 in the bank, and Howard wanted to have campaign managers in all fifty states," Trippi recalled, laughing. As a response to Dean's stubborn insistence, Trippi wrote a memo to the campaign staff arguing that "few successful national campaigns have garnered that success by embarking on a full blown fifty-state strategy. The demand on time and resources has almost always led to failure." In his office, Trippi scribbled four things on a giant whiteboard: Iowa, New Hampshire, Internet, and $. "If you came in to talk to him about anything else, he said 'Get the fuck out of my office,'" said his deputy, Paul Blank. "And believe me, he didn't say it nicely."

But as donations skyrocketed and supporters flooded the website, Dean's implausible fantasy suddenly became a workable concept. Soon enough, this fifty-state strategy became a badge of honor inside the campaign, another symbol of how Dean was running a different kind of campaign. As e-mails poured into headquarters, local volunteers were asked to begin organizing their states by holding meetups and recruiting more volunteers. Zephyr Teachout called it "hiring people for free." The campaign as a whole still focused primarily on Iowa and New Hampshire, but broadening beyond the usual battlegrounds gave Dean the tactical advantage of being organized in places his opponents were not—generating a ton of press and money as a result—and took on the larger significance of involving people in places the party had long ago written off. "The campaign got so much excitement everywhere that you had to have a fifty-state strategy," explained Blank, "because how could you turn down all these people who were excited about politics for the first time ever just because they lived in Montana? That's ridiculous. So we had to get them involved, and that's where technology was so helpful, because it meant they could get involved."

In August 2003, when George Bush retired to Crawford for his summer vacation, the campaign made a surprise decision to place a TV ad in Bush's backyard. Looking relaxed in a blue oxford shirt, Dean stood behind a row of trees and looked directly into the camera. "In the past two and a half years we've lost over two and a half million jobs," he said. "And has anybody really stood up against George Bush and his policies? Don't you think it's time somebody did?" The ad ran only in Austin and cost less than $200,000 to produce and air. Nonetheless, it generated a torrent of publicity for the campaign and $1 million in donations over the Internet. Texas became Dean's latest red-state obsession. Later that month, he visited both Austin and San Antonio on the Sleepless Summer Tour, drawing huge crowds. "In Dean, some backers see hope for Texas' ailing Democratic Party," the *Austin American-Statesman* reported. At the end of September, five hundred Texans spent a weekend knocking on doors in Iowa and New Hampshire, sharing their firsthand stories of disgust with George W. Bush. That same weekend, the campaign set the Guinness world record for conference calls, connecting 3,557 different phones in all fifty states. By early fall, Dean got his wish, and the campaign hired organizers in the states following Iowa and New Hampshire on the primary calendar: Arizona, New Mexico, Oklahoma, South Carolina, Michigan, Washington, Wisconsin, and Oregon.

Along with attempting to reshape the political map, the Dean campaign strived to reinvent the everyday practice of politics, fusing the birth of the new with the renaissance of the old. In many ways, grassroots organizing dates back to the beginning of the American Revolution and formed the bedrock of political campaigns until the spread of television. But during the TV era, old-school organizing went out of style. Political consultants who made their fortunes off thirty-second ads—and politicians and pollsters who loved the instant gratification of television—now dominated the landscape. Then-journalist Sidney Blumenthal called these consultants "the new political bosses." Paradoxically, it took the emergence of the Internet—a medium everyone thought would turn its users into antisocial automatons—to make old-school organizing relevant again and reestablish the sense of community that TV destroyed. Few people knew this storied world better than Marshall Ganz, a rotund, mustachioed sixty-year-old lecturer of public policy at Harvard University and expert on community organizing who became a key figure in the Dean campaign.

In the summer of 2003, Karen Hicks, the state director for Dean in New Hampshire, went to see Ganz in Cambridge. Hicks—a thirty-four-year-old native of Concord and a live free, die hard veteran of Granite State politics—had been running a pretty traditional campaign, relying on underpaid college students to knock on doors in support of Dean. Unfortunately, even though New Hampshire bordered Vermont, few voters in the first primary state knew who Dean was back then or were prepared to commit to his campaign. After knocking on seventeen thousand doors during the spring and summer, the campaign netted only three hundred new supporters, a horrendous return rate.

Hicks had thrown her support behind Dean, and not an established candidate like Kerry or Gephardt, in part because she wanted to try something new. She'd spent the 2002 cycle working on the Senate campaign of former New Hampshire governor Jeanne Shaheen, who ran against freshman incumbent John Sununu. It was a nasty, multimillion-dollar race, with attack ads on both sides. Shaheen lost by twenty thousand votes, and a GOP political operative later went to jail for jamming the phone lines in Shaheen headquarters on Election Day. When it was all over, Hicks realized, "we had increased the bar on cynicism rather than invite more people in." After the election, she went to India for six weeks and lounged on the beach in Goa, detoxing. Shaheen became national cochair of Kerry's campaign, and most of her campaign staff followed suit.

When Hicks returned, she heard all the candidates speak, but only Dean moved her. She first heard him at a house party in Concord hosted by Gary Hirshberg, the president of Stonyfield Farm yogurt, a local New Hampshire institution. "I remember being just shocked," Hicks remembers. "Literally, I went ahhh"—she grabbed her throat and inhaled deeply for emphasis—"when he was speaking. At that time nobody was saying anything close to what he was saying." She wanted to run a campaign that matched the unconventionality of the candidate and the grassroots energy he'd unleashed. "I knew I wanted to do something different, but I didn't really know what or how."

That's how she and her deputy Tom Hughes ended up having coffee with Ganz at Henrietta's Table in Cambridge.

"We're not getting the numbers we need," she told him. "What if we tried community organizing?"

"Oh, that would be interesting," Ganz responded. "We haven't done that for a while in electoral politics."

Not since the 1980s, when he'd helped elect a promising California liberal named Nancy Pelosi to the U.S. House of Representatives. Phillip Burton, his brother John, and his wife, Sala Burton, had represented San Francisco's Fifth Congressional District since 1964. In 1987, before Sala passed away in office, she named Pelosi as her designated successor, though she still faced a stiff challenge from San Francisco supervisor Harry Britt, a mainstay in the city's influential gay community. Pelosi had no organization, so Ganz and his partner Paul Milne decided to hold house meetings in the city to spread the word of her candidacy, a grassroots model pioneered by César Chávez and the United Farm Workers. "We had eighty-one house meetings in three weeks, and she went to seventy-nine of them," Ganz recalled. Pelosi won the special election narrowly, by 4 percent.

The idea of house meetings came from Chávez's mentor, Fred Ross Sr., a protégé of legendary Chicago community organizer Saul Alinsky. At the time, Ross and Chávez were trying to get Mexican-Americans in Los Angeles to join the Community Service Organization, a precursor to the United Farm Workers of America. The predominant organization in the area, the Catholic Church, opposed the union. So Ross and Chávez started holding house meetings "to go direct to the people," Ganz said. In a sense, house meetings created a social network long before so-called social-networking tools, like Facebook, existed. That's what Ganz wanted to do in New Hampshire for Dean.

Ganz grew up the son of a rabbi in Bakersfield, California, and headed east to Harvard in 1960. He dropped out in 1964 and became an organizer with the Student Nonviolent Coordinating Committee (SNCC), the campus arm of the civil rights movement, in McComb, Mississippi—the site of SNCC's first voter-registration drive. He lived with a black family in a KKK stronghold near the Louisiana border, registered voters for the integrated Mississippi Freedom Democratic Party (the reigning state Democratic Party was aligned with segregationist Dixiecrats), and taught Sunday school at the Sweet Home Baptist Church. The Klan in Mississippi famously lynched three college students that year, and there were twenty-four bombings in McComb alone. Ganz had a front-row seat to the violence and injustice that marked the struggle for political power in America, forever changing the way he saw the country. He called it "Mississippi eyes."

In 1965, he returned to Bakersfield. Thirty miles north, thirty-eight-year-old César Chávez was leading striking farmworkers, agitating for a union and basic political rights. Ganz joined Chávez as an SNCC representative. In 1968 they organized East Los Angeles for Bobby Kennedy in the California primary, proving that long-disenfranchised minority voters could be a force in electoral politics. Ganz helped transform the United Farm Workers into one of the most politically astute unions in California, then started his own organizing institute, but soon became dismayed by the rise of the "consultocracy." In 1980, for example, Democrat Alan Cranston spent $2.5 million on a winning Senate campaign in California. By 1986, Cranston had unloaded $20 million on his reelection. Pollsters and admen dominated the process, squeezing out organizers like Ganz, who made a living the old-fashioned way, talking to people. Ganz quit politics altogether in 1991 and went back to Harvard to resume his studies and teach. There was no place for him in the money-infested Democratic Party of the 1990s. "I never got Clinton," he said. "It was just never there for me."

It wasn't until Dean that he became reengaged with politics and the Democratic Party. In 2003, he kept hearing his students talk about the insurgent governor from Vermont. "It was clear there was this kind of energy that, to me, resonated with my experience back in the sixties," he said. When he asked his students why they liked Dean so much, it was all about one thing, he remembers: courage. "Dean was the one guy who said the emperor had no clothes," Ganz said, "and everybody else was chickenshit." He agreed to help.

On a scorching weekend that July, Hicks, Ganz, and all the principals of the Dean campaign in New Hampshire gathered for a retreat at the Browne Center in Durham, a bucolic town on the Oyster River. Campaign staffers slept and worked in small, spartan wooden yurts in the woods and showered at the local gym. Standing in an exceedingly warm, thirty-foot-wide circular room, Ganz plastered the walls with a series of large charts describing the building blocks of community organizing. He told his own story and asked those assembled to tell theirs, explaining how the campaign would be different from now on. "Organizing is not about marketing an idea as a cause or a service to customers," he said. "It is about entering into a relationship with one's fellow citizens."

Dean staffers would identify local leaders in New Hampshire through one-on-one sessions, recruiting top supporters, who would then invite fifty people or so over for a house meeting. They'd watch a short New Hampshire Public Television special about the candidate, and then the organizer and the host would tell their stories of how they came to work on behalf of Dean. "The story," as Ganz called it, was the most important part of the meeting, "a connection between the activist, the organizer and the campaign," Ganz said, and the vehicle through which the Dean campaign could build enduring relationships and multiply the number of committed supporters in a way no other campaign could. At their best, these meetings combined the social atmosphere of a Tupperware party with the intimate fervor of a church.

It took a while for organizers on the campaign to grasp this different kind of model. "They'd been told, well, organizers have no personality, and what you do is just carry the message of the candidate," Ganz said. "I was saying the opposite, 'No, you draw on your own experience, you establish relationships.'" Two of Ganz's graduate students, Lauree Hayden and Jeremy Bird, became top organizers on the campaign, covering New Hampshire's two sprawling congressional districts. Like their mentor, neither took a conventional route to politics, especially Bird, a bespectacled, hyperactive twenty-five-year-old. Hicks thought it was hilarious that when Bird joined the campaign, he thought GOTV—"get out the vote," the most common of political acronyms—stood for "go on TV."

Bird told his personal story at meeting after meeting. He grew up in a trailer park in High Ridge, Missouri, an outer-ring suburb of St. Louis, where his mom was a secretary at a high school and his dad a janitor at a gas station. They were conservative Southern Baptists who didn't much care for politics. Around the kitchen table, the family talked about how they were going to pay for groceries or send the kids to a doctor. As a child Bird needed Forrest Gump–style leg braces, but his parents couldn't afford them. "The kid's not too clumsy, he'll be okay," the doctor assured them. Quite taken with the church, Bird won a scholarship to Wabash College, a nine-hundred-person all-male school in the woods of Crawfordsville,

Indiana, where he studied religion and aspired to be a missionary. In 1999, he studied abroad in Israel at the University of Haifa. At the time, Ehud Barak was running for prime minister against the hardliner Benjamin Netanyahu, and the intense support for Barak on college campuses left an impression on Bird. "Most people go to the Middle East to find religion," he said. "I found politics."

He decided to attend Harvard Divinity School, with the goal of one day doing conflict resolution overseas. In 2003, he took Ganz's class Organizing: People, Power, and Change. Ganz required all his students to volunteer in the community, and Bird linked up with the Boston Youth Organizing Project, based in the tough, working-class neighborhoods of Roxbury and Dorchester. He helped forty or so kids fight for better funding for the area's crumbling schools. When Boston mayor Tom Menino ignored their request, Bird and the students directly lobbied Boston's city council, convincing them to veto Menino's budget and add $11 million in education funding. It was Bird's first experience with community organizing, and it opened his eyes to the possibilities of the work. "It was a formative experience," he said. "I always wonder, if it had been an utter failure, would I have been like, 'Oh, organizing, that doesn't work.'"

In March 2003, Bird heard Dean speak at the John F. Kennedy Library in Boston. "I thought he was honest and he spoke to a lot of frustration that I had toward the Bush administration at the time," he said. He graduated from Harvard that summer and went to New Hampshire to work for Dean full-time, overseeing the entirety of western New Hampshire, the political hub of Manchester, and the coastal bedroom communities on the southeast tip of the state. Instead of sitting in an office and supervising a bunch of deputies, he went to more house meetings than practically anyone. "Jeremy was going to be a priest," Hicks liked to say, "but we converted him to Howard Dean."

Stories like Bird's, defined by improbability and seemingly immovable obstacles—much like the birth of the Dean campaign itself—gave the house meetings their power. The *Washington Post* likened them to a "secular tent revival, winning over individual souls one at a time." As with a church service, becoming a believer required a bit of a leap of faith. Hicks wasn't sure if the strategy would work, but Kerry had sucked up most of the traditional power players anyway, so it couldn't hurt to try. With an added boost from the Internet, which helped voters find the events and allowed the campaign to closely monitor who attended, house meetings spread like wildfire throughout the state in a span of just a few months. A third of New Hampshire voters, one poll found, reported being invited to a Dean meeting. By the end of November, the campaign had held its thousandth event. For the first time in many years, the organizers and the supporters, rather than just the candidate, became the stars of the campaign. Dean's mantra of empowerment had finally found its organizational expression.

Unfortunately for Dean, Iowa came before New Hampshire.

On a rainy, unpleasantly windy Saturday in September, three thousand Iowa Democrats gathered twenty miles south of Des Moines in a gigantic hot-air-balloon field for Senator Tom Harkin's annual Steak Fry. Iowans like their food fried. The Iowa State Fair featured such delicacies as fried Mars bars, fried Twinkies, and fried pickles. So what better way to kick off the fall season of the Democratic primaries than over a plate of panfried steak, baked beans, and potato salad?

Bill Clinton first spoke at the Steak Fry in the fall of 1992, a boyish young governor in a pink and green plaid shirt spinning folksy yarns. He came back four years later during his reelection campaign. And there he was on September 13, 2003, dominating the spotlight and overshadowing the would-be applicants for his former job. Clinton appeared relaxed in a denim shirt and blue jeans, voice slightly hoarse with age. Unlike in 2000, when Al Gore barely mentioned his name on the campaign trail, each of the candidates praised Clinton and his legacy. "I am tired of Democrats walking away from Bill

Clinton and Al Gore," said John Edwards. "I think they're both going to help us a lot," Dean echoed. Clinton went out of his way to
praise all of the candidates, but Dean's advisers couldn't shake the
feeling that Clinton preferred the one candidate who was not there:
former NATO supreme commander Wesley Clark, who was due to
enter the race any day. "Folks, go ahead and fall in love, be for somebody," Clinton told the crowd. "But when the primaries are over, let's
fall in line." That sentence, in particular, aroused a great deal of suspicion among Dean supporters. "It was hard to mistake that for anything other than a shot across our bow," wrote Dean pollster Paul
Maslin, "and in our minds it clearly indicated that Clinton was, as
the rumor mill suggested, secretly pushing for General Clark."

In fact, as Dean gained steam, it was hardly a secret that Bill and
Hillary had encouraged the worldly, photogenic general to enter
the race. "Bill particularly was clearly talking up his virtue," super-
lawyer Alan Dershowitz reported after seeing Clinton in Martha's
Vineyard. "You could tell he was Bill's kind of guy." Upon Clark's
entrance into the race, Clinton's former campaign chairman Mickey
Kantor immediately signed on as a top adviser, as did former Clinton adviser Rahm Emanuel. In his book *You Have the Power*, Dean
tells the story of how Clinton called up a friend and told him: "I
need you to be for Wes Clark...I'm from Arkansas and Wes is
from Arkansas, we need to be for Wes." The friend said that he was
supporting the Vermont governor. "Dean forfeited his right to run
for president when he signed the civil unions bill," Clinton replied.
"He can't win."

Much of Clinton's former circle went to work either for Clark or
against Dean. Chris Lehane, Clinton's top spokesman at the DNC,
did both. A combative thirty-six-year-old, Lehane specialized in
the war room clashes of the 1990s, defending Clinton from the
"vast right-wing conspiracy" (he coined the phrase for Hillary) and
earning a reputation as a "master of disaster." Lehane started out
with John Kerry but quit when the candidate wouldn't step up his
attacks on Dean. He later joined the Clark campaign and arrived in

Washington in early December with a three-ring binder of damaging material on the Vermont governor, which he circulated to influential political reporters. "The Clark campaign did not single-handedly destroy Dean," *The Atlantic*'s Josh Green later concluded, "but [it] could certainly be charged with aiding and abetting Dean's collapse."

Lehane was hardly alone. Clinton's most famous political consultant, James Carville, lobbed bombs at Dean on a nightly basis from his perch on CNN's *Crossfire*. *Newsweek* called Carville "dean of the 'Stop Dean' spinners." "No Democrats closely associated with the Clintons are working for the Dean campaign," *The New Republic* reported. "In fact, it's hard to find a Clintonite who speaks favorably of the former Vermont governor. This evident schism is not just about Dean's opposition to the war—or even his prospects in the general election. It's a turf war to decide who will control the future of the party."

Dean, throughout his years in politics, had been close to Clinton. In February 1992, when Clinton's campaign was reeling in New Hampshire following the release of a letter expressing his opposition to the draft in Vietnam and revelations of an alleged affair with Gennifer Flowers, Dean—at the time a political novice—endorsed the Arkansas governor. Hillary traveled to Vermont to accept the endorsement. From that point on, Clinton became Dean's political role model. Both were moderate governors from small, rural states who supported balanced budgets, free trade, the death penalty, and welfare reform, often drawing the ire of their more progressive constituents. "I was a triangulator before Clinton was a triangulator," Dean said. But as he thought about running for president, Dean became convinced that the times required a fresh approach. "Bill Clinton got us back to the White House," Dean said, "then we needed to remember why we were there." Clinton's loyalists, in Dean's view, had trouble adapting to a new era in politics. "The problem is, after they won in '92, they didn't change. And time passes on and, you know, it was a different America."

Two Democratic parties had emerged over the course of the 2004 primary: one led by the Clinton wing and Washington Democrats who rallied around Clark, Kerry, Gephardt, Edwards, and Lieberman; and another allied with Dean, the emerging "netroots," and dissident members of the political establishment. The *American Prospect* dubbed them "the New New Democrats." So it came as quite a surprise when Al Gore, a longtime member of the former group, announced he was siding with the latter.

Dean had never been personally close to Gore. In December 1997, Dean went to see the vice president at the White House and told him he was considering running for president in 2000. Gore reacted coldly to the news, but Dean, naively, asked that the conversation remain between the two of them. Before Dean's plane had touched down in Vermont, Gore's aides had leaked the news of Dean's budding presidential ambitions to the Vermont press. Vermonters were furious that Dean was preparing to abandon the governorship, and his poll numbers plummeted. Dean quickly put his presidential bid on hold and endorsed Gore in 2000 before the New Hampshire primary. When he did run for president, Dean called Gore often for advice. At the campaign's urging, Dean's supporters also wrote Gore handwritten letters asking for his endorsement. Finally, Gore told Dean at the end of a forty-five-minute phone conversation from Tokyo on December 5, 2003: "I've decided I want to endorse you."

Four days later, just half a block from Bill Clinton's Harlem office, Gore, looking comfortably beefy in a black suit and blue tie, clasped hands with Dean. "Howard Dean," Gore declared, "really is the only candidate who has been able to inspire, at the grassroots level all over this country, the kind of passion and enthusiasm for democracy and change and transformation of America that we need in this country." Gore made it clear he was endorsing not only the candidate but also the new style of politics embodied by Dean's campaign. "We need to remake the Democratic Party; we need to remake America; we need to take it back on behalf of the people of this country," he said. If you were paying attention to politics in the Bush era, Gore's endorsement of Dean made sense. After all, Gore had opposed the war in Iraq, criticized the Patriot Act, and given a series of highly touted speeches before MoveOn.org. Still, it was a bracing moment, a passing of the torch from one leader of the party to another.

In early January 2004, Trippi, the political consultant Tom Ochs, and a sardonic, mustachioed Chicago reporter turned political strategist in a schlumpy red sweater and baseball cap named David Axelrod sat in the dark, mahogany-paneled bar of the Hotel Fort Des Moines, the premier watering hole for politicos in the state. That day, Bill Bradley had just endorsed Dean in Manchester, adding yet more gravitas to his juggernaut campaign. Axelrod had been working for John Edwards but was in the process of being pushed out because of strategic differences with the candidate's wife, Elizabeth. Over red wine and beers, the three old pros shared war stories from the business and talked about the unexpected rise of the Dean campaign. As far as the other campaigns were concerned, Axelrod said, Dean was "a pimple on the ass of progress." The recent Gore endorsement had only made Dean more of a marked man. Yet it was clear that Axelrod had been paying close attention to Dean's unorthodox campaign. The Chicagoan had worked for both Clintons and flew down to Nashville in September 2002 when Gore was deciding whether to run for president again. "He said, 'Look, if I run for president,' and he started outlining his campaign," Axelrod told Trippi and Ochs. "He said, 'I'm not gonna take any contributions over some figure.' He said, 'I think you can raise a lot of money over the Internet. I'm gonna take some positions that you traditionally can't take.' He completely described what you guys are doing."

Axelrod saw the potential of this new politics outlined by Gore and put into motion by Dean. "You guys are the Green Bay Packers of politics," Axelrod said. "Everybody owns a share. I think you got a base of people who feel a total sense of ownership . . . They get it. The big question for you guys is, will it play that way in the universe at large?"

In 1988, Axelrod worked on the presidential campaign of Illinois senator Paul Simon, a morally upright, avuncular intellectual. Axelrod ran ads in Iowa showing cartoons of Simon with his bow tie and horn-rimmed glasses, turning his bookishness into an asset. Though never a favorite, Simon narrowly lost to Gephardt in the caucus that year. "I think people are so resistant to the politics of bullshit that authenticity is enormously important," Axelrod said he learned. "That's why McCain did well, that's why you guys are doing so well. I just don't know how far you can ride that."

Axelrod's newest client, a young state senator from the South Side of Chicago, also kept an eye on the Dean campaign during his run for the Illinois Senate. In August 2003, Dean stopped in Chicago to raise some money. While in town he called in to a popular radio show, *Beyond the Beltway*, hosted by radio veteran Bruce DuMont. In the studio that day sat Barack Obama, looking relaxed in a black blazer and white shirt. When Dean called in, DuMont put Obama on the line.

"Congratulations to you," Dean told Obama. "I see a lot of people around with Obama buttons on. I didn't know who you were until I saw those buttons and asked."

Obama smiled widely. "I like that," he said. "I like that." He then told Dean, "You were out front in opposition to Bush's policies in Iraq and I actually share many of your views." In the run-up to the invasion of Iraq, Obama also opposed the war, saying at an antiwar rally in downtown Chicago, "I am not opposed to all wars. I'm opposed to dumb wars."

When Dean got off the line, DuMont asked Obama what he thought of the Vermont governor. "I like Dean a lot," Obama replied. "One of the things that is striking about where Democrats are right now is there is an enormous hunger for plain-speaking Democrats. His major advantage as a governor is that he is not subject to some of the equivocation that the senators who are in the presidential race seem to be having problems with. He takes a clear stand, he speaks his mind, and I think that resonates very well with Democratic primary voters. Obviously, that also means he's alienating some potential general election voters, but in the primary that's a real strength."

Yet just as the Dean campaign was supposed to fully come together, it was in the process of falling apart. For all its innovation, the campaign failed to master some of the most elementary basics of campaigning. For starters, the celebrity campaign manager, Joe Trippi, was not a manager, nor was he totally in charge of the campaign. "When I hired him, I said, 'Joe, you're not a manager, but we need your help, and in September we'll make another change,'" Dean said. "Of course in September we were in first place, so we couldn't exactly make the change." Trippi never had control of the campaign's checkbook, nor would it have been a good thing if he did. As the campaign progressed, Dean and Trippi rarely spoke. "He was a terrible manager and emotionally strung out all the time," Dean said. The Vermont faction of the campaign, loyal to Dean during his years as governor, severely mistrusted Trippi, and vice versa. Trippi and O'Connor shared an office in Burlington separated in the middle by a huge piece of duct tape on the floor. Each side operated in separate worlds.

Trippi liked to say that he ran "the old campaign" during the day, talking to elected officials and political operatives, and "the Internet campaign" from 10:00 p.m. until 3:00 a.m., chatting and conversing with techies and bloggers until the wee hours. For nine months he operated on a few hours of sleep, adding an even harder edge to his already irascible personality. He threw phones, knocked over desks, and screamed at overworked staffers. "Petty jealousies and staff rivalries, when combined with a full dose of Trippi, led to a very dysfunctional organization," pollster Paul Maslin wrote in a campaign postmortem in *The Atlantic Monthly*. "It may have seemed like Mardi Gras but deep down we were squabbling the whole time."

Compounding the problem, every week, it seemed, the candidate himself made a statement that got him into trouble with the media or rival campaigns. The same qualities that made Dean a compelling insurgent, his tenacity and tendency to openly speak his mind, turned him into a lousy front-runner. Many of these statements, such as his contention in December that "the capture of Saddam [Hussein] has not made America safer," may have been prophetic but sent the campaign spinning into damage control at a time when it should have been consolidating support. "We desperately needed an 'adult,'" Maslin wrote. In a sense, Dean knew this better than anyone. "I think the largest flaw in my campaign by far," he said after it was all over, "was both the lack of discipline in the candidate and the campaign."

The most glaring problems occurred in the only state that initially mattered. In many ways, the campaign in Iowa was the inversion of New Hampshire—bereft of strong local leadership, and missing a coherent strategy and organizational structure. Before the top brass knew there was a problem, Dean's young organizers in Iowa felt their supporters slipping away.

Buffy Wicks, an organizer in Des Moines, was one of them. Tall, blond, competitive, and built like a brick, Wicks grew up outside of Sacramento and spent five hours a day in the pool as a girl training to be an Olympic swimmer. After college, she organized antiwar rallies prior to the invasion of Iraq in San Francisco. "I was really frustrated by the direction of the Democratic Party and felt like it didn't represent me," she said. Like every young progressive organizer, she struggled with the question of "do you change the system from within or from outside?" The night the war began, she got a call from her best friend and roommate. He'd tested positive for HIV/AIDS, he told her, and didn't have health insurance. She wondered what kind of country would invade another nation, unprovoked, but refuse to provide health care for its own people. That same week, on the news, she heard Dean speak at the California Democratic Party's state convention, where he repeated his infamous "What I Want to Know" speech from the DNC. "I was so moved by his ability to pierce into the heart and soul of the Democratic Party at the time," Wicks recalled. Within a few weeks, she got into her car and drove to Iowa.

She took six counties in and around Des Moines and quickly became one of the campaign's best organizers—tenacious, persistent, and quick on her feet. She realized that the seventy-year-old farmers she met had the same concerns about Iraq that she did. She also grasped, soon enough, that Dean's organization in the state wasn't all it was billed to be. "When you're riding a wave of momentum, you think everything's fine," she said, "but people in the field feel it first." In late November, Wicks picked up *The New York Times* and read an article about the organizing successes of the Dean campaign in New Hampshire. "That's what we need here," she thought. A group of Iowa organizers held an intervention and voted to adopt the house meeting plan. Wicks called Bird, who relayed her concerns to Hicks. Soon enough, Ganz's partner, Paul Milne, and two organizers from New Hampshire were dispatched to Iowa.

Unfortunately, it took months to build and refine the house meetings in New Hampshire, and the organization couldn't be transported overnight. Nor did the top brass in Iowa and Vermont ever really commit to the program. In a few places, such as Wicks's sections of urban Des Moines, the house meetings solidified the campaign's support, but by the time the model was imported to Iowa—in early December—in most places there was no enthusiasm to try something new and it was already too late. "If it had been the statewide mandate and they'd have started as early as they did in New Hampshire," Milne argued, "Dean would've had Iowa sewn up."

Instead, the campaign shifted to plan C.

Tim Connolly arrived in Des Moines the third week of October. A former Army Ranger in Desert Storm, the fifty-year-old Connolly served in the Clinton administration as the principal deputy for special operations at the Pentagon, a portfolio spanning everything from the Green Berets in Somalia to humanitarian relief in Chechnya to the drug war in Colombia. He's the guy you call when there's a disaster brewing. Connolly loved covert operations and guerrilla political campaigns, so naturally he gravitated to Dean. Commanding the ground troops in Iowa, as the campaign's new field director, would in many ways be his most daunting mission yet. Though Dean had become the consensus front-runner in Iowa by the fall, "when I came in, the campaign had a fairly small operation with a fairly small footprint," Connolly said. "It had a lot of talented people," such as Wicks, but "there wasn't a vision of how to leverage the talents of people on the ground." A lot of innovative young staffers were "woefully underutilized," he found, "leaving 90 percent of their talents on the table." Connolly took over a windowless second-floor bunker across the street from the campaign's headquarters in downtown Des Moines. His main job was to figure out how to integrate the thousands of volunteers who were planning to stream into Iowa that winter for the caucus and were dead set on coming whether the campaign wanted them there or not.

That's where his Special Forces training came in especially handy. Connolly set up dozens of winterized camps known as fire bases, recruited teams of ground captains and local responders, and distributed hundreds of cell phones. Volunteers would be given orange wool caps for safety and identification purposes. All the logistics would be managed over the Internet; Connolly controlled the entire operation without ever having to speak to a single volunteer. He picked a storm metaphor to describe the operation. First came the Brewing Storm, beginning the day after Christmas, followed by the Emerging Storm (January 2–4), the Gathering Storm (January 9–11), and, finally, the Perfect Storm in the days before the caucus. The goal was to assemble a massive, all-volunteer strike force of "storm troopers" that would blanket the state and overwhelm the opposition.

The plan sounds like a bad imitation of *Star Wars* in retrospect, but the logic at the time seemed sane enough. If each Stormer brought ten voters to the caucus, the campaign would have the thirty-five thousand supporters it needed to prevail. "We were going to just flood the state," said Maslin, "and make up for whatever leadership difficulties we had with sheer numbers."

Yet Connolly was mainly a logistician, not a political strategist. The head of the Dean campaign in Iowa, Jeani Murray, a former executive director of the Iowa Democratic Party, turned out to be no match for Michael Whouley, the legendary über-strategist who parachuted into Iowa in November and rescued the Kerry campaign. A balding, rail-thin Bostonian who swore like a drunken sailor, never talked to the media, and somehow transformed political campaigns without ever being seen, Whouley was like a ghost. Every political operative had a story about him. Connolly liked to tell the one about how, while working for Gore in New Hampshire in 2000, Whouley allegedly created strategically placed traffic jams on Election Day to prevent Bradley voters from getting to the polls.

In Iowa, Kerry ran a traditional by-the-book campaign, relying on neighborhood leaders known as precinct captains in the business. Iowans talked to Iowans in the Kerry campaign, a far cry from the out-of-state Deaniacs who flooded the state. As the Dean campaign came unglued, Whouley maintained ironclad discipline among Kerry's loyalists. Whouley knew everything there was to know about Kerry's campaign in the state. Dean's campaign was just the opposite.

"What happened in Iowa is the same thing that happened in Iraq," Connolly said. "At its very elemental level, the entire operational plan was predicated on bad intel."

Quite simply, the Dean campaign had far fewer supporters than it thought it did. As the primary got closer and the combined attacks from the other candidates and negative media coverage of Dean sharply increased, that problem only got worse. (Roughly two weeks before the vote, a tape surfaced showing Dean on Canadian television in 2000 calling the Iowa caucus "dominated by special interests." Following its release, Dean dropped ten points in the campaign's internal polling.) Dean desperately needed a Whouley. Trippi, a veteran of four presidential campaigns in Iowa, was the closest he had. Around Thanksgiving, Dean asked Trippi to decamp to Iowa full-time. He refused. "He was afraid there would be a palace coup" back in Burlington, Dean recalled. Trippi said he conveyed his worries about Iowa to the candidate in early October, but Dean had no recollection of such a conversation. "If he knew it," Dean said, "he should have gone out there and fixed it."

Trippi worried that if he went to Iowa, the national campaign back in Burlington would fall apart. Campaign aides nicknamed him Eeyore—after the donkey in *Winnie-the-Pooh*—because he always fretted that the sky was falling. In late November, Trippi made another trip to Des Moines, bringing along a half dozen aging political consultants that Connolly dubbed "the white hats." He instructed Connolly to hire a staggering 175 new organizers over the next two months to keep parity with Kerry. Suddenly computer programmers in Burlington were dispatched to the cornfields of Iowa to manage the complicated caucus. Then the Stormers showed up. "Here's the irony of the Storm," says Connolly. "It was by far the largest operation in the entire Dean campaign, both in terms of numbers and complexity, and *nobody* cared about it. Trippi did not feel compelled to micromanage it." The Stormers, Dean's advisers believed, didn't wreck the campaign to anywhere near the extent the media portrayed, but there was no denying that the biggest asset Dean had—his band of committed supporters, many becoming engaged with electoral politics for the first time—turned into a thoroughly mocked PR circus and an ineffective organizing weapon. Instead of expanding Dean's support in Iowa, they repelled caucus voters, who resented being told how to vote by a bunch of kids from out of state wearing bright orange hats. Said one gleeful Kerry volunteer: "I kept telling everybody, in *The Perfect Storm*, everybody dies at the end."

So many different factors, exhaustively chronicled in the weeks that followed, contributed to Dean's dramatic collapse. No one explanation is sufficient to explain why he tanked in Iowa; Dean was done in by a combination of self-inflicted gaffes and mistakes, subpar organizing, heightened media scrutiny, attacks from the other candidates (particularly concerning his temperament and electability), the rabidity of his supporters, and the belated efforts by Kerry and Edwards to co-opt his message of change. By January 19, many caucus-goers doubted whether Dean could really defeat President Bush and possessed the qualities necessary to be an effective candidate and president. Iowans, ultimately, concluded that he was too risky a pick for such an important election and turned to the two safest alternatives, the war hero and the charismatic Southerner.

The outrage and despair that Dean had tapped into, which Axelrod and Obama identified as a short-term strength but potential long-term weakness, catapulted Dean a long way, but could take him only so far. During the campaign, Bill Clinton gave Dean at least one piece of valuable advice. The two spoke roughly every month, even when it appeared that Clinton preferred Wes Clark. "Now that you're the front-runner," Clinton told Dean in the weeks before the Iowa caucus, "if you want people to vote for you, you have to act like a president." Dean knew Clinton was right, but he couldn't leave the insurgency behind. It was as if his supporters and opponents saw only one side of Dean, the fiery, antiwar, throw-caution-to-the-wind crusader, and blocked out the rest of his record and biography. Even when he knew he needed to modulate his image, reminding people that he could actually win and govern, the candidate got sucked into the excitement just like everyone else.

"I was intoxicated at the same time," Dean admitted. "If you go before adoring crowds, you pump your fist in the air, and they go absolutely crazy, there's a certain amount of addiction that goes with that. I realized it was happening to me in Iowa, and it was a terrible feeling because it was too late to do anything about it. I was realizing what was happening in Iowa in the last two weeks. I was still drawing huge crowds everywhere I went, but it was the same people.

When we got on the bus and drove to the next stop, they got in their cars and went on to the next stop. So it became almost like the Grateful Dead. It was the same people over and over again, and that's not how you win races." His opening acts, in the last week, included liberal comedian Janeane Garofalo and aging rocker Joan Jett. Not exactly the types of people you want closing the deal in a place like Iowa.

Still, polls in the last weeks showed him ahead—or at least tied—and the campaign expected to prevail. In the weeks before the caucus, Trippi spent millions of dollars on ads and staff in Iowa, New Hampshire, and the half-dozen states that soon followed. The campaign went from a patient fighter preparing for a long bout to a hungry would-be champion intent on delivering a swift knockout blow. Ali turned into Foreman. The strategy backfired completely when Dean came in a distant third in Iowa. His campaign bungled the expectations game and blew $41 million. In perhaps the biggest irony of all, the fiscally conservative governor had looted the cookie jar. "We were in good shape in every state but Iowa," Dean later admitted, "which was the one state I didn't understand." But Iowa came first, a harsh reality Hillary Clinton would learn four years later. "It's a terrific exercise in organization," Dean said of the caucus. "We flunked it totally."

Though Buffy Wicks and many of her counterparts would go on to bigger and better things, the scars from the first war zone of the 2004 election never disappeared. "I left my heart in Iowa," she said.

The results were as follows: John Kerry, 38 percent; John Edwards, 32 percent; Howard Dean, 18 percent. "Dean! Dean! Dean! Dean!" a raucous crowd of eight hundred supporters chanted at Dean's "victory" party in Des Moines, trying mightily to mask the utter disappointment of the news.

Kate O'Connor described the night's result as "the shocker of the century." The campaign may have been slipping in the polls, but few predicted such a poor finish. "No one thought we were going to lose," she said. "So there was never a discussion of 'what do we say if we don't win?'" Ten minutes before he was due to speak, Dean sat on his campaign bus with his shell-shocked top aides. The atmosphere was akin to a funeral. Steve McMahon told Dean to remember Bobby Kennedy's famous speech in the black ghetto of Indianapolis following Martin Luther King's death in 1968, when Kennedy's raw yet eloquent words soothed a wounded and angry crowd.

Trippi had just surveyed the manic scene inside the Val Air Ballroom. He and Dean, barely on speaking terms by that point, conferred for a few minutes on the bus. "You've got three thousand people in there," Trippi reported, unintentionally overstating the number. "This is a big blow for them. You've got to go out there and cheer them up." He handed Dean an orange hat, which the candidate stuffed in his back pocket.

Inside the retro ballroom in West Des Moines, furnished with a massive disco ball, the crowd blanketed the place with American flags and chanted, "Let's take our country back!"—the campaign's motto and emblem on the giant black banner overhead. Dean came out defiant, took off his black suit jacket, and rolled up the sleeves of his blue shirt in trademark fashion. He wasn't going to let a distant-third-place finish ruin his planned celebration. He grabbed the orange hat from his back pocket, held it high above his head, and emphatically chucked it into the frenzied mob below, eliciting wild cheers. Dean smiled broadly and exchanged a boyish high five with Iowa senator Tom Harkin, his top supporter in the state. The candidate looked ready to rumble—short, squat neck bulging out of its tight collar, mic in his left hand, jabbing intently with his right. There was no script or formal speech in sight.

"I was about to say, you know, I'm sure there are some disappointed people here," Dean said at the outset. The crowd booed. "You know something, if you had told us one year ago that we were going to come in third in Iowa, we would have given anything for that." He was in a fighting mood. There would be no concession speech or acknowledgment of defeat. "Not only are we going to New Hampshire," he informed the crowd, "we're going to South Carolina and Oklahoma and Arizona and North Dakota and New Mexico. And we're going to California and Texas and New York . . . And we're going to South Dakota and Oregon and Washington and Michigan, and then we're going to Washington, D.C., to take back the White House!" As he yelled out the upcoming primary states, Dean's face turned redder and redder and his voice plunged deeper and deeper, taking on the wild inflection of a WWF announcer. Then, voice cracking, right arm swinging forward, he let out a high-pitched "Yeah!" for exclamation that sounded, at least to a TV audience, more like an unhinged "Yeeeeeeeearrrrrrhhhhh!" The crowd went crazy. Dean let out a big chuckle. "We will not give up!" he exclaimed, caught helplessly in the sheer bravado of the moment. "We will not give up in New Hampshire! We will not give up in South Carolina! We will not give up in Arizona! Or New Mexico! Oklahoma! North Dakota! Delaware! Pennsylvania! Ohio! Michigan! We will not quit now or ever! We want our country back for ordinary Americans!" Voices in the crowd called out the names of those states Dean had somehow forgotten to mention. "And we're going to win in Massachusetts!" Dean responded excitedly. "And North Carolina! And Missouri! And Arkansas! And Connecticut! And New York! And Ohio!" he repeated mistakenly. It was almost a shame he never got to all fifty.

Three of the longest minutes in political history elapsed before Dean turned to the "polite" part of his remarks, calmly thanking his campaign staff and volunteers. He was supposed to talk about how his supporters had changed politics forever, even in defeat, but that message never broke through. Those in the room didn't know it yet, but the millions of people who watched on TV—some of them seeing Dean for the first time—viewed the speech as a requiem for a terrifying campaign. Cable news instantly replayed "the scream" on an endless loop, amplifying Dean's yelp for maximum effect (you could barely hear him inside the earsplitting room), and the clip became an early Internet video sensation. Dean's political obituary was penned virtually overnight.

In the blackness of the next morning, Dean and staff flew to New Hampshire, arriving at 3:30 a.m. for a rally at an airport hangar in Portsmouth. Then he went to sleep. He woke up the next morning to footage of the scream, which he saw for the first time on his campaign bus. He was flabbergasted—but not entirely surprised—by the media's portrayal of him as an unhinged lunatic. "It is what it is," he told O'Connor. "What are we supposed to do about it now?" No amount of damage control could push it off TV. Cable news eviscerated him; then the late-night comedians dumped Dean's remains all over the floor.

Leno: "Cows in Iowa are afraid of getting mad Dean disease."

Letterman: "Here's a little tip, Howard—cut back on the Red Bull."

Conan: "Afterwards Dean said, 'Iowa is behind me. Now I'm looking forward to going to New Hampshire and screaming at voters there.'"

Game. Set. Match. "In forty years of observing presidential contests," wrote Bill Greider in *The Nation*, "I cannot remember another major candidate brutalized so intensely by the media."

Before Iowa, Dean comfortably led Kerry and Clark in New Hampshire. Afterward, he plummeted to third place in the polls. Bird and his organizers fought and clawed to get the candidate back to a respectable showing. Whouley later admitted that he feared the Dean campaign might pull off a miraculous comeback. Alas, it was not to be. Dean took 26 percent of the vote, losing to Kerry by thirteen. If it hadn't been for the endless loop of the scream, Bird argued, Dean would've won the state despite his lopsided defeat in Iowa and had a shot in the ensuing contests. The campaign held its core supporters—the undecideds just broke the other way. If New Hampshire had come first, everything might've been different.

The oldest story in presidential politics had once again played itself out. The insurgent came out of nowhere, captivated everyone for a while, and then flamed out, soon to disappear into oblivion. Dean was just another Hart or Bradley or Bruce Babbitt. Like clockwork, the old politics had conquered the new. Iowa and New Hampshire represented yet another "triumph" for "the original Comeback Kid, Bill Clinton," the DLC argued, and a vindication for "the Blair Democrats who supported the war in Iraq." The brief reign of the Dean Democrats had come to a crashing end.

Such widespread establishment chatter proved to be a rather self-serving and myopic bit of hackneyed political analysis. Many of Dean's sharpest critics, who as it happened would end up on the losing end of the following presidential election, saw only the campaign's dysfunction and demise rather than its unrealized potential.

2 ★ STORMING THE CASTLE

We see the party made up of grandees and peasants. And we peasants think things should be done in a different way. —Hayes McNeill

At 9:00 p.m. on July 27, 2004, a rollicking blues tune filled the Fleet-Center, and a soft female voice introduced "the man who energized our party." With that, Howard Dean strolled to the stage of the Democratic convention in Boston, flashing two thumbs-up with a big, sheepish smile on his face. This was step one on his comeback tour. Following the stunning collapse of his presidential bid, most influential Democrats wanted Dean simply to disappear. He was thought to be too angry and divisive, practically radioactive—the type of person you didn't want to be seen in public with. Even his top strategists cautioned him to take some time off, relax for a while, see whether he couldn't rehabilitate his image down the road.

As the primaries wound down, Dean was angry and bitter at the way he'd been treated. He flirted briefly with the idea of joining or starting a third party. It was Al Gore who ultimately "talked me down off the ledge," Dean wrote, persuading him that the fight ahead mattered more than his bruised ego. Patience had never been Dean's foremost virtue, and he wasn't much for reflection. After his presidential campaign ended on February 18, with yet another distant-third-place finish, this time in Wisconsin, Dean retired to

Burlington for a few weeks, cleaned out his garage, fixed up his house, then got back to work.

He flew to San Francisco on March 18 and gave a speech announcing the creation of Democracy for America (DFA), a spin-off of his campaign organization. "We are going to fundamentally change the Democratic Party," Dean, standing in front of a giant American flag, told a jam-packed room of one thousand supporters at the Palace Hotel. Dean's advisers modeled DFA after the Christian Coalition, which built a farm team of religious-right Republicans following Pat Robertson's presidential bid in 1988. A decade later, they'd practically taken over the Republican Party. DFA didn't aspire to be as radical as the Christian Coalition; Dean, for all his fire, never wanted to lead a Robertson-style ideological crusade, but he did believe that grassroots Democratic activists needed to be given a larger megaphone in order to save the Democratic Party. That spring and summer Dean crisscrossed the country—just as he'd wanted to do as a presidential candidate—stumping for candidates of all different stripes, from a soil and water district commissioner in Florida to an opponent of House majority leader Tom DeLay in Texas.

The first group of candidates DFA endorsed, known as the Dean Dozen, included a little-known Illinois state senator who'd just won a crowded primary race. "DFA volunteers all over Illinois helped Barack Obama win his primary," Dean wrote to his supporters in May 2004. "Now it's time to help him win the general." A spokesman for Obama's initial Senate opponent, Jack Ryan, used the endorsement as ammo against Obama, saying, "With a record and an agenda that's far outside the mainstream, it's no surprise that Barack Obama was endorsed last week by Howard (I-have-a-scream) Dean, a fellow outside-the-mainstreamer." (Ryan later withdrew from the race after news broke that he frequented Parisian sex clubs with his wife, actress Jeri Ryan.) A month after the endorsement, Dean flew to Chicago and took in a Cubs game at Wrigley Field, spoke before a large health-care rally in Lincoln Park, and met Barack and Michelle at a swanky fund-raiser at the Four Seasons, delivering a $5,000 check for his campaign. He immediately sensed Obama's potential. "Right then and there I thought, This guy could be president," Dean said. In July, Dean and Obama spoke on the same night of the Democratic convention. Their time in Boston marked the beginning of Obama's historic run for the presidency and the next chapter in Dean's political career.

His advisers weren't sure what kind of reception Dean would get. "Dated Dean, Married Kerry," went a popular slogan in the run-up to the Iowa caucus. Judging by the response when he walked onstage, many of the delegates at the convention never quite got over their first love. Dean received a two-minute standing ovation that night, which he repeatedly tried to quiet. "My lord," he remarked in surprise, as hundreds of delegates stood and applauded. I SCREAMED FOR DEAN, said one sign in the audience. NOW I SCREAM FOR KERRY.

Though he'd lost as a candidate, his message could still prevail. "Tonight," Dean said with a feisty glimmer in his eye, "we are all here to represent the Democratic wing of the Democratic Party." His fervent belief in competing everywhere, reinforced more than ever during his travels with DFA, formed the backbone of his speech. "We're going to be proud to call ourselves Democrats, not just here in Boston," Dean said. "We're going to be proud to call ourselves Democrats in Mississippi. We're going to be proud to call ourselves Democrats in Utah and Idaho." Polite claps turned into boisterous cheers. "And we're going to be proud to call ourselves Democrats in Texas," Dean said, referring to President Bush's home state. He smiled mischievously and the crowd roared.

Yet as much as Dean believed that the party—if only it tried—could make inroads everywhere, the Kerry campaign, scarce on resources and confined by traditional electoral calculations, was preparing to go the opposite route, concentrating all its time and money on a few precious battleground states. The next day, at a skybox behind the stage, Dean met with eighteen local Democratic

Party leaders from across the country. They came from places like Kansas and Nebraska and Wyoming and Montana and Mississippi and Alabama and Texas. These state chairs, who worked practically full-time (and then some) for no pay, tended to be invisible cogs in the Democratic machine, but formed the backbone of the Democratic Party back home, or at least what existed of it. And they were angry and frustrated that no one was listening to them. The chairs had compiled a list of states that were either too red or too blue to warrant any attention from the national Democratic Party. Dennis Langley, the former chair of the Kansas Democratic Party who now held the number two position in the South Dakota Democratic Party, gave a presentation detailing the woes of the non-targeted states. Langley dubbed them "the Big L" because of their shape on the map, stretching from the Mountain West through the Great Plains all the way down to the Deep South, state after state of barren Democratic territory.

At the meeting with Dean, Langley told a story about going down to Nashville and visiting Al Gore in 2000. Gore's advisers gave Langley and two hundred other party aficionados a sneak preview of his general election strategy, which concentrated solely on sixteen carefully selected swing states. Langley was asked what he thought of Gore's narrowly tailored battle plan. "You're playing your cards too close to the vest," he bluntly told the vice president. "If anything goes wrong, you're going to lose. You have no safety valve." Such criticism did not go over well at the time, though it proved prescient after the fiasco in Florida. Now the state chairs feared that Kerry was about to make the same mistake. They asked Dean to help them raise some money to invest in their forgotten state parties.

Dean got the message, loud and clear. "They were all talking to me about how hard it was to win governorships and Congressional seats and state legislative races because nobody would put any money in," he recalled. He'd seen firsthand from his presidential run just how much the party had atrophied organizationally, "lurching from one election to the next," slicing the electorate into narrower and narrower targets, eventually betting everything on Florida in 2000 and, soon enough, Ohio in 2004. The meeting with the state chairs confirmed his worst fears. "I realized we weren't a national party anymore," he said.

That night, accepting the vice presidential nomination, John Edwards would speak passionately about the existence of "two Americas"—one for the rich and one for everybody else. The great irony was that you could've said the same thing about the Democratic Party. There was one party in Washington and another one pretty much everywhere else, especially outside of the prized swing states. The two worlds barely coexisted. "You know what's so tragic about this party?" Dean told DFA's executive director, Tom McMahon, as they left the meeting. "The day our VP nominee is about to give a speech in July, before the election, we've already determined that we're not going to put any resources into any of these states because they're not viable enough." McMahon nodded along. "The unfortunate thing," Dean continued, "is that we hadn't planned ahead and thought about how we can make more of these states more viable in this election." It turned out that Dean had a few ideas (or "idears," as he said in true New England fashion) for how to right that wrong. The party needed what he'd first articulated in his presidential campaign and Kerry had ignored: a fifty-state strategy.

The Kerry campaign ran a single-state strategy in the final weeks of the general election, betting everything on Ohio. The electoral map following his defeat terrified despondent Democrats. Most of the country was a mass of red, with the only blue pockets confined to both coasts and the upper Midwest. The country had become deeply balkanized. Blue states blamed red states for Kerry's loss, and red states blamed blue states for the nation's many woes. It was as if America were at war with itself—gay versus straight, rural versus urban, red versus blue.

Over e-mail and on the Internet, Democrats rationalized their defeat by resorting to bitter sarcasm, finding new ways to insult Bush country and prove the intellectual and cultural primacy of blue America. "With the Blue States in hand," read one widely circulated e-mail, "the Democrats have firm control of 80% of the country's fresh water, over 90% of our pineapple and lettuce, 92% of the nation's fresh fruit, 93% of the artichoke production, 95% of America's quality wines, 90% of all cheese production, 90% of the high tech industry, most of the US low-sulfur coal, all living redwoods, sequoias and condors, all the Ivy and Seven Sister schools, plus Amherst, Stanford, Berkeley, CalTech and MIT.

"The Red States, on the other hand, now have to cope with 88% of all obese Americans (and their projected health care cost spike), 92% of all US mosquitoes, nearly 100% of all tornadoes, 90% of the hurricanes, 99% of all Southern Baptists, virtually 100% of all Televangelists, Rush Limbaugh, Bob Jones University, Clemson and the University of Georgia." In another e-mail, the state of California drafted a letter of secession. "God is going to give us the Pacific Ocean and Hollywood," the e-mail read. "God is letting you have the KKK and country music (except the Dixie Chicks)." Yet another e-mail declared, "Fuck the South. Fuck 'em. We should have let them go when they wanted to leave."

Despite the vulgarity of the message, "fuck the South," in particular, proved a surprisingly popular sentiment among Democrats, first made (in kinder terms) by University of Maryland political science professor Tom Schaller, who argued in an influential November 2003 *Washington Post* op-ed that Democrats should no longer compete for votes in a region that had once been their most loyal base. "Trying to recapture the South is a futile, counterproductive exercise for Democrats," Schaller wrote. "It has swung. Richard Nixon's 'Southern strategy' of 1968 has reached full fruition." Moving forward, he argued, "Democrats would be better served by simply conceding the South and redirecting their already scarce resources to more promising states where they're making gains, especially those in the Southwest."

The results of 2004 supposedly strengthened Schaller's argument. After all, Kerry hadn't won a single southern state, and Democrats lost close Senate races in Florida, Georgia, Kentucky, Louisiana, North Carolina, and South Carolina (in addition to Alaska, Oklahoma, and South Dakota), reducing their Senate minority to forty-four seats. Schaller soon expanded his argument in a bestselling book called *Whistling Past Dixie*. Unfortunately, his thesis risked becoming a self-fulfilling prophecy. Even if Democrats flourished out west, as Schaller predicted, abandoning a dozen states in the South wouldn't give Democrats much room for error in the next presidential election, nor would it help them regain their majorities in the House and Senate.

As Democrats drifted toward hapless regionalism, conservatives boasted of finally assembling Karl Rove's permanent Republican majority. "Republican hegemony in America is now expected to last for years, maybe decades," predicted *The Weekly Standard*'s executive editor, Fred Barnes. Virtually every prominent Republican politician and pundit—and more than a few envious Democrats—echoed this line of thinking. Soon enough, a proliferation of books would hit the shelves chronicling the dominance of the GOP's electoral machinery in near-pornographic detail, with titles like *Building Red America*, *Painting the Map Red*, and *One Party Country: The Republican Plan for Dominance in the 21st Century*.

In those dark days, seemingly every politician and pundit had a prescription for what ailed the party.

Be populist! Thomas Frank, in his wildly successful book *What's the Matter with Kansas?*, wrote that Democrats had abandoned the economic populism that had once made them a successful "party of the people," allowing Republicans to convince the blue-collar denizens of Middle America to vote against their economic interests by pushing culture war issues like abortion, gay marriage, and gun rights.

Get tough! *The New Republic*'s editor Peter Beinart, a gaggle of wonks at Washington think tanks, and influential senators like Joe Biden argued that Democrats needed to be tougher on foreign policy and more willing to exercise the use of military might in an age of terrorism. In the words of former UN ambassador Richard Holbrooke, all Democrats must become "national-security Democrats."

Get religion! A wide-ranging coalition of religiously minded Democrats, spearheaded by the evangelical preacher Jim Wallis, author of *God's Politics: Why the Right Gets It Wrong and the Left Doesn't Get It*, urged Democrats to more openly talk about their religious faith and support policies that encouraged the expression of religion in public life (without violating the Constitution, of course).

Start framing! University of California–Berkeley linguist George Lakoff, author of *Don't Think of an Elephant!* became a cause célèbre in Democratic circles by detailing how Republicans were better at "framing" issues and by suggesting a politically palatable vocabulary for Democrats, a notion embraced by nearly every leader in the party, from Harry Reid to Nancy Pelosi.

Move to the right! The DLC blamed MoveOn and Michael Moore for pushing the party too far to the left. "What leftist elites smugly imagine is a sophisticated view of their country's flaws strikes much of America as a false and malicious cartoon," wrote Will Marshall, president of the DLC's Progressive Policy Institute. "Democrats should have no truck with the rancid anti-Americanism of the conspiracy-mongering left."

Move to the left! The likes of MoveOn and many netroots Dean activists, in turn, blamed the DLC for pushing the party too far to the right. "Democrats can't keep ignoring their base," Joe Trippi wrote in a *Wall Street Journal* op-ed titled "Only the Grassroots Can Save the Democratic Party." "Running to the middle and then asking our base to make sure to vote isn't a plan. And to those who say talking to your base doesn't work—Read the Rove 2004 playbook!"

None of these remedies alone seemed sufficient to Dean (though he did pen the foreword to Lakoff's book). He didn't believe the

Republican hold on power was nearly as secure as Rove maintained, and he didn't think that Democrats could win by becoming a regional party, nor should they accept such an outcome as inevitable. He also didn't believe it would do much good if Democrats behaved more like Republicans, nor would simply "framing" their issues more effectively or talking about God put them back in power. For too long, he argued, Democrats had communicated with too few voters in too few states. That was the first thing that needed to change, and from there everything else would follow.

As Democrats struggled for answers to their electoral misery, Dean considered his options. Would he run for president again in 2008? Go back to Vermont and wait until a Senate seat opened up? Keep doing Democracy for America? He contemplated running for president again, but didn't believe he could win unless the party reformed dramatically, nor did he think he could defeat Hillary Clinton if she ran in 2008. He reached the rather startling conclusion that he'd be most effective by taking on the ultimate insider job, DNC chair, and overhauling a party desperately in need of deep repair. "I concluded it's faster to change the party from the inside," he told Tim Russert on *Meet the Press* in December 2004. He conceded, however, "I'm not much of an insider, and this is a pretty insider game." Dean told me: "I basically believed that it didn't matter who we nominated for president, we were never going to win unless we revamped the party."

Before reaching a final decision, Dean called Gore, who'd become a trusted adviser. "Why would you ever want to become DNC chair?" Gore asked him. "It's thankless." Senate minority leader Harry Reid summoned Dean to the Capitol and told him point-blank not to run. "He thought I scared the hell out of the Washington establishment," Dean said.

His own advisers in Washington thought he was nuts. Mark Squier laughed in disbelief when Dean walked into his northern Virginia office and broke the news that he was strongly considering a bid for chair. "Howard, this is the most brutal, treacherous electorate there is," Squier told him. "You're now going to go into a closed election of 447 people. You want to subject yourself to that?" Squier's partner, Steve McMahon, assembled a host of DNC insiders to advise Dean on the decision. Just like Gore and Kerry, nearly everyone urged him not to run. (Trippi, by then estranged from Dean, endorsed Simon Rosenberg of the New Democrat Network.) "The general tenor was, it's a job where you basically put on a referee shirt every day and you go to work and blow a whistle," McMahon said. "There's a lot of racial politics, there's a lot of cultural politics, and there's a ton of fund-raising and most of it is big-donor fund-raising and that's not what you like to do." Dean's brother Jim pleaded with him, in a handwritten letter, not to enter the Washington "cesspool."

These were all perfectly reasonable reactions. Chairman of the party, historically, had never been a glamorous job. Party chairs tended to receive their marching orders from the White House and/or Congress, and usually that meant forking over large sums of money, no questions asked. Inevitably, the president or congressional leaders wanted more money, or had differing priorities, and the DNC chair was the sad sack caught in the cross fire. "The number-one sport in Washington is to take shots at the DNC chair," joked one former high-ranking DNC official. The last memorable party chairman dated back to Lee Atwater, the blues-playing, mudslinging, southern-bred hatchet man for George H. W. Bush, whom *The New York Times* dubbed the "most controversial and successful political operative in America." But he was an anomaly inside either political party; the job of party chair usually went to a revolving door of yes-men. Dean was undeterred by this history—he figured that it would take someone of his stature and persistence to make the kind of tough, transformative decisions that party chieftains had heretofore avoided. Over Christmas, Dean called Parag Mehta, the deputy political director on his presidential campaign, and asked him to help with the chair race.

"That's a terrible idea," Mehta told him.

"Why?" Dean asked.

"You're the guy on the outside throwing rocks at the establishment, trying to keep them honest," Mehta responded. "My fear is that if you win, you're going to go on the inside and become part of the problem."

"Parag," Dean told him, "change only happens when the outsiders come in and make it happen. So what do you say, do you want to go and storm the castle?"

On December 8, 2004, Dean gave a speech at George Washington University titled "The Future of the Democratic Party," which became the blueprint for his DNC campaign. "Let me tell you what my plan for the Democratic Party is," he started the speech. "We're going to win Mississippi . . . and then we're gonna win Alabama . . . and Idaho . . . and South Carolina!" Dean mused, openly mocking his disastrous "scream" speech. But he was only half joking. Dean believed that the party not only had to modernize to reflect the technological changes of the twenty-first century but also had to get back to the business of old-fashioned political organizing—showing up, everywhere, and asking people for their votes. The big-city political machines and influential labor unions that powered the Democratic Party in the twentieth century no longer cut it.

"We cannot any longer be a party that seeks the presidency by running an eighteen-state campaign," Dean said. "We can't be a party that cedes a single state, a single district, a single precinct, or even a single voter." That meant drastically changing the way the party did business. "The way to rebuild the Democratic Party is not from the consultants down, it is from the ground up," said Dean. Woody Allen famously claimed that "80 percent of success is showing up." Dean's favorite quotation, which he repeated over and over, was Louis Pasteur's "Chance favors the prepared mind." The way Dean saw it, you never knew when any state, even a place like Mississippi, might get a jolt of blue. If Democrats in Oklahoma didn't define what they stood for, then Rush Limbaugh and Bill O'Reilly would.

"I had learned a couple things from running for president," Dean said. "One, there were Democrats everywhere, and we were grossly underestimating the hunger for change in places like Idaho and North Dakota, and, more importantly, in places like Colorado, Arizona, New Mexico, Nevada, and Montana. Two, that we needed a strategy to be able to win even without Ohio and Florida, and if we couldn't develop a broader strategy, then we couldn't rely on the White House. And, three, we needed what the Republicans had, which was a long-term business plan for winning elections." Dean's passion for showing up in areas that the Democratic Party had long ago confined to invisibility was based not on wishful thinking or stubborn naïveté but on political necessity.

The Democratic Party is one of the most recognizable institutions across the globe, but few people know what actually constitutes it. The DNC itself happens to be the longest-running political organization in the world, or at least claims to be, created at the Democratic convention in 1848, when the short-lived Free Soil Party attempted to end the Democrats' long-standing support for slavery. They failed, but the assembled Democrats in Baltimore created a committee to run the party's elections and plan upcoming conventions. It tended to be a rather exclusive club for party bosses until the 1960s and '70s, when reformers like James Q. Wilson and George McGovern pushed through a series of rule changes that democratized the party to reflect its newfound diversity. Since then, the DNC has served as a hub for the various arms of the party, especially when it came to campaigning and, most notably, raising money. Its 447 members were composed of local party leaders, a few elected state and national politicians, and an assortment of representatives from the party's different allied interest groups—an odd mix of insiders, quasi-insiders, and rank-and-file activists who didn't feel part of the club.

At the beginning of the DNC chair's race, "the 447," as they're known, liked Dean's message but still weren't sure whether they trusted the messenger, a secular governor of a tiny New England state who'd just spectacularly imploded as a presidential candidate. Dean himself brought up these doubts, unprompted, at a forum with the nine prospective candidates for DNC chair in Atlanta in early January. "What's a Vermont Yankee liberal doing down here in the South trying to convince you all that I oughta lead the party?" he asked rhetorically. "Members of the DNC knew three things about Dean," said Steve McMahon. "Number one, his presidential campaign brought a lot of new people into the political process. Number two, he had given a speech that caused their jaws to drop. Number three, now he was back promising to resurrect the party nationally. And the question for all of them was, this is what we want to do, but is he the one to take us there?"

Just like his presidential campaign, Dean's bid for DNC chair faced an outpouring of opposition inside the Beltway. Influential Washington Democrats couldn't agree on much back in those days, but they did concur on one thing: Dean needed to be stopped. "We knew we were going to run into an enormous amount of resistance," Dean said. "Everybody was terrified because of the image that had been created by my opponents in the primary—that I was a left-wing radical." Republicans, meanwhile, mocked and reveled in the prospect of Dean running the Democratic Party. "If [Democrats] have a true death wish, he'd be the perfect guy to go with," Newt Gingrich told Fox News. "After 10 years, you wonder if Democrats are running out of ways to say no," said Tom DeLay. "But then again, if they make Howard Dean the party chairman, I guess you could scream it." Predicted former RNC chairman Richard Bond: "He will reinforce all of their worst instincts. His style and message is one that will narrow his party's options rather than expand them."

Not to be outdone by the likes of Gingrich and DeLay, high-profile political pundits also chafed at the idea of Dean becoming chair, as if it were both unwise and undignified. "Making Dean their spokesman is exactly the wrong way to go," *The New Republic* editorialized. "Dean is even less suited to run the DNC than he is to run for president," Jonathan Chait wrote in the *Los Angeles Times*. "He reinforces all the party's weaknesses . . . With his intense secularism, arrogant style, throngs of high-profile counterculture supporters and association with the peace movement, [Dean] is the precise opposite of the image Democrats want to send out." With Dean in charge, the *New York Times* columnist David Brooks wrote snarkily, "Democrats are sure to carry Berkeley for decades to come."

Dean's team viewed all this chatter as mere noise and distraction. "Our mantra was basically 'If they don't got a vote, they ain't shit,'" said Tom Ochs, Dean's campaign manager during the chair's race. A gregarious, bellowing New Yorker from Long Island, Ochs cut his teeth in the bloody world of New Jersey politics as a young aide to Bill Bradley. He went on to produce TV ads for Clinton in 1992 and 1996 and became intimately acquainted with the DNC, working at every Democratic convention since 1980. He loved the pomp and pageantry of politics and called himself "Mr. Convention." Ochs worked hard and partied hard in those days, eventually losing a wife and almost a career. In 2004, he joined the firm of Dean's media consultants, McMahon Squier and Associates. The disheveled Ochs made Dean look like a *GQ* model. He wore faded old T-shirts, left his balding brown hair comfortably unkempt, and drove a bright green Saturn SUV ("the green machine") whose color could charitably be described as guacamole.

Ochs described his personal politics as "all over the map" but gravitated toward Dean prior to the invasion of Iraq, when he became "really, really antiwar." He particularly liked what he termed Dean's "fuck you to the establishment," which may have sounded somewhat counterintuitive given all the time Ochs had spent inside the corridors of power. "Considering what I've done for about thirty years, you'd think I'd lean toward the establishment," Ochs said, "but as I get older and I do this more and more, I see that shit needs to be blown up." In December 2003, Ochs went out to Iowa at Mc-Mahon's request and saw firsthand how disorganized things were on the ground with the Dean campaign. Ochs told Dean that the chair's race would be the opposite of his presidential campaign—tight, disciplined, and on message. The entire race would last four months, target fewer than five hundred people, and cost only half a million dollars. Between Thanksgiving and the first week of January—before he officially entered the race—Dean personally called all 447 DNC members and solicited their opinions on the job. Many didn't believe it was actually him—after all, no one of his stature had ever run for DNC chair *after* losing a high-profile presidential campaign. After announcing his candidacy in early January, Dean called each DNC member again asking for support.

The race became a textbook illustration of the current and coming change in the Democratic Party. In years past, the party leadership simply installed a handpicked caretaker in the job. Kerry, believing that he still had the clout of a presidential nominee, tried to nominate Tom Vilsack, the supremely vanilla departing governor of Iowa. The pick excited no one. Kerry then tried to persuade former New Hampshire governor Jeanne Shaheen to enter the race, but she'd just finished a grueling losing Senate campaign and begged off. The party leaders in Congress, Nancy Pelosi and Harry Reid, wanted Tim Roemer, a clean-cut conservative Democrat from Indiana who opposed a woman's right to choose and supported privatizing Social Security, which was to be the centerpiece of Bush's second term. No way, rank-and-file Democrats responded. Any high-profile endorsement from D.C. quickly became a "kiss of death" for Dean's challengers, *The Hotline* reported. The ham-handed attempt by marquee Democrats to try to stop Dean became a hilarious exercise in futility.

Just consider the tragic story of Leo Hindery Jr. A multimillionaire media mogul from New York, Hindery was a longtime Democratic donor and close friends with former congressional leaders Dick Gephardt and Tom Daschle, and figured that was as good a reason as any to run for chair. So he fired up his private jet to Orlando, where the first informal meeting of prospective chairs was taking place. Over the course of his flight, a group of Democratic bloggers loyal to Dean found out that Hindery had donated $100,000 to fund a sleazy attack ad in Iowa that compared Dean to Osama bin Laden and had previously voted Republican and generously bankrolled the GOP. The bloggers quickly circulated the information around Orlando. Upon landing, Hindery was informed by his aides that he didn't stand a chance. Rather than brave a hostile environment, the candidate flew straight back to New York. That night, reported *The New Republic*, "in Hindery's abandoned hotel suite, a gaggle of Democratic operatives raided his mini-bar and mockingly toasted the death of his absurd candidacy: 'To Leo!'" Concluded the magazine: "In hindsight, the boozy requiem wasn't just for Hindery, but for an era. The DNC chair race has exposed deep fissures within the Democratic Party. Some of these are ideological, but the real story of the race is the diffusion of power away from Washington and to new people and entities that have rushed to fill the vacuum at the top of the party."

When Vilsack, Roemer, and Hindery flopped, the remaining candidates included a sleepy former congressman from Texas, two promising but youthful political operatives, a former mayor of Denver, and a former head of the Ohio Democratic Party. Not exactly the party's A-list. So the search for a credible anti-Dean candidate went on. Bill Clinton and New York senator Chuck Schumer tried to get current DNC chair Terry McAuliffe to consider staying on. When he declined, Governors Bill Richardson of New Mexico and Ed Rendell of Pennsylvania frantically searched for a suitable replacement. Richardson had previously said that he, along with Reid and Pelosi, was "planning to endorse" a candidate who was "not a high-profile liberal"—a not-so-subtle dig at Dean. But neither he nor Rendell found anybody the governors could agree on. "Nobody wanted Howard," Ochs said, "but there was no consensus candidate."

During President Bush's second inaugural ceremony in late

January, Clinton pollster Mark Penn held a party at his $5.1 million town house in Georgetown, feting Bill and Hillary, among other high-profile Clintonistas. "There was a ton of positive energy at the house," a guest told *Newsweek*, "except for the fear and loathing of Dean." A few weeks earlier, Harold Ickes—a deputy chief of staff in the Clinton White House and the son of FDR's powerful secretary of the interior—had briefly entered the chair's race, but failed to gin up any enthusiasm for his bid. At the first meeting in Orlando, Ickes, an old-time New York pol known for his colorful profanity and moody temperament, was asked how state parties could get more financial support from the DNC. "Let me tell you something," Ickes responded, scornfully looking at the questioner as if he'd just shot his dog. "I know all the major donors. The last thing they're interested in doing is helping state parties. They think the money just gets pissed away." So much for playing to the crowd. "Ickes was the personification of why the states were frustrated with the DNC," said Neel Pender, executive director of the Oregon Democratic Party. Before the final DNC chair meeting in New York, Ickes dropped out and endorsed Dean. He made it clear that his endorsement "does not reflect Senator Clinton's opinion."

"We fully expected somebody to be a stalking horse for Hillary, who at that point was the presumptive nominee [for 2008]," Dean adviser Mark Squier said. "We were surprised that that never really formed. It's still one of the most baffling things to this day. Some people think it's the very, very beginning seeds of her not pulling off the nomination. You have to question, well, maybe they should have paid more attention to the party apparatus two years out."

Part of the reason the "anybody but Dean" bandwagon never got rolling was that Dean's many detractors in Washington never made any attempt to understand the roots of his appeal. "Deanism isn't about turning to the left," the *New York Times* columnist Paul Krugman astutely observed. "It's about making a stand." Dean's popularity within the DNC didn't stem from pure ideological affinity. The genius of the fifty-state strategy, a plan national in scope but local in focus, was that it transcended typical ideological barriers and gave disparate Democrats from Colorado to Indiana to North Carolina a common purpose. "The only knock against Howard Dean is that he's seen as too liberal," Scott Maddox, chairman of the Florida Democratic Party, said when he endorsed Dean. "I'm a gun-owning, pickup-truck driver and I have a bulldog named Lockjaw. I am a chairman of a Southern state, and I am perfectly comfortable with Howard Dean as DNC chair . . . What our party needs right now is energy, enthusiasm and a willingness to do things differently. I think Howard Dean brings all three of those things to the party."

The final last-ditch attempt to stop Dean came in New York City, when the executive committee of the state party leaders, known as the Association of State Democratic Chairs (ASDC), hastily called a meeting at the Roosevelt Hotel to endorse a candidate. By a vote of 8 to 6, the executive committee sided with Donnie Fowler, a hip-looking thirty-seven-year-old political operative from South Carolina with floppy brown hair and bookish black rectangular glasses. It just so happened that Fowler's dad, Don Senior, had been head of the DNC under Clinton, and his soon-to-be stepmom, Carol, was a member of the ASDC's executive committee. In addition, Fowler had just run the Kerry campaign in Michigan, and the head of the ASDC served as the state chair of . . . you guessed it, Michigan! Fowler called the ASDC endorsement "a watershed event," but it looked to other members of the DNC like the very sort of backroom deal that Dean was running to stop. "They've ruined their credibility," Wisconsin state chair Linda Honold, a Dean supporter on the committee, told her colleague Paul Berendt of Washington, a fellow Deaniac.

The executive committee scheduled a conference call for the next day with all the state chairs and vice chairs—by far the largest bloc of delegates in the DNC—to ratify the Fowler endorsement. Berendt, who'd taken a red-eye from Seattle to attend the meeting, went back to his hotel room and called every ASDC member he knew until the wee hours, making sure they were on the call and with Dean. Dean aides woke up supporters in Hawaii and Guam to ensure that they voted. That Monday, the executive committee's endorsement backfired, and the ASDC supported Dean by a vote of 56 to 21. DNC members were tired of being told what to do and whom to vote for. Once Dean won the allegiance of the state party chairs, by pledging to invest real time and money in their state and local parties, the race was his. All of the candidates for DNC chair had pledged to back a fifty-state strategy, but Dean seemed like the only one with the clout and base of support to actually make it happen. He was unanimously sworn in as chair two weeks later.

The Clinton wing of the party, which had ruled for over a decade, was particularly apoplectic. "The thing that stuns me is that this is supposed to be a rigged deal—chairman of the party!" James Carville, the bald and belligerent "ragin' Cajun" Svengali to Clinton in 1992, proclaimed in a moment of characteristic bluntness. "The congressional leadership, the fund-raisers, people like that are supposed to decide. You [DNC members] are supposed to get a call and are told who to vote for! You're not supposed to really vote on this shit!"

No one could've described the old way of doing politics better. It was precisely the kind of smug, insular arrogance that helped drive the Democratic Party into a ditch. Nowhere had this good ol' boy syndrome been more prevalent than at party headquarters. Clinton, while president, used the DNC as his personal expense account for TV ads and staggering legal bills. The lines of communication traveled one way, from the White House on down. His last DNC chair, Terry McAuliffe—a.k.a. the Macker—had the distinction of being Bill's best friend and a high-flying schmoozer and incessant name-dropper who titled his memoir *What a Party! My Life Among Democrats: Presidents, Candidates, Donors, Activists, Alligators, and Other Wild Animals.* McAuliffe was great at raising money and loved appearing on TV but didn't care much about the nuts and bolts of grassroots politics, which is precisely where Republicans had been kicking the Democrats' asses. "You are about to become a human fire hydrant," McAuliffe told Dean when they dined on veal paillard at Cafe Milano, the Macker's favorite see-and-be-seen Georgetown dining establishment. "You will get blamed for every loss. You will get zero credit for any win."

Nancy Pelosi and Harry Reid, speaking with a whiff of royal entitlement, reacted dismissively to Dean's new perch. "I think that Governor Dean would take his lead from us," Pelosi said. "The Democratic chairman has a constituency of 447 people," Reid asserted. "Our constituency is much larger than that."

In fact, Dean would soon have a far broader constituency than Reid ever imagined. The same forces that propelled Dean to power in Washington were just as prevalent in the states the DNC chairman would now oversee.

Nowhere was this "silent revolution" in the Democratic Party—as the blogger Jerome Armstrong of MyDD called it—more deeply felt than in North Carolina. On December 21, 2004, the Raleigh *News & Observer* ran an article headlined: "Easley Wants Raleigh Man to Lead State's Democrats." The story began: "Ed Turlington, a Raleigh lawyer who was the right-hand man for such Democratic leaders as Jim Hunt, Terry Sanford and John Edwards, has been tapped to lead the North Carolina Democratic Party during the next two years. Governor Mike Easley has signaled that Turlington, 47, is his choice to become the new state Democratic Party chairman." The article detailed Turlington's impeccable résumé: chief of staff to four-term governor Jim Hunt, executive director of the state party, cochair of the Kerry-Edwards campaign in North Carolina, top aide to presidential candidate Bill Bradley, and confidant of the state's reigning Democratic governor. "Easley's choice will have to be approved by the State Democratic Executive Committee, which meets early next year," the *N&O* noted casually. It was considered a foregone conclusion that state party members would simply rubber-stamp the governor's pick.

Two days later, the *News & Observer* ran another article headlined "Meek Won't Let Easley Anoint a Party Leader." That was Jerry Meek, a thirty-four-year-old, six-foot-eight trial lawyer and party activist from Fayetteville with a deep southern drawl and dry sense of humor who resembled Cameron from *Ferris Bueller's Day Off*. Meek had wanted to run for chair two years earlier but was told to wait in line. He took the number two position of vice chair instead. Now he was being instructed by the governor to wait again. Not this time, he decided. "The governor is one of 570 State Executive Committee members allowed to vote," Meek told the paper. "I'm sorry I won't be having his vote." The *N&O* didn't think much of his chances. "The State Executive Committee has not in recent memory—and probably never—rejected a Democratic governor's choice," it reported. Meek was unfazed by this history. There's nothing he loved more in life than the Democratic Party, and he had quite a few deeply held convictions about the direction it needed to follow in North Carolina. He'd been prepping for this position ever since he was thirteen.

In the summer of 1983, young Meek—a gangly, brainy teenager— wanted to be an astronaut and attended space camp in Huntsville, Alabama. That year Ohio senator John Glenn, the first American to orbit the earth, ran for the Democratic nomination for president. Meek thought it'd be the coolest thing in the world to have an astronaut as president. He started volunteering for Glenn and then Walter Mondale when he won the Democratic primary. One day, at a popular music festival in Fayetteville—a Democratic stronghold since Reconstruction—Meek passed out five thousand flyers for Mondale and felt a tremendous sense of satisfaction. But as he turned the corner to walk home, Meek found a trash can overflowing with Mondale flyers. It was his first taste of the harsh realities of electoral politics. Mondale lost forty-nine states to Ronald Reagan that year, including a twenty-four-point drubbing in North

Carolina. Meek's career in Democratic politics, however, had only just begun.

He became president of the state teen Democrats at fifteen, giving speeches all over the state at rallies and barbecues, where he ate hush puppies and drank sweet tea. He'd take the bus from Fayetteville to Raleigh every weekend. When Meek got his license, at sixteen, he drove to Washington on his first road trip and met Mondale. Feeling emboldened, he drove to Plains, Georgia, the next weekend and met Jimmy Carter. A year later, he became the youngest delegate ever to the Democratic convention in Atlanta. He earned a law degree from Duke at twenty-seven, commuting to Durham from Fayetteville, where he was now running the Cumberland County Democratic Party. He finished law school early and ran for the statehouse against an incumbent Republican. For the first time in his life, Meek lost an election.

He moved to Dallas and became a lawyer specializing in mental health cases. In 2002 he came back to Fayetteville and was "disgusted with the way the state party interacted with the county party," he said. "There was no respect by the state party for how county party leaders thought about what should be done." The canvassers hired by the state party to knock on voters' doors in the days before the election "looked like they came straight from a homeless shelter and probably did," Meek remembered. He decided to run for party chair against Barbara Allen, a genteel former energy executive who was popular with the politicians and donors in Raleigh. Allen cut a deal with Meek—he would become her deputy, and she wouldn't run again in two years, paving the way for his ascension.

Meek had bought a single-engine Cessna prop plane for $64,000 in Dallas and learned how to fly. Nearly every weekend, as vice chair, he flew to the most remote parts of North Carolina to train county parties, averaging six thousand miles a month. Usually a courtesy car, in the form of a 1970s beater with a nominally functioning AM radio, would be waiting for him at the airport. He'd written four different training manuals and would give a three-hour seminar to local party leaders detailing the nuts and bolts of fund-raising, voter targeting, and volunteer recruitment. "I wanted county parties to think more like businesses," Meek said. The local parties, for the most part, tended to be insular, aging institutions with no budget and little funding. Strengthening these parties, Meek thought, held the key to rebuilding the Democratic brand in a conservative state like North Carolina.

When he prepared to run for chair in 2004, Meek heard whispers that Governor Easley—a popular former district attorney from eastern North Carolina who didn't tend to care much about party affairs—was recruiting another candidate, which turned out to be Turlington. Meek, who was regarded as a bit of a rabble-rouser in Raleigh, asked one of the governor's top lieutenants if this was the case. "Yes, it's true," the aide responded. "The governor appreciates all your hard work and would like to find another way to reward you." "At that point," Meek said, "I made up my mind that I was definitely running." The state party, he thought, had become far too closely identified with the wishes of the governor and elected officials in the state capital. "If the activists aren't going to have a role in the party," he wondered, "then where is their voice going to come from?"

The state's entire Democratic congressional delegation and nearly every statewide elected official, in addition to heavy hitters like John Edwards and Bill Bradley, supported Turlington. Meek received exactly one statewide endorsement—from Jim Long, a short, chubby, backslapping state insurance commissioner since 1984 from rural central Carolina. After the *News & Observer* named Easley's pick, Meek called Long and asked if he was still with him. "Hell yeah," Long responded. "Now more than ever." Long circulated a letter in support of Meek to every member of the state executive committee. "While there are some advantages to having a State Party Chair with 'national connections,'" he wrote, "it's time for us to focus our efforts on North Carolina."

Turlington versus Meek became a classic insider versus outsider contest and a microcosm of the DNC chair race, with Meek playing up his distance from Raleigh and his diligent work in the far-flung sections of the state. "Anybody who is anybody is supporting my opponent," he told members of the state executive committee, "but when this election is over, do you think they're going to care about you?" Meek—mirroring Dean's fifty-state strategy—promised to devote resources to every part of the state, most of which he'd already visited, and "leave no county behind." Like Dean, he asked, "Are we going to take our party back?"

As with the DNC, Democratic activists in North Carolina wanted the party to become more relevant and inviting and resented being told how to vote. The state was less red than most outside observers believed—Democrats had just retained the governor's mansion and had controlled the statehouse and senate for decades. But they'd also lost two close U.S. senate races in recent years and watched the Kerry campaign pull out of the state before Labor Day even after putting a favorite son on the ticket. Kerry won only twenty of the state's one hundred counties that year. Local parties, meanwhile, languished in despair, especially in the most heavily Republican pockets of the state. "We see the party made up of grandees and peasants," Hayes McNeill, chairman of the Forsyth County Democrats in Winston-Salem, told the *News & Observer.* "And we peasants think things should be done in a different way."

One afternoon, Bill Bradley—corralling votes for Turlington—called McNeill's friend Delmas Parker, a seventy-two-year-old longtime Democratic activist from the mountains of Western North Carolina known for his loquaciousness. Parker kept Bradley on the line for half an hour, complaining about how the state party always took the votes and concerns of rural mountain folk for granted. After listening to Parker's diatribe, Bradley got around to asking if he'd support Turlington. "Well, Senator, I'm supporting Jerry Meek," Parker told Bradley, "for reasons you wouldn't understand because you're not from North Carolina."

The originally scheduled vote got postponed for three weeks due to "inclement weather"—snow fell hard in the Blue Ridge

Mountains—conveniently giving Turlington's side more time to rustle up votes. Bradley, Edwards, Hunt, Easley, and Lieutenant Governor Bev Perdue all called members of the executive committee on behalf of Turlington. The day of the vote, the executive director of the National Education Association came down from Washington, at Turlington's behest, to lobby teachers on the committee.

On February 19, 2005, the 570 committee members gathered in a fluorescent-lit conference room inside a giant slab of concrete on the campus of North Carolina State University to elect a new party chair. Under the rules, whoever was nominated second advantageously got to speak right before the voting began. Neither side wanted to speak first. At the start of the nominations, nobody uttered a word for three to four unbearable minutes. Jim Long sat at the front of the room with his arms folded and stared down Jim Hunt, the powerful former governor and a beloved figure in the state who was used to getting his way. Hunt, miraculously, budged first and stood to nominate Turlington. Then Long introduced Meek, praising his "fresh leadership and fresh ideas." Meek thought he had the votes but wasn't positive. Before he spoke, his team passed out little packets of grass seeds to signify his commitment to the grass roots. "I believe that our state party has lost touch with the local party," Meek said. "I'll create a party of inclusion where grassroots workers have a real say and power isn't just limited to the Raleigh insiders." It took two hours to count all the votes. When the final tally came in, Meek prevailed by twenty-nine votes, 271 to 242. Wild cheers erupted after the announcement, while Turlington loyalists sat slack-jawed in shock. One Meek supporter from Raleigh declared simply: "The people have won."

Following the vote, the state press, reflecting a common sentiment in Raleigh, immediately savaged Meek and his followers. "Insurgents don't realize that their party in North Carolina is skating on some exceedingly thin ice," wrote Rob Christensen, the top political columnist for the *News & Observer*. His colleague on the editorial page Jim Jenkins concurred. "Party activists now act like people who, if you invited them to an archery tournament, would wear bull's eye sweatshirts," Jenkins wrote. "North Carolina politics is exactly where we expect it to be: somewhere between utter chaos and just north of mayhem."

Like Dean, Meek was stereotyped as a left-wing radical and his supporters miscast as fringe activists. In truth, Meek's candidacy drew strength from urban liberals and rural moderates, both of whom believed the state party no longer represented them. "People felt like the state party was more interested in what was happening in Raleigh and more focused on a small clique of insiders than in giving real power to more people," Meek explained after the vote. "And so it very much ended up being an insider versus outsider campaign, whether you were an outsider because you were ideologically on the left, or you were an outsider because you were in a rural county that nobody cared about. Oddly enough, those two groups shared a common perspective on things. When I was running for chairman, I was able to unite the two."

The outcome in North Carolina turned out to be a harbinger of things to come rather than a distinct anomaly. Across the country, in states as different as Arkansas and Colorado, outsider insurgents swept to power in state party elections. *The Washington Post* dubbed them "The Democrats' Mini-Deans."

As Meek walked to the parking lot after the vote, he received a call from Chairman Dean, who'd been following his race closely. "Congratulations, Jerry," Dean told him. "This is part of a national shift that's about to happen. How can I help you?"

Meek asked Dean to help pay for state party staff outside of Raleigh. Within a month, North Carolina became the first state to have a fifty-state strategy organizer on the ground.

3 ★ MIDTERMS

People started coming out of the woodwork. They said, "Oh my God, the Democratic Party is actually alive." —Mark Hufford

On a soggy Saturday morning in late April 2006, Democrats in Boone, North Carolina, held their first canvass of the new year. This was no small deal around these parts. The DNC had organized a series of nationwide canvasses as part of the fifty-state strategy—and it was fitting that Watauga County came first. Democrats here did grass-roots politics better than just about anyone, creating a small refuge of blue amid mountains of red. Starting in the spring, they'd knock on every conceivable door in the county, block by block, week by week, until the midterm election in November. It didn't matter if you were a Democrat, Republican, or Independent. They believed everyone could be converted and anyone could be beat.

Nestled three thousand feet into the lush scenery of the Blue Ridge Mountains in Western North Carolina, Boone is home to Appalachian State University—one of North Carolina's best public universities—and has many of the trappings of a crunchy college town: a pizza place named Mellow Mushroom, a video store with an extensive kung fu collection, a preserved downtown lined with coffee shops, art galleries, and a retro greasy spoon. Drive a few minutes out of town, however, and the county turns real red, real quick. The mountain folk of Western North Carolina (more commonly known by the acronym WNC) are about as conservative as you can get—religious, traditional, resistant to change. Much of the region feels frozen in time. If Howard Dean wanted to craft a national party, he'd need to start in places like this, which establishment Democrats had long ignored.

The seventy-odd Democrats assembled that morning in 2006 wore bright red T-shirts that said "Democratic Pride" in large white lettering, with the phrase "We're on your side" written below in cursive. "Watauga Co. Democratic Party" was stamped on the back of the shirt in big block lettering. There was no mistaking this crowd. State party chair Jerry Meek drove three hours from Raleigh for the occasion. Also present was his new field director for WNC, Mark Hufford. Hufford faced a daunting task—of the thirty-three counties in his sprawling mountainous region, every single one went for President Bush in 2004. Watauga was in better shape than most; Kerry lost the county by only six points (in some of the neighboring counties, Bush won by fifty), and Democrats swept all the local races. Meek and Hufford wanted to know how and if the "Watauga Model" could be transferred to the surrounding red counties.

The pre-canvass training and pep talk was led by Pam Williamson, a lively fifty-three-year-old woman with short curly blond hair and a bawdy sense of humor. In a land of despondent Democrats, Williamson was a fearless partisan and master strategist, the closest Democrats in Watauga had to a Karl Rove. "I am only out for blood," she said in her raspy drawl, "and that is Republican blood. I want every one of them out." Williamson's family were farmers from the mountains of rural southwest Virginia, "rode hard and put up wet," she said. Her father taught biology at North Carolina State University and, over the years, became a staunch Republican. "Rush Limbaugh poisoned him," she said. Williamson went to school at Appalachian State, lived for a time in Washington working for "big business" (Ernst & Young), then returned to Boone in 1983, marrying a former professor of hers. She'd been doing politics pretty much ever since.

That morning, Williamson fired up the troops by hammering home her motto: "No matter what the issue is, Democrats are always better than Republicans!" She had her volunteers practically shouting the slogan by the time they went out to knock on doors. "*Do not* argue about hot-button issues like abortion and gun control," she told the volunteers. "You won't change their minds." She urged them to emphasize local concerns or more favorable national terrain like health care and the economy. "If you sense a soft Republican, try persuasion," she said. "If you sense a strong Republican, move on." Williamson was a big believer in the efficacy of door knocking to spread the Democrats' message—she relied on research by Yale political scientists Donald Green and Alan Gerber, who found that door-to-door canvassing increased the probability of voter turnout by up to 10 percent, a more effective route than calling a potential voter or sending a piece of mail from the candidate. "We were in a Republican county," Williamson said, "and we kept asking ourselves, what are we gonna do to win?"

Democrats started getting their act together in Watauga after what many in the party considered one of the darkest moments in the state's political history. Back in 1990 and 1996, when Harvey Gantt ran for the Senate against Jesse Helms, whose Bible-thumping conservatism became the face of southern Republicanism, the local Democratic Party didn't lift a finger to help Gantt, the first African-American student admitted to Clemson University. Gantt studied architecture and graduated with honors from Clemson, earned a master's degree in city planning at MIT, and went on to become a popular mayor of Charlotte. Yet race played a major role in both of his campaigns, especially when Helms ran the infamous "White Hands" ad alleging that because of racial quotas, black workers stole white jobs. Gantt narrowly lost both elections. "There was no difference between the parties," said Williamson. Democrats had been captured by the town's business elite, which supported Helms. Williamson and other young Gantt volunteers were so furious at the party's old guard that they decided, in 1997, to stage a coup. They recruited enough volunteers to elect their own officers at the party's next organizing meeting, unexpectedly ousting the longtime regulars. The bitter old-timers said Democrats would never win again.

Finding local issues that would divide Republicans and unite Democrats became the blueprint for the party's success. Williamson and company rebuilt the Democratic brand by linking Republican candidates to crooked businessmen and shady developers. "If the Democrats didn't stand up for poor and sick people," she asked herself, "then what good were we?" In the following years, Watauga Democrats blocked the construction of an asphalt plant on a scenic river, stopped the demolition of a historic African-American neighborhood, and prevented the residents of a long-standing trailer park from getting thrown out of their homes by a developer. "Neighbors Working for Neighbors" became the slogan of the party. Long before it was in vogue, Williamson nurtured a fleet of community organizers, many of whom ran for office themselves. One of the leaders of the coup, Loretta Clawson, a cheerful woman in her sixties, became mayor of Boone.

That Saturday in April, Williamson sent Meek out canvassing with Ingrid Kraus, a local psychologist. "Take him to a lower-income neighborhood," she instructed her, "and make sure he learns something." Kraus took Meek to her hometown of Meat Camp, a mountainous enclave a few miles outside of town, where small Baptist churches practically outnumber people and legend has it that Daniel Boone stored his meat in a cave on hunting trips. Meat Camp was Williamson's favorite place to canvass. The terrain rose sharply from a base of rolling farmland into the thick of the mountains. A creek snaked alongside Meat Camp Road, where an old buckwheat mill used to be. Locals used to farm tobacco and corn on the hills with a horse plow. Now they mostly raised cattle, herding the livestock into rusty old wood barns. Many of the two thousand residents of Meat Camp worked for the city or the university, if they worked at all. The Meat Camp Fire Station and Meat Camp Baptist Church, founded in 1851, were the only public markings for the area. Otherwise, the place resembled a lot of WNC, with a mix of trailers, small ranch houses, and a few nicer properties up near the mountains populated by retirees from Florida. That day, Meek and Kraus visited a relatively poor section, where few people had health insurance and many didn't bother to vote. In one of the first houses Meek stepped into, his foot went crashing through a wooden plank near the entrance. "I feel like I'm in Mexico," he told Kraus.

"It was the kind of place you think of when you read *What's the Matter with Kansas?*" Meek said. "You wonder why these people are voting Republican, but they are." Abortion and gay marriage were big issues in Meat Camp. So were guns, evidenced by a popular shooting range in the valley, where locals fired at clay pigeons and into the mountain embankment.

One day, a few years earlier, Williamson received a call that a developer wanted to store his sewage tanks on the top of a nearby mountain, where the runoff was likely to infect the area's water. She drove out to see a family on the northeast end of Meat Camp, where a sparse road turns into rough gravel and climbs sharply. She abandoned her van and went up to a ramshackle house on a hill. On the porch sat a guy wearing an NRA cap and a shirt with an image of a target filled with arrows. His brother wore a blue shirt that said "C.O.P.S." in white lettering, short for "Christians Obediently Preaching Salvation." This is my kind of place, Williamson thought to herself.

"I'm here on behalf of the Watauga County Democratic Party," she told them. "What can we do to help?" Neither man seemed thrilled that a woman from the Democratic Party was standing on his porch. "Has the Republican Party been here?" she asked them. It hadn't. The brothers confirmed that a developer wanted to store the sewage near their land.

Williamson sued the county. She lost and appealed the decision. When that failed, she made the developer very unpopular with the county commissioners, which eventually led him to pull out of the project. Meat Camp became one of the first communities where party activists knocked on every door. Despite its cultural conservatism, Williamson hoped to get 50 percent of the vote there in 2006. Her brand of grassroots activism, neighbors working for neighbors, underscored a broader electoral strategy—remake the Democratic Party by owning local issues and addressing people's everyday concerns.

From that first canvass, Watauga Democrats could tell that county residents had begun to sour on the GOP. In 2004, even good Democrats kept telling Williamson that George Bush deserved a chance to finish what he started. No longer was that the prevailing sentiment. Residents now protested the deteriorating situation in Iraq, the slowdown in the economy, and the escalating price of health care. They complained most vociferously about the rising cost of gas prices, which had neared $3 a gallon in North Carolina and across the country—sending Bush's approval rating to an all-time low. When he got back to Raleigh, Meek fired off a press release: "Gas Price Crisis Continues to Burn North Carolina Working Families." "Bush Republicans," he wrote, "have given a free pass to oil and gas companies that are charging record prices even as they reap record profits." It was the type of message, Meek assured himself, that would play well in a place like Watauga. Now he just needed to get WNC's thirty-two other counties in the same shape.

When Hufford came on board as a DNC organizer in the spring of 2005, he drove his Subaru wagon to all the counties in his region to see firsthand what kind of shape they were in. He was startled, but not necessarily surprised, by the condition of many of the local parties. "A lot of them at that time didn't have e-mail," he said. "Most county parties didn't have websites." A squat forty-eight-year-old with a jovial demeanor, Hufford was almost always the youngest person in the room. When he tried to get the locals to go out and knock on doors, he often heard: "Well, that just ain't the way things are done around here." Hufford and Meek hoped they could help turn things around, convening a Western Task Force to look at everything east of Winston-Salem as an interconnected region rather than a series of essentially abandoned counties.

Hufford knew this turf well. He grew up in D.C. but had lived in WNC since 1980. He started a nonprofit wildlife organization and brought hawks and owls into schools to teach kids about the importance of conserving the environment. Over time, he realized that his congressman, a wealthy banker and farmer named Charles Taylor, controlled the purse strings for the national parks by virtue of his position in Congress and had been systematically gutting their funding. Environmental groups dubbed Taylor "Chainsaw Charlie." In 2004, Hufford managed the campaign of Taylor's opponent, Patsy Keever, a county commissioner from Asheville. Keever ran a spirited campaign but ultimately lost by ten points. The race convinced Hufford of the need to revive the Democratic Party in the area—a Democratic stronghold since the Civil War that had turned bright red since the Reagan and Gingrich revolutions. Democrats still technically outnumbered Republicans, but lost election after election.

Meek put Hayes McNeill, a gregarious fellow with a snow-white beard and a singsong southern accent, in charge of the Western Task Force. McNeill grew up in Wilkes County, once known as the Moonshine Capital of the World, then moved to Winston-Salem to work at Wake Forest University, most recently as special assistant to the president. He lived in a spacious 1950s brick house in a tidy university neighborhood. His office also doubled as a ramshackle antiques shop for all his political memorabilia. On the far wall hung a poster of his father, R. H. "Bob" McNeill, a bottler of Coca-Cola who ran for county commissioner in Wilkes. "He got more votes than Kennedy," McNeill said. "They both lost." According to McNeill, the county hadn't voted for a Democratic presidential candidate since the days of Andrew Jackson. As he told it, there were really three Democratic parties in North Carolina: the governor's party, the legislature's party, and "the real one," which McNeill described as "us poor bastards out in the foxholes." That's who he wanted to serve.

The task force studied how Democrats were viewed in the region. "We're perceived as spineless, wimpy complainers who don't stand for anything," Hufford wrote. Republicans had been successfully hammering Democrats for years on issues like abortion. Hufford and McNeill realized that Democrats needed a few wedge issues of their own. They consulted a Pew report from May 2005, which said that while Democrats were divided on social issues, Republicans were torn over the proper role of government. Democrats could make inroads by pushing issues like lower gas prices, retirement security, better funding for public education, and conserving the environment.

When the thirty members of the task force convened for a meeting at the governor's western residence, a brick and dark wood Americana home in the verdant hills overlooking Asheville, Hufford pitched the idea of resurrecting the old Burma-Shave ad campaign, a series of rhyming jingles for shaving cream that became popular roadside billboards from the 1920s to the 1950s, before the explosion of the interstate highway system. (A sample from 1932: "You'll love your wife/You'll love her paw/You'll even love/Your mother-in-law/If you use/Burma-Shave.") Those old enough to fondly remember the folksy jingles especially loved the idea. Hufford raised $40,000 in two days and printed up four hundred sets of blue and red signs, plastering them all over WNC. The first set went up in the spring of 2006 and focused on gas prices. It read: "The high price of gas/Greatly impacts us/But Big Oil's politicos/Still avoid taxes/WNC Democrats/Emphasize energy independence." (Hufford's catchier initial draft—"When filling your tank/Empties your pocket/Terrorists win/Without launching one rocket"—was deemed too provocative by the house and senate caucus.) It may not have seemed like much, but the ad campaign galvanized Democrats in the area. "When the Burma-Shave signs started going up," Hufford said, "people started coming out of the woodwork. They said, 'Oh my God, the Democratic Party is actually alive.'"

Every month or two, a tight-knit group of black women Democratic political operatives—who called themselves, affectionately, the "Colored Girls"—met for dinner in Washington. The group included Donna Brazile, the tart-tongued, Bayou-born campaign manager of Al Gore's 2000 presidential run; Leah Daughtry, a Pentecostal preacher from Brooklyn who served as Terry McAuliffe's chief of staff; and Tina Flournoy, a high-ranking official with the American Federation of Teachers. The "Colored Girls" formed an unlikely inner circle for Dean when he came to Washington. They'd risen from obscurity to become mainstays in D.C., even if they didn't always feel part of the capital's old (mostly white) boys' club. "We'd all worked in Washington for a long time," Flournoy said, "but we believed that the party had to be bigger than the candidate. Dean's emphasis on really working with the states was something we found appealing."

In the winter of 2005, they invited Dean to dinner at Nora, a fashionable organic restaurant on a tree-lined street in Dupont Circle. They brought along Cornell Belcher, one of only two prominent black pollsters in the Democratic Party. Dean immediately liked Belcher. "He and I just clicked," Belcher said, "because—although some of my friends are big in the establishment column—I've never really been an establishment sort of guy." The thirty-five-year-old from Norfolk, Virginia, liked to think and dress outside of the box, sporting a short, curly salt-and-pepper Afro, round black glasses, and a trim goatee. The day I first met him, Belcher wore a well-tailored gray-tweed three-piece suit, a black polka-dot tie, and a pink-and-black-striped shirt, paired with black Converse sneakers. Daughtry had just asked him to survey "values voters" in eight red and purple states, such as North Carolina, Iowa, and New Mexico. He found that religious voters, who made up a huge percentage of the electorate on both sides of the aisle, were drifting away from the party at an alarming rate. In 2004, Bush won voters who said their most important issue was "moral values" by sixty-two points. Unless the Democrats began to cut into the GOP's advantage on some of this terrain, they could very well be a minority party forever.

Dean believed the poll's findings buttressed his plan to target voters unaccustomed to hearing from Democrats and asked Belcher to be his pollster at the DNC. He kept Daughtry on as his chief of staff and put Flournoy in charge of getting the DNC up and running. In addition, Dean recruited Karen Finney, a tall, intense African-American woman who'd been a top aide to Hillary Clinton, as his communications director. Longtime Dean aide Tom McMahon, a reliable Midwesterner from Omaha, became his executive director. He also hired Pam Womack, a Virginian with a deep southern drawl and gravelly laugh, as his political director. Womack knew Dean from her days at the Democratic Governors Association and had been in her fair share of smoky back rooms, becoming acquainted with all the major players in state politics. To update the party's technology, Dean brought on a pair of young techies from his campaign, Joe Rospars and Ben Self, who'd just founded a company called Blue State Digital.

For all the talk of traditional conservatism, when it came to politics, Republicans were far more innovative and experimental than Democrats. Ever since Richard Nixon ambled up to Madison Avenue in 1968, Republicans had understood the power of television ads, and later direct mail and the Internet, as a means of reaching voters well before the Democrats did. In 2000, Democrats viewed George Bush's win as an aberration, stolen by the Supreme Court and lost by a dismally run, cardboard-stiff Gore campaign. But in the 2002 midterm elections, Karl Rove blindsided Democrats with an impeccably planned turnout blitz known as the 72-Hour Plan, rapidly increasing the Republican vote in fast-growing suburbs and driving up GOP turnout in rural areas Democrats had long abandoned.

In 2004, Rove expanded the plan and borrowed Amway's famous volunteer-based organizing model, using churches, gun clubs, and other local groups as recruiting centers. By February 2004, the RNC knew precisely how many volunteers it needed on the ground in Ohio, where they would be, and what they'd be doing. The Democrats didn't even begin organizing in key swing states like Florida until well after the Democratic convention in July. Short on money and behind on planning, the Kerry campaign outsourced much of its ground game to new 527 groups (named after their tax code) like America Coming Together, which could raise unlimited sums of money from large donors but couldn't legally coordinate with the party and never built a base of support in most communities. "We sent fourteen thousand people into Ohio from elsewhere," Dean explained on *Meet the Press*. "They had fourteen thousand from Ohio talking to their neighbors, and that's how you win in rural states and rural America." In fact, it's how you win everywhere. Republicans used a combination of polling, census, and commercial data, through a burgeoning technology called microtargeting, to identify pockets of potential voters that Democrats never bothered to find, such as Russian Jewish émigrés in suburban Cleveland. In 2004, Bush won ninety-seven of the one hundred fastest-growing counties in America. No wonder Rove thought his permanent majority was just around the corner.

Everything came together for Republicans at the Republican National Committee (RNC). The GOP could plug in nearly any candidate, even one as hapless as Bush, and get him elected president. "In the years of Republican dominance, one of the things that was striking was how institutionalized the RNC was," said Elaine Kamarck, a top strategist under Clinton and lecturer at Harvard University's Kennedy School of Government. "They had stable teams, personnel; it wasn't a revolving cast of characters. It was really the place they built a base of strength from."

The DNC, on the other hand, had often been a laughingstock, chronically broke and maligned. When Ron Brown, a former aide to Jesse Jackson and future commerce secretary under Clinton, took over the organization in 1989, Daughtry remembers, staffers were forced to ration Xerox paper. Things didn't get a whole lot better even when Democrats controlled the White House, as Clinton's many legal bills sent the committee into a staggering level of debt. "Democratic presidents worked assiduously to personalize their parties," wrote Northwestern University political science professor Daniel Galvin, "but they took few steps, if any, to leave behind a more robust party organization able to persevere over the long term." When McAuliffe took over in 2001, the DNC still had a Republican landlord in an office that "smelled *terrible*," he said. There were left-over pizza boxes and papers everywhere. The RNC had 150 million names of voters in their database, while DNC staffers still used Windows 95.

McAuliffe found a new headquarters across the street, on the abandoned south end of Capitol Hill, next to a busy freeway and a large coal plant, which resembled the color of week-old salmon on the outside. It was, however, quite nice on the inside—airy, modern, and loftlike. "We had a great building and no debt," Dean said when he took over. "But there was essentially no technological infrastructure and no political infrastructure of any worth." McAuliffe didn't much care for the state parties, who, by and large, had been left to fend for themselves. Dean had to make the case that creating such "infrastructure," the kind of resolutely unsexy word that conjures the gray morass of the Soviet Union, could spark the party's electoral revival.

He looked to the GOP as a model. "I hate the Republicans and everything they stand for," Dean, in classic form, told a gathering of Democrats in New York City in February 2005, "but I admire their discipline and their organization." During the race for DNC chair, the state chairs asked Dean and the other contenders to pledge $200,000 a year to each state party. Dean enthusiastically embraced and enlarged the plan and gave every state the resources to hire three or four staffers and access to a high-tech database of voters the DNC was constructing. He immediately sent out teams of political operatives as forensic scientists to undertake a thorough assessment of every state party and make recommendations that would inform the structure and composition of the fifty-state strategy. Not every state was treated equally—a marquee battleground like Ohio still got more money than an emerging swing state like Colorado, which received more funding than a deep red state like Idaho. But every state got something. That might not sound like much, but it was tantamount to a paradigm shift within the Democratic Party, which tended to view the DNC as a PR agency and ATM for the White House and/or Congress. As Caroline Valand, executive director of the North Carolina Democratic Party, put it: "You can do a whole lot more with three people than you can do with zero."

Yet no Democratic Party leader had ever made the case that this was how the party should spend its money. "It was a revolutionary thought!" said former DNC chair and Dean confidant Steve Grossman. "Dean said the Democratic Party is only going to be as robust and as vibrant as its weakest link." In truth, there were more than a few weak links, and not just in hopelessly red states such as Utah. "There were *a lot* of states that were in terrible shape," Dean said. Democrats were behind Republicans pretty much everywhere, outside of a dozen reliably blue states.

"The Democratic Party had, unfortunately, been guilty of far too much elitism for too long in its fund-raising, in its Washington-centric approach, in its rather narrowly defined view of the political battlefield," Grossman said. In many states, the party had abandoned the battlefield before the battle had even begun. Dean saw his strategy as the only corrective, both philosophically and practically, to the negative perception many potentially persuadable voters had of the party. "I wanted to move the power outside Washington," Dean said, "because inside Washington it had become the handmaiden for elected officials, and that's not how you expand the party." Over time, the idea was to turn red states less red, purple states blue, and blue states bluer. "Sometimes you need a simple idea to cut through a lot of BS," said then Virginia governor Tim Kaine. One of the most thankless jobs in Washington became the laboratory for one of the most exciting experiments in Democratic Party history.

Transferring authority away from Washington, not surprisingly, didn't sit well with those accustomed to running the show inside the corridors of power. It didn't help that Dean himself got off to a rocky start as DNC chair. He usually did fine when he traveled the states, kicking off a red-state bus tour, fittingly, in Kansas, and receiving boisterous receptions in places like Mississippi and Tennessee, where party operatives were convinced the Vermont Yankee would never play. But Dean kept making statements in the summer of 2005 that got him into trouble back in D.C. At the Massachusetts Democratic Party convention on May 14: "I think Tom DeLay ought to go back to Houston, where he can serve his jail sentence." Before a liberal gathering in Washington on June 2: "A lot of them [Republicans] never made an honest living in their lives." At a June 6 fund-raiser in San Francisco: The Republicans are "a pretty monolithic party. They all behave the same. They all look the same. It's pretty much a white Christian party."

Some of these remarks were perfectly defensible in their proper context; others were not. All of them provoked sharp and rapid disavowals from the party's presidential aspirants and would-be standard-bearers. "He doesn't speak for me with that kind of rhetoric," said Joe Biden, "and I don't think he speaks for the majority of Democrats." "It may get to the point where the party may need to look elsewhere for leadership," warned Tennessee congressman Harold Ford Jr. Wyoming governor Dave Freudenthal said simply: "I don't care about Howard Dean." The GOP eagerly exploited every one of these media controversies. After the "white Christian" remark, Dean's communications director, Karen Finney, told him that if he screwed up again, he was done. Dean's executive director, Tom McMahon, urged him to stop playing off the crowd and stick with the script, however limited it might be. "Don't listen to the voices," McMahon told his boss in jest.

The uproar over Dean's words overshadowed the early successes of his strategy. In 2005, Democrats elected the first African-American mayor of Mobile, Alabama, and the DNC put $5 million into the successful gubernatorial campaign of Tim Kaine in Virginia. In April 2006, Tulsa, Oklahoma, elected a Democratic woman as mayor. Yet this news failed to capture the headlines. Once Dean became more disciplined and his gaffes largely subsided, the talk turned to dollar signs. "Forget Howard Dean's mouth," read a subhead in *The Boston Globe*. "The real issue facing the Democrats is dollars."

Dean had been raising money at a good pace, but he was also spending it at a fast clip, putting organizers in the field and building a centralized, high-tech database of voters. The party had gone from zero to sixty practically overnight. As was usually the case, the DNC had far less cash in the bank compared with the RNC. McAuliffe and those close to him, ever protective of his legacy, began spreading the word that Dean wasn't raising as much as he should be. "Democrats Losing Race for Funds Under Dean," ran a *Washington Post* headline. Few of the stories mentioned that Dean had raised more in 2005 than McAuliffe had during 2003. "We raised 20 percent more than Terry did before the [2004] nomination," Dean complained, "so this business about Dean, the reluctant fund-raiser, is bullshit." At the same time, the RNC, flush with Bush Pioneers and Rangers, had been hauling in more than ever before. The traditional big donors to the DNC never liked Dean to begin with, and the small donors from his presidential campaign didn't always readily follow him over to the party, which felt more opaque and stagnant than a high-voltage presidential campaign. At the beginning of 2006, the RNC had $34 million in the bank, compared with just $5.5 million at the DNC.

Yet all the cash in the world couldn't mask the escalating scandals of the Bush administration and the Republican Congress, from Hurricane Katrina to Tom DeLay to Jack Abramoff. The 2006 midterm elections had suddenly become surprisingly competitive, and the predicted Republican stranglehold didn't feel so secure. But at the very moment when Democrats should have banded together to exploit Republican weakness, they turned their fire on each other. In the spring and summer of 2006, Dean had the misfortune of picking a fight with two of the most ambitious, power-hungry, media-savvy, cutthroat operators in all of Washington. An epic battle about how and where to spend the party's limited resources had been simmering for months and now boiled over.

In early May, Rahm Emanuel and Chuck Schumer, the leaders of the House and Senate Democratic election committees, went to see Dean at the DNC. They each brought along a top aide and sat on plush tan leather couches—cushy remnants of the McAuliffe era—in Dean's third-floor corner office. The atmosphere was anything but relaxed. Dean and his staff knew a fight was brewing.

Rahm wanted Dean to give him $150,000 to $200,000 each for forty targeted House races. When Dean insisted that DNC money be spent solely on the fifty-state strategy, Rahm flew into a rage. Such verbal aggression was certainly not out of character for the rail-thin, ballet-trained, hyperactive drill sergeant from Chicago whose political style was memorably described by his friend Paul Begala as "a cross between a hemorrhoid and a toothache." Rahmbo, as the lore goes, lost half of his much-used right middle finger in a meat grinder in high school, once sent a dead fish to a pollster he disliked, and regularly taunted reporters and political enemies in unprintable bursts of vulgarity. The son of a pediatrician and a social worker, he grew up in a hypercompetitive family on the North Side of Chicago, with two brothers, Ari, a high-powered Hollywood agent and inspiration for the foulmouthed bully Ari Gold on HBO's *Entourage*, and Ezekiel, a prominent bioethicist at Harvard. Rahm majored in liberal arts at Sarah Lawrence College and earned a master's in speech at Northwestern University before working as a top lieutenant for Chicago mayor Richard M. Daley, the son of the famed city boss and overseer of a powerful Democratic machine.

Rahm became a relentless fund-raiser for Bill Clinton and entered the Clinton White House as its political director at thirty-three. His brash demeanor quickly alienated top Clinton aides, including Hillary Clinton. When White House chief of staff Mack McLarty ostensibly fired him, Rahm refused to leave, accepting instead the lowly position of "director of special projects." Yet soon enough, he was back pushing major bills through Congress, like the North American Free Trade Agreement—which rankled many of the president's liberal allies—and the 1994 crime bill. He survived as a senior adviser to Clinton and left the White House in 1998 for the lucrative world of investment banking, where he quickly made millions in Chicago.

In 2002, with Daley's blessing, he threw his hat in the ring for Illinois's Fifth Congressional District seat—a heavily Democratic Polish-American enclave of North Chicago—when Rod Blagojevich vacated the post to run for governor. "You don't get any lower on the food chain," Rahm said after entering the House in January 2003. To no one's surprise, however, he rapidly climbed the ladder in Congress, accepting Nancy Pelosi's offer to run the Democratic Congressional Campaign Committee (DCCC)—an instant springboard for ambitious young members—after the 2004 election. Engineering an improbable takeover of the House would put Rahm on a fast track to realizing his lifelong dream—becoming the first Jewish Speaker of the House. He wasn't about to let anyone, least of all Howard Dean, stand in his way. "Everybody is a fucking idiot to Rahm," said his longtime ally James Carville. Now Dean was the biggest fucking idiot of them all.

Rahm didn't think much of the fifty-state strategy or the organizers Dean had hired. "I've met the kids," he told Nancy Pelosi. "I've been in sixty districts. They couldn't find their ass with both hands tied behind their back." In the meeting with Dean, Rahm asked the DNC chair what he planned to do for each of his competitive races.

"Don't worry, there's going to be a ground game," Dean told him. "There will be money going out into the states—we're putting that piece together." Rahm wanted specifics. He turned to Dean's political director, Pam Womack, whom he also distrusted, and pointed his finger menacingly at her. "All right, what are you going to do in these forty districts?" he asked her. "Go through them right now." Womack said that many of the organizers hired by the state parties would help out with Rahm's races. Rahm was unsatisfied with her answer. He raised his arms in exasperation and slammed his fists down. "Your field plan is not a field plan," he told Dean. "That's fucking bullshit. It's not real."

The typically pugilistic Dean stayed calm, mostly just listened, and assured Rahm that the DNC would meet its end of the bargain. Dean could be as stubborn as they come, and he wasn't about to be bullied by Rahm's antics. "He wasn't going to use it for the things I thought were important," Dean said later. "We didn't give anybody any money—not Schumer, not Rahm—unless it had a long-term purpose as well as a short-term purpose." Dean and his aides feared that Rahm would spend the DNC's money on expensive and often frivolous TV ads, which did little to build the party and conveniently lined the pockets of the same select group of increasingly discredited Washington consultants. "There's frustration inside the Beltway because I want to do things differently," Dean said at the time, "but if we don't do things differently, we'll be extinct as a party."

After he was done speaking his piece, Rahm stood up abruptly and said, "I have to go vote." He slammed the door on his way out and swore as he left the office. DNC chief of staff Leah Daughtry kept a swear box on the desk of her office, which adjoined Dean's. When someone cursed, he or she had to make a contribution. If Rahm had been a paying customer as he walked out, Daughtry would've been rich.

Schumer, ever the deal maker, apologized for Rahm's behavior and tried to have a productive discussion. "Look, that's not what my viewpoint is," he told Dean. "We want the DNC to do what it can do. The biggest thing we want you to do is tell us on the front end what you think you can do and when, so we can plan accordingly."

"You should know me by now, Chuck," Dean responded. "You might not always like what I have to say, but I'll be totally straight with you."

Though they had their fair share of disagreements, Dean and New York's senior senator remained amicable. On the other hand, his face-off with Rahm had only just begun. According to Dean, Schumer wanted the money but was willing to negotiate the terms; Rahm was not. "For Schumer it was all about the money," Dean said. "He had a job to do, and in order to execute the job, he needed more money, and once he got the money, we were out of the line of fire." With Rahm, Dean said, "it was about more than that. Rahm likes to do it his way and I like to do it my way, so that's the way it was." He made the clash sound almost inevitable. "I've never met anyone in politics who enjoys a fight as much as Howard Dean," said Bob Rogan, Dean's longtime aide in Vermont. One could easily have said the same about Rahm.

The two didn't speak again until Election Day, but their paths crossed often in the press. Soon enough, details of the confrontational meeting hit all the major papers. Dean refused to talk about it publicly and instructed his aides to hold their fire; Rahm exercised no such restraint. He knew all of Washington's best reporters and didn't hesitate to tell them what a disaster Dean was. Practically every week, a damning article about Dean appeared in a major paper. *Washington Post*: "Democrats Are Fractured over Strategy, Funds." *New York Times*: "Dean and Party Leaders in Money Dispute." *Chicago Tribune*: "Democrats Fear Rifts Risk Midterm Victory; Dean, Emanuel at Odds on Strategy for Party." Rahm fueled all of this coverage. "[Dean's] management of money has left us at a historic disadvantage at a historic time," Rahm told his biographer, the *Chicago Tribune*'s Naftali Bendavid. "I don't know how else to say it." Things went on like this for months. Because so much attention had gone into rebuilding the party for the long haul, the DNC was initially ill prepared for 2006, and Rahm was singularly obsessed with it, saying of his GOP opponents: "I have my knee on their verte-brae and I'm not going to let up until I hear the vertebrae snap."

Rahm had a point. The impact of the nascent fifty-state strategy varied widely from state to state and even within different parts of a state. To get the states to buy into the program, the DNC purposely gave state parties, many of whom were initially skeptical, a lot of leeway on how to implement it. Success depended in large part on the competence of the state chairs, whom they hired, and how they used that staff. When Dean took over, many of these parties were in bad shape. As they received an infusion of resources, growing pains, missed opportunities, and outright failures occurred. Some chairs hired political cronies to fill the DNC positions, while in other states organizers disappeared into the wilderness with little ac-countability. Yet despite these inherent flaws, and as important as Rahm's task of taking back the House was, Dean argued persua-sively that his experiment needed time to work. He wasn't simply going to abandon his strategy halfway into the first major election cycle. No matter how valid Rahm's tenacious criticism, he didn't seem to realize how the party had changed. As former DNC chair Joe Andrew put it, "Rahm forgot that Dean didn't work for him."

In addition to empowering local activists, Dean wanted Demo-crats to draw sharper contrasts with the GOP on the issues of the day. The congressional leadership, Rahm included, tended to be su-premely cautious. Starting in 2005, Dean began pushing a plan drafted by two foreign policy experts at the Center for American Progress to pull U.S. troops from Iraq within two years. Rahm didn't want his candidates to talk about withdrawal, fearing it would make Democrats look weak. He said of the war in December 2005, "As for Iraq policy, at the right time, we'll have a position." In May 2005, Dean also labeled the swelling Republican scandals in Congress "a culture of corruption" during an appearance on *Meet the Press*. A high-ranking congressional aide called Karen Finney and told her the phrase was too harsh and Dean shouldn't use it. In a matter of months, however, such wording became a key part of the Democratic message for 2006.

Dean versus Rahm prompted a more fundamental discussion of what a political party, particularly the Democratic Party, should stand for. Rob Johnson, a major Democratic Party donor and former chief economist on the Senate Banking Committee, once argued that the real fight among leading thinkers in the Democratic Party and the progressive movement pitted "party subsidizers," those who simply wanted to elect more Democrats, against "climate changers," those who wanted to change the paradigm in which politicians operated (not to be confused with global-warming advocates). The analogy fit perfectly in this case. Emanuel and Schumer wanted Dean to subsidize the party; Dean wanted to change it. "I was fighting for a new idea," he said. "And there are always people who resist anything new, and in Washington the resistance is at its height."

Dean told me more than once that the fight with Rahm was the best thing that ever happened to the fifty-state strategy. "Political writers will rarely write about substance," he explained, citing his lifelong distrust of the press. "But they like to write about combat, so every time they did a column, which was once every two weeks, first of all it would end up on the front page, because there wasn't that much going on, and secondly, in order to write about what the fight was about, they had to explain what the fifty-state strategy was, usually somewhere in the first four paragraphs. So on the front page of almost every major paper in the country, every two weeks, was something about the fifty-state strategy. And the average Democrat in the country thought, 'Hey, this is great, this fifty-state strategy. I matter again. You know, there's somebody in Washington that cares about us.'"

That may have been true, particularly among the party's grassroots activists, but the fight with Rahm certainly weakened Dean's standing in Washington and made him an easy target for subsequent criticism. He'd undertaken a difficult juggling act, ceding power to the states while trying to win respect for his long-term vision inside the Beltway during a crucial election year. "I know how hard it was and the kind of criticism he took," said Donna Brazile, "when all they wanted the DNC to do was raise money and send it downstairs to the DCCC and across the street to the Democratic Governors Association and down the block to the Democratic Senatorial Campaign Committee. And Dean said no: we're going to play, we're going to have a role, we're going to be a part of this."

The brutal day after the 2004 election, when most Democrats sank into a prolonged depression, Terry McAuliffe huddled with his staff at the DNC to figure out how to explain to his top donors why his party had just lost another election they were supposed to win. As one of his key projects, McAuliffe had poured millions into compiling a database of voters, known as Demzilla, which he promised would be on par with the vaunted Republicans' system. That day, McAuliffe's tall, white-haired tech guru, Laura Quinn, went through a PowerPoint presentation detailing the GOP's remaining advantages. "Republicans have better targeting," said one of the slides.

"Wait, wait, wait," McAuliffe responded. "What do you mean, we can't do what the Republicans do?"

Quinn explained that Demzilla hadn't worked as seamlessly as planned.

McAuliffe launched into a red-faced, expletive-filled tirade. "No wonder we lost," he said.

In the fall of 2004, the Kerry campaign had commissioned an evaluation of Demzilla by the consulting firm Booz Allen. After the election, Dean saw the report. You're only as good as your data, the saying goes in politics, and the Democrats' data was no good. If you punched in the city of Fort Lauderdale, for example, Fort was a city and Lauderdale was a country. There were more Democratic voters listed in Colorado than the population of the state as a whole. The state parties particularly disliked the national database and used their own, which varied from state to state. Campaigns came and went and took all their precious information with them when it was all over. As a result, each new campaign had to start from scratch, causing a colossal amount of redundancy and repetition every election cycle when it came to identifying voters. Dean wanted one central database, which every state would buy into, that would improve from election to election. That simple proposition turned into "the great insider argument," Leah Daughtry said.

Dean brought his own team of young Deaniacs into the DNC to develop a new database, which he called Vote Builder. "We hired a bunch of smart twenty-five-year-olds who slept under their desks for four years," he liked to say. Quinn was angry she had not been retained by the DNC and teamed up with Clinton adviser Harold Ickes to start their own data firm, Catalist. *The Washington Post* labeled the new effort "a vote of no confidence" in Dean. "It's unclear what the DNC is doing," said Ickes, a potent behind-the-scenes operative. The criticism perpetuated the idea that Dean was throwing money down a sinkhole at the very time when Democrats had their best chance in a decade to recapture power.

"He says it's a long-term strategy," the Democratic consultant Paul Begala said on CNN in May 2006. "But what he has spent it on, apparently, is just hiring a bunch of staff people to wander around Utah and Mississippi and pick their nose."

The stinging barbs from the likes of Rahm, Ickes, and Begala—all prominent Clintonites, perhaps not coincidentally—rallied Dean's backers outside Washington, particularly the besieged state chairs who were becoming a force of their own. Party leaders from Utah, Mississippi, and all across the country fired off angry letters to Begala, pointing out the progress in their states. "Shame on you, Paul Begala," the netroots organizer Zack Exley wrote on *The Huffington Post*. "I'll tell you what this onslaught by Clinton '92ers looks like," Exley wrote. "It looks like you guys are stuck forever thinking about that one big election you won. And it looks like you haven't noticed that, ever since then, your way of approaching elections has kept Democrats in a tailspin."

Begala posted an apologetic reply, calling Exley's response "a good deal more thoughtful than my offhand comment insulting Democratic Party organizers." He insisted, "I strongly believe in a fifty-state strategy," citing his own Texas roots. What Begala meant to say was that the party needed a message. The solution? His new 349-page book with Carville, *Take It Back: Our Party, Our Country, Our Future.*

Still, as the midterm forecast for Democrats kept improving, Dean was under a great deal of pressure—from the congressional leadership, DNC donors, and influential political operatives—to strike some sort of deal with the election committees. In September, Dean reached an agreement with Emanuel and Schumer, transferring $2.4 million to the DCCC and $5 million to the DSCC, through the state parties. (He later gave Schumer an $8 million loan, principally for Jim Webb's Senate race in Virginia.) By that time, however, the story of the election had already been foretold inside Washington. No matter what happened, Dean lost.

In Washington, you were either with Dean or with Rahm. In reality, out in the states, the argument was never that clear-cut. The great irony is that in a number of high-profile races some of Dean's best organizers helped to elect some of Rahm's favorite candidates. Western North Carolina was a prime example.

In the fifteen westernmost counties of the state, Rahm recruited Heath Shuler, a former star quarterback in college (and prolific bust in the NFL), to unseat Chainsaw Charlie Taylor, who'd become embroiled in a variety of colorful scandals that included conspicuously missing a crucial last-minute vote on an unpopular trade deal with Central America and investing in a shady Russian bank linked to the KGB. It wasn't hard to tell why Rahm pushed so hard for Shuler to enter the race: he grew up in the Smoky Mountains on the North Carolina–Tennessee border, became a standout quarterback at the University of Tennessee, and played briefly in the NFL before returning home. The thirty-four-year-old family man had a pretty wife and two young kids (named Navy and Island) and cut a dashing figure in the district with his broad shoulders, chiseled jaw, and sky-high name recognition.

In many ways, Shuler was an atypical Democrat: a pro-life Southern Baptist endorsed by the NRA who strongly denounced illegal immigration and gay marriage. At the same time, Shuler's dad, a postal worker, had been a lifelong Democrat, and Shuler shared his father's populist streak, supporting a raise in the minimum wage and opposing the lopsided trade deals that had ravaged North Carolina's once-thriving textile industry. He promised to be a good steward of the environment and fight for new jobs and better health care for his mountain constituents. Democratic activists were desperate enough to defeat Taylor, who'd been in Congress since 1991, that they agreed, sometimes reluctantly, to forgive Shuler's ideological transgressions and rally around the Democratic hopeful.

Shuler came around at a time when the Democratic Party was going through a rebirth of its own in WNC. The success of the "Watauga Model" and work of the Western Task Force reached the most unlikely of places, such as tiny Polk County, located one hundred miles south of Boone in the wooded foothills of the Blue Ridge Mountains, near the South Carolina border, past ski slopes and Christmas tree farms and roads shaped like Richard Serra sculptures. Polk had been something of a destination in the early twentieth century, when a passenger train from New York snaked through the mountains and stopped overnight in the placid hills of Tryon. As passengers such as F. Scott Fitzgerald, who was visiting his ailing wife, Zelda, in nearby Asheville, disembarked, locals brought them homemade wine from the nearby vineyards. Fitzgerald, largely penniless by that point, stayed on the top floor of the Oak Hall Hotel and ate frequently at the Misseldine's Pharmacy down the hill, scrawling a poem in its honor on a napkin. The area's horse farms, wooded trails, and warm weather proved popular attractions. Eventually, conservative retirees from Charlotte replaced the New York literary types, and the county, like the rest of the state, moved to the right in the 1980s and '90s. By 1994, known as the year of "the angry white male," Republicans held every county seat. Like most of the counties in Taylor's rambling district, Polk was predominantly white, Baptist, blue-collar, and rural. George W. Bush received 57 percent of the vote there in 2004.

Mark Hufford moved to Polk County just after the Republican takeover, in 1995, living in an old cabin built by Cherokee stonemasons up on Skyuka Mountain, near a clear and expansive lake. In 2002 he became active in the local party, which he described as "stagnant and barely functional." The Democrats that remained held bean dinners and pancake breakfasts but did very little voter contact or candidate recruitment. Hufford was the only one in the room without gray hair.

Things began to change when Margaret Johnson moved to town from Memphis, by way of Indiana, in 2003. Her father had been a district attorney in Nashville and a close friend of Senator Albert Gore Sr.'s, and Johnson shared her father's doggedness. She found the suburbs of Indianapolis too conservative and stifling, so she moved to Polk County with her teenage son, which felt more like home. She worked hard for Gore in 2000 and, after the Supreme Court threw the election to Bush, decided to get more active in politics. She'd been a nurse in the Air Force and a health administrator after that, and looked more like a PTA mom than the stereotype of your typical Democratic activist, with wire-rim glasses, a short, sensible bob of salt-and-pepper hair, and a fondness for cardigan sweaters. After getting situated in town, she paid a visit to the Democratic Party headquarters in Columbus—population 992—a small white 1940s-era former church located between the jail and the fire station. As she went to the door, a pickup truck drove by. The driver poked his neck out of the window and hollered, "Lady, don't you know there ain't no Democrats in Polk County?"

Johnson looked back and replied, "Well, there are now."

She became chair of the local party in 2004 and decorated the building to her liking, putting up donkeys everywhere: gray donkey decals on the walls; a blue flag of a donkey atop the state (the official logo of the Polk County Democratic Women's Club); a porcelain donkey with a straw hat on, next to a picture of Bill Clinton. After 2004, Johnson and her fellow Democrats were devastated by yet another loss. They held only the office of county clerk. "We were pulling our teeth out, saying, what on earth can we do?" she recalled. They needed money and a message.

Johnson read Lakoff's popular book *Don't Think of an Elephant!*, and showed an accompanying DVD at a party meeting. "We've gotta do a better job of letting people know that we're good people," she said. The party started a community action club and decided to lead by example. They picked up trash on the highway, winterized homes for poor families, sponsored a bowling night for needy kids, and donated money to a local wildlife conservatory. Every time they did an event like this, Johnson soon realized, they got a story and a picture in the local paper, the *Tryon Daily Bulletin*, which billed itself as "the world's smallest daily newspaper." After a while, Johnson's Republican neighbors started coming up to her and saying, "I may not agree with your politics but I sure like what you're doing."

The state party designed a website for Polk County Democrats, gave them access to a database of voters in their area, and organized online canvassing training with Pam Williamson. Hufford's Burma-Shave signs went up all around the area and were a "big hit," Johnson said. Early on, the party organized "meet the candidate" events at barbecues and picnics, recruiting a popular Hispanic soccer coach to run for sheriff and two reputable candidates for county commissioner seats, beginning to build a farm team for local Democrats. Heath Shuler visited the county often. He helped raise money for the nature conservatory when he came to town, met scores of voters at a local parade, jumped into a horse-drawn wagon for a classic old-time North Carolina photo op, and spoke before a predominantly Republican retirement home where Democrats hadn't dared to venture in years past. The increasing baggage of the Republican Party on so many fronts—stagnation in the economy, violence in Iraq, corruption in Washington—prompted the denizens of Polk County to look more favorably on the arguments of the opposition for the first time in a long while.

In previous elections, whatever money from Raleigh or Washington that flowed through the local party, however limited, would've gone straight into the congressional race. This year all the local races took priority, which Dean believed was the key to rebuilding the party from the bottom up and creating a base of support for national races. For the first time in ages, the party developed its own get-out-the-vote plan. "People don't have to hold their nose to vote Democrat in Polk County anymore," Johnson said. As a result, on Election Day, Democrats won practically everything in this once-abandoned, insular red county. They elected two Democratic county commissioners and a Democratic sheriff and threw their votes behind a Democratic congressman for the first time in a decade. Though he was outspent by $2 million, Shuler handily defeated Taylor, including in Polk. The rain came down hard that night, but 250 Democrats crammed into the diminutive party headquarters for a riotous victory party. The Raleigh *News & Observer*, which just a year earlier had written disparagingly about Meek and Dean, drove four hours to witness the occasion. "It's a sight I'll never forget," Johnson said.

The same jubilation among Democrats could be heard across WNC on election night. Up in Watauga, Williamson and her activists elected a retired Baptist preacher to the state senate and a former radio broadcaster to the statehouse and knocked off yet another Republican county commissioner. Over in Waynesville, a railroad town deep in the heart of the Smoky Mountains, a charismatic architect named Joe Sam Queen defeated an incumbent Republican to pick up another statehouse seat. (Just a year earlier, a pastor at East Waynesville Baptist Church had expelled nine members of his congregation for committing the sin of voting for Kerry.) Overall, sixteen new Democratic county commissioners swept into office on

Hufford's turf. Groused one losing Republican candidate: "All over the mountain area, the Democrats were organized. They smelled blood two years out. They outworked Republicans, no question about it." Outside Democratic headquarters in Raleigh, an august white colonial mansion, Meek unfurled a giant banner on the porch of a donkey kicking an elephant in the ass.

A month after the election, Democratic leaders from Hufford's thirty-three counties gathered for "An Early Thanksgiving" at a stately white banquet hall in Morganton, a quaint city of twenty thousand seventy miles northwest of Charlotte, to share their stories. The place crackled with excitement. "Everyone saw the miracle that had happened here and knew it could happen anywhere," Hufford said. In the interest of brevity, each county chair had ninety seconds to speak. Those that went overtime had to donate $100 per minute to the Democratic coffers of WNC's Tenth Congressional District, which remained in GOP hands. Hufford was already looking forward to the next election. "We can win North Carolina in '08," he boldly predicted in his speech. "The time to start planning is now." All of a sudden, that didn't seem like such a crazy aspiration.

The returns on election night from around the country stunned even the most optimistic of Democrats. As night became morning, Democrats had taken control of both houses of Congress for the first time since 1994, picking up eight seats in the Senate and thirty-one seats in the House. Seventeen of those victories came in states Bush won in 2004. Indiana—which Bush carried by twenty-one points in 2004—led the way, with Democrats electing three new Democratic congressmen and flipping the statehouse. "We're a poster child for the fifty-state strategy," Indiana Democratic Party chair Dan Parker said after the election.

Near midnight, the party's top leaders graced the stage of the Hyatt Regency ballroom on Capitol Hill for a smashing victory party. Confetti fell from the rafters as Pelosi, Reid, Schumer, and

Emanuel clasped hands, raised their arms, and bowed in a triumphant victory salute amid deafening applause. "Schumer, Emanuel Engineer Party's Win," the Associated Press reported afterward. Rahm had already been dubbed "the architect," the same nickname Bush bestowed upon Rove.

Dean was nowhere to be found that night, opting instead to do a round of TV interviews from a Capitol Hill studio a few blocks away. There would be no confetti or heralded embrace with the party's glitterati for the Democratic chairman. He was still an outcast in his own party. Eight days later, despite the victories, two of Rahm's closest allies, James Carville and former Clinton pollster Stan Greenberg, revived the preelection skirmishes and fired the first retaliatory shots at Dean.

In the winter of 1966, Godfrey "Budge" Sperling, an upstart Washington correspondent for *The Christian Science Monitor*, decided to organize a monthly 8:00 a.m. breakfast where Washington's best-known newspaper and magazine reporters could interview one of the city's prominent news makers in an extended and casual setting. The exclusive, invite-only Sperling Breakfast soon became a must attend for the Beltway's top columnists and reporters. Carville and Greenberg were frequent guests and used the occasion of November 15 to lambaste Dean, knowing the remarks would travel far and wide. Despite a Democratic takeover of the House and Senate, the two strategists were unhappy with Dean's performance, believing the DNC should have spent more money on Rahm's competitive House races.

"There was a missed opportunity here," said Greenberg. "I've sat down with Republican pollsters to discuss this race: They believe we left 10 to 20 seats on the table." When asked if Dean should be replaced, Carville responded, "In a word, do I think? Yes." He continued: "I think he should be held accountable. I would describe his leadership as Rumsfeldian in its incompetence." The ragin' Cajun added in a subsequent interview with *The New York Times*: "Do we want to go into '08 with a C minus general at the DNC?" When asked for a comment, Rahm echoed Carville's bromide. "More resources brings more seats into play," he said tersely. "Full stop." Soon enough the "dump Dean" news was everywhere. Carville, who talked to Rahm every morning, continued bashing the Democratic chairman in the press, floating Harold Ford Jr., a failed Senate candidate in Tennessee, son of a Memphis political machine, and chairman of the right-leaning DLC, as a replacement.

Dean, though no stranger to controversy, felt the criticism hit him like a sucker punch. "That was low," he told me. "That was pathetic. That was the last gasp of the old guard of the Democratic Party."

Under closer inspection, Carville's and Greenberg's outlandish claims were quickly debunked. *National Journal's Hotline* blog, the ultimate insider source in D.C., examined every competitive House race and concluded: "Extra money could have made a small difference, but certainly not to the degree that Carville has been suggesting. Dean may have made strategic blunders in the past, but his fiscal responsibility here seems like the wiser course." Even Dean's old foes among the party establishment found this particular criticism of the DNC chair utterly preposterous. Don Fowler Sr., the tall South Carolinian and former DNC chair under Clinton whose son, Donnie, ran against Dean for the job, told the *Times*: "Asking Dean to step down now, after last week, is equivalent to asking Eisenhower to resign after the Normandy invasion. It's just nonsense. Carville and Greenberg—those people are my friends—they are just dead wrong. They wanted all that money to go to Washington consultants and speechwriters and pollsters." Added the new Senate majority leader, Harry Reid: "I didn't support [Dean's] running for DNC chair . . . I was wrong. He was right: I support his grassroots Democratic Party–building."

With Dean in the hot seat, Rahm started receiving a little scrutiny of his own, as candidates who were largely ignored by the DCCC registered surprise upsets or lost narrowly while many of Rahm's favorite candidates went down as expensive failures. Ac-

cording to the final tally, of the twenty-one candidates Rahm first
endorsed and funneled large checks to, a mere nine won. Of the
sixty-two candidates the DCCC endorsed in total, only half prevailed. The top three candidates Rahm spent the most on (nearly
$10 million combined)—Tammy Duckworth in suburban Chicago,
Lois Murphy in suburban Philadelphia, and Ken Lucas in western
Kentucky—all lost. Rahm supported primary challenges to four
other winners and snubbed a number of compelling grassroots candidates who nearly made it, such as Larry Kissell, a high school social studies teacher and former textile worker from the rolling
Piedmont of central North Carolina who didn't get a dime from the
DCCC and lost by 329 votes.

Tim Walz from Mankato, Minnesota, and Nancy Boyda from
Topeka, Kansas, were two such freshmen who barely made a blip on
the DCCC's radar screen until the last weeks of the election. Both
shared their stories at a DNC forum in Washington a month after
the election. A burly geography teacher, high school football coach,
and twenty-four-year veteran of the Army National Guard, Walz
became just the sixth Democrat ever to win in rural southern Minnesota's First Congressional District, which stretched from the plains
of South Dakota to the bluffs of the Mississippi River. The fertileness
of the land gave Walz's home county the name "Blue Earth." The
state Democratic Party put a staffer on the ground in southern Minnesota in 2005, who worked closely with Walz as he knocked off a
six-term Republican incumbent, Gil Gutknecht, that few thought
could be beaten. "Thank you for a vision that I know has been somewhat controversial," he said at the DNC meeting. "I am here to tell
you there is no controversy in how this was done. It was pragmatic,
it was a great use of resources . . . and because of it, we are sitting in
the majority."

Boyda told an even more implausible story. A chemist, mother
of seven, and Republican until 2003—when she left the party as
it moved far to the right—Boyda pulled off a stunning upset in an
eastern Kansas district that extended from the Nebraska to the

Oklahoma border, which Bush won by twenty points. Boyda first ran in 2004 and lost by fifteen points to incumbent Jim Ryun, a protégé of Kansas senator Sam Brownback, one of the GOP's highest-profile social conservatives. Boyda didn't know whether she had it in her to run again. This time, however, thanks to an influx of DNC resources, the Kansas Democratic Party had something tangible to offer her. "[I] decided to run again," she told Dean, "because it [the fifty-state strategy] was in place." Bush and Cheney both visited her district in the waning days of the election, but Boyda held on. "Nancy who?" operatives in D.C. asked themselves on election night. Thomas Frank's Kansas—a national symbol of entrenched right-wing Republicanism—now had a glimmer of blue.

The clunky attempt to oust Dean and sideline the party's newly energized activists and organizers soon backfired on its perpetrators. "Howard Dean, vindicated," Joe Conason wrote in *Salon* in the days following the election. A subsequent study by Elaine Kamarck in the University of California–Berkeley's political science journal *The Forum* found that in congressional districts where DNC organizers had been on the ground for over a year, Democratic performance more than doubled compared with the rest of the country. Even though Dean always viewed his experiment as a long-term investment, in some cases "the fruit ripened early," said Leah Daughtry.

In mid-November, Rahm called Dean—only the second time they'd spoken since their infamous blowup—to say that although he shared some of Carville's complaints, he wasn't behind the push for his ouster. At the same time, rampant speculation inside the Beltway posited that Carville wasn't offering an unsolicited opinion but rather carrying water for the presumptive Democratic presidential nominee, Hillary Clinton. After all, it was Hillary who called Rahm in early 2006 and told him, "You've got to do something about Howard Dean." A few months before the midterm elections, *The New Republic* reported that Clinton's camp had begun "laying the groundwork to circumvent the DNC in the event that Clinton wins the nomination." This shadow DNC had a number of integral parts: Ickes would develop state-of-the-art technology to help Clinton reach prospective voters; EMILY's List and Clinton's allies in organized labor would launch an unprecedented effort to turn out supporters, especially women; McAuliffe would raise untold sums from wealthy donors and the business community; and communications honcho Howard Wolfson would direct an unrelenting war room. Dean could remain at the DNC, as a figurehead, only if he stayed in line.

Soon enough, however, Hillary would learn that it wasn't so easy to simply push Dean and his supporters aside. More important, a new kid on the block would quickly present the Clintons with a slew of problems they never expected to face.

4 ★ CLINTONISM VS. CHANGE

We pioneered it and Obama perfected it. —Joe Trippi

In January 2005, Joe Hansen, a blue-collar meat cutter from Milwaukee and president of the United Food and Commercial Workers
(UFCW), placed a call to Paul Blank, the twenty-nine-year-old former political director of the Dean campaign. For twenty years, the
UFCW had been frustratedly attempting to unionize employees at
Walmart, filing ignored workers' complaints with the federal government, and futilely trying to negotiate with management. The effort
bore little fruit. Hansen wondered whether the grassroots, agile
movement-feel of the Dean campaign could be translated to the
corporate world. Rather than targeting Walmart internally, hoping
for scraps of concessions here and there, Hansen wanted to pressure
the company from the outside, improving conditions for workers by
changing the way everyday consumers and decision makers viewed
the retail behemoth. He asked Blank to start a new group called
Wake Up Walmart. That spring, Blank called two of his old colleagues from the Dean campaign, Jeremy Bird and Buffy Wicks, and
asked for their help.

After Iowa and New Hampshire, Bird and Wicks stayed with the
Dean campaign until its fitful last stand in Wisconsin. After the
campaign, both were fed up with electoral politics. "I had no inter-

est in working for another presidential campaign," Wicks said. They liked the idea of fighting an organization as feared and controversial as Walmart, where their organizing work—if successful—could make a tangible difference in people's lives. Bird's mother had worked at the company for four years, when his family lived in a trailer park outside St. Louis and struggled to pay the bills. Wicks became the group's organizing director, and Bird directed its ground strategy. Each brought different skills to the table.

Wicks, a tall, blond, sturdy twenty-seven-year-old Californian, was the most persistent organizer Blank had ever seen. One day, she needed a quick answer from Hansen, knowing full well that the union (or any union) didn't always make decisions in the timeliest fashion. So she marched up to the president's office, plopped herself on the floor, and told his assistant, "I'm not going to leave until he comes out, and I'm going to be the first person he sees." Sure enough, she got an answer that day. "She's a bull in the china shop," Blank said, "but she leaves all the china on the shelves."

Bird, a short, geeky, high-octane, bespectacled twenty-six-year-old from Missouri, was the most disciplined. In the summer of 2006, he almost single-handedly planned a thirty-five-city, thirty-five-day, fifty-four-event bus tour—to raise awareness about Walmart's working conditions—across eight thousand miles. Longtime union officers told Blank that Bird could one day be president of the UFCW if he wanted. The tour started in the Bronx and ended in Seattle. As the red, white, and blue bus, adorned with the group's logo of a frowning yellow smiley face, stopped in presidential battlegrounds such as Ohio and Iowa—attracting presidential hopefuls like Joe Biden and Bill Richardson—Bird and Wicks once again caught the campaign bug.

They were especially intrigued by Barack Obama, whose memoir—in part about his experiences as a community organizer in Chicago—appealed to the activist in both of them. "We wanted to work for someone who saw community organizing as a means to victory and not just a talking point," Wicks said. In November

2006, the group persuaded Obama to participate in a conference call kicking off a holiday campaign urging the company to provide a living wage and affordable heath care to its employees. On the ten-minute call with Walmart employees, Obama cast the issue in moral terms. "This is a much broader issue than Wal-Mart," he said. "Folks on Wall Street and people in the top 1 percent of the income bracket are getting more and more of the productive resources, while ordinary folks are finding themselves systematically in jobs where they don't find adequate wages, no health-care benefits, and no significant form of retirement security."

Through the call, Wicks came to know Steve Hildebrand, an openly gay political operative from South Dakota who was helping the Illinois senator explore the possibility of a presidential run. "If this guy runs, we're going to go work for him," Wicks and Bird told each other. When Obama officially announced his candidacy on the steps of the Old State Capitol in Springfield in February 2007, Wicks launched what she called "a campaign to get on the campaign," repeatedly badgering Hildebrand about a job. Bird did the same. Wicks joined Obama's burgeoning staff a month later; Bird followed shortly thereafter.

At the start of the 2008 election, Hillary Clinton began her campaign with nearly every possible advantage, short of being an actual incumbent. For starters, her husband was not only a popular former president but also widely considered among the savviest strategists in all of politics. Her brusque chief strategist, Mark Penn, oversaw one of the world's largest PR and lobbying firms, Burson-Marsteller, and boasted a reputation for "undisputed brilliance," according to *The Washington Post.* Her boisterous campaign chairman, Terry McAuliffe, was regarded as the best fund-raiser in the Democratic Party. Her communications guru, the balding, tight-lipped Howard Wolfson, put fear into the hearts of his rivals. Veterans of past Clinton campaigns owned Washington's Democratic turf. Rank-and-file Democrats adored the Clinton brand, Penn argued. "We have incredible image strengths," Penn wrote in a fawning early strategy memo. "We have the highest levels of early enthusiasm for any Democratic candidate in modern history—people don't just like Hillary Clinton, they love her." How could she not win?

In their preview of the 2008 election, *The Way to Win*, journalists Mark Halperin and John Harris devoted fifty-four pages exclusively to Clinton and never once mentioned Obama. Penn didn't seem too concerned about him, either. "We are the candidate with the money, the ideas, the operation, and the determination to win," he wrote in December 2006. Penn cited the Democratic base—"the most liberal, activist, difficult group of voters in America"—as one possible obstacle but concluded, "The brie and cheese set drives fundraising and elite press but does not drive the vote. Kerry beat Dean. Gore easily defeated Bradley." Clinton would defeat Obama. "Obama is unelectable except perhaps against Attila the Hun," Penn confidently asserted in March 2007.

Obama's team consisted of the prized leftovers, who were either unwilling or unable to work for Clinton. Even many political junkies had never heard of his campaign manager, David Plouffe, a camera-shy thirty-nine-year-old from Delaware who swore like a trucker, worked as a strategist for Dick Gephardt in 2004, and advised Deval Patrick's successful gubernatorial campaign in Massachusetts in 2006. Obama's top strategist, the wry, mustachioed David Axelrod, had worked closely with both Clintons and powerful Chicago mayor Richard Daley but was hardly a household name outside of the Windy City and had been fired from John Edwards's presidential campaign in 2004 after clashing with the candidate's wife. Much of Obama's inner circle, like Plouffe, chief of staff Pete Rouse, and deputy campaign manager Steve Hildebrand, came from the staffs of former House and Senate leaders Dick Gephardt and Tom Daschle. They were, on the face of it, a pretty traditional lot. But Obama's advisers knew that if they ran a second-rate version of the Clinton campaign, they would lose. That's why Dean presented an intriguing model.

After the Dean campaign ended, Axelrod hired Jim Brayton, a thirty-four-year-old techie from Dean's staff in Burlington, as Obama's new-media director. Brayton stayed on when Obama entered the Senate and heard a lot of outside chatter about a presidential run, but no inside confirmation. Nate Tamarin, the political director of Obama's political action committee, Hopefund, told him in the beginning of 2006 that there was a 90 percent chance that Obama would not run in 2008. Things began to change that fall, when Obama drew massive crowds on his book tour for *The Audacity of Hope* and campaigned for Senate candidates in the reddest of red states. Obama admitted on *Meet the Press*, in October 2006, that he was thinking of running. When he went to Hawaii to mull it over during Christmas break, nobody knew what he'd decide. After he came back and chose to pursue the presidency, the campaign immediately scrambled to get an operation in place. Clinton had spent years planning for this; Obama now had a month.

Plouffe came on board and ran Obama's exploratory committee out of his consulting firm on K Street in downtown Washington. Brayton's wife was due to have another baby in the winter, and he'd already given notice at work. A lot of people now wanted his job— Joe Trippi lobbied him, as did former MoveOn and Dean organizer Zack Exley and popular blogger Jerome Armstrong of MyDD.com. "I became a very popular person," Brayton joked. Brayton wanted Joe Rospars, a twenty-five-year-old blogger on the Dean campaign who later ran the new-media shop for Dean at the DNC, to replace him. "I just knew that he could take a lot of the lessons that had been learned from Dean and could hit the ground running for Obama," Brayton said. "I wanted somebody I knew, that I trusted."

Rospars's friends on the Dean campaign liked to joke that they knew him when he was a baby-faced idealist. He'd grown a beard since then, bought a few designer suits, and adopted a rather gruff, introverted demeanor. He was fiercely loyal to Dean and wasn't sure he wanted to work for Obama.

Rospars grew up in Oyster Bay, Long Island, Teddy Roosevelt's hometown. His siblings were much older and his father passed away when he was four, so he spent most of his childhood around his mother, who worked two jobs, as a nurse and a paralegal, attended Catholic Mass regularly, and didn't much care for politics. He was a precocious kid who enrolled at George Mason University in suburban Virginia when he was sixteen, studying philosophy before switching to political science when his philosophy books became a little too thick for his liking. He moved to Sweden after college and started blogging about Dean from afar.

While back in New York visiting his mom in June 2003, he drove up to Burlington for Dean's announcement speech. Six weeks later, he packed his bags in Sweden, left his girlfriend, and moved to Burlington. The Web operation had just taken off, and space was tight inside headquarters, particularly in the makeshift new-media section outside Trippi's office. Brayton was kind enough to offer him a folding chair, an Ethernet cord, and a power outlet. Rospars had a knack for writing and began sending out e-mails and blogging for the campaign. All the young tech geeks were aware they were making history; they just didn't know which kind. "This campaign is either going to end in the White House or in a start-up," Jascha Franklin-Hodge, a Dean programmer, told Rospars.

It ended in at least two start-ups. After the campaign, Trippi invited Dean's Web team to his rustic farmhouse on the Eastern Shore of Maryland. On the drive down, Rospars and three friends from the campaign—Franklin-Hodge, an MIT dropout from Boston; Clay Johnson, a boisterous Georgian; and Ben Self, a courtly Kentuckian—brainstormed the name of the tech company they planned to launch together. They settled on Blue State Digital, Rospars's last choice. He borrowed $2,500 from his mom to get the company off the ground.

After the weekend, Brayton and a half-dozen other campaign alums started a rival shop, EchoDitto. They retained Trippi as a consultant, who persuaded Axelrod to hire them for Obama's Senate campaign. Rospars and Blue State Digital stayed with Dean, helping him launch Democracy for America and run for DNC chair. After he won, Dean asked Rospars and Ben Self to undertake a thorough thirty-day review of the DNC's technology. "We found a mess," Rospars said. When they presented Dean with their findings, he told them, "Now you need to stay and fix it." Self went down to the basement, euphemistically known as the "garden level," to reconstitute the DNC's technology and voter database. Rospars took up an office near Dean and began overhauling the DNC's relationship with its online constituents, redesigning the website, conversing over blogs and e-mail, making sure grassroots activists knew their state party officials and vice versa. The idea was to do for the DNC what he'd done for the Dean campaign. He designed a website called PartyBuilder, modeled after Facebook, where activists could plan and publicize their own events and network with supporters in their area.

Rospars left the DNC in April 2006 and began to grow Blue State. The company moved to the top floor of a town house in Dupont Circle, next to a bar called the Big Hunt, and lined up heavy hitters like George Soros and AT&T as clients. He'd just landed a gig running Ted Kennedy's new-media operation when Brayton called and asked him to meet with Plouffe. Like nearly everyone, Rospars was intrigued by Obama. He'd gone home in the summer of 2006 and found a postcard of the Illinois senator on his apolitical mom's fridge, much to his surprise.

"Where'd you even get that?" he asked her.

"I dunno," she responded. "I just like the guy."

Rospars agreed to meet Plouffe, though not without a little apprehension. He'd never heard of him before, and the only video he could find online was a clip of Plouffe ripping Dean on CNN's *Crossfire* when he worked for Gephardt. Rospars knew that Obama's communications director, Robert Gibbs, had assisted a shadowy attack outfit in 2004 that compared Dean to Osama bin Laden in a

TV ad. He'd soon learn that Gibbs's deputies, Bill Burton and Dan Pfeiffer, had worked for Rahm at the DCCC in 2006. He wondered what kind of campaign Plouffe envisioned running.

They met in Obama's temporary campaign office on K Street. Plouffe had a lean build and a chipmunk face. As was his nature, he got right to the point. "Hillary's got all the party infrastructure, all the donors, all the political support," Plouffe told Rospars. "And if we're going to be successful, the only way is that it has to be organic and from the bottom up." Deval Patrick had used Internet video throughout his campaign in Massachusetts, and Plouffe saw first-hand the potential of the Internet to reach supporters in unconventional ways. He asked Rospars if Dean's success online in raising money and attracting volunteers could be replicated. Rospars thought it could be.

A week later, Rospars met with Obama at his Senate office. The senator was taping a weekly podcast, about Iraq, when he walked in. Obama sat on a tan couch across from a dark wood coffee table. Near his desk hung a giant, iconic black-and-white photograph of a young Muhammad Ali standing triumphantly over a fallen Sonny Liston, taunting the aging fighter. A pair of signed Ali boxing gloves rested next to the photo. Rospars saw Obama as a rare breed: an egghead constitutional law professor, street-savvy organizer, Lincolnesque orator, and hypercompetitive jock rolled into one. Obama described his own background as a community organizer—how, at twenty-four, he'd helped tenants in a depressed housing project remove asbestos from their buildings and fought for jobs in blighted neighborhoods devastated by shuttered steel plants. "Change won't come from the top, I would say," Obama wrote in his memoir, *Dreams from My Father*. "Change will come from a mobilized grass roots." Two decades later, such words guided his budding presidential campaign.

The country would soon receive a not-always-accurate crash course in community organizing, with the previously obscure likes of Saul Alinsky—a product of the Jewish ghetto of Chicago in the early twentieth century, author of *Rules for Radicals,* and godfather of the community organizing movement—becoming household names. Obama's supporters viewed his work on the streets of Chicago as the inspiring core of his candidacy, while his opponents, on the right, and sometimes on the Clinton campaign, saw a radical, shadowy endeavor everywhere they turned. Obama explained to Rospars how he wanted his own experience as an organizer to animate the campaign. "Even if we don't win," Rospars said Obama told him, "how we do it, by getting people involved and building a grassroots movement, will leave the political process and the party better off for having done it that way." Rospars liked what he heard—he didn't want to be part of a boom-and-bust carnival that left all the garbage in town when it was over. He agreed to come on board.

They didn't have much time. Obama's campaign website consisted of only a video of the candidate talking about his exploratory committee, while the e-mail list of his political action committee contained only fifty thousand names. "We basically had nothing," Rospars said, "and we had to build it from scratch." He wasn't sure if they could pull it off. "I expected it was going to be very hard," he said, "and that it was going to be very lonely."

From the start of Obama's run, Rospars saw a number of striking parallels and divergences between his old boss and his new one. Both Dean and Obama rode to prominence because of their early opposition to the war in Iraq; both were outsiders to D.C. who had a tremendous following among rank-and-file Democrats and grassroots activists; both ran against established candidates who had compromised on the big issues of the day, weighing them down with baggage; both talked at length about giving power back to ordinary people in the political process. "Dean certainly built a movement," said Hildebrand, "and that was our mission from the very beginning."

The differences between the two candidates, however, were almost as considerable as the similarities. Dean started as a nobody, whereas Obama jumped into the ring with a significant national following. Plouffe was the polar opposite of Trippi—methodical,

intensely private, and extremely loyal to his boss. And Obama, stylis-
tically, couldn't have been more different from Dean—scripted, poetic, always striving for consensus. Obama's cautious communications
team downplayed any similarities to Dean, fearing the comparison
would make the campaign look flaky and faddish.

Dean himself readily acknowledged the differences between his
campaign and Obama's. From the outset, "they were incredibly better organized and more disciplined than we were and they had a
much more disciplined candidate than we did," Dean said. "I would
maintain that while we started a lot of stuff that Obama was able to
build on, I was a transitional candidate while Obama was the first
candidate of the new generation." Dean admitted that he possessed
a "willingness to stand up against the established order, but I didn't
really have a definition of what the new order looked like. But by the
time Obama came along, he was the definition of the new order."
Dean tapped people's anger, including his own, while Obama appealed to their aspirations for the future. Dean came during the
middle of the hotly contested Bush era, Obama toward the end. By
the time Obama announced his candidacy, disasters from Iraq to
Katrina had thoroughly discredited Bush and the GOP. The country
was ready to move on.

Obama was more of a modernizer than a pure innovator. Unlike
Dean, he became an insurgent by circumstances, not temperament.
He tended to be more conciliatory than fiery and often distanced
himself from the hard-edged populism that usually catapulted insurgent candidates, Dean included, into the spotlight. As a result,
Obama was neither a typical insurgent nor an established front-
runner, but rather somewhere in between. That gave him the ability
to run a traditional campaign and attract experienced talent while
also incentivizing his staff to be flexible, experimental, and open to
new ideas and strategies. "We studied your campaign really carefully," Obama's chief operating officer, Betsy Myers, told Dean when
they met at a DNC fund-raiser during the primary. "We got rid of
all the stuff that didn't work, and we took the stuff that did work and

made it better." Clinton, as a juggernaut from day one, had no similar incentive to rewrite the rule book. After all, her husband and his advisers had pretty much written it.

In March 2007, the Obama campaign based its headquarters in the 33,000-square-foot eleventh floor of a black and glass skyscraper in downtown Chicago, across from Lake Michigan. Rospars moved into a corner office overlooking bustling Michigan Avenue, originally overseeing a staff of half a dozen in the small new-media shop, which reported directly to Plouffe. On the Dean campaign, the rush of online activity had failed to translate into votes at the polls. Rospars wanted to be certain that didn't happen again, so he quickly moved to integrate new media with the organizers out in the field knocking on doors and targeting voters. The campaign's top brass studied the Dean campaign closely and learned from its mistakes. "One of the biggest lessons coming out of their campaign was, just because someone signs up on your e-mail list doesn't mean they're a supporter or willing to be helpful," said Hildebrand. "We always had the sense that anybody who came to our website, we had to work to take them off-line, and if we could get them involved off-line, we could really count on them." No candidate had yet merged the online and off-line worlds before; doing so would represent a major innovation. "The first thing new media did," said the Illinois state director, Jon Carson, "it just found people you don't find otherwise."

Rospars found them—or, rather, they found the campaign—by turning the DNC's PartyBuilder website into the home page my.barackobama.com, which became known as MyBO. (*The Guardian* of London helpfully instructed readers that it was pronounced "My-Beau.") The site became the Facebook of the Obama campaign, where supporters communicated and organized online. It just so happened that Brayton had recently hired Facebook cofounder Chris Hughes, a twenty-four-year-old Harvard graduate who looked like Zac Efron. Rospars put him in charge of MyBO.

In those early days, the campaign focused almost entirely on Iowa. "Every staff meeting, David would ask, 'What did you do today to help us win in Iowa?'" said Hughes. Given the perceived dominance of Clinton, Obama needed to finish first or a strong second in Iowa in order to have any shot at winning the nomination. When he wasn't obsessing over Iowa, Plouffe tended to the three states that immediately followed: New Hampshire, Nevada, and South Carolina. Rospars gave each early state its own new-media director, even if it didn't much want one initially.

At an early rally in Iowa, Rospars sent a young videographer, Chris Northcross, to shoot footage of Obama backstage. "Who the hell are you?" barked Obama's Iowa director, Paul Tewes, a feisty, balding Minnesotan who managed the caucus for Gore in 2000.

"I'm with the website," Northcross informed him.

"What fucking website?" Tewes responded.

As they helped out with the four early states, Rospars's department kept an eye on the other forty-six through MyBO. "We were always fighting to devote some minimum level of resources to everybody else," he said. On the day Obama announced, over one thousand different volunteer Obama groups sprung up on MyBO within twenty-four hours, all across the country. That was more than during the entirety of the Dean campaign. The website almost crashed from the traffic overload. Even Rospars didn't anticipate such a sudden rush of activity. It was the first of many "holy shit" moments.

As the campaign grew, Rospars viewed himself as a dogged protector of Obama's grassroots brand. He was usually a curt and icy presence at headquarters, stubbornly persistent and not very popular with the other departments. He refused to ask supporters for money until he established a relationship between them and the campaign, over e-mail, on the blog, through MyBO. As a result, he didn't send out a fund-raising e-mail until March, infuriating the campaign's finance director, Julianna Smoot. They screamed at each other during a conference call with Plouffe. Relations didn't thaw until Obama raked in a stunning $25 million in the first quarter of

April 2007, matching Clinton and far exceeding expectations. A hundred thousand people donated to the campaign, twice as many as Clinton, and $7 million came in online, far more than any other campaign. Rospars had passed his first crucial test.

Plouffe cared about one thing: numbers. He wanted to know precise figures about money raised, volunteers recruited, and voters contacted. When he started the job, Rospars said he could raise $40 million online by Super Tuesday on February 5. Plouffe was skeptical. Rospars ended up raising that much just before the Iowa caucus in early January. When the campaign raked in $55 million a month later, $45 million came through online.

Rospars deliberately kept a low profile and hired other people to be the campaign's public face. Most of them were political novices uncorrupted by the traditional cynicism and ruthless ambition in politics. He convinced Sam Graham-Felsen, a young writer for *The Nation* covering student politics, to blog for the campaign. He asked Kate Albright-Hanna, a producer for CNN who followed the Dean campaign for months as part of a CNN documentary, to be the campaign's documentarian. He made Chris Hughes his chief online organizer, responsible for all the groups on MyBO. They were all lured to the campaign by the unique appeal of Obama, not by the prospect of a cushy job in the White House or on another campaign. Rospars knew they'd instantly understand, chronicle, and channel the larger story of the campaign.

In those early days, the campaign was often an internal battle between tradition and innovation, decorum and experimentation, a few early states versus the rest of the map. Rospars wanted his side to win.

On her thirtieth birthday, Buffy Wicks went to camp. Instead of a tent and marshmallows, she brought a flowchart and a PowerPoint presentation. This was, after all, Camp Obama, a two-day retreat to train the next generation of political organizers. Illinois state director Jon Carson conceived the idea as a way to send eager volunteers next door to Iowa without replicating the fiasco of Dean's storm troopers in their bright orange hats. The Illinoisans learned the basics of community organizing from Mike Kruglik, a tough-talking Alinsky devotee who worked with Obama during his days on the South Side, and received a tutorial on the quirky nature of Iowa politics from campaign staffers, even holding a mock caucus. After watching the early Camp Obamas in Chicago, Wicks realized she could train volunteers to essentially be the campaign in the forty-six states where the campaign hadn't officially landed yet. Rospars promoted the Camp Obamas online and pushed them on the blog. (The campaign's top brass, meanwhile, viewed them as a good way to mollify restless donors in attention-starved places like California and New York.)

On a Friday night in early August 2007, Wicks huddled at the International Longshore and Warehouse Union hall on the waterfront in downtown San Francisco with 120 budding Obama activists, encompassing every conceivable demographic. It sounded like the start of a bad joke: a disabled Puerto Rican lesbian from the South Bronx, a black woman from Salinas engaged to a Republican Iraq war vet, a biracial dreadlocked kid from Haight-Ashbury, a gay man from a small town outside of Sacramento, and a straight man from Eagle, Idaho, walk into a Camp Obama . . .

Here was the new rainbow coalition. Wicks wore a tan blazer, black top, blue jeans, gold dangling earrings, and her blond highlights back in a ponytail. She knew how to command a room, mixing campaign war stories with dry humor and casual asides. This weekend's Camp Obama for Northern California, she explained, would stretch from 8:00 a.m. until 9:30 p.m. on Saturday and Sunday, not including her introduction that night. This information elicited a few groans. "It's pretty intense, I know," Wicks said. "There's a lot riding on this campaign." The first traveling Camp Obama had taken place in L.A. a month before; this was the second. She asked how many in the room had never been involved in a campaign before. Roughly half of the hands went up. "Wow," Wicks said. "That's amazing. That's some serious dedication." That weekend, they'd learn how to contact voters, recruit volunteers, blog and work with media, and manage a voter database. "You guys are our mini-Baracks," she said.

By way of introduction, Wicks told her story of growing up a swimmer in California, how she started in politics, and what she learned from her experience on the Dean campaign. "I don't want this to be the Dean campaign all over again," she confessed. "That was an experience I had that was so raw and so real. There was a lot of potential there as well and a lot of people hungry for change there as well. But it was not organized and I don't want to repeat that. So everything we do on this campaign is through that lens."

The campaign's field director, Cuauhtémoc "Temo" Figueroa, a forty-three-year-old Mexican-American, had also worked on the Dean campaign and didn't want to make that same mistake, either. A week later, at a Camp Obama in New York, Figueroa made a similar point. "What's the main distinction between the Howard Dean campaign and all that enthusiasm and all those big crowds and this campaign?" he animatedly asked a roomful of two hundred New Yorkers gathered at LaGuardia High School on Manhattan's Upper West Side. "What's the biggest distinction between the two? And I'll tell you. It's this. Howard Dean never did this."

Such was the strategic focus of the Obama campaign from here on out; it wanted to turn passive volunteers into active organizers and channel all the enthusiasm Obama had already attracted into a meaningful outlet. "We don't train volunteers," Figueroa liked to say. "We train organizers." Obama didn't want to be just another protest candidate—he wanted to win. "It becomes a contest of power: those who have money and those who have people," Alinsky once said. "We have nothing but people." In the early days, before the money flowed like water, the same could be said of the Obama campaign.

Few understood the nature of power better than Marshall Ganz, whom Wicks had befriended through Bird and invited to lead the training in San Francisco. That Saturday morning, a gray recorder was affixed to his yellow oxford shirt, hung around his neck on a black cord. He stood, with his furry gray mustache and round belly, behind a plethora of large white charts explaining the building blocks of community organizing in a series of sometimes indecipherable diagrams and sketches. One chart listed words commonly associated with disorganization: "confusion, passive, reactive, inaction, drift." Another chart showed the qualities of a good organization: "community, understanding, participation, initiative, action, purpose." The Obama campaign wasn't exactly disorganized in its early stages, but it certainly wasn't organized to the degree Ganz thought it could be.

In an indirect way, Ganz had been at the center of a series of dramatic moments in the country's history and the long arc of the Democratic Party. He was in Atlantic City in 1964, as a young civil rights activist, when the integrated Mississippi Freedom Democratic Party demanded to be seated at the Democratic convention alongside the segregated Mississippi Democratic Party. "We want to register, to become first-class citizens," the group's leader, Fannie Lou Hamer, a granddaughter of slaves and the youngest of twenty siblings, forcefully testified before the convention's credentials committee on live television. "And if the Freedom Democratic Party is not seated now, I question America." Lyndon Johnson offered the delegation a pitiful two seats, which Hamer turned down. When LBJ came out on the balcony of the convention hall to officially accept the Democratic nomination amid a sparkling fireworks display over the festive boardwalk, Ganz and his fellow civil rights activists chanted "Freedom now!" over and over. The civil rights protests eventually ended the Dixiecrats' hold over the Democratic Party and broke up FDR's long-standing New Deal coalition.

Four years later, Ganz turned out the vote for Bobby Kennedy with the United Farm Workers in East Los Angeles. Turnout reached

80 percent on the day of the California primary, handing Kennedy a crucial victory. Ganz was supposed to introduce Kennedy to a group of farmworkers backstage at the Ambassador Hotel after his victory speech when Sirhan Sirhan's bullet stopped the candidate in his tracks. "Talk about feeling history just falling through your fingers," Ganz said.

Nearly forty years later, many had come and gone, but Ganz was still here. "For those in a biblical frame of mind," he said in San Francisco, "forty years of wandering in the desert is just about enough." Applause filled the room. "Amen," he said. "The intent here is to cross the river."

His opening presentation amounted to quite an intellectual tour de force. Ganz quoted Alexis de Tocqueville's writings on American democracy in the 1830s and explored Stephen Jay Gould's theories of time. He picked up a green Hoberman sphere, which expanded from a crunchy ball into a perfectly round dome—a fitting metaphor for the weekend. He asked everybody to read the seventeenth chapter of 1 Samuel in the Old Testament, the story of David and Goliath. "We're going to lay the foundation for a new movement," he said at the end of that first night. He called it "the movement to elect Barack Obama as president."

Early the next morning, on day two of the training, Ganz elaborated on his own story: growing up a rabbi's son in Bakersfield, meeting JFK at Harvard in 1960, going down to Mississippi as a young civil rights activist, working alongside César Chávez during the famed grape boycott, returning to Harvard to get his Ph.D. in sociology and teach community organizing, and hearing Obama's keynote speech to the Democratic convention in 2004, which brought him to where he was today.

In the summer of 2004, Ganz was holed up at a friend's place in Monterey, writing a paper titled "Why the Democrats Keep Nominating Stiffs." There was no TV, so Ganz listened to Obama's speech on the radio. For thirty years, he'd been urging politicians and activists to weave a broader narrative about the hopes and struggles in their lives, rather than just arguing about causes and policy papers. Then he heard Obama. "Holy shit," Ganz thought to himself. "This is quite something." Finally somebody got it. A former community organizer, no less, schooled in the methodology of Alinsky and tested on Chicago's South Side. Though he couldn't see the euphoric reception Obama received that night, it was pretty much love at first sight. "When he decided to run, it was just a no-brainer," Ganz said. He met Obama when the candidate visited Boston in April 2007 and a month later traveled to Chicago to strategize with the campaign's top organizers. In Chicago he met Figueroa, a fellow veteran of the labor movement from rural California whose uncle and nephew belonged to the United Farm Workers. The two immediately hit it off. "Would you do these Camp Obamas?" Figueroa asked him.

That's how Ganz found himself back in California, almost exactly three years after the 2004 convention, deconstructing Obama's iconic speech before a roomful of Obama activists in San Francisco. The Obama campers sat on wooden school chairs, listening intently as if they were in class and Ganz was their professor.

"How many of you saw Barack's speech?" he asked. Every hand went up. "What do you remember about it?"

"There are no red states, there are no blue states, there are only the United States," one man yelled out.

"Why do you remember that phrase?" Ganz asked.

"Because it hits your heart," the man responded.

"What about it hit your heart?"

"No division," the man added.

A young woman with long sandy blond hair chimed in. "It was kind of radical in an election in which everyone said, 'We have to beat Bush, we have to beat the Republicans.' And he just talked about uniting."

Ganz nodded. "What do you remember about Barack?" he asked. "Do you remember his position on policy?"

"No," a few people responded, shaking their heads.

"Do you remember the issues he talked about?" Ganz asked.

"No," another confessed.

"That's very interesting," Ganz said. "Because you read the newspaper, you'd think that's what everybody would remember. So what were the specifics, what do you remember about Barack?"

"He talked about his history and his family. His father being an immigrant," said a young man from the Philippines. "That was very important to me."

"How many people thought his personal story was important to you?"

Virtually every hand went up.

"What else do you remember?" Ganz asked.

"One of the first things he said in the speech was the unlikelihood that he was on that stage," said a man in his thirties.

"Didn't he say 'a skinny kid with a funny name'?" another added.

Ganz played the first seven minutes of Obama's convention speech on a projector. "Let's face it," Obama said as he looked out onto a sea of delegates in Boston holding blue and white signs bearing his name. "My presence on this stage is pretty unlikely." He described his immigrant father, herding goats in Kenya and coming to study in a "magical place" called America. He told the story of his white mother from Kansas, on the other side of the world, how his grandfather worked on oil rigs and farms through the Depression and joined Patton's army during World War II. The family moved west, all the way to Hawaii, "in search of opportunity," Obama recounted. His black African father and white Kansas mother found a short-lived yet "improbable love." Said Obama: "I stand here knowing that my story is part of the larger American story."

While analyzing the speech, Ganz morphed from a rumpled organizer into an urbane lit teacher. "What that talk was all about was bringing values back alive," he said, "interpreting his values to the rest of us and using the vehicle of storytelling to do that." Obama appealed to the raw emotions of the right brain, not just the sturdy logic of the left, associated with stiff, proper, losing Democrats like

Gore and Kerry. "It's not philosophy, it's not statistics, it's lived experiences," Ganz said of the words that elevated Obama to national prominence. The notion of talking about values shouldn't be something the Republicans had a monopoly on, Ganz maintained. Dean had repeatedly made the same argument after becoming DNC chair. "It wasn't that we had the wrong values," Dean said. "It was that people believed we didn't have any."

Democrats might indeed possess better ideas than Republicans, but first they needed to get people to listen to them, especially in those states where the party had failed to venture for so many years. That's where the personal narrative that would drive Obama's campaign came in. That's how Obama's grassroots activists would distinguish themselves from all those high-profile Clinton supporters. They'd build a bigger army and tell a better story.

Ganz wanted the 120 people in the room—and the hundreds he'd subsequently train—to learn how to narrate their own tales and to persuasively explain those stories to other prospective volunteers and voters. "What we did was figure out a way to teach people not to imitate Barack," said Ganz, "but to do their own."

A week later, Wicks took Camp Obama on the road. Her first stop outside of California brought her to Idaho. *Idaho?* She was thinking the same thing. Nampa, Idaho, no less, an old railroad town on the Oregon border populated by hop, sugar beet, potato, and onion fields. Not even Boise, though Nampa was only thirty minutes away. It was the only place where they could find space, in a Hispanic cultural center. None of the unions or local Democrats wanted to be associated with the campaign at that point. You couldn't blame them.

Only twelve people showed up that weekend. Still, Wicks was impressed by what she saw. The fact that there was even a semblance of a campaign in a state like Idaho six months before Super Tuesday was altogether extraordinary.

A group of Mormon expeditioners first settled the Idaho Territory in 1860, mistaking it for the chosen land of Salt Lake City. The initial territory was bigger than Texas, until Montana and Wyoming broke off. The Gem State had once been home to thoughtful liberals like Senator Frank Church, an outspoken critic of the war in Vietnam and author of a sweeping investigation into the CIA in the late 1970s, but those days had long passed. A Democratic presidential candidate hadn't carried the state since 1964. The Clinton years were an especially bad time for Idaho Democrats. "Bill Clinton was intensely unpopular in the state," said Idaho Democratic Party chairman Keith Roark. In 1990, Democrats held the governor's mansion, both congressional seats, and half of the state legislature. By 2000, they retained only one statewide office—school supervisor— and a mere 12 seats in the 135-member legislature. "Clinton's sexual nonsense did great damage to the Democratic Party here," said Richard Stallings, a Democratic congressman from 1985 to 1993.

The influence of the Mormon Church in southern Idaho, the decline of the heavily unionized mining industry in the Silver Valley of northern Idaho, and the influx of conservative Californians from places like Orange County turned the state into a fierce Republican stronghold. The Aryan Nation once called it "the international headquarters of the white race," and apocalyptic outlaws like Randy Weaver in Ruby Ridge flocked to the rugged north. George Bush won 68 percent of Idaho's vote in 2004, his second-best showing after Utah. Despondent Democrats nicknamed their state the "Mississippi of the mountains." Idaho didn't just elect Republicans—it elected crazy right-wing ones. Remember Larry Craig?

Idaho hadn't been relevant to a presidential election since Church briefly ran as a dark horse challenger to Jimmy Carter in 1976. "Usually, they [presidential candidates] fly over between Denver and Seattle and wave as they go by," said Cecil Andrus, Idaho's four-term Democratic governor. Since then, only Howard Dean had been crazy enough to give a damn about the state. He visited three times during his presidential campaign, much to the chagrin of his staff, hell-bent on unearthing a Democratic revival. When he became

DNC chair, Dean paid for the Idaho Democratic Party to hire a communications director and field organizers for the northern and southern parts of the state. "The fifty-state strategy was so obvious here, because we'd had nothing for so long," said Jill Kuraitis, a local reporter and Democratic activist. During the 2008 election, Dean's vision for what could be in Idaho found its unexpected expression, thanks to a black guy with an African-Muslim name from Chicago.

Following Obama's announcement in February, Dave Ficks, an official in the Boise school system, posted a call to arms on MyBO. Ficks was an Independent voter who supported Obama because of his early opposition to the war in Iraq. "I realize Idaho is not the state that anyone thinks of first when contemplating a caucus/ primary, much less electoral victory for Barack Obama," Ficks wrote on February 17. "Despite this, I would like to challenge the supporters of Barack Obama in Idaho to set aside doubt and believe that he can win here . . . After all, if Barack Obama wins Idaho, one of the reddest of red states, there will be no doubt that the vast majority of Americans want new, different, ethical leadership." Ficks held an initial meeting that month at a burger joint outside of Boise with fifteen scattered activists, formulating a volunteer group called Idahoans for Obama. A month later, they hosted a kickoff party for 150 people at a barbecue spot in Boise, the Connector House of Catfish and Ribs. Despite the impressive turnout, even the owner, a loyal Democrat, expressed skepticism about the new group. "If people vote for Obama it will surprise me," said Chantrice Thomas. "It's not a racist thing, it's a Republican thing."

At a small meeting the week after at a pizza place called Papa Joe's, Ficks met T. J. Thomson, a charismatic former student body president at Boise State University plugged into the local Democratic Party. Thomson was handsome in a classically all-American way, with short sandy blond hair, blue eyes, and an athletic build. Ficks asked him to lead the new group. "I was one of the sole people that had political experience," Thomson realized. He could shape the campaign in its own distinct image. "Obama inspired me to personal action by making it a campaign about us, not him," Thomson said, echoing a common refrain among candidate and supporters.

Thomson was raised by a single mother in Idaho Falls, a rigid, heavily Mormon city in southeast Idaho that "makes Salt Lake City look like a pleasure den," the local journalist Michael Ames wrote. While everyone around him paid fealty to the GOP, Thomson became a Democrat at thirteen, licking envelopes for Michael Dukakis, who lost by twenty-six points in Idaho that year. Thomson entered the Air Force out of high school, studied political science at Boise State, and worked as a space analyst at the Government Accountability Office in Washington before returning to Idaho as an auditor for Idaho Power. He'd been all over the world but liked the safe and bucolic City of Trees in the foothills of the Rockies. Boise reminded him of a tiny Portland or Boulder without the hippies. The city became a hub for the high-tech industry in the 1990s, attracting companies like Hewlett-Packard and younger, more liberal residents lured by affordable housing, good schools, and a wealth of outdoor activities. Boise elected a Basque-American Democrat as mayor in 2003 and became one of the state's few Democratic strongholds. Thomson started running Idahoans for Obama out of his house in west Boise, a new part of town filled with lots of identical 1,600-square-foot, two-story vinyl-and-stucco homes.

Thomson e-mailed everybody he could find over MyBO, looking for help. He began conversing with Kassie Cerami, an energetic former cheerleader and youthful-looking mother of two college kids. In 2004, Cerami watched Obama's speech at the Democratic convention and decided she'd do anything to help him, even though she'd never been involved in a political campaign before or really considered herself a Democrat. "I believed him and in him," she said. "I felt that he needed my help, and I wasn't going to sit on the couch and not do everything within my power to get him elected."

After meeting Thomson, she quit her job overseeing marketing for a car dealership and devoted herself full-time to the Obama effort. *The Idaho Statesman* soon dubbed Thomson and Cerami the "Adam and Eve" of Idahoans for Obama. They complemented each other well: she a brash and fiery political novice, he a diplomatic campaign veteran.

On August 5, Cerami picked up Thomson, and they drove five hours south to an Obama event in Elko, Nevada, an old cowboy and mining town where the candidate held a "rural issues listening tour." They helped with logistics and were rewarded with front-row seats as a crowd of nearly one thousand filled the Elko Convention Center. After his speech, they met Obama backstage. Thomson asked the candidate to visit Boise.

"I heard about you guys," Obama responded. "I want to, and I'm going to try."

Cerami heard echoes of the famed *Field of Dreams* line: "If you build it, he will come."

They'd been bugging Wicks for months to hold a Camp Obama in Idaho. Two weeks after Elko, she showed up. They gathered at the Hispanic Cultural Center of Idaho in Nampa, a brightly colored, contemporary adobe structure with an orange base, green and yellow sides, and a purple oval entrance. Cerami was disappointed that only a dozen people showed, but after Wicks had them sit around a table and write down their skills, Cerami realized the group knew more than she'd presumed. As in San Francisco, Wicks helped the new organizers perfect their own stories. Thomson talked about growing up with a mother who suffered from terrible migraines and never had adequate health insurance. When the pain grew too overwhelming, she took her own life at fifty-two. It happened in 1995, but Thomson had scarcely talked about it since. That day, he realized his own experience had the power to move even skeptical Republicans. "People can't argue so much with, 'No, your mother didn't deserve insurance,'" he said. He cited his mother's death as a reason he supported Obama and his push for universal health care.

On day two, the group called every identified Obama supporter in Idaho, inviting them to an organizing meeting where they'd lay out the strategy to win the February 5 caucus and assign volunteer leaders for each region of the state. "You guys are the Obama campaign in Idaho," Wicks told them when she left.

Cerami thought they needed an office. Through Craigslist, she found an affordable converted brick-and-stucco fourplex house in an old working-class part of town known as the Boise Bench for its sloped elevation. Starting in late August, Idahoans for Obama shared space with two therapists and a paneling business, who weren't thrilled to have a bunch of Obama supporters running around their office. People donated computers and chairs. Cerami's husband designed a website. Stacy Falkner, a student at Boise State, came by the office nearly every day and contacted students. They printed up shirts and stickers that said "Blue Girl, Red State." By the end of October, Joey Bristol—a recent graduate of the Woodrow Wilson School of Public and International Affairs at Princeton University who postponed a State Department assignment in China to work on the Obama campaign—arrived as Obama's first Idaho staffer. "Before, in Boise, if you were a Democrat, you kept it quiet," Cerami said. "All of a sudden there was Obama stuff everywhere." On November 1, the campaign officially christened the temporary space as an official Obama office. A hundred people crammed in for the party that night, toasting the milestone with wine and cheese. Three months before Super Tuesday, Obama had the state to himself. Ray Rivera, the campaign's western-states director, flew up from Denver for the occasion. The crowd surprised him. "Man, I gotta come to Idaho more often," he said.

On April 11, 2007, Jeremy Bird arrived as Obama's organizer in chief in South Carolina. With his black rectangular glasses, thin stubble, long sideburns, and rapid-fire dialect, Bird looked and spoke more like a hipster from Brooklyn than a political operative from South Carolina, but his fundamentalist Southern Baptist upbringing in Missouri and divinity school training at Harvard served him well in the heavily religious state, where African-Americans made up half of the Democratic primary electorate. He spoke frequently at black churches, where locals called him Pastor Bird. "They refused to believe that I wasn't actually a minister because I went to divinity school," Bird said, "even though I would tell them I'm not ordained."

South Carolina had been known for its mudslinging politics since it became the first southern primary in 1980, and its political campaigns had a familiar feel to them. "Everybody who had ever done South Carolina politics told me, 'They don't do volunteerism down here,'" Bird recalled. "'You have to pay the ministers; you have to pay the state senators. That's just what we do.'"

Obama tried that approach at the beginning, offering a $5,000-a-month consulting contract to state senator Darrell Jackson, a pastor at the eleven-thousand-member Bible Way Church of Atlas Road in Columbia, the state capital. Unfortunately for Obama, Jackson took in $15,000 a month from John Edwards's campaign in 2004. The Clinton campaign promptly quadrupled Obama's offer. Jackson endorsed Hillary in February 2007. Clinton locked up most influential Democratic politicians and preachers through such lucrative contracts or long-standing relationships developed through years of cultivating the state's black community.

Bird didn't have that kind of money to throw around, nor did he want to run such a campaign. In a racially divided state where the Confederate flag still flies on capitol grounds (and hung above the statehouse as recently as 2000), blacks talked to blacks and whites to whites in South Carolina politics. Bird didn't want to do that either. He wanted to direct a campaign in line with Obama's own background as a coalition-building community organizer. After all, that's why Bird himself signed on with Obama. "We had to build from almost nothing," he said. "We didn't have the establishment with us."

The higher-ups in Chicago cared only about how many voters he contacted. Lacking the money or the resources of Iowa, Bird needed a way to train enough volunteers to knock on all those doors and make all those calls. That's where his experience as a Dean organizer in New Hampshire, holding house meetings and developing volunteer leaders to guide and grow the campaign, came in handy. "The basic approach fit beautifully," said Bird's mentor, Marshall Ganz, "because Dean's campaign was an insurgent campaign in New Hampshire, and Obama's campaign was an insurgent campaign in South Carolina."

The short and slender Bird found an unlikely kindred spirit in Anton Gunn, the campaign's six-foot-four, 280-pound political director, a former offensive lineman for the South Carolina Gamecocks who'd spent ten years as a community organizer in Columbia. When Bird came to town, Gunn thought he was just another hired hand from D.C. "At our first meeting, I realized we were singing from the same sheet of music," Gunn said. They knew a lot of the same people, including Ganz. Gunn seconded Bird's house meeting proposal. "We knew if we got people in a living room and had a dynamic conversation about Barack's story and our own, that would be a winning combination."

Bird recruited a bunch of young activists, on college campuses and through Facebook, as his boots on the ground. "You couldn't just go to people who had done it before," he said, "because everybody who had done it before had done it the old way." More so than in any other early state, the battle between Clinton and Obama in South Carolina became a classic top-down versus bottom-up clash. "If he pulls this off," said Inez Tenenbaum, a former state school superintendent who ran for Senate in 2004, "Barack Obama's organization will be studied and replicated in this state for many years to come."

Bird's bosses weren't quite so enthusiastic. "I'll let you try anything as long as you show me it's working," said Los Angeles–based political consultant Craig Schirmer, who'd worked in South Carolina politics since 1998 and supervised the campaign's get-out-the-vote operations. "You have to prove that it's working, and we have to see the results." Steve Hildebrand, who oversaw the campaign's ground strategy from Chicago, doubted whether Bird could import a new model to such a traditional state. "I was one of those skeptics of Jeremy and his crew in South Carolina," Hildebrand admitted after the primary, "as to whether or not through these house meetings, through these gatherings . . . they could build enough capacity to get us across the finish line." The buzz-cut, broad-shouldered South Dakotan thought it was all just a bunch of hippie shit. "I would've shut down South Carolina if I cared about anything other than Iowa," he told a colleague. Still, he allowed Bird to do his thing.

On June 9, the Obama campaign held its first major day of volunteer activity, organizing a series of early door-to-door canvasses in all fifty states called the Walk for Change. Many considered this grunt work, but the hyperkinetic Bird loved it. "I'm pretty impatient," he said. "I get bored when I do a typical desk job." On a ninety-five-degree Saturday in South Carolina—when people carried umbrellas to shield themselves from the sun—more than three hundred volunteers showed up in eleven different cities, including in sleepy rural towns like Orangeburg not known for their Democratic activism. "Most of the presidents you get, they ain't never been on the street," one volunteer from blue-collar North Charleston said that day. "They don't know nothin' about the street. [Obama's] a community organizer, so he understands what it's like." The turnout encouraged Bird. "That was our first realization of, we can do this," he said.

He planned a series of house meetings for the next month. "From your house to the White House," he called it. Rospars sent the campaign's blogger, Sam Graham-Felsen, and videographer, Kate Albright-Hanna, to cover them. Both had worked as professional journalists and now essentially covered the campaign for the campaign.

By documenting Bird's organizing, through video and on the blog, they hoped to inspire Obama supporters to get more involved with the campaign and persuade a skeptical top brass in Chicago that Bird was onto something.

On July 25, 2007, the type of sweltering summer day when the humidity in South Carolina sticks to you like glue, Graham-Felsen and Albright-Hanna met up with Bird in Columbia and drove an hour and twenty minutes east to Florence, a gritty city of 31,000 in the northeastern Pee Dee region, exactly halfway between New York City and Miami. Florence had become a hub for the finance and biomedical industries, but as in so many cities—particularly in the South—there existed a rather prominent gulf between rich and poor, white and black. In 2005, Florence had the highest violent crime rate of any comparable city in the United States. They headed to the depressed west side of town and met the house meeting host Grace Cusack, a spunky, middle-aged African-American woman who ran a day-care center and lived in a small redbrick bungalow with a little porch and grassy lawn filled with children's toys. She wore a leopard-print top, long black skirt, and fire-engine-red lipstick. "I've never had a lot of money," she told Graham-Felsen. "But I'm a trendsetter. I've *always* been a trendsetter," she said, waving her right hand theatrically for emphasis. "Honey, if Grace do it, everybody want to do it." Little did she know that the whole state would soon be following her lead.

Cusack's house meeting had just ended when the Obama staffers arrived, so Albright-Hanna shot footage of another gathering in nearby Timmonsville, a rural, predominantly black farming town twenty minutes from Florence. Ten people, all African-American, squeezed into the small, wood-paneled living room of Reba Martin, a retired educator who proudly displayed family pictures, plaques, and trophies on the walls. Bird observed silently from the back. Ryan Cooper, a twenty-two-year-old organizer wearing khakis and a baggy white T-shirt with an Obama logo, led the meeting.

Cooper grew up in Georgia, starred in basketball in high school, but soon grew disillusioned when a scholarship from a major school never materialized. He dropped out of a community college in Kansas, quit playing basketball, and transferred to the University of Maryland. While watching Obama's 2004 convention speech, he was struck by the candidate's call to "eradicate the slander that says a black youth with a book is acting white." Cooper found an internship in Obama's Senate office, flourished in school, and gave the commencement address at his graduation. After interviewing with Bird in South Carolina, he got the job within five minutes. Cooper told his story at the house meeting. "I don't come from that much money," he said. "My mom's a teacher and my dad's a carpenter. So if we get an administration that only caters to the wealthy, then that means my family gets passed over." He described what drew him to Obama's campaign. "Obama's offering something new," he said. "I tell people, I'm not a campaign guy. I'm really not. I'm a Barack guy. So I will do a campaign for Barack, and I believe other young people will internalize that same notion."

"What's really inspiring me about [Obama]," Reba Martin's daughter told him, "is you."

Graham-Felsen posted an interview with Cusack and snippets from Cooper's house meeting in Timmonsville and another in Columbia on Obama's campaign blog, which soon circulated widely. "No one really knew what we were doing," Bird said. "That video told our story . . . It had a profound impact." That summer, the new-media shop shot a series of short documentaries about the campaign called "The Road to Change: South Carolina." Soon enough, everyone inside the campaign knew what Bird was up to.

Up north, Obama organizers started a program called "Living the Campaign," registering voters and signing up supporters wherever they happened to be. Many South Carolinians congregated at barbershops and beauty salons, so the campaign started organizing there as well. The "B&B strategy" quickly spread across the state. As one barber and Obama supporter put it, "You go to the jailhouse, you see the bad of the community; you go to church, everybody gives you the good side; but you come to the barbershop, you get the real side."

In late August, Bird and a few of his deputies traveled to a Camp Obama in Atlanta led by Ganz. The location was across the street from the first civil rights meeting Ganz ever attended. That day in 1964, young activists held a preach-off to see who could best imitate Dr. King. Now Ganz passed the torch from one generation of organizers to another. He told Bird to trust his instincts. "That kind of creative, experimental spirit is what makes for good organizing," Ganz said.

Still, throughout the summer and into the fall, Obama's South Carolina campaign encountered widespread skepticism from certain quarters of the state's black leadership. "Every Democrat running on that ticket next year would lose," state senator Robert Ford, a Clinton-supporting power broker from Charleston, said of an Obama nomination, "because he's black and he's top of the ticket. We'd lose the House and the Senate and the governors and everything." State representative Harold Mitchell of Spartanburg defected from Obama to Clinton. "Right now, we don't have time for experimentation," he said. Quipped Kevin Alexander Gray, who ran Jesse Jackson's 1988 campaign in South Carolina: "You don't get a revolution from Harvard."

Over the summer, polls showed that black women—the crucial swing vote in the Democratic primary—favored Clinton by thirty-two points. Many openly fretted about Obama's safety and wondered whether he should be running at all. "Personally, I don't feel the country is ready for an African-American," a forty-six-year-old woman from rural Loris, South Carolina, told *The New York Times*. "He would be killed."

In late November, the Obama campaign announced that its yet-to-be-deployed secret weapon, Oprah Winfrey, would start campaigning for Obama. They booked her for Columbia on December 9, reserving the Colonial Life Arena, the eighteen-thousand-seat home of the South Carolina Gamecocks basketball team. After tickets sold out within six hours, Bird sent an e-mail to Obama's events director, Emmett Beliveau, with a picture of the Gamecocks football stadium and the projected weather forecast, seventy degrees and sunny. "I think we could go bigger," Bird wrote. He expected a negative reply. "Let's do it," came the surprise response.

The day before Oprah's arrival, Bird stood on the sidelines of Williams Brice Stadium holding a red bullhorn, addressing three hundred volunteers huddled near the end zone. He wore a black track jacket, blue jeans, and his hair short and spiky. "Tomorrow is going to be a historic day," he said. "No question."

The next afternoon, the largest crowd in South Carolina political history filled the stadium, breaking the Guinness world record for largest phone bank, as 36,426 people each called four names on the back of their tickets. "We know you've got free nights and weekends, so everybody can make this phone call," said Anton Gunn, who played many a Saturday in this stadium. Sixty-eight percent of the crowd had never been contacted by the Obama campaign; half the attendees texted their numbers to Obama's headquarters, allowing the campaign to reach them from here on out. A fifth of the stadium pledged to volunteer for Obama before Election Day. "We were identifying voters in a way the Clinton or Edwards campaigns couldn't possibly do," Gunn said.

Yet the candidate and his top strategists remained fixated on Iowa. Obama's surprise victory in the Hawkeye State on January 3, 2008, exceeded all expectations and changed the dynamic of the entire race. He'd run a hybrid campaign in the opening caucus, mixing a traditional structure with a willingness to experiment. Obama based the effort around local precinct captains rooted in their communities, modeled after Kerry in 2004, while planting young organizers in far-flung counties many months before the caucus, giving them plenty of time to become adopted Iowans. Obama labored to expand Iowa's electorate, putting a particular focus on the state's small African-American population, voters—including Independents and Republicans—who'd never been to a caucus before, and the college and high school students who'd proved so elusive in years past. The Clinton campaign tagged him as a doe-eyed Dean repeat. Obama's supporters "look like Facebook," Mark Penn said derisively. "Our supporters look like caucus-goers," bragged Clinton's media director, Mandy Grunwald.

Unfortunately for the Clintons, the 2008 Iowa caucus didn't look anything like the previous ones. In some locations, seventeen-year-olds with braces counted heads for Obama with calm and precision. Obama's own pollster, Paul Harstad, predicted that no more than 150,000 people would show up for the caucus; in the end, 239,000 Iowans turned out for the largest caucus ever, nearly double the size of 2004. After running neck and neck with his opponents for months, Obama prevailed by a comfortable eight points. He painted Clintonism as a compromised, tired ideology and presented himself as a clean break from the Bush and Clinton dynasties and a fresh face for the country and the world. After his shocking win, the entire nation suddenly paid attention. Plouffe assumed they'd win New Hampshire and lock up the nomination from there.

Only this time the Clinton campaign outhustled Obama in New Hampshire and Nevada. The Obama campaign never built a deep volunteer base in New Hampshire, allowing Clinton to pull off a stunning upset on the night of January 8. In Nevada, Dean New Hampshire alums Karen Hicks and Robbie Mook also used Ganz's house meeting model for Clinton in Vegas, albeit on a smaller scale than Bird in South Carolina, to push Hillary over the top in the first western caucus, even though Obama would eventually take more delegates because of his strength in the state's rural north. (Earlier in the campaign, Hicks wanted to do a big online training for Clinton supporters, similar to Camp Obama, but never got funding from the campaign's higher-ups.) South Carolina now became pivotal. Obama needed a win to get his campaign back on track.

"Iowa showed them that he could win," said Bird, "and then New

Hampshire and Nevada put back a little skepticism that he might not be able to. Obviously, Iowa was a big turning point for us, but we saw more volunteers the day after New Hampshire than we did the day after Iowa. And it was with more urgency and a lot more energy. They felt that it mattered more." By Election Day, Bird had recruited fifteen thousand volunteers and held more than two thousand house meetings across South Carolina. He found 283 neighborhood team leaders just like Grace Cusack, who each oversaw five to ten precincts in his or her area (the average precinct contains eleven hundred registered voters), and put organizers in every pocket of the state. Hillary's network of paid politicians and ministers was no match for Bird's grassroots army.

Ganz spent Election Day in the "upstate" city of Greenville—a former "Textile Center of the South" and site of a famed civil rights sit-in at Woolworth—alongside a vivacious young organizer with a perfect southern name, Peachy Myers. Hillary had all but abandoned the state in the final days, yet Bill insisted he could pull out a strong showing for his wife, owing to his reputation as "the first black president." His harsh criticism of Obama, however, only weakened Clinton's cause, sparking a particular backlash among black South Carolinians. Former South Carolina Democratic Party chair Dick Harpootlian likened the ex-president to another South Carolinian, the Republican hatchet man Lee Atwater. Clinton blew up at a CNN reporter when he heard the comparison.

Ganz almost crossed paths with the ex-president in Greenville. In the end, the precincts Clinton visited in the city voted 80 percent for Obama. "It was just classic David and Goliath," Ganz said. "Classic. Goliath is so consumed with mocking David that that's exactly when David gets him with the stone."

Obama carried the state by twenty-eight points. Five hundred and thirty-two thousand people voted in the Democratic primary, up from 293,000 in 2004. Twenty-seven percent had never voted before. Despite the red hue of the Palmetto State, Democrats outnumbered Republicans by 97,000 voters in their respective primaries.

"The cynics who believed that what began in the snows of Iowa was just an illusion were told a different story by the good people of South Carolina," Obama said at his raucous victory party in Columbia. After his speech, as he worked the rope line, the candidate spotted Bird and gave him a big hug. "I'm really proud of you," Obama told his protégé. Bird's work in South Carolina became a model for the rest of the campaign.

After South Carolina, in the ten days leading up to Super Tuesday, Plouffe and company made a brilliant strategic decision to largely ignore blue-state metropolises and rack up as many delegates as possible in the small red states deemed insignificant by the Clinton campaign. On January 29, Obama stopped in his grandfather's hometown of El Dorado, Kansas, population 12,718, picking up the endorsement of Kansas governor Kathleen Sebelius. From there he headed to Kansas City, Denver, Phoenix, then off to East Los Angeles before a debate in California. He was planning a trip to Utah when the campaign got word of the death of a prominent Latter-day Saints leader. Holding a political rally in the state didn't seem appropriate. The campaign chose Boise as the alternate location.

On January 31, Kassie Cerami and T. J. Thomson received notice: Obama was coming to town on the morning of February 2. They had two days to find a venue. Within minutes, the news leaked to all the major papers and TV stations.

"What's the biggest high school gym you have?" Katie Ingebretson, a young staffer sent from Iowa to Idaho, asked Cerami.

"You've gotta be kidding me," Cerami responded. "We need the biggest venue in the state." The Obama campaign already had five offices in Idaho, including in deep red Idaho Falls, and nearly twenty organizers on the ground. Nineteen of twenty-six Democrats in the state legislature had endorsed Obama. Finding a crowd would not be a problem, Cerami assured Ingebretson. The fourteen-thousand-person Taco Bell Arena (formerly known as the Pavilion), home of the Boise State Broncos basketball team, fit the bill. The campaign passed out free tickets to supporters who made two hundred calls for Obama. Suddenly a bunch of new volunteers showed up at the office.

Thomson woke at 3:30 a.m. on February 2, took a shower, and practiced his lines. He arrived at the arena downtown, a block from the Boise River, in blackness at 5:00 a.m. Despite temperatures below freezing and a bitter wind blowing off the river, a line had already begun to form for the morning rally. A few dozen students spent the night in tents outside, braving the elements. "Saturday's sunrise lines snaked for miles through the Boise State campus, around the Broncos' blue turf field, through pitch-dark parking lots and three fresh inches of snow," wrote Michael Ames, an editor in Sun Valley. Clint Stennett, a Democratic state senator, checked out of the hospital four days after brain surgery and drove three hours from Sun Valley in the dark to get there.

By breakfast time, 10 percent of the city's voting-age population had filled the arena. Two thousand more, unable to get in, listened to the speech on loudspeakers outside. The event streamed live on all three local TV stations. It was the largest political event in the state since Eisenhower visited in 1952.

Cerami's husband picked up Axelrod at the airport that morning. "Where the fuck are we?" Axelrod said in disbelief as he drove by the mile-long crowd queued outside. "This is Idaho?" Cerami met Obama backstage. "You built it," the candidate told her, "and I came."

As the arena filled, Cerami and Thomson went out to energize the crowd, standing on a platform in the middle of the floor behind a giant American flag and a blue CHANGE WE CAN BELIEVE IN banner. Supporters draped homemade signs over the balconies, replacing the o in Boise with the red, white, and blue circular Obama logo. Cerami wore a navy blue "Obama '08" long-sleeve shirt and blue jeans. Thomson had on cowboy boots, blue jeans, and a brown T-shirt with Obama's face on it. "I'm the grassroots guy," he said by way of introduction, punching his left fist in the air.

"Who here has ever been to a caucus?" Thomson asked the crowd. A few scattered cheers bounced around the arena.

"Nice," Cerami responded. "All three of ya."

"I think everyone knows this, but Idaho means a lot this time," Thomson said. "A lot more than previous years. We're on super-duper Tuesday. This is it. Idaho is gonna send a message all the way to Washington."

They led the crowd in Obama's signature call-and-response. "Fired up," they yelled. "Ready to go," the audience responded. It was only 8:00 a.m., but this was the one and only chance for Idaho to do the chant with Obama in the house.

The two organizers introduced Cecil Andrus, Jimmy Carter's interior secretary and Idaho's governor from 1971 to 1977 and from 1987 to 1995. Andrus looked vigorous and energetic at age seventy-six, with two streaks of white hair on each side of his nearly bald head. "Man, what a beautiful sight," Andrus said as he scanned the crowd. "The beauty of this morning is there's a lot of faces out here who are not familiar to me." He told a story about how, as a young lumberjack running for the Idaho senate in 1960, he saw JFK campaign in Lewiston, a timber town in northern Idaho. Kennedy inspired him to run for higher office. Andrus hadn't felt that same idealism until Obama came around. "I'm older now," he said. "Some would suggest in the twilight of a mediocre political career. I, like you, can still be inspired. I can still hope."

The sparkling piano chords of U2's "City of Blinding Lights" filled the arena, and Obama bounded through a black curtain toward the stage. He gave Andrus a big hug as he walked to the podium and took the mic in his right hand. He turned several times and soaked in the incredible sight. Jill Kuraitis described the volume as "just this side of painful." "Wow," Obama said, "look at this . . . Thank you, Eye-da-hoe," he said in his Chicago accent, elongating the last syllable. "What an unbelievable crowd. What an unbelievable reception. I can't believe it." He looked out onto the sea of faces. "They told me there weren't any Democrats in Idaho," Obama said playfully. "I didn't believe them."

You had to wonder: Where was Hillary? A day before Obama's visit, Clinton sent Washington senator Maria Cantwell to Boise, who drew only a placid crowd of fifty. Neither Hillary nor Bill bothered to visit, and her campaign didn't add Idaho to a list of states on its website until nine days before the caucus. "Breaking! HRC Discovers Idaho," the progressive blog Red State Rebels noted sarcastically. Clinton never put a staffer on the ground, opened an office, or spent any money in the state. "I was blown away by it," said the former congressman Richard Stallings, a friend of the Clintons' who chaired the Idaho Democratic Party from 2005 until 2007. "I thought that Hillary would walk away with the state. I should've sensed that she was deaf out here."

At a campaign stop in Indiana, Bill Clinton made a crack about elk outnumbering Democrats in Idaho. "If Bill Clinton had done for elk in Idaho everything he did for Democrats, we'd have far fewer elk," Idaho Democratic Party chairman Keith Roark responded. Throughout the year, Roark had been bombarded by calls from Obama surrogates like Massachusetts governor Deval Patrick and former Senate majority leader Tom Daschle. The campaign flew him out to Chicago to meet with the two Davids, Plouffe and Axelrod. "I never did receive so much as a phone call from a Clinton surrogate," Roark said. He later pledged his coveted superdelegate vote to Obama. "Mark Penn proved himself an absolute idiot," Roark said of the Clinton campaign's decision to bypass red caucus states like Idaho. (In fact, Harold Ickes was supposed to be in charge of tracking delegates, but figured Clinton would do so well in big states like New York that small ones like Idaho wouldn't matter.)

Three days after Obama's rally, eight thousand Boise Democrats crowded into Qwest Arena, home of the Idaho Steelheads hockey team, for the February 5 caucus. The Democratic Party blocked off nearly half the space for Clinton and a chunk for John Edwards, but Obama's supporters took over all the sections, filling the floor and both decks of seating. The place shook with people, especially when the crowd did the wave as if at a sporting event. The hundreds who couldn't get in voted on scrap paper outside. Election officials ran out of ballots and had to fetch more halfway through. The telegenic mayor of Boise, David Bieter, a rising star in the state, spoke on behalf of Obama that night. "We hear Senator Obama say, 'We are not blue states and we are not red states, we are the United States of America,'" Bieter said. "But you know, we are out here in Idaho and it's hard. It's hard to believe, but then he comes here"—the crowd whooped and hollered—"he comes here to Boise, and we have to believe. We simply have to believe."

Twenty-one thousand Democrats turned out to caucus across the state, a fourfold increase over 2004. For the first time ever, Democrats caucused in all forty-four counties. Obama won forty-three of them. He took 86 percent of the vote in Boise—sweeping the county's delegates—and 79 percent of the vote statewide. It turned out to be his best showing of the entire campaign. Obama won fifteen of Idaho's eighteen delegates that night, narrowly amassing more delegates than Clinton on Super Tuesday, even as she pulled out big wins in populous blue states like New York, Massachusetts, New Jersey, and California. "If Mrs. Clinton won by nine points in California and Mr. Obama won by 62 points in Idaho, does that make us 71 points more conservative than the 'Great Potatoes. Tasty Destinations' state?" the author Dave Eggers mused in *The New York Times* afterward. Obama's delegate margin would prove insurmountable as the campaign churned on. He won the campaign right here, in small red states like Idaho and Utah and Kansas, which few expected to matter and his chief competitor chose to ignore.

A few months later, sitting in a living room in Indianapolis, Obama explained how his campaign did so well in such far-flung locales. "People wonder, 'How did this guy win all these states? How'd he win Idaho by forty points?'" Obama underplayed his own margin of victory, smiling as he once again accentuated the state's syllables. "It was because volunteers got together and they really built the campaign. We weren't even there, in Idaho, and suddenly we get a call from somebody saying, 'Hey, I'm here in Idaho and I'm organizing, and can the senator stop by sometime?' So we didn't have, originally, big plans for Idaho, but people made this structure."

Meanwhile, one month and eleven contests after Super Tuesday, Cerami went down to Texas for the Obama campaign and ran into Bill Clinton at a coffee shop in Austin. She had on a blue Obama shirt. "What's a pretty girl like you doing wearing a shirt like that?" Clinton teasingly asked her.

"Because this pretty girl's got a brain," the forty-something Cerami tartly responded. The ex-president just stood there as she put a dollar in the tip jar and walked out.

For most of its history, the Democratic Party selected its presidential candidates in an anything-but-democratic manner, intentionally empowering front-runners like Hillary Clinton and thwarting pesky insurgents like Barack Obama. Party bosses picked the nominee in the back rooms of the conventions, disregarding the will of the voters in primaries and caucuses. In 1968, Hubert Humphrey won 2 percent of the vote in the primaries but 67 percent of convention delegates in Chicago, more than enough to become the Democratic nominee. When student activists protested outside the convention hall downtown, Chicago's mayor, Richard J. Daley, a legendary Democratic power broker, brutally unleashed his police on them. Amid the chaos of the convention, supporters of Robert Kennedy and Eugene McCarthy passed a rule mandating a study of how the party chose its nominee. The rather innocuous effort led to a commission helmed by South Dakota senator George McGovern, whose 1971 report, *Mandate for Reform*, led to a sweeping revision of party politics. The McGovern Commission greatly expanded the number of primaries and ensured that convention delegates were roughly proportional to vote results, drastically reduced the power of party officials to serve as delegates and dictate the choice of the nominee, and mandated a greater role for the ascendant future of the party—young people, women, and minorities. The new rules helped catapult two dark horses to the nomination, McGovern himself in 1972 and Jimmy Carter in 1976.

The old guard was furious. "There's too much hair and not enough cigars at this convention," groused a longtime delegate in 1972. "We aren't going to let these Harvard-Berkeley Camelots take over our party," vowed the AFL-CIO political director, Al Barkan. By 1980, the powers that be had seen enough, striking back with a commission of their own, led by North Carolina governor Jim Hunt. The Hunt Commission returned power to elected officials and party regulars, adding hundreds of unpledged delegates known as superdelegates, comprised of members of Congress, governors, and the DNC. They existed, in great measure, to prevent another McGovern or Carter from becoming the nominee.

Four years later, Senator Gary Hart launched an insurgent challenge to the front-runner, Walter Mondale. Hart won sixteen primaries and caucuses to Mondale's ten, and barely lost the popular vote. Nonetheless, when Hart solicited support from superdelegates, he found that Mondale had locked virtually all of them up before the primary had even begun, leveraging his connections as Carter's vice president. Hart probably would've lost anyway, but the superdelegates sealed his defeat. From then on, the Democratic primaries followed a familiar rhythm: a captivating insurgent always emerged to challenge an established front-runner, only to run out of gas as the primary churned on. In 1988, conservative southern Democrats bunched nine southern primaries together on Super Tuesday as an additional obstacle to liberal insurgents. The showdown became a contest between a priest and a warrior, *Los Angeles Times* columnist Ron Brownstein wrote in an influential column. The warrior always won. In 2008, it wasn't hard to figure out which candidate assumed which role. Before Super Tuesday, Hillary the warrior held a massive advantage among superdelegates, 184 to Obama's 95. From there, however, everything went off script.

Obama amassed a significant delegate advantage by narrowly besting Clinton on Super Tuesday and racking up eleven straight victories in the weeks following. Superdelegates now faced tremendous pressure to follow the will of the voters. Messy new tensions, meanwhile, spilled out into the open. Managing the primary became especially chaotic for Chairman Dean. He faced botched contests in Michigan and Florida that resembled phony elections in a banana republic. Superdelegates, a word and entity most people had never heard of, became a national buzzword and source of frenzied anxiety—uniquely able, by virtue of their numbers, to tip a deadlocked race.

Dean was criticized for being both too passive *and* too forceful. Both the Obama and the Clinton camps believed he favored the other, even as the Democratic chairman remained fastidiously neutral throughout. "I didn't even vote in my home state primary, even though it's a secret ballot," he said, "because I didn't even want to know, myself, who I favored." He believed both Obama and Clinton would be equally strong candidates in a general election—Obama might appeal to more places, such as Virginia and North Carolina, but Clinton would run strong in traditional battlegrounds like Florida and Ohio.

Many of Dean's supporters and former aides, however, viewed the Clinton-Obama contest as a referendum on Dean's legacy as a presidential candidate and party chair. Not surprisingly, they lined up with Obama. In the Internet era, elder statesmen sitting in smoke-filled rooms (these days they're probably smoke-free) often mattered less than millions of people organizing locally around candidates and issues. Obama, like Dean, understood the changing nature of the party and embraced it. Clinton did not. "They looked at '04 and said, 'If Howard Dean lost, these tools must not have worked,'" argued Joe Trippi. Hillary's candidacy, since its inception, represented the polar opposite of what Dean embodied: dominated by an inner circle of Washington-centric top strategists, with little room for grassroots input; impervious to new social-networking inventions like Facebook and YouTube; dismissive of long-ignored red states; reliant on large financial contributions from a small group of high rollers, which became the main reason money dried up so quickly as the primary dragged on. After Obama's wins on Super Tuesday, the Clinton campaign criticized delegates chosen in red-state caucuses like Idaho as undemocratic "second-class delegates," arguing that Clinton's victories in large blue states like California and Massachusetts—places certain to go blue in November—should matter more. Markos Moulitsas of the popular blog Daily Kos labeled Clinton's complaints the "insult 40 states" strategy.

In contrast to Clinton's campaign, Dean's argument for how to rebuild and expand the party for the long haul found its perfect short-term exponent in Obama, whose legions of small donors, bottom-up foundations, and big-tent appeal to Independents and disaffected Republicans planted Democratic roots in unfamiliar soil. "The mentality that Dean had of the fifty-state strategy, whether the top Obama people would acknowledge it or not, was the same mentality that the Obama campaign had," Paul Tewes said. That philosophy represented a natural progression rather than a mere coincidence. "We pioneered it," Trippi said, "and Obama perfected it."

Aside from influencing a new political playbook, Dean inadvertently boosted Obama in two critical ways that spring. By prohibiting the sham elections in Michigan and Florida from counting—as Clinton wanted—Dean helped Obama win the Democratic primary. And by refusing to shut down the extended primary—contrary to Obama's preference—Dean presented his nominee with a larger playing field for the general election. States like Indiana and North Carolina, which didn't vote until May and normally would not have mattered, now took center stage.

Unable to match the intensity of Obama's grassroots supporters, the Clinton campaign resorted to ridiculing them. The new meme quickly stuck in the press. "The Obama campaign seems dangerously close to a cult of personality," Paul Krugman wrote in *The New York Times*. "The Holy Season of Lent is upon us," cracked ABC News's Jake Tapper. "Can Obama worshippers try to give up their helter-skelter cultish qualities for a few weeks?" Said one headline from the watchdog group Media Matters: "Media Figures Call Obama Supporters' Behavior 'Creepy,' Compare Them to Hare Krishna and Manson Followers." Clinton adviser Sidney Blumenthal e-mailed the article to an influential list of reporters and politicos. It wasn't hard to figure out why the Clinton campaign resorted to such an attack. "Nothing will take the air out of a movement like being told that its enthusiasm is 'creepy,'" Cora Currier noted in *The Nation*.

After a flawless run following Super Tuesday, Obama began to stumble. He lost both Ohio and Texas on March 4, giving Hillary a second—or possibly third—wind. Later that month, ABC News unearthed the incendiary "God damn America" sermons of his pastor, Jeremiah Wright. Obama quelled the uproar with a well-received speech on race. A month later, however, another controversy emerged when Obama explained his difficulty winning over blue-collar voters during a fund-raiser in San Francisco. "You go into some of these small towns in Pennsylvania, and like a lot of small towns in the Midwest, the jobs have been gone now for twenty-five years and nothing's replaced them," Obama said. "And they fell through the Clinton Administration, and the Bush Administration, and each successive administration has said that somehow these communities are gonna regenerate and they have not. And it's not surprising then they get bitter, they cling to guns or religion or antipathy to people who aren't like them or anti-immigrant sentiment or anti-trade sentiment as a way to explain their frustrations." Though his analysis contained a hint of truth, the resulting furor, known as Bittergate, crushed Obama's chances in the Pennsylvania primary on April 22, which Clinton handily won by nine points.

Pundits began likening Obama to a long line of Democratic failures. Columnists Maureen Dowd and George Will compared him to Adlai Stevenson, the egghead Illinois senator who twice lost to Eisenhower. *The New Republic*'s John Judis saw ghosts of George McGovern, a starry-eyed idealist backed by fervent students and antiwar liberals who lost forty-nine states to Richard Nixon. Still others, such as Paul Begala and Christopher Hitchens, viewed Obama as the heir to Michael Dukakis, the staid, emotionless technocrat from Massachusetts. Many political analysts assumed that Obama's poor showing among segments of Clinton's base—working-class whites, elderly women, Hispanics—would carry over to the general election. Historian Sean Wilentz lumped Obama with a series of "beautiful losers"—McCarthy, McGovern, Hart, Tsongas, and Bradley. Would the righteous priest succumb yet again to the bare-knuckle warrior?

Having already amassed a near-intractable delegate advantage, Obama needed a victory in North Carolina and a strong showing in Indiana on May 6 to prove his skeptics wrong. More important, he had to knock Clinton out of the race to prevent the battle from going all the way to the convention.

On April 17, 2008, Obama traveled to Greenville, North Carolina—an old tobacco town of eighty thousand in the state's low coastal plain—for a boisterous rally at East Carolina University. Eight thousand people, as diverse as the state itself, filled the Pirates' basketball stadium. Obama was exhausted from the long primary, but his supporters in North Carolina were just getting started. The candidate entered to Bruce Springsteen's "The Rising," standing on a square platform in the center of the arena floor. At the beginning of his speech, he urged the crowd to sit, but many chose to stand. "You can sit down," Obama joked. "I won't be insulted."

The race in North Carolina had the intensity of a campaign that wasn't supposed to happen. The new North Carolina wanted so badly to erase the bigotry of the old, avenging the crushing defeats of Harvey Gantt and the right-wing rage of Jesse Helms. The Tar Heel State had changed dramatically in the past decade, with 1.5 million people moving in between 1996 and 2006. As the tobacco and textile mills closed, banks and hospitals and tech firms arrived. Demographically, North Carolina fit the profile of an Obama state, with a large African-American population, lots of students at good universities, and a plethora of well-educated, white-collar professionals in the Research Triangle (Raleigh, Durham, and Chapel Hill) and Charlotte. Half the population lived in North Carolina's three largest metro areas. To win, Obama had to both harness and expand the state's emerging electorate.

Still, Clinton was determined not to give the state away. She sent down her best turnout operative, Ace Smith, and deployed her husband to the small, rural, predominantly white country towns that backed George Wallace in 1972, when he upset favorite son Terry Sanford in the North Carolina primary. Clinton also had the support of North Carolina governor Mike Easley, a popular former district attorney. "This lady right here makes Rocky Balboa look like a pansy," Easley said during his endorsement.

A week before Obama arrived in Greenville, "Bittergate" exploded, with the Clinton campaign eagerly painting Obama and his supporters as condescending snobs. At a forum in Pennsylvania, Clinton called Obama's words "elitist, out of touch and, frankly, patronizing." Early in his speech, Obama refuted the charges. "People are angry and frustrated," he said. "They're frustrated about losing jobs. They're frustrated about seeing their communities deteriorate. They're frustrated by not being able to afford college. They're frustrated about schools that aren't working. But let me tell you something—this campaign started because we want to transform that frustration into hope." As an illustration, he told a story about the enthusiasm among everyday people his campaign had generated in the state.

"I met a gentleman just backstage, one of the volunteers, who said that he had taken a week of his vacation time to go and register voters," Obama said. "He works in a restaurant. Not a wealthy man, I'm sure he doesn't get a lot of vacation time. Took a week off to just go out and register voters. He said that it was the best vacation he ever had"—the crowd laughed and applauded—"because he's getting ready to bring about change. There is something in the air in this election."

That man was Daniel Ayala, a thirty-four-year-old immigrant from El Salvador who lived in Durham, North Carolina. He drove two hours east in his 1984 Toyota pickup to meet Obama backstage with fifteen other volunteers who led the campaign's massive voter-registration drive. Ayala stood a compact five feet six, with shaggy black hair and a black mustache. He wore a red button-down shirt, black tie, and a pin that said "New Way Forward."

Ayala grew up in the war-torn mountains outside of San Miguel, near the Pacific coast, in rebel-held territory during the country's decade-long civil war. In 1986, when he was twelve, U.S.-backed military forces bombed his hometown, firing an 80 mm mortar twenty feet from his adobe house. The thick walls protected him as he hid in the family's bread oven. He fled to Guatemala two years later, then on to Mexico, eventually claiming political asylum in the United States.

He moved to North Carolina in 1990, lived in Durham for a while, then bounced around from place to place. He cooked in a restaurant in New York's Chinatown for half a year, bunking with three other people in a tiny apartment, then moved to Miami in the late 1990s, working at high-end restaurants in Miami Beach. He returned to Durham in 2001, finding work at hotels and country clubs as a cook and sous-chef. He moved in with a woman from Germany who worked at Duke Medical Center, living in a tidy one-story brick house on a quiet, sloping, tree-lined street.

Ayala never cared much about politics, but the anti-immigrant sentiment of congressional Republicans and demagogues like Lou Dobbs opened his eyes. "After five years of Bush, I could start seeing the difference," he said. "The Hispanic community had been targeted." Ayala had twice been pulled over by the police recently for no apparent reason while driving on I-95. He started researching the presidential candidates and, during a January 31 debate in California, watched Obama answer the sensitive question of whether illegal immigrants drove down wages for black workers. "Before the latest round of immigrants showed up, you had huge unemployment rates among African-American youth," Obama responded. "To suggest somehow that the problem that we're seeing in inner-city unemployment, for example, is attributable to immigrants, I think, is a case of scapegoating that I do not believe in." Ayala liked Obama's answer and decided to support him. "Obama seemed like a guy who was very consistent and, quite frankly, honest," he told me.

He began writing letters and e-mails to the campaign, but never heard back. Then he found out about a group called Durham for Obama. A creative-writing professor at Duke, the aptly named Faulkner Fox, and a Durham public schools teacher, Elizabeth Ahten-Anderson, had met over MyBO and started the group. They held the first meeting at the Durham Public Library on February 18, expecting a crowd of maybe twenty on a Monday night over Presidents' Day. They planned to raise some money and send volunteers to Texas and Ohio. One hundred and thirty-five people showed. They immediately built a website, formed six different committees, and put a special emphasis on voter registration. Ayala came to the next meeting two weeks later, with 250 people at St. Joseph's AME Church, one of the first autonomous black churches in America. He offered to help register voters. Often overshadowed by its trendy neighbor, Chapel Hill, Durham had a gritty, not-quite-realized feel to it, reminiscent of parts of Brooklyn in the 1980s. The Bull City voted Democratic since its inception, but Obama needed a big turnout in the Triangle to offset the more conservative parts of the state likely to go for Hillary.

The economy had slowed down anyhow, so Ayala took all his vacation time from a diner in Chapel Hill and started registering voters from sunrise until sundown, even waiting for the college bars to close at 2:00 a.m. He started on Good Friday, March 21, at a popular flea market on the outskirts of town where many Hispanic locals bought fruits and vegetables. More than one thousand people, he estimated, came and went that day. Ayala stood at the entrance and asked everybody, "Estás registrado para votar?" Are you registered to vote?

"No puedo votar," came reply after reply. "I can't vote." He stood there from 7:00 a.m. until 4:00 p.m. By the end of the day, he'd registered thirteen people.

This isn't working, Ayala said to himself. So he tried a different tack, focusing on Durham Technical Community College, where he took classes. He figured out the class schedule for the entire school and took his table and forms from building to building as students came out. He often wore a black T-shirt with a picture of Dick Cheney brandishing a light saber and a reference to Shakespeare's *Henry VI*: "First thing we do is kill the lawyers."

"I can't vote," Ayala told the students. "You can compensate for me." Though he could work legally, it took a long time for political refugees to become American citizens and Ayala was still waiting in line.

When he wasn't at Durham Tech, Ayala hit all the high-traffic spots: Food Lion, Walmart, large apartment complexes. "I was constantly on the move," he said. "Every second that passed, if I could get one more person, there was a better possibility that North Carolina would go for Obama." Outside Walmart, he met a nineteen-year-old African-American kid named Charlie who worked in a cafeteria at Duke.

"I don't vote," Charlie told him.

"Why not?" Ayala asked.

"I don't care," Charlie said.

"C'mon, just register," Ayala urged.

"Nope," Charlie replied. "Not interested."

Later that day, Ayala passed Charlie again at a Food Lion in the same shopping center. Not recognizing him, he asked, "Are you registered to vote?"

"You just asked me, man," Charlie snapped. "Don't ask me no more."

A few days later, Ayala knocked on an apartment door in Chapel Hill. Who else but Charlie opened the door. "You again?" Charlie said.

"You don't vote, right?" Ayala replied.

"Yep," he said, shutting the door.

A short while after, as he distributed Obama stickers at Duke, Ayala bumped into Charlie a fourth time. "Man, are you for Obama?" Charlie asked.

"Yep," Ayala said.

"You've seen me four times," Charlie responded. "I've been thinking about it, and today I'm gonna register to vote." He filled out the form, went into the kitchen, and brought five of his coworkers with him to register. He wore a white chef's uniform and a French baking hat, and smiled broadly. "Okay, now you'll leave me alone," Charlie said.

On Friday, April 11, the last day of voter registration for the primary, Ayala spent from 7:00 a.m. until lunchtime at Duke, adding one hundred new registrants. He then hit a corner store downtown, signing up twenty-three more. He'd acquired quite a reputation within Durham by this point, and a student from Duke followed him that day for a documentary film class. Finally, he handed in the forms to Obama's office. He estimated he'd registered anywhere from seven hundred to one thousand people in a three-week span. "I made up for all the votes I couldn't cast," he said.

Longtime North Carolina Democrats couldn't quite believe the sudden flood of activism. "This is immodest, but I think we had the best grassroots organization the state's ever seen," said former governor Jim Hunt, who led the state from 1977 to 1985 and from 1993 to 2001. "But Obama was better at reaching people who had never registered, never voted, who just had not participated in democracy.

It was amazing to see and really gratifying, because these people had been left out of their own country. They never had a voice."

As in so many states, the hard work of the Obama campaign began long before the campaign officially arrived. During the primary, 165,000 new Democrats registered to vote in North Carolina, helping the candidate win the primary by 230,000 votes. Obama's grassroots base had come through for him at another crucial time. On May 6, Ayala watched the election returns at a bar in Durham. As Obama delivered his victory speech in Raleigh, the race in Indiana, where Hillary was heavily favored, was still too close to call. She never got the landscape-altering victories she so desperately needed. The next day, the cover of the *New York Post* displayed a picture of Clinton's face with the headline: "Toast!"

5 ★ NATIONALIZE THIS

It's the damnedest thing I ever saw. —Tony Rand

On June 3, after voters went to the polls in Puerto Rico, Montana, and South Dakota, the Democratic primary finally ended. A few days later, Hillary Clinton officially dropped out of the race and urged her supporters to back Barack Obama. On June 6, the presumptive Democratic nominee stopped by his Chicago office to thank his campaign staff and prepare them for the grueling five months ahead. The candidate received boisterous applause as he walked through his expansive office. Deputy campaign manager Steve Hildebrand gave his boss a high five and passed him the mic. "I might have something really inspiring to say," Obama joked at the outset when the sound malfunctioned.

The last time he addressed his entire staff in Chicago, in August 2007, Obama trailed Clinton by thirty points in national polls and "everybody had written us off," he recounted. He echoed what he said back then. "When I started this campaign, I wasn't sure that I was going to be the best of candidates," Obama said slowly and deliberately, "but I was absolutely positive . . . that there was the possibility of creating the best organization." He credited his old organizing mind-set. "It's not just a gimmick, it's not just a shtick, I actually believe in it," he said.

He relayed the same message now that he'd conveyed to Joe Rospars in January 2007. "Even if we had lost, I would be proud of what we built, because nobody thought we could build it," Obama said. "Everybody thought, at some point, this thing was all going to be a flash in the pan. Collectively, all of you—most of whom I'm not even sure are of drinking age," he needled, "you've created the best political organization in America, and probably the best political organization that we've seen in the last thirty, forty years. That's a pretty big deal."

The candidate repeated his well-worn motto that the campaign was not about him. "I know that sometimes it may come off as just a line," he said. "But I really mean it. This campaign has been about you and you guys discovering your collective ability to make history and just move an entire nation in a new direction. And that is a remarkable feat. It is just an astonishing feat. Everybody's marveling at it. Everybody's marveling at it," he repeated.

The eighteen-month primary, exhausting and exhilarating as it was, served as a mere tune-up for the coming general election. "We're gonna have to work twice as hard," Obama told his staff. "We are gonna have to be smarter, we're gonna have to be tougher, our game is gonna have to be tighter. We are gonna be attacked more viciously. We're gonna have to respond more rapidly. We are gonna have to raise more money. I am gonna have to be a better candidate. Each and every one of you, whatever it is that you do, you are gonna have to do it better, longer, and probably without break between now and November 4."

Obama succinctly laid out the stakes ahead. "We don't have a choice," he said. "Now, if we screw this up, all those people that I've met [on the campaign trail] who really need help, they're not going to get help. Those of you who are concerned about global warming, I don't care what John McCain says, he is not going to push that agenda hard. Those of you who are concerned about Darfur, I guarantee you, they're not going to spend any political capital on that. Those of you who are concerned about education, there'll be a bunch of lip service, and then more of the same. Those of you who are concerned about making sure that there's a sense of fairness in our economy, it will be less fair. So now everybody's counting on you, not just me. And I know that's a heavy weight. But also, what a magnificent position to find yourselves in, where the whole country is counting on you to change it, for the better. Those moments don't come around very often. And here you are, five months away from having transformed the country." He ended the stirring pep talk with a final command: "Let's go win the election!"

After addressing his staff, Obama jumped on a conference call with Howard Dean and the fifty state party chairs. The day before, Obama announced he was keeping Dean at the DNC and sending the architect of his Iowa caucus victory, Paul Tewes, to run day-to-day operations in Washington. Obama assured the state chairs that Dean's fifty-state strategy would morph into the fifty-state campaign, with offices and staff, to varying degrees, in every state. "I am proud of the fact that we're the first campaign in a generation to run a fifty-state strategy," he'd later say.

There were some notable differences between the two approaches. As DNC chair, Dean ran his strategy through the prevailing organs of the Democratic Party, namely, the state parties. Obama attracted a ton of new people to his campaign, a decent percentage of whom didn't identify as Democrats and never would. A number of state party chairs, based on long-standing relationships, backed Clinton during the primary, creating friction between the two camps in places like Indiana and Pennsylvania. Obama's insurgent campaign felt, at times, like a third-party candidacy. He couldn't simply run his campaign through existing institutions—he had to create new ones while taking advantage of what the DNC and state parties had already built.

Luckily for Obama, the DNC offered his campaign a number of crucial assets that wouldn't have existed in years past. During the primary, detailed information on every Clinton supporter went into the DNC's massive new voter database, which Tewes called "easily the best there's ever been," allowing Obama's team to quickly court the eighteen million Clintonites once the primary ended. The DNC also developed a state-of-the-art online tool allowing volunteers to find and contact potential supporters in their neighborhoods, which greatly enhanced the Obama campaign's grassroots organizing prowess during the general election. The DNC's best organizers, like Fadia Halma in eastern Philadelphia, soon jumped over to the Obama campaign.

Yet despite his lofty rhetoric, Obama never intended to run a true fifty-state campaign. (The first and last candidate to do so was Richard Nixon in 1960, when he promised at the Republican convention to campaign in every state, thereby calling attention to Eisenhower's admission of Hawaii and Alaska to the Union the year before. He came to regret the decision when, the Saturday before the election, he was forced to trudge all the way up to Alaska. He narrowly won the state but lost the election.) Based on extensive electoral projections, fewer than half the states would be targeted with a massive influx of staff and cash. Volunteers in non-targeted states like Idaho were urged to call and visit their neighbors in competitive battlegrounds like Colorado and Montana. Still, the campaign's strategy represented a dramatic improvement over the eighteen-state battleground calculus that had long typified presidential politics.

During the primary, Rospars's new-media shop created individual campaign websites for every state. Days after winning North Carolina, the campaign launched an extensive fifty-state voter-registration drive called Vote for Change. Obama had already shaped a new electorate in the primary, registering 200,000 new Democrats in Pennsylvania, 165,000 in North Carolina, and 150,000 in Indiana. "There was an understanding that we could not win it conventionally," said Cornell Belcher, who polled for the DNC and the Obama campaign. "If we couldn't change the face of the electorate and broaden the playing field, we wouldn't have a chance."

After the primary ended, Obama's top crop of state organizers, including Jeremy Bird and Buffy Wicks, conferred in Chicago with the field director Jon Carson to develop the organizing manual that would guide them through the fall. (Bird ran Ohio, and Wicks took Missouri for the general.) They compared notes, plowed through interviews with more than two hundred organizers, and adopted the mantra of the campaign in Iowa for the title of the resulting 368-page tome: "Respect. Empower. Include."

"Empowerment requires creating structure that allows all members of the team to make this campaign his or her own," the manual stated. "We must go beyond simply assigning volunteers tasks, to allowing well-trained and supported volunteers to have real ownership within the campaign." This wasn't just dry, feel-good campaign-speak. In the middle of June, the campaign trained thirty-six hundred new Obama organizing fellows across the country, drastically expanding its grassroots army. "The campaign itself became an organizing school," observed Marshall Ganz. "Nobody had done anything like that since John L. Lewis in the CIO," he said, referring to the legendary United Mine Workers leader who organized hundreds of thousands of workers in the coal, rubber, auto, and steel industries through the Congress of Industrial Organizations from 1935 to 1955.

Thanks to the Internet, money and manpower weren't problems. (Rospars now oversaw more than one hundred staffers at headquarters in the new-media department, the largest on the campaign.) To supplement perennial battlegrounds like Ohio and Florida, the campaign set up unprecedented operations in emerging swing states like Colorado, Nevada, and Virginia, and targeted a dozen states that went for Bush in 2004, including Iowa, Indiana, Missouri, Montana, Georgia, and North Carolina. Obama's team wanted as many different pathways to 270 electoral votes as possible. They'd create new swing states and expand the electorate in existing ones, deploying resources to the reddest of red counties. *The Huffington Post* called Obama's game plan "the first truly national test of the viability and prescience of Howard Dean's 50-state strategy."

Since 2004, Obama had been preparing for this moment. "There's not a liberal America and a conservative America," he said famously at the Democratic convention. "There's not a black America and white America and Latino America and Asian America; there's the United States of America. The pundits like to slice and dice our country into red states and blue states: red states for Republicans, blue states for Democrats. But I've got news for them, too. We worship an awesome God in the blue states, and we don't like federal agents poking around our libraries in the red states. We coach Little League in the blue states and, yes, we've got some gay friends in the red states. There are patriots who opposed the war in Iraq, and there are patriots who supported the war in Iraq. We are one people, all of us pledging allegiance to the Stars and Stripes, all of us defending the United States of America." Were those guiding words hopelessly naive or ambitiously hopeful? In the strenuous coming months, Obama would find out.

In July 2005, when Dean first visited Colorado as DNC chair, Elbra Wedgeworth, a popular councilwoman from Denver who grew up the youngest of six in a tough inner-city housing project, approached him with a plea: hold the 2008 Democratic convention in her hometown. "If we can host Pope John Paul II and the NBA All-Star game," Wedgeworth told him, "I think we can do this."

Thirty-five cities initially bid on the convention, which shrank to three—Denver, St. Paul, and New York City. When the Republicans picked St. Paul for their convention, Dean chose between the Big Apple and the Mile High City. The latter didn't seem to stand a chance. Denver had already bid for the Democratic convention in 2000 and 2004, losing out both times, and hadn't hosted a convention in nearly a hundred years, when Democrats nominated the

Great Commoner, William Jennings Bryan, for a third and final time (he lost all three presidential elections). The West hadn't been particularly welcoming to Democrats at the beginning of the new century, either. In 2002, Republicans controlled every governorship in the eight states of the Interior West. Only two Democrats carried Colorado in presidential elections since 1948, LBJ in 1964 and Clinton in 1992. At the start of the 2008 election, registered Republicans outnumbered registered Democrats by 150,000 voters in the state.

From his first day at the DNC, Dean believed the party needed to look west. He knew Democrats couldn't rely on Florida or Ohio to win the White House and the West seemed like fertile yet undiscovered turf. Sure, Democrats had been saying that for a decade, but Dean thought the time had finally come. The GOP's right-wing extremity had alienated moderates and libertarian-minded conservatives, while younger residents and new immigrants kept flocking west, creating an unlikely melting pot in cowboy country.

It made sense for Democrats to start with Colorado. It had the most electoral votes of any Mountain West state, and Democrats had just taken back the statehouse and state senate, along with a U.S. Senate seat in 2004, bankrolled by a new quartet of progressive philanthropists known as "the gang of four." Beyond Colorado, Democrats had picked up five governorships and two Senate seats in the Interior West since 2002, and two dozen state legislators in 2006 alone.

In his first major decision of the 2008 election, Dean gave Denver the nod. "I have long believed that the essence of a Democratic victory goes through the West," he said during a conference call on January 11, 2007, announcing his decision. "If we're going to have a national political party, we're going to have to have Westerners vote for us on a consistent basis. At the end of the day, that's what tipped it to Denver." The decision held obvious ramifications for the impending presidential election, all but ensuring that Colorado—and possibly three or four more western states—would become competitive battlegrounds. "If we win the West," Dean predicted, "we will win the presidency."

Elbra Wedgeworth wept when she heard the news. No one thought a quiet mountain city, where the most famous hotel is called the Brown Palace, could prevail over the glitz and glamour of New York. "I can't tell you how cool this is," she said at the Hyatt Regency in Denver. "It'll be the best damn convention they've ever had."

Dean found a willing partner in Pat Waak, the chair of the Colorado Democratic Party. Her own story mirrored the broader changes in the West's political topography.

Waak had a motherly demeanor and a fondness for the colors of the Southwest, particularly turquoise. She moved to Colorado in 1980. Reagan was in, Carter was out, and she was down a job in Washington. Waak needed space. Colorado seemed as good a place as any to start anew. After all, that's why people moved there all the time, scrapping old lives and creating fresh ones. She found a patch of land thirty miles northwest of Denver, on a hill surrounded by sunflowers and prairies. She could watch the stunning sunsets over the towering peaks of the Rockies from her porch. Only two roads were paved in her new hometown of Erie, founded by Italian coal miners in the nineteenth century. The "New West" had yet to arrive.

Weld County wasn't exactly filled with Democrats. There were no elected Democratic officials when she got to town, and Democrats often didn't bother to run a candidate in the gigantic Fourth Congressional District, which stretched from southern Weld County all the way to the eastern plains on the Nebraska border and up to Wyoming. Still, the churches and cowboys reminded her of home.

Waak grew up the oldest of four in a poor family in East Texas, the daughter of immigrant German farmers and tri-racial "Red-bone" cowboys (white, black, and Native American), all Democrats. "They believed the Democratic Party cared about what happened to working folks," she said. She studied nursing at Tulane and joined the Peace Corps in Brazil before moving to Washington. She served in the Office of Population at USAID in the Carter administration, then left for the Audubon Society. A jack-of-all-trades, she later got a master's in psychology and a doctorate in ministry.

Like Colorado itself, whose population grew by 30 percent between 1990 and 2000, Weld County had changed dramatically in the past twenty years. It was now the richest agricultural county east of the Rockies, a leading producer of cattle, dairy, grain, and sugar beets. Nearly all the roads were paved, and natural gas derricks dotted the landscape. People kept moving there and commuting to Denver, in search of good jobs and cheap land. "Drive until you can buy," the saying went. Weld became the fastest-growing county in the state.

Colorado had always been something of a schizophrenic state politically, electing liberals like Gary Hart and embracing the environmental movement in the 1970s; moving right during the Reagan years and the oil boom of the 1980s and '90s, attracting transplants from Orange County and Texas; shifting back to the center in the new millennium, as moderate and liberal residents from Los Angeles County began to outnumber their conservative brethren. Both feminist liberals (Pat Schroeder) and fire-breathing conservatives (Tom Tancredo) called the state home. Hart likened Colorado to California twenty-five years ago, holding on to a fabled past while rapidly creating a new future. "It is, in my lifetime, literally a swing state," Hart told me. Yet one constant remained in Weld County as recently as 2004: Republicans outnumbered Democrats two to one.

Waak took the reins of the state party after the 2004 election, upsetting the incumbent chair by three votes. "The party was not an activist party," she said, explaining her decision to run. "The only time you saw the chair was at an official meeting." Rank-and-file Democrats believed the party focused only on Denver, concentrating power in too few hands, to the detriment of the rest of the state. "The real issue is whether we're going to be a grassroots party," Waak said after her election. "The party wanted to go in a different direction, and I was willing to go out and say it."

She immediately adopted a sixty-four-county strategy, and didn't need to look much further than her own backyard. "Poor Weld County," the denizens of nearby Fort Collins would say, "there's no

Democrats over there." In May 2006, she decided to hold the state party's annual convention in Weld County's most populous city, Greeley. It was not an obvious choice.

Greeley's cosmopolitan neighbors looked down on the place as a backward cattle town, in view of the Rockies but with the conservative culture of the eastern plains. "You can smell Greeley, Colorado, long before you can see it," Eric Schlosser memorably wrote in *Fast Food Nation*, referring to the town's large meatpacking plant. James Michener once called it "a city of wide streets and narrow minds."

GREELEY—AN ALL AMERICA CITY, read an official green sign at the city's entrance. That may have once been true, but the sign now seemed like a bad joke to those inhabitants hanging on to a pastoral, homogeneous existence that had long since vanished. Starting in the 1980s, migrants from Mexico and Central America came to work in Greeley's slaughterhouse and beet fields, inexorably altering the previously white, heavily WASP city of a hundred thousand. In 1917, the architect William Bowman built a spectacular classical-revival county courthouse downtown, punctuated by towering columns and intricate stained-glass windows. Ninety years later, a grassy pavilion with a gazebo in the center sits across the street. That's about all there is. FOR RENT signs and Mexican restaurants are the only markers of life in the slumbering town center. At the time of the state convention, state representative Jim Riesberg, a gerontologist who ran for office at sixty-one, was the only elected Democrat in Greeley. When I asked Riesberg what's changed since he moved there in 1986, he responded, "The downtown went away." The small glass facade of the Weld County Democratic Party office sits a block down from the courthouse. A printing store next door sells typewriters in the window. Before the state convention, local Democrats, like the downtown itself, seemed on the verge of extinction.

Since 2002, Republican Marilyn Musgrave, an antiabortion activist and strident culture warrior, represented Greeley in Congress. She was best known for pushing a constitutional amendment to ban gay marriage, calling it the most important issue facing the country. Every two years, Musgrave handily lost Fort Collins, a poor man's Boulder, but racked up enough of a margin in Weld to hold on to her seat. "If we could just find five thousand votes in Weld County," Democrats said to themselves. Waak hoped the state assembly would boost Musgrave's challenger, state representative Angie Paccione, and candidates statewide by activating Democrats in the third-largest and ninth most populous county in the state. Indeed, five thousand Democrats converging on the town for a weekend provided a powerful shot in the arm. "The Democrats' assembly surprised us," *The Denver Post* editorialized. "It was a smooth session that could easily have fractured." Just two hours south, the Republican convention in Colorado Springs had turned into a civil war between moderate and conservative factions. The GOP crack-up offered more proof that the state itself no longer bled red.

The day before the 2006 election, Republicans dispatched all their heavy hitters to Greeley—including President Bush. Five thousand Republicans crowded into a newly built auditorium near the cattle plant, watching the president's helicopter fly in. A truck outside posted a fitting homage to Musgrave: STOP GAY MARRIAGE NOW SO OSAMA DOESN'T GET AWAY. The deep piano chords and ominous guitar riffs of Van Halen's "Right Now" filled the darkened auditorium, the drums kicking in as Bush took the stage. "It's good to be in country where the cowboy hats outnumber the ties," the president said in his Texas drawl. He gave a rousing endorsement of Musgrave and told his flock, "Go from this hall and turn out the vote."

On Election Day, Democratic gubernatorial candidate Bill Ritter narrowly carried Weld County by a surprising three hundred votes, but Musgrave hung on by two points. If only Democrats could've found those five thousand votes.

In Weld County Democratic headquarters there's a large map of Greeley. The west side is red (Republican), the middle, near downtown and the University of Northern Colorado, is green (up for grabs), and the east is blue (Democratic). The west side has golf courses, office parks, shopping malls, and the fast-growing bedroom communities of Denver. The east side has the meatpacking plant, railroad tracks, and tightly spaced bungalows and trailer parks where much of the city's Hispanic community lives. On the outskirts of the east side, next to the Poudre River and along the railroad tracks, sit an expanse of barbed chain-link fencing and a series of dreary white buildings that make up the JBS Swift beef plant, the largest employer in town. Employees enter the plant via an underground tunnel from a giant parking lot across the street, enduring the harsh smell of manure as they walk into work.

At dawn on December 12, 2006, the holiday of Our Lady of Guadalupe, a heavily armed fleet of Immigration and Customs Enforcement (ICE) officers stormed the plant in riot gear, arresting 265 workers and deporting dozens in a coordinated seven-city raid known as Operation Wagon Train, a key front in the Bush administration's "war against illegal immigration." The largest ICE raid in U.S. history ruptured the sleepy city, split apart families, drew national headlines, and sparked a heated debate inside the city. When Greeley's Republican mayor, Tom Selders, criticized the government's heavy-handed tactics and testified in Washington about the detrimental impact the raids had in his community, he was ousted by a right-wing challenger, Ed Clark, a hulking police officer who showed little sympathy for those rounded up. (Clark later got in trouble for allegedly assaulting a teenager and showing schoolchildren a $3 bill portraying Obama in a Saudi headdress.) Some conservatives argued, in the wake of the raids, that white locals would fill the jobs. When that didn't happen, Somali and Burmese immigrants came in, adding a new layer of tension to an already divided town. The Somalis asked to observe Ramadan on the job, setting off a firestorm among nativist locals, who formed the Coloradans Against Sharia Task Force to protest "stealth jihad." It didn't help that fast-growing and economically anxious Weld County led the country in foreclosures that year. Said one Hispanic activist, "This has been our Katrina."

Hispanics make up 35 percent of Greeley's population, and the raids deeply affected nearly all of them, including those who were born in America, spoke English as a first language, and paid their taxes just like everyone else. People like Joe Perez, who dutifully drove a bus for the city for twenty-nine years. "I was heartbroken," the sixty-three-year-old Perez said. "I had flashbacks to memories of what my father told me about seeing the Klan burn the cross." After growing up in the conservative panhandle of western Nebraska, Perez always felt on edge. "I've tried to do everything I could as an American," he said. "I graduated high school, went to college, served in the military for twenty-four years, have always voted and supported my family. But I always felt like I was a step behind."

Perez had always voted Democrat—his family identified with the social justice teachings of the Catholic Church—but nothing more. After watching Obama's 2004 keynote speech, however, he told his son, "If he ever runs, I'm going to support him." Obama's appeal to inclusion moved Perez. "When he said 'We're not black Americans, we're not Latino Americans, we're not Asian-Americans, we're Americans,' that's what I've always wanted to be," Perez said. "Just an American."

During the summer of 2006, Perez took an Obama sign down to the Greeley Stampede parade, the world's largest Fourth of July rodeo. U.S. senator Ken Salazar said it was the first Obama sign he saw in Colorado. Perez was tall and broad shouldered, with a dark complexion, brown eyebrows, a gray mustache, and a distinctive long gray ponytail. He usually wore cowboy boots and blue jeans. Though he considered himself a soft-spoken kind of guy, he threw himself into the Obama campaign with a missionary's zeal. When Obama came to Denver in March 2007, Perez was the first in line. In May, he went to the first organizing meeting Buffy Wicks held in the state. By early summer, he and three friends had started Greeley for Obama. "We had no idea what we were doing," Perez said. During

Obama's national Walk for Change in June they went downtown to the farmers' market and public library wearing Obama shirts, hoping to get the word out about their candidate. To their surprise, many in Greeley still had yet to hear of him. "Barack Obama?" people asked. "Who's he?"

The next day, Perez heard Obama speak again at an airport hangar outside Denver. "That ignited the fire even more," he said. After Obama's win in Iowa, Perez went to an organizing meeting in Fort Collins, a college town forty-five minutes away. He met Joe Duffy, a twenty-two-year-old organizer from Illinois who worked on the campaign in Iowa. Duffy asked for help getting the Obama operation off the ground in Greeley.

"What do you need?" Perez asked. Duffy said the campaign needed an office.

"Let's have it in your garage," his friend David Carrier suggested to Perez.

"Will people come to the east side of Greeley?" Perez wondered. In 2006, he'd finished a detached white and blue garage in his leafy backyard off a modest two-story house on a quiet cul-de-sac. He'd recently fixed it up to accommodate country-and-western dance classes. A car aficionado, he otherwise housed his 1952 Chevrolet Biscayne sedan and pink 1968 two-door Chevy pickup—the first truck his father ever bought—in the new structure. He stashed a 1968 Mustang convertible, his first car, behind an RV in the backyard. For his own ride, Perez drove a red Dodge 4 × 4 plastered with Obama and Air Force stickers on the back.

Duffy stopped by a few days later. "This is perfect," he said. Joe's garage became the official Obama office in Greeley. Thus the lore began. Joan Kato, a pretty, diminutive Californian who ran Obama's Hispanic outreach in Iowa, soon showed up. She trained volunteers and held mock caucuses in the garage. Perez opened up the back gate, and his sleepy side street filled with cars. THE ROAD TO THE PRESIDENCY RUNS THOUGH GREELEY, said a banner on the wall. "It turned into a big party," Perez said. The effort unfolded organically, far away from state or national headquarters. "I didn't train Joe," said Colorado state director Ray Rivera. "I didn't make Joe. He was there. We just gave him some resources."

In Greeley and throughout Colorado, the Clinton campaign could only scoff at Obama's operation. "Clearly, they've taken the Starbucks approach to the campaign," said Clinton's state director Tyler Chafee. "Pretty soon, they'll have [an office] on every corner." Obama handily won Weld County by twenty-eight points en route to a landslide victory in the state's caucus.

Once the general election began, Plouffe cited Colorado as a key battleground. At a bare minimum, the campaign knew it could win the election if it held Kerry's states and added Virginia and Colorado, which both looked ripe for the taking. "If we win these two, we win it all," Obama's campaign manager often said. The Obama campaign immediately dispatched 150 organizers to Colorado; a few hundred more soon followed. Artie Blanco, a native Texan, worked as the DNC's western-states director before leading Obama's Hispanic outreach in Colorado. "We had organizers in every single county," she said. "No place was left untouched."

Perez needed someone to help cover his own turf. In early July, he drove down to Obama headquarters in Denver and spotted Rogelio "Roger" Chanes, a young activist of Mexican descent from Brownsville, Texas. Perez introduced himself and asked Chanes to breakfast. "I need a Latino organizer in Greeley," Perez told him. Three days later, Chanes moved into Perez's basement. When he left Denver, no one told Chanes about Greeley's splintered history or recent raids; they only warned him about the smell. The worst came on Thursdays, when the Swift plant boiled cows' blood just a few miles from Perez's house. Otherwise the place was all right.

The city's large Hispanic community had not been a particular priority for the campaign up to that point. One of Chanes's bosses told him the Latino vote would come from Denver and Pueblo, a blue-collar steel town in southern Colorado. Greeley was something of an afterthought. Because of the raids, many Hispanics were reluctant to publicly support Obama. "Don't make any waves," locals told him. Behind closed doors, high-profile Hispanic officials confessed that they were Republicans because Democrats couldn't be leaders in the community.

Over the summer, Chanes started to build a volunteer base, holding one-on-one sessions and house meetings with potential volunteers, just as in South Carolina. The gatherings in Perez's garage always had the best attendance and most enthusiasm. Interest began to build around the Democratic convention sixty miles south. Perez's activism caught the eye of the campaign in Denver, which soon dispatched high-profile surrogates to Greeley, including Joe Biden and Bill Richardson. Senator Salazar, former governor Roy Romer, and agricultural commissioner John Stulp opened a new office in a small storefront near Northern Colorado's campus. Salazar spoke of a time when Democrats were told to stay away from the plains east of I-25, the state's main interstate. "We don't believe that and Barack Obama doesn't believe that," he said.

Visits from celebrities like Kevin Costner, Eva Longoria, and Kal Penn brought Hollywood glamour to the isolated cow town. More important, four new organizers arrived from Washington and Boston to help turn out the vote in the Hispanic community. Greeley suddenly witnessed "an eruption of activity," Perez said. He'd come home from work, take a quick nap, and head out to register voters. "We reached into neighborhoods that people were generally leery to walk into," he said. One afternoon, he found a father, mother, daughter, and grandmother from Mexico who'd just become U.S. citizens. The elderly grandmother had never voted because her husband told her women weren't supposed to. Perez assured her it was safe. The campaign in Greeley became a point of pride among Hispanic activists. "Especially in the Hispanic community, people would come up to me and say, 'I'm gonna go work in Weld County and Greeley,'" said Rivera. "Greeley was an example of us going to places people didn't expect."

Indiana was another. When Karl Rove dreamed of his permanent Republican majority, he probably envisioned a place like Hamilton County, Indiana. In 2004, Bush won 74 percent of the vote in the populous suburbs north of Indianapolis, filled with well-manicured golf courses, tidy town squares, upscale malls, European roundabouts, gleaming glass hospitals, and exclusive developments with streets called Prosperity Road and Cheswick Place, home to man-made ponds and brick McMansions. Following World War II, Hamilton County became a refuge for suburban white flight and more recently a haven for well-to-do newer arrivals from outside Indiana, lured by all the benefits of living in the state's fastest-growing, most affluent county, the so-called playground of Indianapolis. Since as long as anybody remembers—and well before that—Hamilton County had been a Republican stronghold, electing just two Democratic sheriffs since its inception in 1823, the last of whom left office in 1934.

Chuck Lasker moved to Indiana in 1985 from Long Island, found an engineering job in Indianapolis, and settled in the Hamilton County suburb of Westfield in 1998. He and his wife purchased the sixth house in the cul-de-sac of Carey Commons for $130,000, a white two-story home with a grassy backyard. Lasker voted for Reagan in 1984 and had been a straight-ticket Republican ever since. "I was the worst kind of negative-campaign Republican," he said. He passed out fake get-out-of-jail-free cards in 1988, ridiculing Michael Dukakis's furlough of Willie Horton, and in 2004 Photoshopped a picture of his house just to annoy his liberal brother, embellishing a giant Bush-Cheney sign on the roof and plastering a photo of Bush grinning like a Cheshire cat on his garage. Lasker became a right-wing Baptist and for a time attended the Indianapolis Baptist Temple, which the IRS seized in 2001 after the church refused to pay $6 million in taxes. The Anti-Defamation League, citing its links to segregationist pastors and militia groups, listed the church as one of the top two hundred hate groups in the country. One congregant wore fatigues every Sunday and invited Lasker to shoot machine guns on his property after service. The ushers all kept guns in their holsters, preparing for the government to attack.

Lasker had a compact build, spiky black hair, and a trim goatee. His political "awakening," he said, began with a "growing dislike for Bush" after the 2004 election. He felt the president spent recklessly and plunged the country deep into Iraq when he should've kept the target on Al Qaeda in Afghanistan. Lasker had always considered himself a "libertarian with a small *l*" but now questioned his loyalty to the Republican Party. He watched Obama's speech in 2004 and liked what he saw, if not everything he heard. He disagreed with some of Obama's policy positions—on abortion, gun control, and the role of activist government—but "loved" *The Audacity of Hope*, particularly "Obama's sincerity and optimism," which reminded him of Reagan. During the 2008 election, he printed up a special sign to replace the Bush-Cheney paraphernalia in his backyard: HAMILTON COUNTY REPUBLICANS FOR OBAMA, it read, with a picture of a red elephant attached to the blue and white Obama logo. On July 24, 2008, he and his wife, Sharon, who grew up in a Republican family in Charlotte, North Carolina, hosted the first official meeting of Central Indiana Republicans for Obama. "Most of the people there had been secret Republicans for Obama," he said. "They didn't know there were more of us."

Two dozen "whispering Republicans," as he called them, sat on couches in Lasker's brightly lit living room on a Thursday evening, wearing red "Republicans for Obama" stickers as sunlight streamed through the windows and a neighbor's lawn mower blared outside. Guests drank sweet tea and munched on brownies as they revealed their newfound support for Obama and frustration with the GOP. Lasker likened it to a group therapy session. "I'm Chuck Lasker, and I'm a Republican for Obama," he wrote on MyBO.

"Your neighbors are probably wondering, 'What's going on over here?'" one attendee told Lasker.

"I still think of Reagan almost as a grandfather," he said at the meeting. Indiana had once been a haven for Reagan Democrats, the blue-collar, conservative Democrats who flocked to the Gipper in the 1980s. Now the political current was moving the other way. "He's a Democrat," Lasker said of Obama, "but he's not stuck to the partisan wars that are going on."

A wide range of attendees shared similar stories. Becky Kapsalis, an energetic seventy-year-old grandmother of nineteen, moved to the tony suburb of Carmel thirty years earlier, which she described as a "totally 100 percent Republican area." Both her husband and kids opposed Obama's candidacy. "None of my friends are Democrats," she said. Nonetheless, she said, "I'm a registered Republican, and I just feel that Barack Obama is an American. Regardless of party politics, he spoke to my American heart." She'd been volunteering for Obama since the primary began, printing up stickers that read, "USA Begins with *US*," with a picture of Obama underneath the words "The New Hope."

Melissa Achtien, a comptroller for a software development firm, moved to Hamilton County from Orange County, California, in 1995. She grew up in a Republican family and originally supported McCain, but when one of her three daughters dated a soldier at West Point— 70 percent of whom deployed to Iraq—the folly of the war "hit home," and she switched to Obama, partly due to her antipathy toward Hillary. Another woman, Terri Lipscomb, replied that her son was an officer in Iraq supporting Obama.

Achtien described how she knocked on doors for Obama in Ohio with a daughter at the University of Akron, the first time she'd done anything of the sort, and became "hooked" on his candidacy. Her husband was still a staunch Republican, but Achtien estimated she'd knocked on five hundred doors in Hamilton County for Obama thus far. When people often said "I'm a Republican," she responded, "I am too!" Sometimes that worked; other times it didn't. During one particularly contentious encounter, a local Republican told her she had "blood on her hands."

Though they supported Obama, the likes of Lasker, Kapsalis, and Achtien still weren't entirely sold on the Democratic Party and also planned to vote for Republican governor Mitch Daniels in the fall. These split-ticket voters would, in large measure, determine who won the state on November 4.

Hoosiers called the eight heavily Republican counties surrounding Indianapolis "the doughnut" because of their shape, but Obama's campaign termed them "the ring of fire." Democrats routinely got burned there, particularly in Hamilton County. Indiana Democratic Party chair Dan Parker tried to organize the counties after the 2006 election, but nothing much had come of the effort. Even when Indiana voted Democratic in races for the senate or governor, Hamilton County stayed red. The last Democratic presidential candidate visited in 1948, when Harry Truman rolled through on a whistle-stop train tour. So it came as quite a shock when the Obama campaign opened an office in Hamilton County in April and Obama brought his family to the county seat of Noblesville, with its charming town square, antiques shops, and towering brick-and-limestone courthouse, on May 3, three days before the Indiana primary.

The campaign held a "family picnic" for three hundred supporters on a windy, overcast day at a park downtown. Sasha and Malia played on the swings as supporters sat in a circle on blankets and lawn chairs, listening to Barack and Michelle speak under large elm trees. "We're gonna be debating flag pins and sniper fire and comments of my former pastor and all kinds of things that are gonna push us away from each other," Obama predicted of the coming campaign. "But we can't afford that this time, because we've got too much work to do." Due to Senator Evan Bayh's vociferous support for the Clintons, virtually the entire state Democratic Party and every county chair endorsed Hillary or stayed neutral during the primary. Only Keith Clock, Hamilton County's twenty-seven-year-old Democratic chair, endorsed Obama, stunned by the sudden activity in his hometown.

Obama ultimately won 61 percent of the vote in Hamilton County during the primary, and Democrats significantly outnumbered Republicans at the polls. Obama might've carried Indiana if it hadn't been for Rush Limbaugh's "Operation Chaos," which urged Republicans to vote for Hillary and prolong the Democratic primary. Still, given the area's conservatism, few expected Obama would return to Hamilton County or Indiana afterward. His supporters breathed a sigh of relief when the campaign reopened its office in Fishers, a fast-growing town on the southern tip of the county, in July. As a sign of appreciation, locals kept the fridge stocked with Perrier and fresh food. The local party set up shop in a spacious converted buckwheat mill in Noblesville, the first steady party office since the 1980s. Obama added three more offices in the county before the election and assigned three organizers to the area. "Hamilton County is an area that we plan to be very aggressive in," said Obama spokesman Jonathan Swain. Beatina Theopold, a young Obama organizer from upstate New York who'd done stints in Vegas, Texas, and Ohio, arrived during the primary and stayed for the general. "No politician goes to Indiana," Theopold quickly learned. "Republicans don't go because they take it for granted, and Democrats don't go because they're frickin' scared."

Hoosiers hadn't seen a Democratic presidential campaign in forty years, since Bobby Kennedy challenged Eugene McCarthy and Governor Roger Branigin, a "favorite son" stepping in for LBJ, in 1968. Some of Kennedy's advisers originally urged him to skip the state, which they labeled "anti-politician, anti-government, anti-taxation, anti-big-city, and anti-Catholic," but Kennedy ignored the advice, diving into the contest in his typically ferocious manner. "I loved the faces here in Indiana," Kennedy said, "on the farmers, on the steelworkers, on the black kids." Memories of Bobby kept lonesome Indiana Democrats going for decades.

Many Hoosiers still yearned for those days, when a good, solid factory job could support a family and put the kids through college. Now cities like Muncie—once described as a classic slice of Americana—saw their factories shuttered and staggered on the verge of collapse, while others, like Gary, rivaled Detroit in postapocalyptic decay. The farmers and coal miners in the southern part of the state, meanwhile, had more in common with Appalachia than with the industrial Midwest. Indiana voted for sixteen of the last seventeen Republican presidential candidates, with the exception of LBJ. It was known as "the northernmost southern state," and the Klan controlled the state Democratic Party in the 1920s and lingered long after that. Clinton barely set foot in Indiana, and Gore and Kerry never considered it. Because polls closed early, Indiana routinely showed up red before anywhere else on the electoral map.

When Obama came to town, he presented himself as the inheritor of Kennedy's legacy. On March 15, days after the Jeremiah Wright controversy exploded, he spoke at a packed high school gym in Plainfield, a 95 percent white, heavily Republican suburb southwest of Indianapolis. "You know, Bobby Kennedy"—the crowd applauded the mere mention of his name—"gave one of his most famous speeches on a dark night in Indianapolis, right after Dr. King was shot," Obama noted. "Some of you remember reading about this speech; some of you were alive when this speech was given. He stood on the top of a car, in a crowd mostly of African-Americans, and he delivered the news . . . He said, at that moment of anguish, we've got a choice: in taking the rage and bitterness and disappointment and letting it fester and dividing us further, so that we no longer see each other as Americans . . . Or we can take a different path that says we have different stories but we have common dreams and common hopes and we can decide to walk down this road together and remake America once again." Defying all precedents, Obama pledged to put the state in the Democratic column come November.

At the start of the general election, the McCain campaign dismissed Obama's strategy and listed Indiana as "solid GOP" in its electoral projections in June. "We want [the GOP] to put resources in the true battleground states," said Kevin Ober, executive director of the Indiana Republican Party. Tellingly, McCain never opened a headquarters in the state and based his Indiana spokesman in Michigan. A campaign surrogate didn't appear in Hamilton County until August. Otherwise, McCain had no events within one hundred miles of the county, Keith Clock pointed out, while a quick search of Obama's website showed fifty campaign events within fifteen miles of Noblesville. McCain visited the state once in July for four hours, speaking before a national sheriffs' convention in Indianapolis and briefly attending a fund-raiser downtown before telling an aide, "Let's get the hell out of here," and jetting off to Colombia and Mexico. He didn't come back until the day before the election. Plouffe called it "campaign malpractice."

The Obama campaign, to be fair, wasn't always sure of its own strategy, either. Emily Parcell, a twenty-seven-year-old from Mount Pleasant, Iowa, worked as Obama's political director during the Iowa caucus. After Iowa, she oversaw the Midwest states on February 5 (Arkansas, Kansas, Minnesota, Missouri, Oklahoma, and North Dakota) and then planned her wedding. She happened to be marrying the campaign manager for Indiana's Democratic nominee for governor, Jill Long Thompson, but figured the presidential primary would be long over by that point and took a leave from the campaign. She got married in Des Moines on May 17 and watched the Indiana primary from afar. A few months earlier, Obama's Iowa impresario, Paul Tewes, had asked which state she wanted to run in the general election. "I'm gonna be in Indiana," she told him, "either working for Starbucks or the Obama campaign."

"It's not gonna be a targeted state," he responded.

Tewes called again during her honeymoon. "So where do you want to go?" he asked.

"Indiana," she responded for a second time.

"Well, I don't know about Indiana," he told her. She replied that a poll done by Thompson's campaign showed Obama tied with McCain there.

In the first week of June, after a meeting in Chicago, field director Jon Carson handed her the keys to the Hoosier State. By then, Obama's campaign had polled the state and knew it could be competitive. The congressional pickups in 2006 and huge turnout in the primary opened their eyes to the possibilities ahead. "We figured we could win the state on turnout alone," Parcell said. "There's enough Democrats there to win, they just don't vote, because they don't think their vote matters. They'd been told for forty years that a Republican would run away with the state."

She started on June 16. "There's really no model of how to run a presidential campaign in Indiana," she said. "We're breaking new ground." The campaign adopted a similar strategy to Iowa—have a presence in every county, keep it close in the rural areas and Republican suburbs, and run up the margins in cities like Indianapolis, Gary, and Bloomington. The campaign began with eighty organizers and added eighty more after McCain pulled out of Michigan at the beginning of October. Despite the accumulating evidence to the contrary, the McCain campaign never believed that Obama would seriously contest the state. "This is the most cynical, superficial campaign in Indiana's history," said Indiana Republican Party chair Murray Clark. Indiana residents, meanwhile, kept waiting and waiting for McCain to show. "The story was: 'Where is McCain?'" said Obama spokesman Jonathan Swain.

The Obama campaign forced McCain into an unwinnable catch-22: If he contested a deep red state like Indiana, he'd look like a fool nationally. But if he didn't, he risked losing the state and definitely the presidency. "If you had to go spend money in Indiana, you might as well throw in the towel from a Republican perspective," Parcell said.

Yet even as Obama's operation kept expanding, Parcell never knew when and if she'd have to pack her bags. "We felt like every single week we had to prove ourselves to stay on the target list," she said.

Paul Dioguardi oversaw the campaign's Midwestern states from his desk in Chicago. "You don't realize how close it was," he told her after the election. "If the fund-raising hadn't gone well or we had to shift resources to another state, you guys would've been the first to get cut."

As August 2008 approached, Ray Rivera scrambled to accommodate the upcoming Democratic convention. Many local Republicans ridiculed the Democrats' choice of Denver. "Having the national Democratic Party come to Colorado will drive home just how far left and out of touch the national Democratic Party is with Colorado," said GOP state chair Dick Wadhams, an aspiring heir to Karl Rove. But other Republicans worried the convention might solidify the Democratic trend in the state. In July, *The Weekly Standard* ran a cover story by an envious Fred Barnes, who just a few years earlier had predicted Republican hegemony for decades; it was titled "The Colorado Model: The Democrats' Plan for Turning Red States Blue." On the cover, a donkey in red sunglasses snowboarded over the mountains.

McCain's Arizona roots and maverick reputation should have given him a distinct advantage out west. Obama, wisely, never pretended to be something he wasn't. He didn't put on a cowboy hat, snakeskin boots, or a bolo tie, and he never went on a hunting photo op like Kerry. He delivered the same message no matter where he was, convinced that his words had universal appeal. "He wasn't terribly knowledgeable on so-called western issues," said Gary Hart, "but he managed to get by."

Rivera arrived in Colorado the last week of August 2007, the only paid staffer of any presidential campaign in the state. "When I was in town walking around in September, people looked at me cross-eyed," Rivera said, "and said, 'Does your campaign know how it's spending money? Do they understand they should be in Iowa and New Hampshire?'"

Rivera talked so much as a kid everyone just assumed he'd go into politics. He grew up in Albuquerque, the son of a Korean mother and New Mexican father whose family emigrated from Spain in the nineteenth century to work in the mining camps up north. They met when his father served in the demilitarized zone in the 1970s. Rivera already had the perfect family story, along with an intensely driven personality. He planned on going to law school and running for office, but after losing an election for student body president at the University of New Mexico, he decided to become an organizer. In 2004, he got a job with the labor union AFSCME and went to organize in Vegas for Kerry, who narrowly lost Nevada, one of many disappointments out west that year. On his drive back to New Mexico, Rivera's mother urged him to quit politics and reconsider law school. "Why are you a Democrat?" she said. "You guys always lose." Then he got a call from his boss, Ricky Fuller, who told him about the party's unexpected success in Colorado, flipping the statehouse and senate and picking up a U.S. Senate seat. "Pack your bags," Fuller told him. "You're going there."

In 2006, Rivera worked on picking up two more seats in the Colorado Senate. After the election, his colleague Temo Figueroa became Obama's field director and offered him a job. He'd been leading Obama's campaign in Colorado pretty much ever since. The coming convention now seemed like a blessing and a curse for the twenty-eight-year-old. "From my perspective, it was tough," he said. "August was a rough month for us in Colorado." The hype of the convention threatened to overwhelm the actual campaign. "All anyone wanted to talk about was tickets and parties and events," Rivera said. "If we did a press conference on health care, no one cared." A poll on the eve of the convention found the race neck and neck in the state. "Obama was losing ground over much of the summer," found the Denver-based Democratic consulting firm RBI Strategies.

But the convention also became a powerful organizing tool for the campaign. On the evening of August 28, as eighty thousand delegates and politicos filled Invesco Field (formerly known as Mile High), Rivera strode to a podium in front of the faux-Roman columns onstage, held up his BlackBerry, and urged everyone in the audience to text message their phone numbers to the campaign. Forty thousand people signed up within an hour. His bosses said it was a record within the campaign and sent him out twice more to make the same pitch. All the while, organizers on the third floor called unaffiliated voters, urging them to watch Obama's speech. That night, Obama hit it out of the park, so to speak, and his staff went out to celebrate. When boozy Democrats woke up groggy on Friday morning, the McCain campaign had a surprise waiting for them.

In February 2007, Adam Brickley, a.k.a. ElephantMan, a junior at the University of Colorado at Colorado Springs, launched the Draft Sarah Palin for Vice President blog. Brickley, a leader of the College Republicans on campus and an intern at the conservative website Townhall.com, listed Zionism, Vaticanology, and "fighting socialism" among his passions. He was looking for a candidate who was "1) A energetic, young, fresh face who will energize the electorate, 2) Not connected to the current administration, 3) Pro-Life, 4) Pro-Gun, 5) A woman or minority to counter Hillary or Obama and put to rest the idea that America only elects white males." Though sworn in as Alaska governor just two months earlier, Sarah Barracuda fit the bill. "I discovered that she was definitely a new kid [sic] of leader, coming off more as a spunky soccer-mom than a stuffy career politician," Brickley wrote. A year and a half later, his fantasy became a reality. "WE DID IT!!!!!" Brickley proclaimed on his blog after McCain's stunning running-mate selection. "I am positively elated."

Colorado Springs represented a fitting birthplace for the draft Palin movement. Few places better reflected the America she believed in and combined such religious and military might. The city of 400,000, seventy miles south of Denver along the Front Range of the Rockies, was commonly known as the Evangelical Vatican and, to Democrats, the "belly of the beast" for the Republican Party and conservative movement—the home of Focus on the Family, New Life Church, the Air Force Academy, Fort Carson, and NORAD.

Three days after her triumphant introduction to America at the Republican convention, Palin came to town for a rapturous rally at Colorado Springs airport. Hank Williams Jr. sang the national anthem, and a frenzied crowd of ten thousand waved American flags inside the jet hangar as Palin took the stage. "U.S.A.! U.S.A.! U.S.A.!" the crowd chanted, followed by "Sarah! Sarah! Sarah!" McCain put her on the ticket to gin up the base in what she'd later term "the real America," and that's exactly what she'd done so far. Fresh off the convention, McCain now led Obama in Colorado and, for the first time, nationwide.

John and Cindy stood stiffly by her side as Palin revved up the crowd. "It is so great to be here in beautiful Colorado Springs," she said. "And those mountains behind us, they so remind me of home." I'm just like you, Palin implied. Not like that other guy, with the Muslim name and sketchy background who kept "palling around with terrorists." It was the first of three visits for the wannabe veep. Palin's presence delighted the faithful, but was not an altogether good sign for the Republican ticket. After all, Republican candidates routinely won 70 percent of the vote in El Paso County, home to Colorado Springs and its sprawling suburbs. McCain should've had the county locked up long before he picked Palin. For the first time anyone could remember, Republicans were playing defense on their home field.

When Pat Waak ran for state chair, the Democratic delegation from El Paso County asked her, "If we vote for you, will you come back?" She assured them she would. As proof, the state party held the 2008 Democratic state convention right in James Dobson's backyard. If Greeley seemed like an odd choice for a Democratic assembly, Colorado Springs appeared downright insane.

"I don't consider it their territory," Waak explained. "Every place is fair game, and so is Colorado Springs." In May 2008, ten thousand Democrats packed World Arena for a revival service of their own. The *Colorado Springs Independent* called it "The Great Liberal Invasion." The place was so crowded it took over three hours to register everyone, and the first night's gathering stretched well past midnight. "El Paso County is the new capital of the Democratic Party in Colorado," said Speaker of the House Andrew Romanoff. "We're slowly turning it from a deep and ugly red to a bright and beautiful blue."

Still, changing the political hue of Colorado Springs was an altogether herculean—and some would say positively foolish—undertaking. "The state always looked at us as a black hole of Republicanism," said Democratic county chair John Morris, a retired history teacher. "The idea that there were actually progressives and moderates here, people in Denver just couldn't believe that."

Dobson moved his burgeoning religious empire to the Springs from Pomona, California, in 1991, lured by cheap land and plenty of like-minded compatriots. The next year, Dobson lobbied heavily for Amendment 2, which prevented Colorado municipalities from enacting laws protecting gay residents from discrimination. Following passage, Colorado became known as "the hate state" among gay activists, who in New York City dumped Coors beer into the Hudson River, chanting, "We're here, we're queer, we won't drink Coors beer." The Supreme Court struck down the law as unconstitutional three years later, but the issue came to define the city. Also in 1992, another California transplant in the Springs, the antitax crusader Douglas Bruce, successfully lobbied for passage of a Taxpayer Bill of Rights, which severely restricted government spending. The two laws formed the twin pillars of the conservative movement in the state.

North of downtown, past the verdant campus of Colorado College and beyond an industrial stretch of warehouses, sits an area known to Democrats as the Great White North, populated by sandy brown subdivisions with names like Briargate and Chapel Hills. This used to be ranch country, but now it's full of steeples and megachurches and golf courses. The forty-five-acre campus of Dobson's

Focus on the Family, a series of lattice-patterned brick-and-glass buildings with forest green roofs, rests on a hill overlooking the city, with an unobstructed view of the mountains.

Just up the road, off New Life Drive, sits New Life Church, founded by Pastor Ted Haggard in 1984. Before he arrived in Colorado Springs, the native Hoosier smuggled Bibles into the Soviet Union and preached in Baton Rouge, Louisiana. While camping on the base of Pikes Peak one day, Haggard spoke to the Lord and declared the city the home of his budding congregation. He started in his basement, then moved to a strip mall, next to a bar, liquor store, and massage parlor. Haggard put up a banner out front: SIEGE THIS CITY FOR ME, signed JESUS.

"The mega suburban churches weren't here at all, and there was a high percentage of new age and satanic-type activity," Haggard said. He formed a "prayer shield" over the city and instructed his flock to systematically pray over every block—in residential neighborhoods, in vacant lots, outside adult bookstores, and in parks filled with the homeless. "If we weren't doing this," Haggard said, "some of these people would never be prayed for." He claimed crime fell every year as a result. In the early 1990s, Haggard found the perfect patch of land for his ten-thousand-member megachurch. South of the parking lot you could see Cheyenne Mountain, home to NORAD. The Air Force Academy sat across the highway, while Lockheed Martin was just down the street. Haggard said he was "fighting Armageddon in the skies of Colorado Springs." He became a leading GOP power broker, often joking that he differed with President Bush only over choice of trucks. In 2004, Bush received a hero's welcome when he spoke to the Haggard-led National Association of Evangelicals in Colorado Springs. Not surprisingly, Republicans controlled every aspect of the city's politics. Democrats often didn't bother to run for local offices. Bud Gordon, a local progressive blogger, called it "the beat-down syndrome."

"We'd been beaten down so long," Gordon said, "that people were afraid to come out and say, 'I'm a Democrat.'"

Things began to change in 2006, when compelling Democratic candidates ran for local and national offices. John Morse, a candidate for state senate, grew up an Army brat and moved to the city when he was nine. He'd been an EMT, ran a nonprofit, and served as a police chief just south of the city, near Fort Carson. "It's always been conservative," Morse said in reference to the large military population that sprang up after World War II, "but people didn't really care what you did in the bedroom." After all, the libertarian movement, led by Robert LeFevre and his Freedom School, also originated here. "Focus on the Family really changed all that." Morse used to love the town, but he barely recognized it anymore, as the religious right partnered with antitax zealots to turn Colorado Springs into a conservative laboratory. "In the last twenty years, there's no longer flowers on the boulevard," Morse said. "Antigovernment fervor took over and sucked the life out of the place." The city closed parks, cut the number of cops, and no longer inspected restaurants or immunized students. It even canceled its fireworks show on July 4, short on funds. "Our public works department is almost gone," said Vice Mayor Larry Small. "The only thing we're doing in-house now is pothole filling and snow removal." Despite being the second most populous county in the state, El Paso ranked last in tax collection.

Senate President Joan Fitz-Gerald asked Morse to run for office. He initially dismissed the idea, but mulled it over and realized someone needed to make a stand. "That's what's wrong with this town," he said. "It's all Republican! There's never an opposing view. Ever. No one was saying, 'Taxes are how we invest in the community, why are we just cutting and cutting and cutting?'" Amazingly, he won, and for the first time Democrats fielded candidates for every local race. Thanks to a new voter database, the local party could finally figure out where all those closet Democrats had been hiding.

Shortly after the 2006 election, Vinai and Barbara Thummalapally, a couple who attended Occidental College with Obama (before he transferred to Columbia his junior year), began meeting

with other Obama supporters at Meadow Muffins, a dive bar decorated with old movie memorabilia. Vinai, an Indian-American
businessman, roomed with Barack (then known as Barry) one summer and taught him how to cook Indian food. Week after week,
more and more people kept showing up at Meadow Muffins, all
strangers to one another. Mike Maday, a professional mediator from
Minnesota, attended one of the first meetings in March 2007. "Nobody in the group had any political organizing experience," Maday
said. "I had some, but I wasn't James Carville." By default, he became the group's leader. "Most of us couldn't spell 'caucus,' let alone
know how to do it," said Jason DeGroot, a former staff sergeant in
the Air Force.

Maday, fifty-three, was short and thin, with a reddish brown
goatee and bright blue eyes. He was used to sticking out politically.
He grew up in a blue-collar Catholic family in Buffalo, Minnesota,
and, in his first election, caucused for McGovern in 1972 in Hubert
Humphrey's backyard. He came to Denver to get a master's in social
work, moving to Colorado Springs when his wife got a job there.
His new hometown presented quite an adjustment. "There were
some other Democrats, but very few," he said. Maday got involved
with the nuclear freeze movement when the state—particularly El
Paso County—became a proud Reagan stronghold. "It was pretty
lonely back then," he said. After Reagan's landslide victory in 1984,
Maday gave up on Democratic politics. It wasn't until twenty years
later, when his youngest son started following the Kerry campaign,
that he reengaged, or at least tried to. "The Kerry campaign essentially didn't exist in this part of Colorado," he said.

That loss, however, only strengthened his resolve. Maday particularly liked Obama because of his opposition to the war and
appeal among Independent voters, who made up a third of Colorado's electorate. During the Walk for Change in June 2007, two other
people showed up to help him knock on doors in his placid neighborhood of Pleasant Valley: Ann Wallace, a wine merchant, and her
mother, Edna. The campaign gave them a script and a list of Demo-

crats and unaffiliated voters in the neighborhood to contact. Neither Ann nor Edna had canvassed before. "What if people yell at us?" Ann asked Maday. Democrats always ran that risk in Colorado Springs. By the end of the day, however, they'd recruited three more volunteers and knocked on about fifty doors. To his surprise, "the response to Obama was overwhelmingly positive. A lot of people had heard his '04 speech and wanted to know more."

A few weeks later, Maday flew to New York City with Vinai and met Obama during a fund-raiser at the Yale Club. He asked the candidate how he could win over evangelical voters in a place like Colorado Springs. They're not a monolithic group, Obama responded. He mentioned the warm reception he received at Rick Warren's Saddleback Church in California in December 2006. It boded well, Obama thought, for his chances in Colorado Springs.

At the end of July, Maday and Ann Wallace attended a Camp Obama in Illinois. There Maday met Gabe Cohen, a deputy to Buffy Wicks who was organizing a series of early meetings in Colorado. Cohen asked Maday to put together a meeting in Colorado Springs for the next week. On short notice, eighty-five people showed up at the public library downtown for the first meeting of the Colorado Movement for Obama–El Paso County. They appointed leaders for every section of the county and went from there. In September, Maday attended the kickoff of the Obama campaign in Denver at Manual High School, a once-decrepit, predominantly minority school in northeast Denver shuttered by the city (by then superintendent and current U.S. senator Michael Bennet), overhauled, and due to reopen that fall. "We wanted a place where hope and inspiration were being planted," Ray Rivera said. Eight hundred people showed up to meet Rivera, listen to Figueroa (who told Obama's famous "fired up, ready to go" story), and practice a mock caucus, which they called a "mockaus." Maday was one of the few people who had been to a real one before.

He went to Iowa before the caucus, then came back to open an official Obama office in El Paso County in early January. The campaign rented the second floor of an office building in an industrial section north of town, with a conference room and a series of small offices. They expected around sixty on a weeknight in the winter; three hundred showed. Maday and DeGroot ran from room to room to make announcements and accommodate all the people, who eventually spilled out onto the street. This was not your typical Democratic gathering in El Paso County, which could usually fit in a phone booth. A few weeks later, Maday's caucus in Pleasant Valley saw a tenfold increase from 2004, with three camera crews on hand to cover it. Obama took 70 percent of the vote on February 5. (Romney won handily among Republicans, with McCain a distant second.) Afterward, Maday became a delegate to the national convention. In his wildest dreams, he'd never expected to see anything like this in Colorado Springs.

With the general election under way, Obama traveled to the belly of the beast on July 2, delivering a speech on national service at the University of Colorado at Colorado Springs, in the Lions' Den gym. He was introduced by Cori Gadzia, a twenty-four-year-old volunteer with a fiancé stationed at Fort Carson, awaiting an imminent second deployment to Iraq. After his speech, Obama visited the Air Force Academy, toured NORAD, and held a fund-raiser at the Broadmoor hotel, a favorite stop for GOP candidates. In 2004, Bush raised three times as much as John Kerry here. By the end of August, Obama had out-raised McCain in El Paso County. The Obama campaign didn't expect to win the county outright—no Democrat had since 1964—but a big enough turnout would provide a huge boost in Colorado, given his strength in other population centers like Denver, Boulder, Pueblo, and along the Front Range of the Rockies on I-25.

The campaign blanketed the city with offices and organizers. A gregarious Irish-American real estate developer, Chuck Murphy, donated two offices, one above a bank downtown and a main headquarters in an old auto garage ten minutes away. They opened subsequent offices in Manitou Springs, a new age enclave at the base of Pikes Peak, another close to Fort Carson, and a fifth on heavily trafficked Academy Boulevard in the Great White North. The McCain campaign, inexplicably, rented space above a local UFCW union hall. Every time McCain-Palin supporters stopped by, they had to pass a flood of pro-union and Obama signs. By late October, Obama had fifty-one field offices in Colorado compared with only thirteen for McCain. The state had swung from a massive Republican voter-registration edge to nearly even.

Keith Ferguson, a cheerful twenty-six-year-old with a shaved head and red goatee, went to high school in Colorado Springs and came back from New York as an Obama organizer. To the best of his knowledge, McCain held a single canvass in the city, in July. "We were canvassing every single day," he said. Each house meeting Ferguson held spawned another. "You saw people become more and more comfortable being a Democrat in Colorado Springs," he said. The meetings drew an eclectic mix of longtime and closet Democrats, fed-up Independents and Republicans, and unexpected recruits like Kelly Hedgecock, a young evangelical Christian who worked for Compassion International and drove a car with a Jesus fish and an Obama bumper sticker side by side.

Biden visited on October 22, donning a red cap with a gold S at Sierra High School. "We have the best ground operation I think this state or any state has ever seen," Biden said. "I want you to turn off the TV about red states and blue states," he said. "I want you focusing on one thing—get out now and vote now." Michelle Obama arrived a week later for an event at City Auditorium. The fire marshal closed the doors when capacity hit twenty-five hundred, stranding a thousand outside. A cluster of military families stood behind her onstage, holding VETS FOR MICHELLE and VETERANS FOR OBAMA signs. PRO-MILITARY, PRO-OBAMA, said one large banner. "It is good to come back to the states that have given us so much," Michelle said. "Colorado is really one of those states. You guys have been amazing."

With Palin on the ticket, however, enthusiasm peaked on both sides, and the blowback from Republicans became increasingly hostile. "On a day-to-day basis," said Ferguson, "you could count on hearing, 'He's a Muslim. I don't trust him. I don't like where he went to church. He's a racist.'" A lot of Springs' residents said they'd vote only for pro-life candidates, while others responded, "I'm in the military, so I'm voting for McCain." Palin's dire warnings about a socialist takeover of government fed the hysteria. In the days before the election, someone threw a deer head into the parking lot of Obama's main office, its antlers cut off to resemble a donkey.

The repeated visits from McCain and Palin made Ferguson's volunteers increasingly nervous. "Guys, if they're investing any time or money in Colorado Springs in October, it's over for them," he responded. McCain admitted that he needed a hundred-thousand-vote margin in El Paso County to prevail in the state. "I have to win here if I'm going to be the next president," he said of Colorado. To that end, Republican county clerk Bob Balink asserted erroneously that students at Colorado College couldn't register and vote in Colorado if their parents claimed them on income taxes in another state. "Registering to vote in Colorado can have cascading effects," Balink claimed in a letter sent to students, including "criminal penalties" for cars not registered in state and the loss of thousands of dollars of tax exemptions. "At best, the El Paso County Clerk does not understand the laws he was elected to uphold in a nonpartisan manner," Waak responded. "At worst, he is intentionally seeking to intimidate young voters." She traveled down to El Paso County nearly every week to campaign for Obama.

Palin perked up the base, but only to an extent. The religious right no longer possessed the clout of 2004, even in Colorado Springs. In December 2006, a slate of Focus-allied conservatives were ousted from the city's school board. Dobson had never been crazy about McCain—even declaring he'd never vote for him, only to change his mind with Palin on the ticket—and by the fall the economic crisis had caught up with Focus, which eliminated two hundred positions in September and admitted to a "serious" budget shortfall after the election.

Colorado Springs, in particular, had been rocked by the revelations, days before the 2006 election, of Ted Haggard's shocking dalliances with male prostitutes and use of crystal meth. He was told to stay away from the city and the church. The new pastor at New Life, Brady Boyd, kept a low profile and explicitly refrained from endorsing McCain. "The only advice I give is pray, fast and vote, and that can be for any political party," he said. "What's happening to us is less allegiance to the Republican Party, and more to our core principles," Boyd explained. He eschewed the typical social issues, like gay marriage, that still preoccupied Dobson. "To be focused on those issues at a time when people are hurting would really be to the detriment of families," he said.

The economic collapse in September particularly impacted the southeast part of Colorado Springs, near Fort Carson, a largely transient, working-class area hemorrhaging jobs and rocked by the foreclosure crisis. Tidy two-story houses with small front yards form the nicer part of the neighborhood, while mobile homes protected by ramshackle wood fencing, crowded apartment complexes, and tightly spaced bungalows with dry, fenced-in yards make up the rest. There are few pedestrian areas, just highways, stoplights, and patches of housing in between. Near Fort Carson, a desolate highway bridge is decorated with makeshift memorials to fallen soldiers and WELCOME HOME signs for those lucky enough to return.

Robert Andrews grew up in this part of town, a block from Sierra High, where Biden spoke. At age five, he met the legendary Pittsburgh Steelers running back Franco Harris, tried on his Super Bowl ring, and dreamed of playing professional football. When Obama announced he was running for president, Andrews was finishing up his senior year as a star quarterback at Hastings College in Nebraska and negotiating to play in the Canadian Football League and maybe one day in the NFL. A chance for stardom awaited in Calgary. Instead, after just a few months in Canada, he returned to

Colorado Springs and made it his personal mission to help elect Obama in his hometown.

His friends and family were puzzled by the decision. "I feel a greater sense of commitment to social change than I do to changing the scoreboard," Andrews told them. He wanted Obama to replace Michael Jordan as the archetype for young black males like himself. Starting in November 2007, Andrews volunteered for Obama any way he could and officially joined the campaign as an organizer in August 2008. Nothing came easy; southeast Colorado Springs historically had the lowest voter turnout of anywhere in El Paso County. "A lot of people didn't have the hope that Obama preached," Andrews said. Many of his friends from high school were "teetering on the edge," he said, facing bleak futures with few options. He started holding weekly meetings at Sierra High, urging his friends to attend. "I felt like it was my duty to shine a positive light on my city and where I come from," he said.

During his first day on the campaign, Andrews helped open an Obama office—the first presidential storefront in the area since the days of LBJ—just east of Fort Carson, in the blue-collar suburb of Fountain. A month later, the economy collapsed. With the city on edge, Andrews's organizing began to have an impact. "You'd think it would be the opposite, but people actually got more energized and were more hopeful and more willing to do things," he said. "They felt that Obama was actually going to enact some change."

The last week of October, Obama returned to Colorado for a final set of rallies in the state. His campaign expected thirty-four thousand on a sunny Saturday morning in Denver, but triple that showed up, in a scene that the state party vice chair, Dan Slater, called "breathtaking to even the most jaded political eyes." Supporters packed every inch of grass from Civic Center Park to the granite steps of the state capitol. Just a few days earlier, only four thousand people showed for McCain in Denver. Now well over a hundred thousand flocked to see Obama, the largest gathering yet of his campaign. Supporters climbed trees and stood on light posts to get a better view. "The road to the White House in 2008 goes through this park in this city in this state," said Governor Bill Ritter.

"Goodness gracious," Obama exclaimed when he took the stage, peering into the distance. "Who are those folks at the top of the capitol there? Unbelievable." He asked how many people had already voted. A flood of hands went up. (Over 70 percent of Coloradans voted before Election Day.) "That's what I'm talking about," Obama said. He mentioned how Bush had already cast his ballot for McCain. "Colorado," Obama said, "you can finally put an end to the Bush-McCain philosophy!"

From Denver, Obama's motorcade headed sixty-five miles north along the Front Range to Fort Collins in Larimer County, just adjoining Weld. A crowd of forty-five thousand squeezed into Colorado State University's Oval center, a two-thousand-foot-wide grassy pavilion marked by towering elm trees, which glowed bright yellow on the fall afternoon. Mike Maday drove up for a last glimpse of Obama, arriving early to secure a good view. He stood on an elevated rope line directly in back of the stage, watching a sea of people rolling like waves into the pavilion. He knew right then that Obama would win Colorado.

When Obama got to the podium, wearing a familiar black suit and crisp white shirt, he stopped for a minute to take it all in. "It is pretty around here," he said. "I should've gone to school here." He turned and absorbed the crowd behind him. "What a spectacular campus, what a spectacular crowd, and a spectacular day," he remarked. The candidate delivered his ambitious closing argument— stabilize the economy, put Americans back to work, provide every citizen with health insurance, end the country's dependence on foreign oil, combat global warming, bring the troops home from Iraq, repair America's relationships in the world, and restore a dilapidated sense of common purpose.

"This country and the dream it represents are being tested in a way we haven't seen in nearly a century," Obama said. "Future generations will judge us by how we respond to this test. Will they say, 'This is a time when America lost its nerve, when it lost its purpose, when it lost its way'?" Voices in the crowd yelled cries of no. "Or will people look back twenty years from now and say, 'That was another one of those moments when America overcame'?" Obama asked. "That's what this election's about, that's what we're fighting for—to make sure the American promise is there for the next generation." The community organizer made one last pitch. "Colorado, if you will stand with me, if you are gonna go out and talk to your friends, and talk to your neighbors, and knock on doors, and make phone calls, if you are ready to once again believe in the promise of this country, then I guarantee you, we will not just win this election, but you and I together, we're going to change the country and change the world."

After the candidate departed for Ohio, Maday ran into Rivera. They exchanged a big hug, and Rivera brought up that September kickoff over a year ago at Manual High School, when the campaign had been ecstatic to draw eight hundred people. The campaign had grown to proportions nobody, not even the most optimistic organizers or starry-eyed supporters, could have imagined. By the time Obama left Colorado, McCain had all but conceded the state.

In all likelihood, Obama had won the West. But the heartland was still very much up for grabs. The Obama campaign kept two large maps in its Indiana state headquarters in Indianapolis. One showed the unemployment rate of every county in the state, and the other charted the rise in unemployment per county over the past six months. Elkhart County led in both. The campaign's polling showed an unusually large number of potentially persuadable Democratic, Independent, and Republican voters in the area. Bread-and-butter issues were now on everybody's mind, giving a Democrat like Obama an opening in this otherwise culturally conservative county on the

Michigan border, where every other car seemed to have an "In God We Trust" license plate and Bush won 70 percent of the vote in 2004.

Once known as the RV capital of the world, birthplace of Alka-Seltzer, maker of brass instruments, and among the best places in the country to raise a family, the city of Elkhart—an old river town and manufacturing outpost of fifty-two thousand surrounded by rolling farmland—had fallen on hard times. Monaco Coach closed three manufacturing plants in the past year, laying off fourteen hundred workers. Unemployment climbed to 10 percent and would hit 20 percent following the election, the city becoming a national symbol of economic calamity. (MSNBC devoted an entire website to the city's economy, called "The Elkhart Project.") In September, the city council passed a law limiting residents to one garage sale a month. Just south of the preserved Main Street, on the other side of the rail-road tracks, little more than vacant lots, check-cashing stores, and boarded-up storefronts existed. "Elkhart is a real key county for us," said Obama spokesman Jonathan Swain. Even if the campaign didn't carry the county, it hoped to eat into McCain's margin.

The weekend before the election, Satish and Nan Patel's house in Elkhart, on a leafy cul-de-sac ten minutes from downtown, bustled with activity. The Patels housed four campaign volunteers—two twenty-somethings from California (one ran the campaign in Elkhart), a lawyer from Chicago, and a lawyer from D.C. Nan, a whirlwind of energy from Mumbai, cooked chicken tikka masala and made turkey sandwiches for a steady stream of volunteers, kept the TV tuned to MSNBC at all times, and knocked on doors when she had a spare moment. Satish ran what seemed like a never-ending series of last-minute errands for the campaign, shuttling back and forth between his home and the office on Main Street. More and more cars kept arriving from Michigan and Illinois, hoping to swing Indiana blue for the first time in forty-four years.

Such commotion represented a stark break from normalcy. Satish moved to Elkhart in 1978 from Madras, India, for an engineering job, only the third Indian he knew of in town. Nan followed in 1980 from Mumbai. "It was the boonies," she said. "There was nothing here." She had to buy cilantro—a must for her Indian cooking—from a Mexican grocery store in South Bend, forty-five minutes away. The county didn't expand until the 1990s, spurred by growth in the RV industry. Surrounded by Republican neighbors, the Patels voted for both Republicans and Democrats until the late 1990s, when, aghast at Clinton's impeachment, they became ardent Democrats. Their eldest son, Rohan, had worked for Obama since the early days of Iowa.

"My son dropped out of med school for you," Nan told Obama bluntly when they first met in Iowa after the Jefferson-Jackson Dinner.

"Don't worry, Mrs. Patel," Obama responded with a grin. "We're gonna take care of Rohan." After additional stints in Tennessee, Mississippi, and North Carolina, he became the campaign's political director in Indiana, overseeing every aspect of the state's strategy, no detail too minor for his eye.

In early September, Rohan visited the farm of Kurt Bullard down the street from his parents' house, known for its sweet corn, and asked him to paint an Obama logo atop his white barn. A few months earlier, Bullard, vice chair of the Elkhart County Democratic Party, had introduced Obama inside a barn at the neighboring St. Joseph County fairgrounds. "There were already quite a few Obama barns in Ohio," Bullard said, "and they wanted to get some in Indiana." He put a new coat of white paint on top and added the campaign's signature red, white, and blue Obama '08 rainbow. He used paint, he said, that would last for eight years. Similar Obama barns could soon be seen across the state. Bullard's brother, Kevin, a registered Republican, ran the farmers' market next door and didn't care for the Obama barn, which he called bad for business. He put up a sign of his own: IT'S NOT OUR BARN. Such were the tensions within family and among candidates in once solidly Republican Elkhart County. The Patels had three Obama signs stolen off their lawn in one week. There was no point in reporting it, Nan said. Though the town had a Democratic mayor, local law enforcement was solidly behind McCain.

Like Hamilton County, Elkhart had become another unlikely battleground. Obama opened two offices during the primary, visited briefly in May, and bested Clinton by nineteen points. The campaign reopened the glass storefront office on Main Street in early August—the first ever for a Democratic presidential campaign during a general election—just before Obama returned for a highly publicized visit with Indiana senator Evan Bayh, then a rumored VP selection. Supporters assembled outside Obama's office at 6:00 a.m. just to get tickets, waiting for eight hours during a heavy thunderstorm. On August 6, Obama spoke before a packed crowd of three thousand at Rohan's old school, Concord High, addressing the energy crisis in particular—NEW ENERGY FOR AMERICA, said a sign on the podium—a salient topic in a place where high gas prices had devastated the local automobile industry.

"When George Bush took office, you were paying $1.50 at the gas tank," Obama said. "Remember that?"

"No!" a few voices in the crowd yelled out.

"You don't remember?" Obama laughed. Those days seemed like an eternity ago.

"We need help," one questioner after another told the candidate during the Q&A.

"The American people . . . are anxious right now," Obama replied. "Things don't feel like they're getting better for people. And I know they don't feel like that here in Elkhart." Keep in mind, this was *before* the economy collapsed.

McCain never made it to Elkhart. Neither did Palin, though she did make three stops in the state—belatedly fighting to fend off Obama—including one in Hamilton County, where Republicans, for perhaps the first time ever, were on the defensive. The local Republican Party opened a barely functional office in Elkhart a few weeks before the election, with a few posters in the window but never any

people around. Shortly thereafter, construction began on that portion of the street, blocking easy access to the Republican office—a
fitting metaphor for the state of the GOP and McCain campaign.

Indiana's embrace of Obama and his exotic biography ranked as
one of the more surprising developments of the general election.
The day before the election, the salt-of-the-earth head of the United
Steelworkers in Illinois and Indiana, Jim Robinson, campaigned in
a working-class section of Elkhart with gubernatorial candidate Jill
Long Thompson. Photos of John Kerry windsurfing or Monica Lewinsky's stained blue dress did Democrats no favors in the Hoosier
State, Robinson contended. "We've been waiting for a candidate to
come to Indiana and talk to us about our issues," he said.

Obama had done just that. On October 23, he held one last rally
in Indianapolis, his second in the past month. He stood on a raised
platform on the north end of the American Legion Mall downtown,
behind his signature CHANGE banner and an array of American and
Indiana flags, the latter blue with gold stars and a torch in the center.
Behind the candidate sat the beautiful, columned old city library and
the stately limestone headquarters of the American Legion (once a
hotbed of right-wing conservatism), with its sunken garden, cenotaph, and four columns of black granite with golden eagles on top.
Before Obama, another huge crowd of thirty-five thousand assembled on a brisk fall weekday morning, among the most racially and
ethnically diverse the state had ever seen, framed by yellow trees and
somber memorials to the country's foreign wars. An absolutely massive American flag hung on the end of the mall, in front of a hundred-
foot gold-capped obelisk and towering granite Civil War memorial.
By the time Obama came out, the sun had peeked through the
clouds.

The beauty of the day stood in stark contrast to the terrifying
news of the moment. The economy was in a tailspin. "Now, more
than ever," Obama said, "this campaign has to be about the prob-

lems facing the American people." He looked into the crowd and saw a panorama of Americans struggling to weather the crisis. "I see some sheet metal workers," Obama said, pointing into the crowd with his right hand. "I see some carpenters up here. I see some teachers out here." He raised his voice a few notches and, in a rare moment, diverged from his prepared remarks. "Who's looking out for steelworkers?" Obama asked. "Who's fighting for carpenters? Who's fighting for teachers? Who's fighting for Teamsters? That's the president I want to be."

A day before the election, McCain swooped into Indiana to try to save face. The white, blue, and yellow "Straight Talk Express" Boeing 737 landed on the tarmac at Indianapolis International Airport at 4:00 p.m., the candidate quickly disembarking and strolling to the nearby podium for a brisk seventeen-minute speech. COUNTRY FIRST, read the large blue banner behind him, the crowd of five thousand wearing red for the occasion, the only color the state had known for a generation. "The Mac is back!" McCain proclaimed. The crowd repeated the chant. Judging by McCain's itinerary, it certainly didn't seem that way. He'd started the day in Tampa and would end it in Prescott, Arizona, with stops in between in Tennessee (targeting the Virginia and North Carolina border), Pennsylvania, Indiana, New Mexico, and Nevada—all states (with the exception of Pennsylvania) that Bush carried in 2004. "Indiana, I'm counting on you," McCain said. Gone were the days when the Republican ticket could reliably depend on the state.

Obama one-upped McCain by returning to Indiana for a surprise rendezvous the next day, his forty-ninth visit and only campaign stop on Election Day. On Tuesday morning, the candidate landed in Indianapolis and headed south to a modest UAW get-out-the-vote location, where two dozen volunteers worked the phones in the campaign's final hours. The former organizer rolled up the sleeves of his white shirt and got busy. "This is where the work is done, over here," Obama said when he walked in. "That's what I'm talking about." He made thirteen calls, ranging from phone to phone, which he joked was his only exercise of the day. His staff hoped the visit would spur those outstanding voters to get to the polls. "He was here to ask Hoosiers for their votes," said Dan Parker. "And he followed through on that—to the final day." It was hard to believe that just a few years earlier Parker and the Indiana Democratic Party had no money, scant staff, and few prospects for victory in places like Elkhart and Hamilton counties. "I think we can win Indiana," Obama said. "Otherwise I wouldn't be in Indiana." No matter what happened that night, one thing was for certain: Indiana would no longer be the first state to show up red on the electoral map.

After Obama locked up much of the West and most—if not all—of the heartland, the South remained the difference between a slim mandate and an electoral landslide for his campaign. He'd long counted on Virginia and poured a ton of money into Florida. With Georgia and Mississippi looking out of reach, his best chance for an unexpected pickup came in North Carolina.

The modern political history of the Tar Heel State can be summed up in two words: Jesse Helms. "The influence of Helms can't be overstated," said Richard Starnes, professor of history at Western Carolina University.

The Jesse Helms Center sits just off Highway 74 in the small town of Wingate, past the strip malls and big-box stores thirty miles southeast of Charlotte, in the red-clay exurbs of Union County. Outside the brick-and-glass building is a huge sculpture of a bronze bald eagle, advertised as the largest in the world, a symbol of rugged American freedom. Inside there's a model replica of the United Nations Security Council (whose U.S. dues Helms withheld for half a decade as chairman of the Senate Foreign Relations Committee), clips and cartoons poking fun at Helms's controversial reputation (*Time* magazine, May 30, 1988: "Scourge of the Senate"), and T-shirts of Senator No's jowly, bespectacled mug, with the tagline "30 Years of World Domination." The eponymous center celebrates Helms as statesman, humanitarian, and visionary—the man who saved the UN, defeated the Evil Empire, and energized the New Right. Not surprisingly, there's no mention of his cozying up to dictators, calling gay people "weak, morally sick wretches," singing "Dixie" in front of a black colleague in the Senate, or filibustering a national holiday to honor Martin Luther King.

As went Helms, so went North Carolina. When the popular radio commentator-cum-senator bolted the Democratic Party in 1970, many conservative Jessecrats followed, ending one-party rule in the state. Even as North Carolina consistently elected Democrats to local offices, the state had voted for every Republican presidential candidate since 1976. Helms's bombastic brand of backlash politics—marked by vehement opposition to civil rights and the social movements of the 1960s and '70s—defined the state to the outside world. In 2001, the esteemed *Washington Post* columnist David Broder called Helms "the last prominent unabashed white racist politician in this country."

"Where did Jesse Helms come from?" a friend once asked the renowned black historian John Hope Franklin.

"From hell," Franklin responded.

Helms died at eighty-six, on July 4, 2008, no less, smack in the middle of the presidential campaign. By contesting North Carolina, Obama wagered that the Helms era had ended, or at least receded, and the state was ready, finally, to start anew.

On October 5, Obama strolled down a series of winding concrete steps on the charming grounds of Asheville High School, picking up babies and shaking a throng of hands along the rope line as he made his way onto a stage on the school's football field. Under a clear blue sky, with the temperature unseasonably warm in the low seventies, onlookers packed the field, bleachers, and any space on the hills atop Memorial Stadium. The sheer size of the crowd—twenty-eight thousand—didn't make the Sunday afternoon rally particularly noteworthy. After all, Obama drew enormous crowds everywhere he went. Geography and timing marked the significance—Obama was not only in North Carolina a month before the election but in the heavily Republican western portion of the state, home to places like Watauga and Polk counties, which in normal times voted for GOP candidates in election after election. Asheville advertised itself as a liberal enclave in the foothills of the Blue Ridge Mountains, but the surrounding counties—first targeted by state chair Jerry Meek and DNC organizer Mark Hufford—couldn't have been redder. Bush won the region by eighteen points in 2004; now Obama narrowly trailed McCain in Western North Carolina (WNC) and ran neck and neck in the state.

Obama had decamped to Asheville for a few days before the second presidential debate across the border in Nashville, Tennessee. His campaign wisely fit in a Sunday afternoon rally and, the night before, a surprise appearance at the North Carolina Democratic Party's annual Vance-Aycock fund-raising dinner, named after two of the state's most famous governors (and both ardent segregationists, reflecting the state's checkered racial history).

"When we started this campaign, we said we were going to change the political map," Obama said in the ballroom of the Grove Park Inn, perched on the city's verdant hills, where he'd been staying during debate prep. "And people said, 'No, it can't be done.' And we kept on coming down to North Carolina. And people said, 'What's he doing spending so much time in North Carolina?'" Seven hundred Democratic partisans applauded loudly at this observation. Obama wasn't exaggerating. On July 1, *Whistling Past Dixie* author Tom Schaller wrote an op-ed in *The New York Times* urging Obama to "write off" the state and region. That's what Democrats had done in 2000 and 2004, when Bush twice won North Carolina by thirteen points, solidifying Republican domination since 1976. "They'd talk a good game in late July," former governor Jim Hunt said of previous Democratic campaigns, "but by the time September was over with, they were long gone and there wasn't a soul left." It was now early October, and to the surprise of Hunt and many others, Obama showed no signs of jumping ship. He had 625 volunteer teams of four to six people in North Carolina, each overseen by a campaign staffer, covering every one of the state's 2,762 precincts.

"Thirty days out, we are right in the hunt in North Carolina," Obama said to cheers. He had been enjoying his time in town thus far—shooting hoops with Senate candidate Kay Hagan at Asheville High; picking up ribs, brisket, pulled pork, corn pudding, and sweet tea at a popular barbecue joint; and taking long walks in the early evening on his hotel's picturesque golf course. In fact, Obama had now visited North Carolina three weekends in a row.

"I have to say, if there's a prettier state than North Carolina, I have not seen it yet," Obama said, hamming up the crowd. "I confess that I haven't been to Alaska," he added with a mischievous grin.

"You can see it from Russia," yelled a man in the back of the room.

Even though Governor Mike Easley joked that "Barack is Hawaiian for Bubba," Obama's visits "had nothing to do with guns, or NASCAR, or 'life,' or 'faith,' or any of the sorts of cultural shtick national Democrats have trotted out so uncomfortably in the South," *The Nation*'s Bob Moser, a native North Carolinian, noted. Obama kept the message focused squarely on jobs and pocketbook issues. The first state-specific TV ad the campaign ran told the story of a Carolina Mills plant that produced threads for American flags and, in a cruel twist of globalization, had since relocated to Asia. Not even American flags were made in America anymore. In recent years, Carolina Mills had shut down seventeen plants in central and western North Carolina, eliminating twenty-six hundred jobs. McCain, the ad stated, supported the slanted trade deals that shuttered once-thriving factories and shipped good textile and manufacturing jobs overseas. "North Carolina," said the ad's narrator, "just can't afford more of the same."

On that October Sunday, before Obama spoke, Bricca Sweet, a

fifty-five-year-old Army vet and educator from Watauga County, stepped onstage to recite the Pledge of Allegiance. Surveying the crowd in disbelief, she couldn't help but get an extra word in. "Hel-loooo, Obama voters!" she said, her words echoing loud and clear on the fall afternoon. The crowd roared back.

Sweet grew up in Seattle, San Francisco, and Idaho, the daughter of a nuclear physicist who followed the trail of the Atomic Energy Commission. While teaching in Idaho in the 1970s, she joined the Army because she wanted to see the world. Though she was based in D.C., her turf as an intelligence officer "stretched from Thailand to Turkey, the long way around," her boss liked to say. She married a fellow intelligence officer from North Carolina, the son of a retired Methodist minister, and moved to Watauga County in 1995. They bought a sixteen-acre farm west of Boone, raising goats and chickens amid the lush forests and jagged mountains. Sweet earned two master's degrees and a Ph.D. in education from Appalachian State University (ASU), using up her GI Bill and then some, she joked.

She registered as a Republican when she got to town, outraged by Clinton's sexual indiscretions in the White House. But the local Republican Party's opposition to land conservation soon pushed her into common cause with Pam Williamson and Watauga County Democrats. With the Kerry campaign absent in North Carolina, she called in to Ohio a little bit in 2004 on behalf of the Democratic ticket. "The Republican Party violated everything about what I believed the United States of America stands for and what I wore a uniform to serve and protect," she said of the Swift Boat attacks on Kerry's military service. Feeling terribly guilty for not having done more, she became a registered Democrat in 2007 and supported Obama because of his cross-racial appeal and her belief that Hillary wouldn't be able to get anything done even if she was elected. Her father, husband, and son, who followed the family trade as an intelligence officer, with two tours of duty in Iraq, remained staunch Republicans. She didn't discuss politics with any of them. Still, she encountered a surprising number of Republicans and Independents who "felt like their country had betrayed them" and were voting for Obama.

In June 2008, Sweet attended a three-day training in Raleigh and became an Obama organizing fellow. She was the oldest person in the room. All the young organizers called her "ma'am," which she found cute but a little annoying. Nothing, not even the Army, prepared her for the intensity of a sixty-hour-a-week campaign. "I have not worked anywhere that was as demanding as volunteering for the Obama campaign," she said. She opened a campaign office in Boone and started a group called High Country for Barack Obama, with a logo of the campaign's insignia over a blue and white backdrop of the mountains. Williamson paired the newly arrived Obama staffers with locals like Sweet who knew the terrain. "You better look like you're from here if you go to Meat Camp and knock on a door," she told them.

The day after McCain picked Palin, Sweet went canvassing with Obama staffer Mark Powell, a young Air Force vet from Chicago. They drove down a dusty road in a sparsely populated part of the county and found a small trailer surrounded by mangy-looking dogs, one of which had testicles the size of balloons that practically dragged on the floor. Sweet remembered Williamson's maxim—"never skip a door"—but prayed no one would answer. The guy who did looked like a human-size Paul Bunyan, wearing a plaid flannel shirt on a hot August day, with a scraggly beard and bowl haircut. He pushed aside some dog excrement on the floor and invited them to sit down. Sweet entered apprehensively, wearing her "Veterans for Obama" button. "I just want you to know, I'm not gonna vote for that guy," the man said angrily. "You know, what's his name? The one who put a woman on the ticket!"

Sweet almost swallowed her tongue. It took all kinds in WNC. "No disrespect to you," he added. He said he and his wife were voting for Obama. "Every single vote counted," Sweet said wryly, including, it turned out, one from a raving antifeminist hillbilly. Helms would be rolling in his grave.

Elsewhere in Watauga, Harvard Ayers, a white-bearded anthropology professor who specialized in recording rare Eskimo tribes in northern Alaska, devised a unique system for targeting students at ASU in Boone. Instead of standing outside classes with a clipboard and voter-registration forms day after day, he convinced forty professors teaching big lecture classes to let him register their students, en masse, at the beginning or end of class. Somehow no one had thought of that before. On average, he said, a fourth of students registered for the first time or shifted their registration to North Carolina; Intro to Biology proved particularly fruitful. As an added boost, Williamson convinced the board of elections to place an early-vote location on campus, which Ayers urged students to visit after class.

In June, Ayers flew to Obama headquarters to pitch the idea of adopting the program nationwide. Though his strategy fell on deaf ears in Chicago, it paid big dividends in Watauga—roughly 70 percent of ASU's fourteen thousand students voted by Election Day, favoring Obama over McCain 65 to 35 percent according to exit polls, the kind of margin that went a long way toward flipping the county and state. Democrats added 360,000 voters to the rolls in 2008, compared with only 85,000 for the GOP. The state's mix of young voters, minorities, white-collar professionals, and new arrivals from the Northeast helped put fast-growing North Carolina in play. *National Journal*'s Ron Brownstein dubbed it the "coalition of the ascendant."

McCain, meanwhile, seemed curiously indifferent to the state and didn't visit after the primary until October 14 (notwithstanding a customary pilgrimage to see an ailing Billy Graham and his son Franklin in June at their mountaintop retreat outside Asheville), a stunning case of Indiana redux. His first appearance took place at the aptly named Cape Fear Community College in Wilmington. During his six stops in the state, McCain spoke to 17,900 people, the Raleigh *News & Observer* estimated; through the general election, Obama made twenty-one trips and addressed 194,000.

By the end of the campaign, North Carolina had become the

most competitive state in the nation, with close races for president, governor, House, and Senate. So much for whistling past Dixie. "People came to trust him and appreciate his possibilities," Jim Hunt said of Obama. "In the South and in North Carolina, to a certain extent, it was a matter of him not becoming threatening or scary." Obama spent the day before the election in the former Confederate strongholds of Florida (Jacksonville), North Carolina (Charlotte), and Virginia (Manassas).

North Carolina's old-guard white Democratic establishment, which grew up during segregation, watched the campaign unfold with keen interest and a unique mixture of pride and bewilderment. Hunt's law school classmate Tony Rand had served as the theatrical majority leader of the North Carolina Senate since 2001, representing Fayetteville in the body for twenty-seven years. A crafty pol plucked straight from *The Wire*, the white-haired sixty-nine-year-old had a thick, unhurried drawl and a fondness for pin-striped suits and the baby blue ties of his beloved alma mater in Chapel Hill. Rand kept a wall of framed cartoons in his senate office ridiculing his penchant for backroom horse-trading. One showed his round face on a pyramid. "So," said one onlooker to another, "what are the chances that Senator Rand will return from Egypt and explain how legislative pension amounts became secret?"

He grew up in Garner, North Carolina, at the time a segregated cotton town outside of Raleigh. "I never went to school with a black person," Rand told me. "I had only two black law school classmates. You can't imagine what it was like. When I was growing up, a black person didn't come to your front door. They'd come to your back door, knock on the door, and step back." He paused for a few moments, reflecting on his words. His great-great-grandpa had been a slave owner. In July 2008, Rand found out that the family patriarch, William Harrison Rand, had two families: seven kids with his wife and seven with his black mistress. He was reportedly run out of the state because of the affair.

Rand endorsed Obama during the primary and campaigned

across North Carolina for him. The state he was born into seemed so far removed from the North Carolina of the present. The prospect of an Obama victory almost didn't seem real. "It's the damnedest thing I ever saw," he said. "In many ways, I have trouble envisioning all of this occurring."

On July 17, Dean traveled down to Crawford, Texas, which he'd always wanted to do as a presidential candidate, to kick off a five-week, cross-country voter-registration tour on a red, white, and blue biodiesel bus at the behest of the Obama campaign. He parked across from a dusty RV lot on a sweltering, sunny Texas morning, wearing a rumpled white polo shirt and khakis. The site of Bush's beloved ranch, Dean said, would make a nice "retirement home" for the soon-to-be-ex-president.

Later that day, at a rally in Austin, the DNC chair named a few of the states he planned to visit in the coming days, starting with Louisiana, Mississippi, Georgia, and North Carolina. "I'm not supposed to give you lists anymore," he joked, letting out a mild "yee-haw" and swinging his right arm, mimicking "the scream." "We're gonna win in states we haven't won in a long, long time," he predicted. "This is an opportunity to undo thirty years of bitter, ugly, divisive, scapegoating, hate-based politics, where one party believed they're more important than our country."

At first Dean felt as if he'd been exiled by the Obama campaign as far away from the action as possible, but he came to enjoy the bus tour. It turned out to be a fitting conclusion to his tenure at the helm of the party, the once-controversial chairman receiving a warm welcome in states from New Mexico to North Carolina, where many forecast he'd never play.

As the election approached, the battlefield kept expanding. On November 3, Dean arrived in Tucson, Arizona, for one last rally, in McCain's backyard. "I wanted to do Arizona earlier, but the Obama campaign didn't want to waste their money," Dean told me. "They thought McCain was unbeatable there." But surprising new polls showed McCain only narrowly trumping Obama in the state he'd represented for twenty-five years. "I only get asked to come to states where Barack Obama can win," Dean said to sustained cheers before a crowd of 150 outside the Pima County Democratic Party. "Earlier in the week I was in North Dakota. These states weren't on anybody's lists a while ago, but they are now." If McCain hadn't been the GOP nominee, his campaign manager, Steve Schmidt, asserted after the election, Republicans would've lost Arizona, too.

By the time Dean reached Chicago on election night, he believed Obama's campaign had vindicated his strategy. After TV networks called the election, which now had the makings of a momentous landslide, Dean walked toward the stage in Grant Park. Amid the euphoria, he spotted a young Obama staffer wearing a sticker that said "50 State Campaign."

"I like your sticker," Dean said with a satisfied grin.

6 ★ BLOWBACK

You've got to be [an] optimist to be a Democrat, and you've got to be a humorist to stay one. —Will Rogers

A month after the election, near the end of his tenure as DNC chair, Howard Dean caught a JetBlue red-eye to San Diego for the winter meeting of the state party chairs, held at the Hotel del Coronado, a massive white Victorian beachfront structure with red turrets and a dark mahogany interior that resembles a giant gingerbread castle at Disney World. The location provided the backdrop for Billy Wilder's iconic *Some Like It Hot*. It was a perfect place to throw a victory party.

Unlike four years earlier in Orlando, when the party bemoaned its losses and searched for a leader, Democrats in San Diego had plenty to celebrate. Speaking behind a giant banner of a red, white, and blue gavel (the logo for the state chairs), party leaders from New Hampshire to Kansas to Nevada described how their states had been transformed politically, with Dean's help, since 2004. The head of the Nevada Democratic Party, Sam Lieberman, proudly noted that the state Republican Party closed its office in November after running out of money, with the executive director handling operations from his parents' basement. He subsequently went into retail.

At the beginning of the gathering, the chairs passed a resolution praising Dean for taking "on all foes to defend the inherent bril-

liance" of the fifty-state strategy, and naming him "the most successful Democratic chairman in decades." Under his tenure, Democrats
elected a president and picked up six governorships, fourteen Senate
seats, fifty-five House seats, and fifteen state legislative chambers. Not
too shabby a record for someone whose political obituary had been
penned immediately following his failed presidential campaign.

"The landscape of this country has been changed," Dean said during his short speech. "President-elect Obama won nine states that
President Bush won in 2004 [three in the West, three in the Midwest,
and three in the South]. We picked up seven Senate seats and twenty-
four additional House seats [in 2008]. There are now twenty-nine
Democratic governors. Democrats control at least sixty of the ninety-
eight state legislative chambers." The party's many factions appeared
unusually united, belying Will Rogers's famous quip: "I belong to no
organized party. I am a Democrat."

"It is great to have one Democratic Party," Dean said, "from top
to bottom. I consider the top to be the grass roots and me to be at the
bottom and not the other way around." After receiving a rousing
standing ovation at the end of his remarks, the DNC chair smiled
bemusedly and took a bow.

Every state chair tasted a piece of the victory cake. Colorado's
Pat Waak wore an Obama button on her blazer, next to a brooch of
a sparkling red, blue, and silver apple, a gift from her counterpart in
New York. Any lingering tension over Dean's choice for the Democratic convention had long since subsided. Democrats in Colorado
now controlled the governor's office, five of seven congressional seats,
the state senate, and the statehouse, a total reversal from five years
earlier. "Seeing the Obama campaign pick up the fifty-state strategy,
which was already showing success, and mirroring that just kept
the momentum going for us," Waak said. On Election Day, it wasn't
even close. Obama carried Colorado's nine electoral votes by nine
points. Though he didn't win either, Obama posted the best showing of any Democratic presidential candidate in conservative Weld
and El Paso counties since 1964, registering the biggest vote shifts of

anywhere in the state. Over in the Fourth Congressional District, Betsy Markey, a successful businesswoman from Fort Collins and former aide to Senator Ken Salazar, handily defeated Marilyn Musgrave, carrying Weld County by a comfortable six points en route to a double-digit victory few saw coming. Finally, Democrats found those five thousand votes Waak had spent a decade and a half mining. In southeast Colorado Springs, a Filipino-American peace activist and community organizer, Dennis Apuan, won a stunning upset to the statehouse by 539 votes, thanks to a 10 percent increase in voter turnout from 2004. And even El Paso County overwhelmingly rejected a statewide ballot initiative pushed by the Christian Right to define a fetus as "personhood."

At the hotel bar, Indiana's Dan Parker toasted Obama's victory. "Twenty-two points!" he proclaimed, Bud in hand, referring to the difference between Bush 2004 and Obama 2008 in Indiana—from twenty-one down to one up for the Dems, the largest swing of any state. Indiana went from the first place called on Election Day to nearly the last. Obama's state director, Emily Parcell, stayed at the campaign's boiler room in downtown Indianapolis until 3:00 a.m. on election night, frantically hitting refresh on *The Indianapolis Star*'s website long after Obama's victory speech in Grant Park. She heard the news driving to work the next morning—Obama had carried the state by 28,391 votes. Despite losing both, Obama improved upon Kerry's take by 15 percent in Elkhart County and 13 percent in Hamilton County. Astoundingly, Democrats increased their margins in every county in the state. McCain won a dozen counties with populations under fifteen thousand, but Obama crushed him in cities like Indianapolis, Gary, and Bloomington. The Hoosier State turned from deep red to "baby blue," as Donna Brazile put it.

North Carolina's Jerry Meek, newly married to state representative Tricia Cotham, was off on his honeymoon, so his executive director, Caroline Valand, stood in for him in San Diego. North Carolina witnessed the closest finish and most dramatic turnaround of any state. Obama carried its fifteen electoral votes by 14,177 votes while Democrats swept competitive races for governor, Senate (the seat once held by Jesse Helms), and House. Turnout increased by 9 percent in the presidential, the largest jump in the nation, as Obama flipped thirteen counties, including Watauga and Buncombe (home to Asheville) out west, Wake (Raleigh) in the Triangle, and Pitt (Greenville) to the east. "Nobody believed it would be a battleground, maybe myself included," Valand admitted. "North Carolina really was the perfect storm of a weakened president, people very frustrated with what was going on nationally, and changes in the state."

If Indiana and North Carolina were long ignored by the national party, then a place like Alaska—three thousand miles from Washington—didn't exist. Dean was roundly mocked, including in a *New York Times Magazine* profile, for visiting and investing in the Last Frontier. "The idea that you're going to put money in a place like Alaska seemed insane," Dean said after the election, "because you could take the same amount of money and maybe win a House seat in California with it. That was the thinking here. The problem is, that's a totally short-term strategy." The DNC's investment quadrupled the full-time staff of the Alaska Democratic Party, rather humble to begin with, from one to four. Similarly important, "it made Alaskans proud to be Democrats again," said state chair Patti Higgins.

When opportunity struck, Democrats were ready. Not only did former Anchorage mayor Mark Begich knock off longtime senator Ted Stevens following his indictment (later overturned) for lying to federal investigators about accepting favors from a top campaign donor, but Democrats ran their strongest challenger in years to Alaska's lone congressman, the notoriously corrupt Don Young, who's held the seat for thirty-five years. His challenger, Ethan Berkowitz, was, of all things, an Alaskan Jew (paging Michael Chabon). A few polls even showed Obama leading in the state—with his campaign planning a visit (the first for a presidential candidate since 1960)—before McCain tapped Palin. Higgins subsequently dubbed Palin "AWOL from Alaska," which proved prophetic in more ways than one.

Obama didn't win Idaho, either. In fact, he lost by twenty-five points. But Idahoans elected a Democrat, Walt Minnick, a successful entrepreneur and former political Independent, to the deeply conservative First Congressional District—which stretches from Nevada to Canada—for the first time in fourteen years. The state Democratic Party's communications director and field organizer for northern Idaho, both funded by the fifty-state strategy, proved instrumental to Minnick's campaign. Shortly thereafter, the Obama superactivist T. J. Thomson won a seat on the Boise City Council.

Much amusement in San Diego stemmed from the news that even Republicans, having seen their strongholds reduced to the Deep South, now wanted to emulate Dean, with candidates for RNC chair and local GOP leaders proposing their own version of the fifty-state strategy. "We're gonna bring this party to every corner, every boardroom, every neighborhood, every community," the new RNC chair, Michael Steele, said in his victory speech. "Everybody laughed when Howard Dean said he was going to make the Democratic Party competitive in all 50 states," wrote John Feehery, a former top aide to Speaker of the House Dennis Hastert, after the election. "Nobody is laughing now. The fact is that Republicans are becoming dinosaurs in too many states, especially north of the Mason-Dixon line." GOP Web strategist Patrick Ruffini blogged in late December: "Republicans have come down with Howard Dean Envy."

Dean's legacy finally seemed secure. "Dean won the argument," said DNC insider Elaine Kamarck. "There's no doubt about it."

Yet Washington has a strange way of penalizing success and rewarding failure. During a speech in early December before the 92nd Street Y in New York City, an audience member asked Dean about his future plans. "I have no *idear* what's in my own future," he responded, "and that won't be determined by me." He flashed a sly grin, and the audience cheered. Dean seemed to be hinting, not so subtly, that a position in the new administration was in the cards.

And then, silence. Dean waited and waited, but his phone never rang. "The constant nothing was just hard to understand," said his chief of staff, Leah Daughtry. "There were points at which, honestly speaking, it was painful to watch."

On election night in Chicago, Dean talked with Obama confidant and former Senate majority leader Tom Daschle about joining the administration. Daschle suggested that he take the lead on health-care reform, as Obama's health czar, while Dean would run the Department of Health and Human Services (HHS), a position the DNC chair had fancied since 2000. After all, as a physician and former governor who'd extended health insurance to nearly every child and pregnant mother in Vermont, Dean understood the nuts and bolts of the health-care system better than just about anyone. "It wasn't my call," Dean said, "but I was hoping I'd get HHS." But the White House wanted Daschle to fill both positions.

With HHS taken, a few top labor officials, including the AFL-CIO's John Sweeney and SEIU's Andy Stern, floated Dean's name for secretary of labor, but after the withdrawal of Bill Richardson as commerce secretary the administration needed another high-profile Hispanic in the cabinet. Labor went to California congresswoman Hilda Solis. Daschle eventually called and offered Dean a position as director of the Office of Global Health Affairs in HHS, a backwater in the Bush administration that Daschle promised to revitalize at an ambassador level. "Tom, if I was forty or seventy, I would take it," Dean told Daschle. But he was only sixty, still in the prime of his political career, and yearned to be a major player in the coming fight for health-care reform. He didn't want to direct an international aid mission or take a largely symbolic position like surgeon general.

Then Daschle himself withdrew amid controversy. HHS opened up again. Dean allies in Congress, like Iowa senator Tom Harkin and Arizona congressman Raúl Grijalva, lobbied for him in conversations with administration officials, but Dean never made the short list. The job eventually went to the governor of Kansas, Kathleen Sebelius, an early Obama supporter. "He would've been a great HHS secretary," said Harkin, "but there were people around Obama—I don't need to mention any names—that were not about to let that happen."

There were many explanations for Dean's absence from Obama's cabinet—he was too partisan for the "post-partisan" Obama era (even if such a utopia was unlikely to be achieved in modern-day Washington), too gaffe prone, too divisive, too undisciplined—but much of the speculation led to a simple one-word rationale: Rahm.

Before Obama had even won the presidency, he asked Emanuel, the party's most outspoken critic of Dean and the fifty-state strategy, to be his chief of staff. Rahm was a groomsman at David Axelrod's wedding and knew Obama well from Chicago, where they ran in similarly high-powered circles. "We were facing an emergency," Plouffe wrote in his book, *The Audacity to Win*. "Obama would need a strong general." According to Plouffe, Obama's top brass saw in Rahm "a strategist with deep policy expertise, considerable experience in both the legislative and executive branches, and a demeanor best described as relentless."

A hawkish political centrist and cutthroat Beltway insider known for recruiting conservative Democrats to run for Congress, Rahm also had a rocky relationship with the party's base and a notorious capacity for holding a grudge. There's nobody in Washington whom he loathed more than Dean, several plugged-in Beltway observers told me. "I wouldn't describe them as key allies," John Podesta, the head of the White House transition team, said, laughing. Parag Mehta worked as the DNC's training director for three years before joining Obama's transition staff in November. Whenever he floated Dean's name for various appointments in transition meetings, he was told, "It's a nonstarter." He didn't need to ask why. For all the talk of a team of rivals, the administration, it turned out, wasn't big enough for Dean and Emanuel.

Those with firsthand knowledge of the transition process said that Emanuel, an infamous score settler, made his intentions regarding Dean perfectly clear. "There was never any intention to hire Dean, and in fact there was a great deal of satisfaction at dissing him," said a senior member of the transition team. "The orders were coming down from Rahm that Dean was not to be considered for anything [high-ranking] and he didn't want anything to do with him." Podesta, a former chief of staff to Bill Clinton and president of the Center for American Progress, offered a different take on how things went down. "We talked about Dean for a variety of jobs in the administration, and indeed he was offered some jobs," Podesta said. "So I don't think he was blackballed. But in terms of trying to put together a balanced cabinet, he wasn't a must-have, either." Obama, not Emanuel, made all of the final appointment decisions, Podesta said.

On January 7, White House political director Patrick Gaspard, a former top labor organizer from New York, called DNC executive director Tom McMahon. Gaspard told McMahon that Obama planned to name Virginia governor Tim Kaine as his new DNC chair and wanted to make the announcement at the DNC the following day. Gaspard asked if Dean would be around.

Dean's planning to be in American Samoa, the last U.S. territory he'd yet to visit as DNC chair, McMahon responded. (He'd logged 741,000 miles on the job.) Should he postpone his trip?

If he's already planning the trip, don't tell him to cancel, Gaspard replied. It would be better, in other words, if Dean wasn't there. Administration officials didn't want Obama to face any questions at the press conference about why Dean hadn't received a plum position in the White House. One snub led to another.

Gaspard, ironically, worked on Dean's campaign in 2004, but now served a higher office. "The decision was made by Rahm and Plouffe and [deputy chief of staff] Jim Messina," said the senior transition member. "I was specifically told by a senior administration official, 'It comes from those three guys. They specifically want to do this to Dean.'" Even the new Camelot wasn't above a little revenge.

Dean was 5,798 miles away in Pago Pago when Obama introduced Kaine. It was a surreal scene—Obama and Kaine praising the outgoing DNC chair while he was on the other side of the world.

(Administration officials attributed Dean's absence to a scheduling conflict.) "Having steered the Democratic Party through two successful elections, Howard deserves enormous credit for ushering in a new era in Washington," Obama said. He called Dean a "visionary and effective leader" and "an outstanding chair." He also thanked him, rather bizarrely, for "working with my chief of staff Rahm Emanuel" in 2006.

"I've got huge shoes to fill," Kaine added.

Dean's communication's director, Karen Finney, listened in dismay from the back of the room. "It was so kind and gracious what Obama said," she remarked. "And I was like, why couldn't he say that with Dean standing there?"

Dean, ever the stoic WASP, refused to publicly talk about his rough dismissal. But privately he fumed. "Some of those Obama guys have very sharp elbows," he told Vermont's attorney general, Bill Sorrell. When another friend broached the topic, Dean responded angrily, "I don't want to talk about those assholes."

His close friends and family were deeply hurt by the turn of events. "I thought the press conference was disgraceful," said his younger brother Jim, who runs Democracy for America. "It was so incredibly petty. Obviously he deserved better." Even Joe Trippi sympathized with his estranged former boss. "He's no saint," Trippi said, "but nothing justifies the shit they've done to him." When asked if he felt "vindicated" by the success of the fifty-state strategy, Dean jested, "I might have been right, but I'd rather be chief of staff."

Obama's kind words on election night notwithstanding, his inner circle didn't seem particularly eager to credit Dean with laying the groundwork for Obama's victory. Plouffe disliked Dean from his days working for Gephardt, privately blamed him for the lengthy controversy over Florida and Michigan during the primary, and mentioned the DNC chair only in passing in his book. "They hate it when Obama is called Dean 2.0," one Dean staffer told me. The administration regarded Dean's large and boisterous following, which couldn't always be controlled, as a bothersome nuisance.

"A year in which Democrats were running against a party freighted by the most unpopular president in history—and amid an economic collapse—is probably not the best laboratory for measuring the success of his experiment," Adam Nagourney of *The New York Times* wrote of Dean in a skeptical postelection analysis. "The argument that Mr. Dean's actions set the stage for Mr. Obama's broad win in a presidential campaign may prove more problematic." Nagourney's article reflected the prevailing or once prevalent opinions among many of Washington's current and former ruling class, who looked askance at Dean and his strategy. In his latest book, *40 More Years: How the Democrats Will Rule the Next Generation*, James Carville, continuing his jeremiad, maintained that "the revitalization of the Democratic Party has occurred despite, not because of, Howard Dean's disastrous tenure as DNC chair." The new regime, much like the old, still regarded Dean as more of a crazy uncle than a political visionary. "You know the expression 'to be a prophet without honor in your own land,'" said former DNC chair Steve Grossman. "That's Howard Dean."

Dean's snub didn't matter because of one man's bruised ego or thwarted ambitions. Rather, his shabby treatment would come to represent a broader abandonment of the party's grassroots base, especially as Obama packed his White House with well-worn veterans of previous administrations who embodied longevity over innovation and connections over change—quite an irony given his critique of Hillary as a washed-up Washington insider during the primary. Obama's administration soon bore an eerie resemblance to Clinton III, with a little bit of Bush here and there.

A day after Obama's inauguration, Dean officially passed the party's chairmanship to Kaine during the DNC's winter meeting at the Marriott in Washington's leafy Woodley Park. Dean liked Kaine, put $5 million into his campaign for governor in 2005, and recommended him as a successor. But the Virginia governor, with his flat-top haircut and background as a missionary in Honduras and as a civil rights lawyer in Richmond, in some ways was everything Dean was not: disciplined, uncontroversial, easygoing, and amiable. Obama's team viewed his blandness as an asset. In a tightly wound White House that valued orderliness above all else, Kaine would make few, if any, waves and take his cues from the top.

"The fifty-state strategy was so simple and so powerful and so true," Kaine said in his gracious opening remarks. "We'll do some new things," he said of the new regime, "because we can never rest on just what worked yesterday, but we will never again, *never again*, write off people or states or regions. The fifty-state strategy," he said emphatically, "is now and forever what Democrats do!"

Hundreds of DNC members erupted in applause. The torch had been passed, and Dean's overarching philosophy still prospered, even if the particulars of his strategy would soon be altered as the former DNC chair once again found himself on the outside peering in. Now came a new test: Could the party's big-tent coalition actually govern?

Heath Shuler rose quickly in Congress, the prize recruit of Rahm's class of 2006. Rahm called his freshmen "moderate in temperament and reformers in spirit." Shuler, the tan and hunky star quarterback, had once been wooed by the GOP while living in Tennessee, but he chose to run as a Democrat, though you wouldn't know it from some of his political stances. "The Democratic Party helps those who cannot help themselves," he said. "That's the Christian that I am." He joined the Blue Dog Coalition of conservative Democrats when he arrived in Congress, shortly thereafter becoming a member of its leadership and whipping votes for the caucus. While in D.C., the devout Southern Baptist stayed at the Capitol Hill town house on C Street run by the secretive Christian right group the Family, bunking with high-profile conservative Republicans like Oklahoma senator Tom Coburn and South Carolina senator Jim DeMint (not to mention disgraced Nevada senator John Ensign, who had an affair with the wife of his top political aide). In his first two years in Congress, Shuler became best known for introducing a tough immigration bill—the Secure America Through Verification and Enforcement (SAVE) Act—that advocated adding eight thousand federal agents on the U.S.-Mexico border, at a cost of $40 billion over ten years, which he touted before Glenn Beck and Lou Dobbs. In his first term, Shuler also voted against legislation to pursue stem cell research, crack down on hate crimes, and expand health care for children, ranking as the most prolific contrarian in the Democrats' freshman class.

Shuler initially backed John Edwards in 2008 but was none too enthusiastic about his party's presidential candidates as the primary churned on, endorsing Clinton only after she carried his Eleventh Congressional District in the North Carolina primary. He scarcely campaigned for Obama in Western North Carolina during the general and was conspicuously absent at most Democratic Party functions. After Obama's election, Shuler enhanced his dissident bona fides by voting against the president's stimulus package, bank and auto bailouts, Consumer Financial Protection Agency, and health-care reform legislation. (He did vote for the pro-union Employee Free Choice Act and legislation to combat global warming, calling the latter "consistent with two of my highest priorities, protecting God's creation and reducing our national debt.") "No Democrat has done quite so much in so short a time to arouse [Nancy] Pelosi's disdain," *Politico* reported.

Yet Shuler was less of an outlier than you might think. There were now dozens of Heath Shulers in Washington, the beneficiaries of the fifty-state strategy's incursion into red America. They quickly became the Democratic Party's leading internal antagonists, causing legislative stalemate in Congress and casting doubt on the viability of a long-term Democratic and progressive majority. Dean- and Obama-inspired activists soon found themselves in similar quandaries across the country, at odds with the once-promising representatives they helped elect.

Unlike some of his fellow Blue Dogs, Shuler didn't have to worry as much about his own reelection. Obama ran surprisingly strong in his fifteen counties, flipping two and barely losing three others deep in the heart of the Smoky Mountains near Tennessee. Although McCain won the district by five points overall, Shuler coasted to re-election by twenty-six points. As a popular hometown football star, he could probably keep his seat as long as he wanted, absent a major scandal or slipup. Though he begged off for a Senate run in 2010, a bid for higher office seemed likely in the not-too-distant future.

Democratic activists in WNC, however, were none too pleased with Shuler's voting record in Congress and had begun to voice their frustrations. Margaret Johnson and Polk County Democrats worked their tails off for Shuler in 2006, holding multiple fund-raisers and public events on his behalf. "We're so disappointed in Shuler," she told me at Democratic headquarters in Columbus, shaking her head. "We laugh when we think about all that we did for him."

In August 2009, Johnson invited Shuler down for a luncheon to discuss health-care reform. She rented out a social hall in a Methodist church in Tryon, F. Scott Fitzgerald's old haunt, and served chicken salad stuffed in fresh tomatoes, picked by a group of sweet elderly ladies at a nearby farm. Eighteen people filled the room, including three ministers, a doctor, a nurse, an attorney who'd held a big fund-raiser for Shuler, and the county's top Democratic organizers.

At the beginning of the lunch, Johnson asked the people in the room to introduce themselves. After the second speaker, Shuler interrupted and took over the gathering. He criticized the health-care bill before the House of Representatives and claimed that energy and commerce chairman Henry Waxman had written it himself (even though the Blue Dog leader Mike Ross consulted extensively on the final draft). When asked why he didn't support a public insurance option to compete with private insurers, Shuler repeatedly said it didn't have enough votes to pass the House. "Why don't you personally support it?" asked Wally Hughes, a forty-two-year-old builder and the local party's liaison to Organizing for America (OFA), the postelection arm of the Obama campaign. Shuler cited the "waste, fraud and abuse" in Medicare—a popular right-wing talking point—and claimed, erroneously, it turned out, that certain doctors in the rural parts of his district wouldn't accept it. He said he trusted private insurers to run health care better than the government.

In 2006, Polk County Democrats printed up T-shirts listing the historic achievements of the Democratic Party—equal rights, Social Security, a minimum wage, Medicare, and so forth. Mary Hardvall, a retired IBM administrator, asked Shuler to sign her shirt when he ran for Congress. "I was so proud to have the T-shirt you signed," she told him at the meeting, holding up the shirt, "and I want to add universal health care to that list."

Shuler just rolled his eyes. When Todd Neel, a nurse practitioner who worked with hospice patients, pressed Shuler on the public option, the congressman turned to his right-hand man, Randy Flack, and said loudly, "This is like talking to a brick wall."

Polk County Dems had come not to expect much of their congressman, but this kind of disrespect was beyond anyone's comprehension. Ted Kennedy had passed away that week, and Johnson noted at the end of the gathering that health-care reform was the cause of his life. "Mr. Shuler, we're counting on you," Johnson said. "You're our Ted Kennedy."

Before Shuler could get a word in, local attorney Jim Carson responded, "You're no Ted Kennedy!" reprising Lloyd Bentsen's famous riposte to Dan Quayle in 1988. The quip summarized the feelings of everyone in the room.

She saw Shuler off politely, but Johnson couldn't believe how rude her guest had been. "He did not want to hear anything we said," she said after. "It's not like we were being hostile or jumping down his throat. He was jumping down our throat. He was belligerent to the people who helped elect him. It really took the wind out of our sails. A lot of our staunch Yellow Dog Democrats are saying, 'We'll never vote for him again.'"

It wasn't as if Shuler had been challenged by protesters from

Code Pink. Johnson and her ilk were well-mannered, hardworking, modest folk of populist inclination—the very types of people Shuler once claimed he wanted to represent in Congress. Now he'd totally disowned them. "He never even said thank you for the food," Johnson remarked.

Shuler seemed to get on better with WNC's right-wing Tea Party movement, whom he warmly met with for over an hour that August, promising to vote against health-care legislation in the House—even though 23 percent of his constituents lacked health insurance. He accepted more money from the health-care industry during his re-election campaign than any other North Carolina Democrat in the House, according to the watchdog group Democracy North Carolina. The small-donor revolution of the Dean and Obama campaigns had yet to trickle down to Congress. Onetime populists like Shuler still routinely did the bidding of the big corporations that funded their campaigns.

Johnson's dealings with Shuler only heightened her broader fear that a small clique of old-guard Democrats were reclaiming their hold on the party in the state. Since Mark Hufford stepped down as a DNC organizer after the 2006 election, Johnson barely saw his replacement, Freddie Harrill, who was said to be a favorite of the Shulerites. Jerry Meek left after 2008 too, accepting a job with a topflight law firm in Raleigh. The new chair, David Young—a county commissioner from Asheville with a scant grassroots following who unsuccessfully ran for state treasurer—had been largely handpicked by the party's previous executive director from the pre-Meek era, Scott Falmlen, a prominent political consultant in Raleigh. Meek's past executive director, Caroline Valand, happened to be dating the new one, Andrew Whalen, Shuler's former communications director. It was hard to imagine a more incestuous tangle. "We worked so dang hard to get our voices heard," Johnson said. "I'm really worried it'll go back to the way it was, that we'll backslide."

Democrats accepted Shuler's apostasy for a while. He was the only kind of Democrat who could win in a place like WNC, everybody said. But the Obama campaign gave Democratic activists a new lease on life. Shuler now seemed like a "perfect rebound relationship" following Chainsaw Charlie Taylor, wrote the Asheville city councilman and progressive blogger Gordon Smith—it was thrilling for a time, but the antics had gotten old. Local Democrats wanted someone they could trust. Maybe they could do better than Shuler, or at least get him to pay attention to their views. What good was a Democratic congressman, they asked themselves, if he voted against nearly every major piece of legislation the leader of his party unveiled?

Paul Choi, an art director and graphic designer by trade, led the Obama activists in the area, co-founding WNC for Obama in the fall of 2007. Choi was born in Asheville, spent most of his childhood in Fayetteville, and returned west in 2006, at twenty-nine. Born to Korean parents, he wore bookish black rectangular glasses and a long hanging beard. He'd never been politically active before and used to tell people in college that it was his right not to vote, chalking his disaffected attitude up to a "naiveté of youth." But after reading Obama's announcement speech with tears in his eyes, inspired by the candidate's call to national greatness, Choi immediately signed up on MyBO, made his first political donation, and attended his first political meeting shortly thereafter.

WNC for Obama grew from a dedicated group of twenty scattered volunteers at the start of the primaries to a well-oiled machine of seven hundred recruits from across the region by the end of the election, helping to register nine thousand new Democrats in Asheville's Buncombe County in 2008. Under the leadership of local party chair Kathy Sinclair, Democratic activists covered every nook and cranny in the county. Obama carried Buncombe by seventeen thousand votes on election night, flipping the county from narrowly red to solidly blue, and Democrats swept every race on the ballot, thirty-six for thirty-six. Afterward, Choi won election to the local party and became a paid staffer with OFA, working alongside a reconstituted WNC for Obama, now called WNC for Change.

Choi took a friendly approach to Shuler when they first met in June 2009. He pitched the idea of making the congressman a spokesman for a national prevention and wellness program for kids. "You're probably the most fit member of Congress," Choi told him. The former football star loved the proposal, but ultimately wasn't convinced to support the broader bill. So Choi and his supporters tried another tack, delivering a petition with five thousand names in support of health-care reform to Shuler's staff and flooding his office with two thousand calls on one day in late October before the House vote. Though Shuler rebuffed the entreaties, Choi told his volunteers, "Keep calling, keep calling." He ate lunch with Shuler's mentor, Randy Flack, once a month to maintain a lifeline to the congressman. "It can't hurt to keep putting pressure on him," Choi said, "despite what his ultimate votes are." He'd opened local OFA chapters in seven surrounding counties, giving Obama activists a wider footprint in the district.

The fifteen Democratic county chairs from across the Eleventh Congressional District, on the other hand, were running out of patience. They met monthly at a Methodist retreat center in Waynesville, Shuler's adopted hometown, nestled in the valley of the Blue Ridge Mountains, on the banks of beautiful Lake Junaluska. Increasingly, the gatherings had become a forum for the local chairs to express their frustration with Shuler and his staff. A meeting in March 2009 took place just after Shuler voted against the stimulus bill, citing its expansion of the deficit and lack of bipartisanship. The chairs were none too pleased that Shuler had cast his first major vote of the new Congress against President Obama—a bad omen of things to come. "In the middle of a recession, sometimes you have to spend money to make money," Marshall McCallie, the chair of Transylvania County, heatedly told Shuler's chief of staff, Hayden Rogers. "Your argument isn't holding water in this economy."

Kathy Sinclair looked across WNC and saw defunct factories and dormant lumberyards in decaying mountain towns. She worked for the state employment commission and knew firsthand how the unemployment picture, pretty bleak to begin with, kept getting worse. The area desperately needed some help—and the stimulus, while imperfect, promised to pump nearly $450 million into Shuler's district and save or create seventy-five hundred jobs, according to the White House. She'd heard just about enough excuses from the Shulerites. "I'm not sure he is really representing his constituents of Western North Carolina," she said. "I didn't vote for him last time, and I won't vote for him next time."

Shuler showed up at one of the chair meetings that July. Once again, he criticized Pelosi and the Democrats' health-care bill, saying he hadn't been adequately consulted. "People in our district are suffering," Johnson told him, "and we need health-care reform—not in the future, but now." Shuler stayed for fifteen minutes and left, saying he had to go babysit his kids.

Local leaders like Johnson and Sinclair prayed that, down the road, somebody better would take Shuler's place. Johnson hoped he'd at least draw a challenger in a Democratic primary. "He's gotta not take us so for granted," she said. Shuler's unpopularity among Democratic activists, she believed, hurt down-ticket Democrats and threatened the prospects of the party in the region. "I'd rather have a real Republican than a fake Democrat," Johnson said. "A real Republican motivates us to work. A fake Democrat de-motivates us."

The Obama activists argued that WNC, though hardly a hotbed of left-wing liberalism, had grown more receptive to a Democratic message. Just look at all the new Democrats registered and the number of previously disengaged organizers. "I don't think it's as conservative as he thinks it is," Sinclair said of the district.

Shuler, on the other hand, bet that Obama hadn't changed his turf much or at all—and Democrats could succeed in formerly red areas only by continually bowing to conservative interests in Washington and back home. A good chunk of congressional Democrats from across the country, particularly down south and out west, evidently concurred. The thirty-nine House Democrats who voted against health-care reform in October 2009 included some of the unlikely faces of the Democratic supermajority: western Idaho's Walt Minnick, northern Mississippi's Travis Childers, western Pennsylvania's Jason Altmire. Over 80 percent of them represented districts won by McCain that were more rural (and white) than the nation as a whole. (The situation was even worse in the Senate, where a few senators from small red states like Nebraska, North Dakota, and Arkansas, elected before Dean became chair and Obama entered the Senate, could essentially hijack the entire caucus, derailing or watering down nearly every piece of meaningful legislation proposed by the party leadership.) Is this what the fifty-state strategy hath wrought? Had improbable success led to inevitable malaise? And, if so, did Dean deserve some of the blame?

Dean challenged Emanuel on how the party should win elections but not on what kinds of candidates they should support. "It's not like I had a preference for one ideology over another," Emanuel said. "It was pure winning." And Dean himself famously and inartfully proclaimed, during his presidential campaign, that he wanted "to be the candidate for guys with Confederate flags in their pickup trucks." The Shulers of the world were about as close as the party would ever get. Desperate to retake Congress, a broad spectrum of Democrats backed candidates who opposed gun control, a woman's right to choose, gay rights, and immigration reform and broke with the party's leadership on core issues of guns and butter. That trend continued into 2008 as dreams of a supermajority expanded. Apostasy once they got to Congress shouldn't have come as a surprise. Governing seemed almost like an afterthought.

Despite the continued defections of red-state Democrats in Congress, Dean didn't question his original electoral strategy. "I'd never back off from the fifty-state strategy," he told me. "If you want to have a majority, you have to be a big-tent party." But he'd recently been pondering the flaws in the tent's construction. "Having a big, open tent Democratic Party is great, but not at the cost of getting nothing done," he said. "Bipartisanship is wonderful but not at the cost of passing legislation that doesn't do anything."

The Republicans had become obsessed with ideological purity, losing their majorities and staggering in the wilderness as a consequence, but Democrats, if anything, weren't ideological enough. Their red-state contingent had so blurred what it meant to be a Democrat that the party itself could barely see. A whole crew of Democrats now roamed the halls of Congress—and, increasingly, the corridors of the White House—standing for little else but political expediency. "That's what makes me nervous about the political process right now," Dean admitted, "because there's always been a streak in D.C. of, do what it takes to get elected, and if that means abandoning issues, go ahead. And that's dangerous because it makes any incumbent worthless." He'd recently been thinking that Democrats might be better off with a smaller and more ideologically cohesive majority—the type of arresting admission you rarely hear from an influential member of the ruling party. "If you have a majority of say sixty people in the Senate, but you can't deliver anything, why not have a majority of fifty-five and not have all this intraparty feuding?" he wondered.

Dean had a favorite saying about political majorities. "If you don't use it," he said, "you lose it."

After stepping down as DNC chair, Dean, failing to land the one job he coveted, pursued many. He joined a high-powered Washington law firm on K Street (which D.C.'s much-reviled lobbyists call home), gave speeches to international political parties overseas, debated the likes of Newt Gingrich and Karl Rove back home before college campuses and business groups, started a charter school with the United Federation of Teachers in the tough Brooklyn ghetto of East New York, consulted for his old group Democracy for America, and, chief among his passions, tried to remain a player in the ongoing fight for health-care reform.

In the middle of February 2009, Dean got a call from David Axelrod, who asked him to come over to the White House for a meeting. The administration was in the midst of picking a new HHS secretary to replace Daschle. "It's not a done deal," Axelrod told Dean. Maybe he still had a shot.

Dean didn't believe him—that day's *New York Times* named Sebelius "the president's top choice"—but he went anyway, interested to hear what the president's top advisers had to say. He toured Emanuel's office, exchanged pleasantries with his old nemesis, whom he'd barely spoken to in two years, and admired a nameplate on the chief of staff's dresser—"Undersecretary for Go Fuck Yourself," it read, an office-warming gift from his two brothers. Over lunch in the chief of staff's office, the three talked about health-care reform and how Dean could help the administration pass a bill. Axelrod and Emanuel wanted to make sure the former DNC chair wouldn't cause the new administration any trouble.

Dean, in fact, was initially quite enthused about Obama's health-care plan, which he called "the most practical, most likely-to-succeed plan I've seen in thirty years." Obama's proposal included the choice of a public insurance option administered by the government, like Medicare, for those Americans who couldn't afford private insurance. Dean believed the public option, as it rather blandly came to be known, was essential to any reform effort. Emanuel and Axelrod weren't so sure. At the meeting, they floated the idea of adding a public option only if private insurers failed to lower costs after a defined period of time. They believed such a "trigger" would play better in Congress. Dean thought a trigger was just a clever way for insurance companies to prevent real competition and pad their profits; they'd rig the system so that the trigger never kicked in. Dean worried, from that moment on, that top administration officials weren't fully committed to pursuing true and lasting health-care reform, a key aspiration of the Democratic Party for the past half century and a centerpiece of Obama's domestic agenda. They wanted to declare victory—no matter what the final bill looked like—and move on. "The Obama people were split," Dean said. "The president really wanted to do health-care reform, and some on his staff were less enthusiastic. And that showed, much to my surprise."

Five weeks later, Dean read an article in *The New Republic* that confirmed his suspicions. Some of Obama's top advisers, including Axelrod, worried that voters cared only about the rising cost of health care, not the escalating number of uninsured Americans, forty-five million and counting. After Obama's election, "a debate raged inside the administration," reported Jonathan Cohn, "with some senior officials arguing that the new president should wade into health care gingerly—or even postpone it altogether—because it would cost too much, distract from other priorities, and carry huge political risks." Obama himself broke the impasse. The American people had waited long enough, he said. It was time to act.

As health-care legislation twisted and turned through Congress in the following year, however, the fight over reform exposed fundamental fissures in the Democrats' governing coalition and raised deeper questions about the priorities of the Obama administration, concerns that weren't likely to dissipate anytime soon. Dean found himself in a somewhat unlikely position, becoming a sharp critic, at times, of an administration and Congress he helped elect.

Three committees in the House and one in the Senate passed portions of the health-care legislation rather swiftly, but things bogged down when the powerful Senate Finance Committee, which largely determines how the government raises and spends its money, took up its own bill. Montana senator Max Baucus chaired the committee. Baucus, long a cautious and conservative creature who backed Bush's tax cuts in 2001 and the Medicare privatization bill in 2003, had a well-deserved reputation as "K Street's favorite Democrat," according to *The Nation*, with a plethora of former staffers ensconced as health-care industry lobbyists. His chief health-care adviser used to be a top executive at the insurance behemoth Well-Point. Reformers like Dean naturally viewed Baucus with suspicion.

But the Obama administration, which recruited Baucus's former chief of staff Jim Messina as Rahm's lead enforcer, seemed oddly accommodating of the Montana senator, giving him months and months to craft a bill to his liking in closed-door fashion, with two Democrats and three Republicans of his choosing. The Finance Committee now set the agenda, and Baucus wanted to jettison any talk of a public option.

In June 2009, as debate over the bill heated up, Dean and fifteen thousand universal-health-care advocates, mostly union members in bright red and yellow shirts, held a boisterous rally on Capitol Hill. Dean looked and sounded as if he were back on the campaign trail, sleeves rolled up and hoarse voice raised. "We are here," Dean feistily announced from a small stage in front of the Capitol. "We're not going away. We voted for change a few months ago. We expect change. And if we don't get it, there's going to be more change!" Yet as Tea Party protests exploded during the August congressional recess, the administration kept distancing itself from Obama's original plan, particularly the public option, which had become a lightning rod on both sides of the political spectrum.

When Baucus finally unveiled his bill in September, absent a public option but mandating that every American purchase insurance, Dean reacted with dismay. "The Baucus bill is the worst piece of health-care legislation I've seen in 30 years," he said bluntly. "It's a $60 billion giveaway to the health insurance industry every year." Never one for subtlety, he added, "This is a bill that George Bush would love." Two months later, after modified legislation passed the House, Dean predicted a "revolt" inside the party if the Senate failed to pass a bill or approved a largely meaningless one. The former DNC chair urged Democrats not to donate to the party's election committees, while Democracy for America launched a campaign urging renegade Democratic senators not to filibuster the legislation. "New Campaign Highlights Growing Rift Between Grassroots Liberals and the Democratic Party," the blog Talking Points Memo reported. "If we don't have a choice [of a public option], this bill is worthless and should be defeated," Dean stated in late November, a year after Obama's triumphant election.

With the public option causing an impasse in Congress, Dean suggested to Senate majority leader Harry Reid that the Senate lower the age of eligibility for Medicare from sixty-five to fifty-five as a substitute, an idea Dean first proposed on his presidential campaign that would drastically expand the pool of Americans in the government-health-care pipeline. "I'll sell it to the left and you can sell it to the holdouts," Dean told Reid and New York senator Chuck Schumer. Reid added a provision allowing younger Americans to buy subsidized insurance through Medicare, and the various wings of the party expressed satisfaction with the compromise. "It wasn't as comprehensive as the public option, but it took us in a good direction," Dean said.

Yet a few days later, as Dean sailed the Caribbean on a cruise sponsored by *The Nation*, perennial mischief maker Joe Lieberman threatened to filibuster the bill unless Reid removed the public option *and* Medicare provision. Shortly thereafter, Emanuel visited Reid in the Capitol and told him to accede to Lieberman's demands. The White House wanted a bill passed by Christmas, no matter the particulars. Dean was furious. He called Axelrod and told him that the bill in its current form was a "disaster" that he could no longer support.

"Would you please not go out with this today?" Axelrod urged him.

"I can't do that," Dean responded.

Axelrod put Nancy-Ann DeParle, director of the White House Office of Health Reform, on the line. Dean remained unconvinced by her arguments. "It was the Washington way of doing things—they were trying to let me think that some reform stuff was in the bill that wasn't really there," he said. "I just concluded that this thing had gone so far down the tracks that it was an insurance company bill and not a health-care bill." From the airport in San Juan, Dean told Vermont Public Radio: "This is essentially the collapse of health-care reform in the United States Senate. And, honestly, the best thing to do right now is kill the Senate bill." Dean advocated that Democrats pass a good bill with fifty-one votes, through legislative maneuvering known as reconciliation, rather than a bad one with sixty votes. His critique circulated far and wide. Liberal Democrats amplified Dean's argument, while devilishly opportunistic Republicans, from Rush Limbaugh to John McCain, appropriated his words.

White House press secretary Robert Gibbs lashed out at Dean at a press briefing the next day. "I don't know what piece of legislation he's reading," Gibbs said. "I think if you talk to members of the Senate that represent a similar viewpoint in the political spectrum that Howard Dean does, they seem to disagree as much with Howard Dean as I think we would." Curiously, administration officials were far more steamed at Dean for criticizing a battered bill than they were at Lieberman for blowing up a health-care compromise he once supported. "They don't seem to be too angry at Lieberman, they're reserving their fervor for Howard Dean," NBC's White House correspondent Savannah Guthrie reported. "They're mad as hell," Dean acknowledged.

Many Washington pundits followed the White House line. "Has Howard Dean lost his mind?" asked the *Washington Post* columnist Ruth Marcus. ("I'll call you from the asylum," Dean joked to MSNBC host Joe Scarborough.) That Sunday, Axelrod and Dean squared off on back-to-back segments on *Meet the Press*. Axelrod, who earlier in the week called liberal opposition to the bill "insane," noted his "respect" for Dean but said that "he just wasn't familiar with some of the aspects of this legislation . . . when you look at the bill in its totality, it doesn't square up with his critique."

Dean responded that the legislation had been improved since he first spoke out from Puerto Rico, but remained structurally flawed. "Here's the major problem," he said. "In an unseemly scramble for votes that have nothing to do with long-range public policy, we have really essentially cut out the idea that Americans will have a choice of a different kind of insurance system." Dean called the debate within the party "a very, very, very sore one." He felt that no matter how unpopular his provocative opinion, someone had to draw a line in the sand. As the administration dissed him, the gulf between Obama and his base kept widening. A poll by the Progressive Change Campaign Committee in late December found that 87 percent of Democrats—and 63 percent of Americans—believed Obama didn't fight hard enough against Lieberman and for the public option. "We've had enough," Dean said at the time. "We've been lied to, compromised, and nobody gives a damn about us." If he had been in Obama's cabinet, Dean later said, he would have resigned in protest. Despite a prolonged economic downturn, Dean viewed health-care reform as the defining issue for the Obama administration and Democratic Congress. "If we can't get health care done right, I think we lose our congressional majority," he predicted. "And then I think next election, President Obama's reelection is in doubt."

As the new year began, Dean toned down his criticism and cautiously supported the efforts of House and Senate Democrats to merge a final bill for Obama to sign. "I got fed up with the right wing making stuff up all the time and I thought that the president needed a win," he said. "Do I think it's a particularly good bill? No. Do I think much more could have been done? Yes. But at the end of the day you either support it or you don't, and I know which team I'm on." But even as legislation passed both houses of Congress, negotiations on a final bill broke down after Scott Brown's upset victory in Massachusetts denied Senate Democrats their crucial sixtieth vote. Brown campaigned vigorously against Obama's health-care plan (an irony given its similarities to what already existed, and Brown supported, in Massachusetts), provoking panic among skittish Washington Democrats.

In the aftermath of Brown's win, dazed congressional Democrats such as Barney Frank eulogized the legislation while Rahm Emanuel pushed for a scaled-back "skinny bill." Obama said little, and the White House seemed gripped by passivity, unsure how to proceed. But a wide spectrum of reform-minded Democrats, from Pelosi to Plouffe to Dean, argued that abandoning health-care reform now, after a year of debate and passage of bills by the House and the Senate, would have a catastrophic effect on Obama's presidency, the Democratic majority, and the country writ large. They pushed for one last up or down vote on a merged House-Senate bill, which the president embraced, persuaded by the urgency of the moment. Discombobulation gave way to hardened resolve, especially in the face of unanimous Republican opposition. "We deserve a vote!" Dean said at an animated rally of reform advocates in downtown Washington in early March, on the same day the health insurance industry held its annual conference at the Ritz-Carlton in Georgetown. "This is a vote about one thing—are you for the insurance companies or are you for the American people?"

Obama inserted himself into the discussion like never before—skillfully debating House Republicans, leading a high-profile bipartisan summit of members of Congress, forcefully making his case in rallies across the country, and personally lobbying more than ninety House Democrats. Here was the inspiring and persuasive president his supporters expected to see from day one. "He proved that he was willing to stand up and do what it took," Dean said. "I, and a lot of other people, had my doubts."

On the night of March 19, sixty-one days after Brown's victory, House Democrats, by a vote of 219 to 214, passed the Senate bill and an additional package of fixes for the Senate to adopt. "Tonight, at a time when the pundits said it was no longer possible, we rose above the weight of our politics," a jubilant Obama said in his midnight remarks from the East Room of the White House. The next morning, Dean called the vote "a huge win for the president," adding, "no one should underestimate how big of a deal this is for the Democratic Party." Four days later, the Senate, following Dean's earlier recommendation, passed the House modifications with 56 votes through reconciliation. Though the process and final legislation left a lot to be desired, it turned out that Democrats were indeed "capable of doing big things and tackling our biggest challenges," as Obama put it.

Still, the full aftershocks of the health-care bill wouldn't be felt for quite some time. A year of infighting and inaction had left Obama's party and presidency in a precarious position, despite an ultimately triumphant and historic vote. During thirteen months of contentious debate, the tension between party subsidizers and climate changers inside the Democratic coalition once again rose to the surface. Dean had wanted to be a climate changer during his run for the presidency and stint as chairman of the party, but had he become a party subsidizer instead, helping to elect a bunch of Democrats who didn't share his values? "Once in a while," Dean admitted, he felt that way. "There's some people, and I won't name who they are, who do things where I'd be happy to exchange them for a Republican." He needed to get the party back in power, Dean believed, before he could change it. "We're going to have a Democratic House, Democratic Senate, and a Democratic president," he said as DNC chair, "and we have to hold their feet to the fire to make sure they do the right thing."

With Obama in charge, though, Dean could influence the party only so much. He was a player at the periphery. And it was sometimes difficult to tell which side the president was on. "My sense is," Obama at one point told Plouffe during the campaign, "that Barack Hussein Obama is change enough for people." He ran as a voice for the grass roots during his presidential campaign, but stacked his cabinet with familiar faces from the Clinton White House and Bush dynasties after the election. "What we are going to do is combine experience with fresh thinking," Obama said. "But understand where the vision for change comes from first and foremost. It comes from me." But Obama himself, startling as his name and image were, couldn't alone change Washington. The new president failed to grasp that his administration would indeed become the sum of its parts. If candidate Obama had said, "I'm running for president to appoint

Hillary Clinton as secretary of state, Rahm Emanuel as chief of staff, Larry Summers as chief economic adviser, Tim Geithner as treasury secretary, and Jim Jones as national security adviser and to keep Bob Gates at the Pentagon," it's hard to imagine he would have enjoyed such enthusiastic support.

Equally troublesome, Obama often displayed a remarkable measure of deference in his dealings with Congress, where institutional inertia almost always trumps innovation. The decision to stock his administration with weathered fixtures of the Beltway establishment and rely on a much-despised legislative branch to slice and dice his ambitious agenda particularly baffled his grassroots backers, given that Obama entered the presidency with a unique eloquence, massive electoral majority, and unprecedented network of politically active supporters. He could've rewritten the rules for how to govern in the twenty-first century, or at least tried. Instead, throughout his first year in office, Obama seemed more like a tepid stabilizer than a great transformer, tweaking the status quo here and there rather than shaking up a corrupt, rotten system. His eventual assertiveness on health care encouraged and excited his supporters, but questions remained about the president's resolve on a host of other fronts.

"Is this really a reform administration or just a much more enlightened administration than what we've had before?" Dean asked. "We don't know the answer to that yet." The fate of the Democratic Party and the country hung in the balance, and there would be plenty more battles ahead. "The election of Obama," Dean said, "is the beginning, not the end."

EPILOGUE: THE NEXT FRONTIER

*The first rule of change is controversy. You can't get away from it,
for the simple reason of, all issues are controversial. Change means
movement, movement means friction, friction means heat,
and heat means controversy. —Saul Alinsky*

On a clear evening in August 2009, a dozen Obama supporters gathered at Julia Demanett's green split-level house in Colorado Springs. They wore stickers that said "I Voted for Change" and spent the Wednesday night calling fellow Obama supporters, urging them to lobby their elected officials in support of the president's health-care reform legislation. A spirited blonde in her late thirties originally from Shenandoah, Iowa, Demanett had been organizing for Obama since the beginning of the primaries, starting her own group, One VO1CE, named after Obama's popular refrain "If one voice can change a room . . ." She lived in a sloping, picturesque subdivision called Antelope Creek, just a few miles away from Focus on the Family in the city's heavily Republican Great White North. "This is totally Focus territory," Demanett said. "We're surrounded."

On Election Day, a large contingent of Obama supporters had assembled at her house for a last round of voter outreach. One of her neighbors, a firefighter, knocked on her door. "So, you're helping to elect that terrorist?" he asked her.

She thought he was joking. After all, he'd been perfectly friendly before. "Yeah, you want to help?" she responded.

"No," he said gruffly. He held a clipboard in his hand.

"Are you campaigning for McCain?" she asked.

"No, I'm campaigning against Obama," he replied.

Anti-Obama sentiment had only become more intense around these parts—and throughout the country as a whole—after the election. The conservative Tea Party movement had hijacked the health-care debate that August, screaming about death panels and socialized medicine and comparing Obama to Mao/Hitler/Stalin. Tensions were running high in Colorado Springs.

A week or so earlier, Demanett's friend Keith Ferguson, a former Obama organizer who grew up in Colorado Springs, visited a farmers' market in the neighborhood and asked people, "Do you happen to be a supporter of President Obama's health-care plan?" Most responses varied from "no" to "hell no" to "you're a Nazi." "There's a new level of animosity," Ferguson said. "The people who oppose Obama are getting scarier." Red America had struck back at blue. One national poll in January 2010 found that 63 percent of Republicans considered Obama a socialist and four in ten thought he should be impeached (for what, they didn't say).

After five years of once-unimaginable success, Democrats in Colorado were coming back down to earth. In a few months, Governor Bill Ritter, dogged by low approval ratings, would forswear running for reelection. Former Denver school supervisor Michael Bennet, whom Ritter appointed to fill the seat of Senator Ken Salazar after he became Obama's secretary of the interior, struggled to fight off a primary challenger and prepare for a tough general election campaign. In states across the country, from North Carolina to Indiana to Nevada, the feeling of euphoria that followed Obama's campaign now seemed like a distant memory. The anti-incumbent rage among voters that threw Republicans out of office and put Obama in the White House had not dissipated since Democrats took charge of Washington. In fact, with the economy still limping and little getting done inside the corridors of power, voter angst had only increased.

Demanett and her group were determined not to let the right

wing win the health-care debate. Obama needed them. "We're his boots on the ground," she said. Like the campaign itself, the participants at her house reflected a remarkable cross section of ages and races and incomes, including two high school students, two retired Air Force Academy professors, an architect, a software engineer, a nurse, and a first-grade teacher. A woman recovering from knee surgery and breathing through an oxygen tank helped out in the den. For a brief moment, it felt as if the campaign had never ended.

Health care, in particular, was not just an abstract issue for Demanett. Fourteen years earlier, on the day before Christmas, she went out for a run. All of a sudden, midway through, she felt as if her spine had been shattered. Her husband rushed her to the ER. She had a blinding headache, intense nausea, and an immovably stiff neck. After extensive tests, the doctor told her that she had a rare form of recurrent bacterial meningitis. Most of the time she'd be okay, the doctor said, provided she took a steady stream of daily drugs, but every month or so the symptoms would flare up bad, just like the first time. He prescribed a cocktail of medicines for the relapses that pretty much knocked her out. She was forced to take a medical retirement from her job as a high school social worker. She had great insurance through her husband's job (he was a school principal), but the cost of the medicine eventually bankrupted the couple and put a severe strain on their previously happy marriage. Now she was going through a divorce. When the divorce finalized, she would lose her husband's health insurance and have no way to pay for the medicine that kept her alive. She wasn't sure what she was going to do. Tears welled in her eyes as she told the story. She placed her hope in Obama.

Demanett had become something of a cause célèbre in local Obama organizing circles, but made it clear she didn't want to be thought of as a martyr. "There are people so much worse off," she said. "That's who I'm doing this for." She didn't want to be stereotyped as a starry-eyed Obamaton, either. "Do I think he's perfect?" she asked rhetorically. "No. Do I think he's a bit too reactive at times?

Yes. I'm not a blind-faith believer." But she wouldn't stop fighting for him anytime soon, as long as her body cooperated. "I know I'm making progress," she said, "because these people are coming back every week." The weekly phone banks at her house would continue without fail, through the highs and lows of the health-care debate, in the months ahead. "It's been frustrating," she said. "But we've gotta keep on keeping on for the good of the cause. I'm not giving up on anything."

That August evening, Demanett and crew, in conversations with fellow Obama supporters, were pushing their elected officials to support a public insurance option. Three days later, however, Obama held a town hall meeting in western Colorado and called the public option just a "sliver" of reform. The official DNC talking points changed again a few weeks later. What had once been an integral element of the Democrats' package was now just a "small part." The malleable nature of the president's plan complicated the task for Obama's sales force. What precisely were they supposed to be fighting for? As the health-care debate dragged through 2009 and into 2010, the number of people making calls on behalf of the bill declined week after week.

While Democrats argued among themselves, the right mobilized. "In the whole period in which we didn't know what Obama was for and nobody was mobilizing or asked to mobilize, it created this huge vacuum," said the Obama organizing guru Marshall Ganz. "So the Teabaggers came in and filled it up." Suddenly conservatives were out in the street, massing their frenzied followers. The Tea Partiers brought much-needed (if not always sane or welcome) energy to the GOP and had begun to infiltrate the party from the bottom up—just as Dean had urged Democrats to do after his presidential campaign. They'd even appropriated the insurgent language of the Dean campaign, pledging to "take back America," and proudly emulated his fifty-state strategy by holding meetings and running candidates across the country, in red and blue states alike. Many Democrats initially dismissed this sudden outbreak of inchoate right-wing rage and scoffed at signs likening Obama to Stalin, but the new regime in Washington seemed powerless to stop it. The enduring Democratic majority appeared just as fleeting as Karl Rove's own master plan for the GOP.

Obama and his followers were no longer the stars of the moment. "The Obama people ran the best campaign I've seen in all my life in politics," Dean said. "But they couldn't translate it into government." The Julia Demanetts of the country would do nearly anything for their president, but it wasn't clear the White House knew what to do with them or recognized their importance. Less than a year after his historic election, what had become of Obama's movement? Where was its leader?

A month after the election, Obama summoned Tim Kaine to Chicago and explained how his presidency and party could prosper going forward.

"How many presidents have tried to meaningfully tackle health care?" Obama asked his DNC chair-in-waiting.

"Every Democrat since Truman," Kaine responded.

"How about energy reform?" Obama continued.

"I remember Nixon saying we were importing too much foreign oil, and now we import three times as much," Kaine replied.

"So if they didn't succeed," Obama asked rhetorically, "was it because they weren't smart enough?"

"No, they were smart," Kaine answered.

"Was it because they didn't know the ways of Washington?" Obama followed up, pressing his point like a vintage constitutional law professor.

"No, they knew the ways of Washington," Kaine added.

"So if I try to do these heavy lifts just like they did, what are my chances?" Obama wondered.

"Pretty much zero," Kaine responded.

"Yeah, so what we have to do is figure out a different way to do it," Obama answered.

"If you just rely on your inside-the-Beltway savvy," Kaine agreed, "that's never going to be enough to make fundamental and important changes, because the forces of inertia inside the Beltway are just going to get into your way."

They both concluded that preserving what Kaine called the "outside-the-Beltway popular muscle" that defined Obama's campaign would be an essential ingredient for the new president's success.

At the same time, a debate raged inside the Obama coalition over the future shape of Obama's powerful campaign arm. Obama organizing veterans like Marshall Ganz and Steve Hildebrand pushed for an independent organization that would be able to pressure Democrats to support the president's agenda and act, at least theoretically, separate from the White House. But most influential Obama advisers, led by David Plouffe and joined by Dean and a chorus of prominent Democrats, saw the DNC as its natural home. An independent entity would needlessly antagonize Democrats and be difficult to structure for legal and financial reasons, they argued. Plouffe and company also didn't want it to seem as if Obama's re-election campaign was starting the day after his election. In the end, Obama for America became Organizing for America (OFA)—a quasi-autonomous entity within the DNC. Mitch Stewart, a promising thirty-three-year-old field organizer who cut his teeth in Iowa and ran Virginia in the general election, took charge of OFA. Jeremy Bird became his deputy.

Despite his locating OFA in the DNC, changing the Democratic Party didn't rank as Obama's foremost priority. He had more pressing problems on his plate. Nor did his followers always march in lockstep. The Obama pollster Cornell Belcher found that 20 percent of Obama voters under thirty-five declined to vote for down-ticket candidates in 2008—a worrying sign for Democrats in the years to come. After the election, *New York* magazine dubbed Obama the "first Independent president," a verifiable "party of one." But in spite of the president's ambivalence, the Democratic Party had changed substantially as a result of his campaign. Obama activists, many new to politics, became county chairs and precinct captains across the country, shifting the power dynamic in their cities and states. In Colorado, Joe Perez took the reins of the Weld County Democratic Party, as did Jason DeGroot, an early member of the Meadow Muffins gang, in El Paso County. These Obamacrats cited the Obama campaign as a model for their areas.

DeGroot, a goateed thirty-six-year-old former political Independent from Sacramento, came to Colorado Springs while stationed at Fort Carson. He became a staff sergeant in the Air Force, specializing in space satellites and calling in bomb strikes from Saudi Arabia at the beginning of the war in Afghanistan. After leaving the military, he looked for ways to get more involved in the community. He first volunteered with the Obama campaign out of a desire to transcend partisan politics. Now, ironically, he was in the most partisan of positions, leading Democrats in Colorado's second most populous county. After the election, the party suddenly had twice as many volunteers, and DeGroot wanted the new recruits to focus on local campaigns and local issues, which he viewed as the best route forward for Democrats in the still heavily red county. "These new people never felt like the Democratic Party was meaningful before," he said. "That's one of the things I hope to really change."

DeGroot had recently attended a phone bank at Demanett's. The party people and the OFA activists didn't seem too impressed by each other. "The old party was chugging along, not moving fast," Demanett said about the campaign. "Then the Obama kids came in, and it was like, whoosh. This isn't the El Paso County Democratic Party," she said of the gatherings at her house. "I don't know that the El Paso County Democratic Party would've made this happen." Demanett was herself a new member of the party's executive committee, but that hadn't changed her opinion of the institution. "They're the talkers," she said. "We're the doers."

A lot of Obama loyalists who committed to the party after the election drifted away in time, leaving DeGroot to battle the party's old guard on his own. "We were trying to move forward and modernize the party," he said, "but some of the people who had been involved for a long time became very resistant." Factions formed and little got done, kind of like in Washington. The party lost a major fight when El Paso County voters overwhelmingly rejected a proposal to increase property taxes to pay for vital public services, and also struggled internally to overhaul its own personnel. During a particularly contentious executive committee meeting in February 2010—fourteen months after he became county chair—DeGroot had seen enough and resigned on the spot. He hoped his departure would remind fellow Obamacrats that unless they dedicated themselves to rebuilding the party, the people who ran things before would once again take over the show.

DeGroot's travails were by no means an isolated occurrence. Following the election, OFA opted to largely circumvent the party rather than enhance it. On November 5, 2008, the DNC's nearly two hundred local organizers awoke to the news that their contracts were expiring at the end of the month. The e-mail from headquarters called it a "bittersweet moment." When Obama's DNC reconstituted the fifty-state strategy a few months later, funding OFA staffers across the country took priority. Unlike the organizers hired under Dean, who worked to strengthen the party at the state and local level, the new Obama organizers were instructed to initially focus strictly on helping to pass the president's legislative agenda, forming a parallel structure to the existing party. "I'm not trying to build a bigger and better Democratic Party," said Colorado OFA director Gabe Lifton-Zoline, a tall mountain man from Telluride.

You couldn't blame Obama for not wanting to take full ownership of the Democratic Party, given its status as a perennial punch line—the Buffalo Bills of politics. In response to the dysfunction of the Democratic Congress, Obama, in his first year in office, kept his own ideology vague, stayed studiously aloof from the specifics of governing, and sought to boost his own "post-partisan" and "pragmatic" brand. He was following a long line of historical precedent. Republican presidents routinely sought to strengthen their parties, while Democratic presidents tended to ignore them, Northwestern University presidential historian Daniel Galvin observed. Galvin thought Obama might reverse that trend with OFA, but he had yet to. The president, Galvin argued in his book *Presidential Party Building*, neglected his party at his own peril. If it atrophied too much, Obama would find himself in a similar situation to Clinton's following the disastrous 1994 midterms, facing an increasingly hostile Congress and unable to push through the transformative change he campaigned on. If that happened, Obama's own election, not to mention the long-term hopes of a Democratic majority, might be in doubt.

Democratic Party officials, as much as they wanted Obama to succeed and saw their fates largely determined by his success, pointed out that they had additional responsibilities, ranging from candidates for governor to county commissioner. If Obama led a party of one, they asked themselves, what happened to everyone else? "We don't own the market on change," Cornell Belcher said. That's why it was so critical to bring Independent and Republican and first-time Obama supporters into the fold. Reagan Democrats, after all, became Republicans after the campaign was over. "There's probably not a more front-and-center issue for the Democratic Party than that," Belcher said. "You'd think they'd build infrastructure at the grassroots level within the party to work that very diverse and younger constituency." One former high-ranking member of Obama's campaign described OFA as a "massive fucking power grab" that siphoned much-needed resources away from the party. (The DNC launched a $50 million effort in June 2010 to persuade first-time Obama voters to vote Democratic in the upcoming midterms.)

There was quite a bit of turmoil regarding how the new Obama supporters were supposed to coexist with the activists of the Dean-era Democratic Party and its predecessors, in theory and in practice. "There's a lot of confusion and miscommunication that goes on between OFA, the DNC, and the White House," said Colorado Democratic Party chair Pat Waak. State and local officials echoed such concerns. "Volunteers and myself are confused—do we do our own community activism or do we become part of OFA?" said Margaret Johnson, county chair in Polk County, North Carolina. "Well, we decided, I guess we'll become part of OFA. But when you're waiting for a big group to tell you what to do, it's slow moving." Dean's strategy decentralized power away from Washington, but under Obama, Washington once again called the shots. "The DNC is just not as energized and connected to local activism as it was under Howard Dean," Johnson said. After the election, pundits predicted that Obama's DNC would launch a "50-state strategy on steroids," but in some places—especially outside of the typical battlegrounds—it felt more like the fifty-state strategy on Ambien.

The state chairs now received far less money than they did under Dean and once again struggled to pay the bills. "They didn't want to give us anything at all," Waak said of her early conversations with Obama DNC officials. One chair called the $5,000-a-month stipend the state parties eventually received "money to shut us up." "If we had what we previously had," said Idaho state chair Keith Roark, "we'd be in far better shape." The gains of the fifty-state strategy were by no means permanent, the chairs warned, and could evaporate as quickly as they accumulated. Indeed, in Obama's first year, the party lost three straight major elections, in states the president won by six, sixteen, and twenty-six points. In Virginia, New Jersey, and Massachusetts, Obama's "coalition of the ascendant"—blacks, Hispanics, young people—failed to turn out in large numbers for the Democratic candidates. For Democratic activists, Scott Brown's stunning takeover of Ted Kennedy's Senate seat in January 2010 was the last straw.

Marshall Ganz was the closest thing to an organizing theorist behind the Obama movement. He mentored organizers like Jeremy Bird and Buffy Wicks who became the backbone of Obama's campaign and trained hundreds of new activists. Ganz hoped, after the election, that these organizers would fundamentally change the nature of governance in the United States. Instead, he watched OFA assemble in secret and the Obama administration squander, in his view, an enormous opportunity to engage its grassroots base in the months after the election. Five days after Kennedy's death, Ganz and Occidental College political science professor Peter Dreier, a fellow veteran community organizer, enumerated their critique in a *Washington Post* op-ed titled "We Have the Hope. Now Where's the Audacity?"

"The White House and its allies forgot that success requires more than proposing legislation, negotiating with Congress and polite lobbying," Dreier and Ganz wrote. "It demands movement-building of the kind that propelled Obama's long-shot candidacy to an almost landslide victory." The institutions that were supposed to channel the movement, namely, OFA, "failed to keep up," they wrote. The administration, they contended, "confused marketing with movement-building."

In December 2008, Dean described his own vision for Obama's DNC. "I'd like the DNC to now mature into a two-way communication between ordinary Americans who want to influence their government and the president of the United States," he said. The Obama campaign, after all, was premised on the idea that the people who elected him would have a say in running the country. "I will ask for your service and your active citizenship when I am president of the United States," Obama said while campaigning in Colorado Springs on July 2, 2008. "This will not be a call issued in one speech or one program, this will be a central cause of my presidency."

Unfortunately, that dialogue from the White House had too often remained typically one-sided: Here's the policy. Go support it. "The White House began to believe that they could mobilize their supporters without hearing what their supporters really wanted in terms of specific change," Dean said. "The principal problem with OFA is the same one the president's having. You can't dictate to your base what's going to happen. It's got to be a two-way deal, and it hasn't been."

OFA assumed the president's policy was always the best possible one. But what about when it wasn't? What were Obama's supporters to do then? They were told to sell the policy, but couldn't influence the shaping of the product. "There's a certain hubris among the people around Obama in the White House that they were above the fray and didn't have to pay attention to the base," said Iowa senator Tom Harkin. "Certainly a president has to govern from the middle, but you've got to reassure your base that what they did and how hard they worked was worth something." Rahm Emanuel, the consummate Beltway insider, had replaced Plouffe, the inner circle's past conduit to the grass roots, as the central figure in Obama's orbit. The insurgency ended once Obama entered the White House.

Obama's organizers on the inside, like Bird, now found themselves in an unfamiliar position. Like it or not, they were tied to the Washington establishment. Following the election, Bird helped plot the formation of OFA. "Anyone who's ever done a sequel knows the expectations are extremely high," he said. Inside D.C., he faced "a lot of false assumptions and expectations" about what the DNC's new organizers could accomplish—as if Obama would just snap his fingers and change would come. "The left is used to organizing in opposition," he said. "No one—Marshall or anyone else—has experience organizing when you are in power."

Bird insisted that he still didn't "feel part of the D.C. pundit, insider crowd" and had been spending as much time as possible outside of the Beltway. In its first year, OFA staff held 937 listening tours in six hundred cities across fifty states. Concerns from activists around the country were transmitted back to the White House political department on an ongoing basis. "I know that Obama cares about that," he said. All the calls made and hours volunteered by Obama superactivists like Julia Demanett, Bird contended, were not in vain, as the passage of health-care reform eventually illustrated. "Almost everything we've touched we've either been successful on or will get there," he predicted. Though many of Obama's campaign promises remained unfulfilled, the last weeks of the health-care debate, as Obama supporters made nearly five hundred thousand calls to members of Congress in the final ten days before the House vote, showed how effective OFA activists could be when Obama gave them something tangible to fight for.

Yet the battle over health care also exposed the organization's limitations. While OFA adeptly lobbied for Obama's top legislative priority, it hadn't ushered in a new progressive era. "Obama's health bill is a very conservative piece of legislation, building on a Republican rather than a New Deal foundation," wrote former Clinton labor secretary Robert Reich, who advised Obama during the presidential campaign. Nor had it repaired a broken political system. Even with the bill's passage, Washington remained a pretty transactional place, and despite the best of Bird's efforts to stay in sync with Obama's grassroots base, he took his cues from the White House. "We can change politics by leading a grassroots political movement inside the Beltway," Kaine loftily proclaimed. But such an aspiration, even Kaine admitted, sounded awfully like an oxymoron.

In fact, during Obama's first year, OFA didn't feel much like a movement or Obama's campaign. Grassroots organizing and Washington sausage making blended about as well as vodka and milk. "It's no coincidence that some of us who are organizers didn't go into the White House," said the former Obama field director Temo Figueroa. "I would've been fired in the first fucking month." OFA was meant to blend the two worlds, but it often floated in a political no-man's-land, tethered to a Washington establishment but unable to change it. Critics like Ganz suspected that was by design. The White House didn't want its activists to disrupt the backroom deals its aides cut with lobbyists and legislators, nor did it want them putting too much pressure on obstructionist Democrats, lest it alienate key swing votes in Congress. The chief of staff memorably called ads run by MoveOn targeting conservative Democrats blocking health-care reform "fucking retarded."

"I'm not looking to pick another fight with Rahm Emanuel, but the contempt with which he held the progressive wing of the party was devastating and incredibly demoralizing," Dean said. "That's basically saying to your own people—you got us here, now FU."

OFA's organizers in the field could do little without approval from D.C. and had to follow Rahm's dictates. The top-down structure was the virtual opposite of Obama's campaign. That struck Ganz as an odd calculation. His supporters, Obama always said, were his most powerful asset. So why didn't he unleash them?

"I definitely think he tried to extend a new model of campaigning into a new model of governing," said White House transition chief John Podesta. "By that, I mean his decision making, his openness, his attempt at broader-based participation, his desire to cool off the intense partisanship in Washington . . . But at the end of the day, the Washington culture is pretty hard to change. So they defaulted to a position that looks and feels a little more like what we experienced in the nineties." Yet only Obama entered the White House with millions of supporters who could theoretically be activated with the click of a mouse; they expected him, however naively, to follow through on his promise to change the ways of Washington. "Our signs didn't say, STATUS QUO '08," remarked former top Obama adviser Paul Tewes.

If a president couldn't lead a movement from the White House, Ganz argued, he could at least encourage its development on the outside, like Reagan did with the New Right. "It takes two hands to make a clapping noise," he said. "Inside and outside. If inside is put in charge of outside, then there's no more outside. The very sources of power that put you there in the first place begin to evaporate." But Obama's White House never felt comfortable with both worlds or fully explored the possibility of governing in a fundamentally different way, despite Obama's initial conversation with Kaine after the election. "There's a core philosophy inside the administration of avoiding conflict and trying to assert control," Ganz said. "That's not how you run a movement."

Obama's movement, in fairness, never adequately prepared for the day after his election. His top supporters dispersed to many individual entities rather than one collective force. Campaign organizers like Buffy Wicks and Ray Rivera and Jon Carson took policy jobs in the administration. Plouffe wrote a book and tended to his family, while Tewes and Hildebrand and Figueroa ran their own consulting shops. Even if Obama's grassroots base had been robustly engaged immediately following the election, a decent percentage would have opted to do something else. The permanent campaign—especially an insurgent one—gets old after a while. Many Obamaphiles—whether Mike Maday in Colorado or Chuck Lasker in Indiana or Daniel Ayala in North Carolina—still supported the president, by and large, but had understandably wandered back to their previous lives. Keeping these activists and their respective states in the mix would be a major challenge in the years ahead.

Obama's new-media savant Joe Rospars, who'd since returned to Blue State Digital, built the campaign for the long haul. He hoped that when Obama found himself torn every which way in the White House by advisers and interest groups and lobbyists, he'd think of the Verizon ad where an army of workers stand behind a company spokesman. "I think he has that network of people outside Washington behind him, but those are delicate relationships that, if not carefully maintained and put to good use, will atrophy over time," Rospars said. Former top campaign officials watched with dismay as what Ganz once termed "the movement to elect Barack Obama," however opaque its policy goals, kept contracting rather than expanding. In his first year, a million people joined Obama's vaunted campaign e-mail list of thirteen million followers, according to Plouffe, but OFA refused to say if the number of people who chose to unsubscribe dwarfed the newcomers. "I haven't really done the math," Kaine replied when pressed on the numbers. "Obama's a learner,"

Ganz said. "He can still learn. The big question is, what's he learning from all this?"

The dramatic revival of health-care reform demonstrated what he'd learned. As Obama settled into year two and successfully fought for the passage of his signature domestic priority, the dynamic and forceful leader who inspired the masses on the campaign trail reemerged. "If he had offered this kind of leadership in the spring of 2009, we'd have had health-care reform far sooner—and much deeper—than what we got," Ganz said. On the night of the House vote, Obama paid homage to his grassroots supporters and specifically credited "the untold numbers who knocked on doors and made phone calls, who organized and mobilized out of a firm conviction that change in this country comes not from the top down, but from the bottom up." As he crisscrossed the country, Obama, more than anyone, seemed to grasp that the future of the Democratic Party would not be fashioned in Washington, no matter how much its decisions impacted the rest of the country. Out in the states, the fight to reshape American politics didn't end after his election, nor would it stop after another. The country continued to morph and adapt, in ways good and bad. If Obama capitalized on these changes, his presidency and party could still be transformative. There were, after all, new frontiers left to conquer.

One postcard of the state of Texas shows a mockingbird and a bluebonnet across from a pecan tree and a pump jack. "Texas: Land of Contrasts," it says. That's true of the state's landscapes, weather, and, most especially, politics. Even for its mammoth size, Texas has always had an enlarged influence on the direction of American politics. It has bounced from one extreme to the other, a Democratic stronghold since Reconstruction to a Republican bastion since Reagan. What other state could produce two Bushes as president alongside Democratic power brokers like Sam Rayburn and Lyndon Johnson in Congress, or pit pugnacious liberals like Molly Ivins against fire-breathing conservatives such as former House majority leader Tom DeLay? The only thing all of these people had in common was their place of residency. "The politics are probably the weirdest thing about Texas," Ivins once wrote.

Between 1848 and 1948, Texas voted for every Democratic presidential candidate with the exception of the New York Catholic Al Smith in 1928, usually by staggering numbers. No Democrat entered the White House without carrying the Lone Star State from 1845 until 1992. The only fight that mattered occurred within the party, between liberal populists and pro-corporate conservatives. As the national party moved left in the 1960s and '70s, those conservative Democrats became Republicans. Texas stayed blue longer than any other southern state, but when it turned red, it was the color of a fire engine. It went for Reagan in 1980 and 1984 and in 1988 sent the first of two Bushes to the White House. By 1994, there were no statewide Democrats left in office. The land of LBJ became the fiefdom of Tom DeLay, leading the country in executions, air pollution, and residents without health insurance (6.2 million and counting).

Yet after the 2008 election, at the DNC's postelection celebration in San Diego, Dean made a stunning prediction: "Texas is next." Like Dean, Obama's team viewed the election not as a mere historical anomaly but as the beginning of a more profound electoral shift. They'd pulled some important states into the blue column, but there were other prizes yet to be had. Texas, with its thirty-four electoral votes and rapidly expanding population, was the biggest catch of all. "If Texas turns blue in a presidential election, it's over for the Republicans," said state Democratic Party chair Boyd Richie. Of course, that's an "if" almost as big as the state itself. "It's an uphill fight with a short stick," Richie conceded.

A short, sturdy lawyer from deep red Wichita Falls ("The City That Faith Built"), near the Oklahoma border, Richie became party chair in 2006. In March 2009, he and an "intrepid delegation" of a half-dozen influential Texas Democrats paid a visit to DNC chair

Tim Kaine in Washington, hoping to persuade him to put some money into the state. "We've been pulling ourselves up by our own bootstraps," Richie told Kaine. "If we have some additional help, we can get over that hill." Democratic operative Matt Angle, a Fort Worth native, showed the DNC chair a PowerPoint presentation of how Democrats could win the governorship in 2010, knocking off the reviled Rick Perry—Bush's lieutenant governor and successor—by maximizing Democratic turnout in urban areas and heavily Hispanic South Texas while keeping it close in the state's vast rural areas. "Texas has po-ten-tial," Richie said in his methodical drawl.

Kaine saw parallels between Texas and his home state of Virginia. When he ran for governor in 2005, Republicans controlled nearly everything in Old Virginny. By the time he left, the situation was practically reversed (though Republicans did win back the governor's mansion in 2009). Kaine said Obama had his eyes on flipping five additional red states blue in 2012. Texas was one of them. "It's a growth stock for Democrats," he said.

That September, the DNC held its first meeting in Texas in thirty years, gathering at the Renaissance Austin Hotel, perched north of the city in the Hill Country. Austin Mayor Lee Leffingwell, a retired pilot with big red cheeks and a self-described "lifelong, dyed-in-the-wool Yellow Dog Democrat," kicked off the festivities. Leffingwell joked that his laid-back liberal city was commonly known as "the People's Republic of Austin." Democrats controlled fifty-seven of sixty seats in Austin's Travis County. "Lately, something strange and very exciting is going on here," Leffingwell proclaimed from the podium. "After many years as a lonely island of blue in a vast sea of red, all of a sudden Austin is beginning to look less like an exception and more like a rule. In cities all across Texas, in Houston, in Dallas, in San Antonio, a sleeping Democratic giant is beginning to stir. And, make no mistake, this meeting and your presence here is an alarm going off in the state of Texas!" Hundreds of DNC members in the chandeliered ballroom cheered loudly.

State senator Leticia Van de Putte, a perky fifty-five-year-old pharmacist and mother of six from San Antonio who wore a bright blue pantsuit, spoke next. Just six years earlier, she led one of the most futile missions in Democratic Party history, fleeing her state with ten other state senators for New Mexico in a desperate attempt to stop DeLay and his henchmen in the state legislature, under GOP control for the first time in 130 years, from redrawing Texas's political map. It was an unprecedented midyear redistricting, designed to ensure Republican majorities for decades to come. And the only thing Democrats could do to stop it, at least temporarily, was to prevent Republicans from getting the quorum they needed to push the change through. So they fled 761 miles to Albuquerque on a moment's notice. Van de Putte's gang became known as the Texas Eleven. They lasted forty-six days, until Senator John Whitmire, a lawyer from Houston soon to be dubbed "Quitmire" by Democrats, came back. DeLay got his new districts, and in 2004 Democrats were booted out of areas they'd held for decades as Republicans sent six new members of Congress to Washington. Yet the power grab had the unintended effect of rallying Texas Democrats for the first time in years. "I want to thank Tom DeLay and Karl Rove for doing something that we couldn't do for ourselves," said state senator Royce West of Dallas, "and that is unite this party."

In 2006, Democrats picked up six seats in the statehouse and two more in 2008. Following the election, DeLay ally Tom Craddick was deposed as the leader of the body and replaced by the amiable moderate Joe Straus, the first Jewish Speaker of the Texas House. Democrats had their eyes on reclaiming the majority in 2010 and gaining a crucial seat on the redistricting board that would determine the fate of Texas politics for years to come. Following the new U.S. Census, Texas stood to gain four more congressional seats and two additional electoral votes. Van de Putte, cochair of the Democratic convention in Denver, was a testament to the melting pot the state had become. "We're part of the South," she said. "We're part of the West. We're part of this wonderful Latina culture." If you mixed Georgia, Colorado, and Mexico in a blender, you'd get Texas. "The real greeting here," she said, "is bienvenidos y'all!" Van de Putte urged the DNC members to tell fellow Democrats in their states, "Texas is coming back. Texas is turning blue!"

The Texas Democratic Party's unlikely revival started, of all places, in Dallas, the city where Kennedy died and the state's Republican takeover began. "Even when there were no Republicans in Texas, there were Republicans in Dallas," wrote one Democratic activist. The Big D had always been the fashionably conservative city of H. L. Hunt, J. R. Ewing, the Dallas Cowboys, and Neiman Marcus. Oilmen, lawyers, and bankers pumped huge sums of money into Republican campaigns and conservative think tanks like the National Center for Policy Analysis and the Free Market Foundation. After leaving Wyoming, Dick Cheney worked out of Halliburton's Dallas office. When he wasn't clearing brush in Crawford, George W. Bush called Dallas home. The city housed more Bush megadonors (thirty-nine Pioneers and Rangers) than anywhere else in the country. Following his presidency, Bush bought a $5 million mansion in the upscale neighborhood of Highland Park, near Southern Methodist University, the future home of the George W. Bush Presidential Library and George W. Bush Institute.

But at the start of the twenty-first century, the demographics of Dallas—like so much of Texas—were shifting in the Democrats' favor, with Hispanics entering and conservative Anglos going. Democrats were supposed to turn it all around by 2002, when the popular former Dallas mayor Ron Kirk ran for the Senate and wealthy businessman Tony Sanchez ran for governor. But it was not to be. Sanchez spent $60 million and lost by eighteen points. Kirk fell short by double digits. Of the twenty-eight candidates Democrats put forward in Dallas County, only one prevailed.

So it came as quite a shock, two years later, when the city elected Lupe Valdez, an openly gay Latina, as sheriff. Valdez was a rare bright spot in what had been an otherwise dismal year for Texas Democrats. The loss of the dean of the Democrats' congressional delegation,

Martin Frost, who represented portions of Dallas and Fort Worth for thirteen terms in Congress, hit especially hard. After the election, Frost's friend Fred Baron, a wealthy Dallas trial lawyer, pledged to spend millions of dollars rebuilding the Texas Democratic Party, which heretofore had been regarded as the worst in the nation, in the hopes of shifting the state's political fortunes. He modeled the Texas Democratic Trust after the "gang of four" philanthropists who bankrolled Colorado's Democratic takeover. In 2006, Dallas became the first test of the Trust's experiment.

The Trust's executive director, Matt Angle, Frost's former chief of staff, saw a unique opportunity where others did not. Between 2000 and 2006, 130,000 Anglos left Dallas and 200,000 Hispanics moved in. Dallas had always been a highly segregated city, with little contact between the predominantly black and Hispanic south and the Anglo north. The southern sector alone was the size of Atlanta. Campaigns tended to do their own thing, and candidates stuck to their own turf. In the process, a lot of Democrats who lived in changing or traditionally Republican neighborhoods kept falling through the cracks. Angle put Jane Hamilton, a slender twenty-eight-year-old from New Orleans, in charge of the effort. "We made a decision to find Democrats wherever they are," Hamilton said. "It sounds really simple, but that was a different strategy." It was the fifty-state strategy on an intensely local scale.

The Dallas County Democratic Party had never run a coordinated campaign before, where every candidate worked together with a unified message and pooled resources, nor had it emphasized straight-ticket voting. An influx of cash from the Trust facilitated a massive undertaking. The party printed up ten thousand blue signs that said, simply, HAD ENOUGH? VOTE DEMOCRATIC. Fifteen different pieces of mail went out to prospective voters. Candidates and volunteers knocked on doors all through the summer and fall, including in heavily Republican suburbs. Hamilton and Angle thought they might win half the races. On Election Day, Democrats won every single one. Almost overnight, every Democrat in the state—and more than a few shell-shocked Republicans—wanted to know how the "Dallas model" could be transferred to their areas.

The effort only expanded in 2008, as the grassroots group Obama Dallas grew to eight thousand people. Six times as many Democrats in Dallas County voted in the March primary as compared to 2004. Though he lost the state overall by twelve points in the general election, Obama won Dallas County by 112,000 votes and carried every major city except for Fort Worth. That included Houston's Harris County, the third most populous in the country, which hadn't gone for a Democrat since 1964. "As goes Harris County, so goes the state," said GOP political consultant Allen Blakemore. In December 2009, the city elected Annise Parker as the first big-city lesbian mayor in the country.

By 2005, Texas had become America's fourth majority-minority state, following Hawaii, New Mexico, and California. There were enough Hispanics registered to flip the state blue in a presidential election if they voted Democratic and 2.5 million more unregistered Hispanics, by some estimates, yet to be brought into the political process. State representative Rafael Anchía—a telegenic forty-two-year-old attorney in Dallas (virtually every prominent Texas Democrat is a lawyer) and son of Mexican immigrants—had already been called the "Hispanic Obama" and "El Gobernador" in the media. He represented the culturally eclectic area of Oak Cliff near downtown, which is majority Hispanic but also boasts a sizable African-American, Asian, gay, and Anglo progressive population—the new face of cosmopolitan Texas. "Dallas County is an instructive model for understanding how the rest of the state might trend," Anchía said. It's only a matter of time, he believed, until the state pulled the lever for a Democratic governor, senator, or presidential candidate. "At some point, there will be a convergence between demographic changes, better candidates, and an increasingly progressive perspective in the Texas electorate," he said. The question is, when?

Many Texans hoped it would be in 2008. But after a brief moment in the spotlight during the primary, the Obama campaign made a cold-blooded decision not to target the state in the general election. As such, the Obama campaign didn't transform Texas politics as it had in North Carolina or Indiana or Colorado. Texans, fiercely individualistic by nature, thus far had done it all by themselves. So while Texas Democrats welcomed the twelve new arrivals from OFA after the election—the largest commitment from the national party in decades—there was also a fair amount of skepticism. What did they want to accomplish? How long would they stay? Would they help turn Texas blue?

On a wet Saturday morning following the DNC's meeting in Austin, OFA held a "community organizer training" at Democratic Party headquarters in Dallas, a one-story white storefront in an industrial neighborhood just south of downtown. Next door, a crew of University of Texas college football fans, decked out in orange, set up a makeshift tailgating party for a game against Wyoming in a massive auto garage. They flashed the team's trademark "hook 'em horns" sign as the Obama activists entered the building.

Fourteen volunteers gathered in a brick-and-linoleum room, sitting on cheap red swivel chairs, munching on doughnuts, and drinking McDonald's coffee. There were eleven women and three men: Anglo, African-American, Hispanic, and African. OFA regional field director Joe Duffy, a twenty-four-year-old Irish Catholic kid from Chicago, led the training. He'd never been to Texas, let alone Dallas, before joining OFA. This was new terrain for himself, the organization, and the state.

Dutifully following Ganz's house meeting model, Duffy introduced himself and asked everyone else to tell his or her own story. He grew up in the Chicago suburbs, attended Southern Illinois University, and joined the Obama campaign as an intern in Iowa. Over Thanksgiving break in 2007, he flew down to Miami and picked up his great-aunt's 1999 Ford Crown Victoria, which he termed the "undercover detective mobile." It had 60,000 miles on it at the time. Now it had 109,000. Duffy traveled all over during the primary and spent the general election in northern Colorado. After the election, his boss joined the DNC and asked him to go to Dallas for OFA. He was now in charge of an enormous region that stretched from the Panhandle to College Station.

"It was half the battle to get Obama in," Duffy told the room. "Even more important now is pushing his agenda and moving the country in the right direction."

"The operative word is 'battle,'" replied Windolyn Mosely, a hearty black woman from Amarillo.

"What really got him elected is people like yourself," Duffy said. "We're going back to what got him in and what President Obama truly believes in, which is community organizing."

A half-dozen activists at the meeting came from Rockwall County, due east of Dallas, the smallest county in the state but the richest per capita, where McCain took 72 percent of the vote. If Democrats wanted to flip Texas blue, they'd need to cut down the GOP's advantage in Republican counties like Rockwall across the state. The local Democratic Party "barely existed" in 2004, said Nancy Sanchez, a youthful-looking sixty-two-year-old nurse. Sanchez was a local precinct captain and leader of a small but committed group of Obama activists in the county. She worked with low-income psychiatric patients and had a daughter who couldn't get health insurance because of a preexisting condition and a ninety-three-year-old father in hospice care. Her Twitter name was Nancylovesobama, and she had a "hope" tattoo on her ankle. "I just love Obama, and I intend for him to succeed and keep his word," she said. "I'm pissed at him, too," she added offhandedly.

"That's what they do to you sometimes," replied her friend Willie Bolden from Rockwall.

"I love him, but he ain't perfect," Sanchez continued. "I will be phone banking every week until the [health-care] bill passes. I don't care how red our stupid county is . . . We're on fire. We're honored you're here, Joe, because nobody ever paid attention to Rockwall before."

Another Rockwallian, Kristi Lara, moved to the state a few years back from Albuquerque, New Mexico. She wanted to work in the reddest of red counties. "I definitely underestimated the difficulty of turning Texas blue," she said.

"Texas used to be blue," pointed out Gene Price, a longtime resident of the state.

"We need to talk about turning it back blue," responded Jacqui Mekias, a fifty-one-year-old health-care activist from Dallas.

After all of the introductions—which lasted more than an hour—Duffy showed a PowerPoint presentation illustrating the contrasts between the electoral map in 2004 and 2008. Texas looked a lot like Missouri or Virginia four years earlier—red in 2004 and brown in 2008.

"We're this close to getting the first domino to fall in Texas," said Windolyn Mosely. "That could be a really big deal in transforming this country."

"They'd rather secede than turn blue," Sanchez said of the Republicans, referencing the governor's infamous remark at the first Tax Day Tea Party in April 2009. "We've got a great union," quipped Rick Perry, a dashing macho man in the John Wayne mold (Ivins dubbed him "Governor Goodhair"). "There's absolutely no reason to dissolve it. But if Washington continues to thumb their nose at the American people, you know, who knows what might come out of that." Perry's comments, and subsequent efforts by conservatives on the Texas Board of Education to rewrite the state's public school textbooks—emphasizing America's roots as a "Christian nation" and deleting liberal icons such as Ted Kennedy from the history books—underscored the degree to which the Texas Republican Party and much of the state remained a bastion of antigovernment sentiment and evangelical fervor.

Jacqui Mekias mentioned that the GOP's congressional campaign chiefs hailed from the state. In the past, national Democrats had swooped in to raise money but paid little attention to Texas politics, which they viewed as unruly and ungodly expensive to compete in.

"When the DNC asked us for ideas, I told them, 'Stop using us as an ATM, goddamn it,'" Sanchez said, apologizing for her language.

"No, that's not happening anymore," Duffy replied. "The DNC recognizes the importance of Texas . . . You're organizing in your state, in your county, in your precincts."

Duffy was asked how the new Obama activists would blend with the existing party structure. "We want to work together," he replied. "But you are going to run into those problems sometimes."

"I can feel a little bit of friction and competition between y'all coming in and what's already there," said Alice Kinsey, a longtime Democrat from West Texas. "We need to bridge the gap between y'all new faces and the longtime people. I kinda feel stretched . . . I want to be on the Democratic side and y'all's side."

"We need to get into the party and transform it," added David Elliott, a middle-aged Anglo who wore a tie-dyed T-shirt that said "If It's Too Loud, You're Too Old." "Thank God people like Joe are coming in. You're our future."

The training lasted nearly four hours, but the newly minted organizers seemed energized on their way out. Before leaving, they stood and ended the meeting by chanting, "Fired up, ready to go!"

Between Dallas and Austin, there's little more than rolling hills and dense brush. The biggest city along the sparse three-hour drive is Waco. Mention Waco to people outside of Texas and they immediately think of David Koresh, the renegade Branch Davidian leader who shaped how the rest of the country viewed Waco and how Waco viewed the rest of the country. When Bush bought a ranch thirty minutes outside of town, his advisers made sure he referred to the area as Crawford, not Waco. "He didn't want the stigma," said Baylor University journalism professor Robert Darden.

Waco used to be solidly blue. Now it's unquestionably red. If Democrats want to recapture the state, they can't just rely on big cities and border towns. Places like Waco have to be part of the plan. Central Texas—south to Austin, west to Abilene, north to Dallas, and east to Lufkin (an admittedly gigantic area)—remains a key swing territory in the state. McLennan County, which includes Waco and Crawford, is the center of that. Locals saw no coincidence in Bush buying a ranch where he did.

In the late nineteenth and early twentieth century, Waco was a hotbed of populist sentiment and an early incubator of progressive public works projects, such as the longest suspension bridge west of the Mississippi and Texas's first skyscraper, the twenty-two-story Amicable Life Insurance Company building. Railroads, cotton mills, and schools sprang up, creating, briefly, the "Athens of Texas." The city developed a burgeoning black middle class and reared Democratic stalwarts like Governor Ann Richards. Downtown still boasts a number of stunning buildings, including a towering Masonic temple, a Romanesque brick Dr Pepper factory, a historic old theater called the Hippodrome, and a white Beaux Arts county courthouse modeled after St. Peter's in Rome. Much of the area was destroyed by a tornado in 1953, however, and never rebuilt. Well-to-do Republicans fled to the manicured white suburbs off Lake Waco. Downtown now feels like a once-grand place abandoned by the natives and left to its own devices, taking on a sad life of its own. The city of 124,000 is the fifth poorest in all of Texas, with mansions converted into halfway houses and splendid Art Deco buildings rotting away. "It's a place waiting for God," said Democratic activist David Gray.

From 2000 on, the area became firm Bush country and the official home of the "Western White House." "When Karl Rove told George Bush to go to Crawford, that stymied us for a decade," said Roy Walthall, a longtime Waco Democrat and instructor of political science at McLennan Community College. Since 1996, the city had a Democratic Party in name only and a county chair who refused to work but wouldn't resign. After the 2008 election, Democrats remained unrepresented in sixty of Waco's ninety-two precincts, and the party had only three hundred e-mail addresses in its database, even though thirty thousand people voted for Obama in McLennan County. "The Politburo would be jealous of the McLennan County Democratic Party," Walthall said. On the face of it, Waco seemed like one of the last places on earth ripe for a Democratic revival.

Yet for all its conservatism, Waco had been represented by a Democrat in Congress, Chet Edwards, since 1991. DeLay targeted Edwards for extinction in 2004, dumping even more Republicans into his already red district, yet somehow Edwards hung on. He ended up on the vice presidential short list for Obama; his biggest booster happened to be Nancy Pelosi, the very sort of San Francisco liberal Edwards often had to distance himself from. Waco was also represented in the state legislature by another Democrat, Jim Dunnam, the minority leader in the statehouse.

Kelly McDonald, an energetic mother of six, first moved to Waco as a foster child in the eighth grade. She left after high school but returned in 1999 to raise a family, buying a farm with twenty acres on the outskirts of town. One of her children had a rare metabolic disorder called PKU that can lead to brain damage and mental retardation. McDonald became active in state and federal politics as a result, trying to get insurance companies to cover the condition. Though never a straight-ticket voter, she became frustrated with the GOP's ties to the insurance industry and told her husband after the 2004 election, "Voting's not enough. We need to do more." She expected to support Clinton because of her expertise on health care but switched to Obama after attending a rally of his in Austin, drawn to the diversity of the crowd. In January 2008, she went to the first meeting of the Obama campaign in Waco at Uncle Dan's BBQ, a popular red-and-white-checkered tablecloth joint owned by a local Democrat. "I haven't stopped since," she said.

During the primary, Bush's backyard saw an explosion of Democratic activism. "I'd never seen anything like this in Waco,"

McDonald said. Over half the people volunteering were new to politics, she estimated. After the primary ended, however, all the professionals got out of town. McDonald left her family behind six weeks before the election and went to organize in Florida. She was originally sent to Gainesville, a liberal college town that felt a lot like Austin. "Is there an area more like Waco?" she asked. They sent her to Lee County, named after the famed Confederate general, on the state's west coast. There were rebel flags all over the place. The former GOP stronghold, which included Fort Myers, had been decimated by economic calamity and foreclosures. Obama cut Bush's twenty-point margin of victory in half. McDonald saw how political organizing could change a community. She wanted to do the same back home.

Luke Hayes, a twenty-five-year-old Obama organizer from the Bronx, came to Waco during the primary. He returned after the election in his new capacity as OFA's Texas state director. Ninety people packed into Poppa Rollo's Pizza, a brightly lit restaurant in a strip mall that shows old movies in its booths, to hear him speak and share memories of the good old days. Hayes promised the county wouldn't be ignored by Obama's post-campaign arm. As proof, McDonald came on board as an OFA organizer in October 2009 and opened an office downtown.

It had been a tough slog so far. Edwards represented the most conservative district in the country for a Democrat, which McCain won by twenty-five points. The Tea Partiers dominated his town halls during the August recess, pressuring Edwards to vote against Obama's health-care bill, which he soon did (twice), along with the president's climate change, jobs, and financial reform legislation. "Democrats here locally are not happy with him, by and large," McDonald said. She tried to get Edwards's back when he did side with Obama, but influential Texas Democrats were wary of OFA's involvement in the area. "It's not gonna help for OFA to be in Chet Edwards's district," said state chair Boyd Richie. Pushing national issues in a place like Waco would only backfire, the operatives argued. The

Obama activists had to become part of the fabric of the state. "If they're not given the freedom to go native," said another well-placed Texas Democrat, "I'm not sure it will be resources well spent." Such were the daily tribulations of a Democratic activist in Waco, Texas. When you weren't fighting Republicans, you had to battle your own kind.

Still, McDonald had reasons to be optimistic. First, Democrats elected a new party chair in May 2010. Second, the city had a large minority population (nearly 50 percent) for a rural county and competitive local and statewide elections on the horizon. Third, the Trust had pledged to put up some money for Waco to run, on a small scale, the type of coordinated campaign that Dallas so successfully executed in 2006. Democrats had to start somewhere if they hoped to encroach on Republican turf. Oscar Boleman, the head of College Democrats at Waco's heavily Republican Baylor University and a self-described "Geeky Mexican" from Galveston, had already printed up special T-shirts for the coming-out party. "Mom, Dad," they said, "I'm a Democrat."

Sending a few of those shirts to the nation's capital might not be such a bad idea. At a time of rampant disillusionment with Washington, the perseverance and tenacity of determined organizers in unlikely locales such as Dallas and Waco, in spite of the news of the day, offers a path forward for Democrats in red and blue states alike. We tend to identify political parties with the professional politicians doing battle inside the corridors of power, locked in a zero-sum game of Beltway paralysis. But at their best moments, both parties, particularly the Democratic Party, live at the grass roots. That's why down here, Dean's vision of rebuilding the party matches Obama's dream of realigning the political map. It may not turn blue for a while yet, but Texas is emblematic of how a place can change, especially when you least expect it.

AFTERWORD: WHITHER THE MOVEMENT?

The movement has to be bigger than Obama. —Howard Dean

Over a weekend in June 2011, Minneapolis, Minnesota—the Land of Nice—became an unlikely political battleground.

At the Minneapolis Convention Center, twenty-four hundred progressive activists assembled for the sixth annual Netroots Nation conference. Two blocks away, a thousand conservatives rallied inside the ballroom of the Minneapolis Hilton—adorned by a gaudy red and blue stage with giant white stars—for the second RightOnline conference. The mood at the dueling conventions could not have been more different. Conservative activists felt proudly ascendant, while their progressive counterparts were deeply uneasy about the political direction of the country. The conservative commentator Michelle Malkin mocked her temporary neighbors as "the spurned progressive Obama lovers confab."

Seven months after a dramatic reversal of fortune in the last election, the wounds were still painfully raw for Democrats. After losing ground in 2006 and 2008, Republicans struck back with a vengeance in 2010, picking up 63 seats in the House of Representatives, 6 seats in the Senate, 6 governorships, and 680 state legislative seats. It was the largest victory of either party in a midterm election since 1938.

In the days and weeks following the election, Democrats at every level asked themselves the same agonizing question: What the hell just happened? How, in such a short period, did the country shift from President Obama's historic election and a massive Democratic majority after the 2008 election to the emergence of the Tea Party and major Republican electoral advances in 2010?

On the first night of Netroots Nation, inside the massive industrial basement hall of the convention center, it felt as if the Democratic Party had been transported back in time. The keynote speakers were Howard Dean and Russ Feingold, the same politicians who led the opposition to the war in Iraq within the party in 2003. Back then, Democratic activists were enraged at their leaders in Congress and on the presidential campaign trail for supporting—or failing to adequately challenge—Bush's radical agenda. In 2011, despite a Democratic president and a Democratic Senate, the crowd at Netroots Nation—a well-educated, high-tech, politically progressive segment of the Democratic base, many of whom came of age politically through the Dean campaign—was similarly anxious about the state of the party. "There has been a lot of angst about whether all the promises have been kept, whether there's been change we can believe in," Dean said in his speech.

Feingold, the former Wisconsin senator who had been regarded by the Democratic base as the conscience of the Senate before losing his seat in 2010, painted a grim picture of the political landscape following the Supreme Court's *Citizens United* decision, which allowed unlimited secret campaign contributions in federal elections. Feingold ominously predicted it could lead to the "complete destruction of our campaign-finance system and domination by corporate interests." Democrats had recently begun forming their own so-called super PACs to compete with the GOP in an ever-more-expensive money race. "I fear the Democratic Party is in danger of losing its identity," Feingold said.

The panels at Netroots Nation had names like "Structural Barriers to Progressive Success," "The Attack on America's Middle Class, and the Plan to Fight Back," and, my personal favorite, "What to Do When the President Is Just Not That into You." The list of grievances with the Obama administration was a long one: a focus on deficit reduction over job creation, a stimulus bill that was too small to spur a lasting economic recovery, the coziness between the White House and Wall Street, no public insurance option as part of health-care reform, no Employee Free Choice Act, no immigration reform, no legislation to reduce global warming, an escalation of the war in Afghanistan and an incursion into Libya without congressional approval, a continuation of the Bush administration's national security state, an extension of the Bush tax cuts, and so on.

A Pew survey in May 2011 found that 84 percent of staunch conservatives strongly disapproved of the president, but only 64 percent of solid liberals strongly approved of him. As the Daily Kos blogger Joan McCarter put it: "The president isn't our boyfriend anymore."

This well-chronicled intensity gap determined the results of the midterm election. The 2010 electorate was older, whiter, and more conservative compared with 2008 and would have voted for John McCain over Obama. Independent voters deserted the Democratic Party, and the Democratic base didn't vote in large enough numbers to make up the difference. By nineteen points, Republicans said they were more excited to vote than Democrats, "the largest gap in enthusiasm by party of any recent midterm elections," according to Gallup.

"The election results themselves did not represent a full-blown realignment, but a more modest shift in existing loyalties," wrote John Judis in *The New Republic*. "In other words, the Republicans did better with their coalition than the Democrats did with theirs." Forty-five million Americans voted in 2008 who didn't vote in 2010, noted Michael Tomasky in *The Guardian*, "and the exits tell us the bulk of them were liberal, young, black, Latino."

The great recession and the country's sky-high unemployment rate provided the shortest explanation for the Democrats' woes. Yet the depth and breadth of the economic crisis—and the inability of the administration to get its message out during it—only told part of the story. The Democratic message in 2010—"we're not as bad as those other guys"—hadn't exactly inspired Democratic voters to rush to the polls. Nor had the promise of the Obama campaign extended in many respects to Obama's Washington. The ugliness of the legislative process in Congress, the seedy culture of moneyed interests continuing to buy influence in government, and the lack of mobilization of Obama's base compared with the mobilization of the Republican base all contributed to massive Republican victories in 2010.

"The Tea Party forces got really well organized and created a lot of momentum," Dean told me after the election. "Obama's political staff was a disaster. It was all inside the Beltway, all the time, and it was not tuned in to what was going on around the rest of the country. And then of course we had the bad economy and the terrible mismanagement of the health-care bill."

The state-based organizing efforts that had inspired Democratic activists since the 2010 election, such as the huge protests in Wisconsin in response to Republican efforts to curtail collective bargaining rights for state workers, had little to do with the national Democratic Party or the Obama White House. Indeed, when organizers at the DNC initially activated Obama's grassroots network in support of the uprising in Madison, they were "angrily reined in" by senior officials at the White House, according to *The New York Times*. "Administration officials said they saw such events beyond Washington as distractions from the optimistic 'win the future' message Mr. Obama introduced with his State of the Union address," reported the paper. The Obama administration seemed disconnected from, if not on the wrong side of, the very fights that were determining the identity of the Democratic Party at the local level. Jim Dean, president of Democracy for America, described the split within the party as "a culture of activism versus a culture of incumbency."

Jeremy Bird spent two years at OFA before moving over to the Obama campaign as its deputy field director. More than anyone inside the upper echelons of the Obama inner circle, he'd tried to stay in sync with the president's base, which had become increasingly disillusioned about the prospects for change in Washington. The day after Dean spoke at Netroots Nation, Bird described how the Obama campaign planned to win in 2012—by expanding the electorate, registering scores of new voters, and reactivating supporters from 2008. "It's gotta be new, it's gotta be innovative, it can't be the same old, same old," he said. In his rapid-fire monotone, Bird quickly outlined the campaign's progress so far. They'd trained 1,650 new summer organizers, held thousands of one-on-one calls and meetings with volunteers from 2008, and would have twenty-five to thirty thousand neighborhood teams in place by the end of 2011.

During the Q&A, Bird's relentless optimism faced push back from the room of current and former Obama supporters. "It is okay that you say that you see enthusiasm [for Obama] out there," said one volunteer from Texas. "I speak to tons of people over the Internet and tons of people face-to-face. We need to do a hell of a lot more on enthusiasm. I don't know what the data says, but we need to do a lot more than we're doing right now."

"I'm not going to say that people are as enthusiastic as they've ever been," Bird admitted. "We do have a lot to do on enthusiasm . . . We have to talk about what the president has done, and we've got to talk about what our opponents are going to do."

Marty Berg, an Obama volunteer from L.A., asked about a key paradox facing Obama in 2012. "I'm confused about the fund-raising strategy of the campaign," he told Bird. News had just broken that Obama had met with twenty top financial executives at the White House under the auspices of the DNC, which looked suspiciously like a fund-raising event. But a day later, the president sent out an e-mail to his supporters claiming that he was "running a different kind of campaign," not financed by "Washington lobbyists or special-interest PACs."

"So which is it?" Berg asked. "Is he taking money from the fat cats and asking for my $5?"

"It's both," Bird answered. "Our fund-raising strategy is multifaceted."

It was a truthful answer that also described the previous Obama campaign. In 2008, Obama raised a third of his money from donors who gave $200 or less and the rest from wealthier donors and corporate interests. For obvious reasons, the campaign chose to emphasize the former narrative over the latter, which continued in 2012.

Obama's 2012 campaign manager, Jim Messina, bragged that the campaign planned to "build the biggest grassroots campaign in American history." Yet simply dropping the phrase over and over didn't make it so. As Micah Sifry of techPresident noted, there was a big difference between genuine grassroots politics and things that seemed "grassrootsy," which had become all the rage following Obama's election. If Obama's grassroots base wasn't part of his governing strategy, would they really have true ownership of his reelection campaign? Thus far, in its attempt to amass a $1 billion war chest for 2012, the campaign had doggedly wooed the fat cats while offering "We Do Big Things" T-shirts to the masses. Of the $86 million the Obama Victory Fund raised in its first quarter of the 2012 election cycle, 40 percent came from 271 bundlers (known as "volunteer fund-raisers") who raised between $50,000 and more than $500,000 each.

This was less an indictment of the Obama campaign per se and more a reflection of the sorry state of American politics. Obama, like any other politician, simply responded to pressures inherent in the political system, and there had been much more pressure on him from the right than from the left since he entered office, from grassroots activists and Washington lobbyists alike. Liberals believed that the mere ascension of Obama and a Democratic congressional majority would somehow shift the political process to the left; in fact, the opposite occurred: the aftermath of the 2008 election further motivated activists on the right while forging a sense of deference and complacency among those on the left. And the moneyed class who prospered during the Bush and Clinton years found a way to kill or water down nearly everything it objected to under Obama. In his new book, *Oligarchy*, the Northwestern University political scientist Jeffrey Winters referred to these disproportionately wealthy and influential actors as the "Income Defense Industry."

The panels at Netroots Nation were largely preoccupied with combating this bipartisan industry, stopping the assault on workers in states like Wisconsin, and exploring new ways to curb the growing influence of corporate money in politics. There was a widespread belief that Democratic activists had to move beyond reliance on Obama and the national Democratic Party and build independent institutions that could more effectively pressure Democrats to support a progressive agenda. You could elect all the Democrats in the world, but if the underlying political system remained fundamentally conservative, the results would continue to be predictably disappointing. After all, even progressive Democratic governors in deep-blue states, such as Andrew Cuomo in New York and Jerry Brown in California, had embraced the GOP's fiscal austerity agenda following the 2010 election, cutting social services for the poor and needy and eroding the power of Democratic-allied labor unions.

"If you're losing the game, change the rules," Darcy Burner, president of ProgressiveCongress.org, told a roomful of activists. "How many of you think progressives are winning the game?"

Not a single hand went up.

With the fifty-state strategy, Dean had tried to build a base of decentralized local activists who would last beyond one election—a permanent standing army for change. But the glue of what held the wildly diverse Democratic majority together—the question of what it really stood for and which principles were nonnegotiable—had never really been elucidated, by either the leaders or the rank and file. "In '06 the glue was Bush," Dean said, "and in '08 the glue was Obama." Ever since then, the organizing focus inside the party had become subsumed by, and subservient to, the president.

"We all came together around the idea of Obama, which was a startling idea, and we all made it happen," Dean said. "But the movement has to be bigger than Obama. It can't be just about Obama." No longer could Obama activists assume that their voices would be heard through the traditional channels run by the Obama machine, such as OFA. "The Obama movement has been institutionalized, to a certain extent, at the DNC and in Chicago, which is a mixed bag," Dean said. "Once you institutionalize it, it's not a grassroots movement anymore." In Minneapolis, a consensus of sorts emerged around this topic: there needed to be a new alternative.

In the most talked-about speech at Netroots Nation, the former Obama green jobs adviser Van Jones described how in 2008 Obama had assembled a "meta-brand" of labor, environmental, racial justice, women's rights, LGBT, and immigrant rights groups. In Jones's PowerPoint presentation, Obama was at the top, and all the groups were below. That was precisely the problem: a supposedly bottom-up movement had been structured in an entirely top-down way. In 2010, the Tea Party created its own meta-brand, uniting various strains of conservative organizations, but as Jones explained: "There is no president of the Tea Party." And that was a good thing.

Many liberal activists had initially dismissed the Tea Party as a top-down, corporate-funded Astroturf organization, rather than an authentic grassroots movement. In truth, it was both. Longtime conservative donors like the Koch brothers and Republican operatives like Karl Rove had used Tea Party activists to further their political agenda and business interests, but these activists had also emerged organically, in a more spontaneous manner. As Kate Zernike writes in her book *Boiling Mad*, there had been numerous attempts on the right to create a Tea Party before, and none had succeeded. FreedomWorks had been trying in vain since 1984. It was only after the election of Obama and the dislocation of the economic crisis that new activists emerged from the woodwork and found a broader audience. Jones and the progressive activists at Netroots Nation vehemently disagreed with the Tea Party's politics but saw its structure and influence as a model for the next phase of the Dean and Obama movements.

After all, the Tea Party brought the GOP back to life quicker than anyone expected. At the very moment that Obama abandoned his political movement, the Tea Party adopted the Dean/Obama playbook and ran with it, fielding insurgent candidates across the country, injecting much-needed energy into the GOP, and systematically taking over local parties at the precinct level. They forced establishment Republicans to pay attention to their agenda, through primaries and protests. The consequences weren't always beneficial to the Republican Party—Tea Party–backed candidates squandered winnable races in places like Colorado, Connecticut, Delaware, and Nevada and cost the GOP control of the Senate as a result—but it's difficult to understate the impact these conservative activists had in 2010.

The Tea Party learned the lessons of 2006 and 2008 better than the Democrats did. "President Obama and Speaker Pelosi can thank Howard Dean's '50-state strategy' for laying the ground work for the Democrat landslide in 2008," said the Tea Party strategist Dick Armey, a former House majority leader and chairman of Freedom-Works. "The Tea Party movement is much the same, and Tea Party groups exist in every state and city across the country." In 2010, for example, Republicans ran more candidates for Congress than ever before. The RNC chairman, Michael Steele, called it "the first time the party has ever engaged in all 50 states of the union."

Establishment pundits and politicians initially discounted the power of the Tea Party, as they did the Deaniacs a few election cycles earlier. "Netroots protests dragged the Democratic Party kicking and screaming into 2006 and 2008," wrote the GOP Web strategists Patrick Ruffini and Mindy Finn in 2010. "Frustrated with the president and health-care reform, the conservative 'tea party' movement has done the same for the Republicans this year." There were some crucial differences between the two movements—namely, the amount of corporate money that fueled Tea Party candidates—but the success of the Tea Party confirmed the dawn of a new political era, where the barriers to entry had been drastically lowered and insurgent candidates in both parties could topple the establishment by mobilizing grassroots activists from the bottom up. If Obama was "Dean 2.0," then the Tea Partiers were the third manifestation.

A few days after Netroots Nation, I met Jones for breakfast in New York City and asked him to explain exactly what about the Tea Party he thought progressive activists should emulate. "The Tea Party is a brilliant innovation in American politics," he said. He went on:

> The most important thing that people don't seem to get about the Tea Party is that the Tea Party itself is not an organization; it's an open-sourced brand. Just under the Tea Party Patriots brand alone, there's 3,528 affiliates.
>
> It's not a coalition where everybody sits around and fights over money. It's a meta-branded network or a movement with a common banner. That approach to politics is really smart. So when you say who is the one leader of the Tea Party, you can't answer the question. Who was the one leader in Madison? Who was the one leader in Egypt? There's something that's changing about the way politics gets done, and we got a taste of it in 2008, and that's why Obama did so well. But now we've got to follow through on the promise of that more open-source, more distributed approach to politics and have it be more people powered and people owned.
>
> The attributes of the distributed approach are that you get a lot more people taking a lot more actions. You have more creativity. You have more small-d democracy. You aren't waiting for one person to get everything right. One thing that some people could argue happened to the movement for hope and change is that in hindsight, at one point everybody put all their chips on the name brand of an individual person—Obama. As beautiful as he is, when he became head

of state, the movement got very confused on how to proceed. Do we just wait until he tells us what to do? Do we challenge the White House? There weren't multiple support centers engaged; it was basically the White House staff and the campaign staff, and it became very centralized. The banner or the meta-brand wasn't about a set of principles; it was about a person. And so the Tea Party is an upgrade . . . They don't just have one leader . . . If Dick Armey makes the wrong call on a piece of legislation, the whole Tea Party doesn't necessarily go in that direction.

Dean agreed with Jones's invocation of the Tea Party as a model for Democratic activists. "When I came in as DNC chair, the Republicans were far ahead of us," Dean said. "We leapfrogged them and did better in '06 and '08 technologically, organizationally, and in terms of how to communicate. Then the Republican Tea Party came back in and leapfrogged us. Their movement is a movement that transcends leadership. And here are the Democrats, who are supposedly the grassroots party, but we haven't transcended leadership yet. So they're really ahead of us, in terms of technology and how to get things done in an Internet-based society. So we're going to have to leapfrog them again."

Tea Party activists could influence the direction of the Republican Party, on issues like taxes and spending, simply by threatening to defeat establishment Republicans who bucked Tea Party orthodoxy. There was simply no equivalent on the Democratic side. "It would be as if the progressives came in and were so well organized that they basically told the Democratic Party if they didn't move to the left, they were going to primary every single one of them, and basically made that stick," Dean said. "The Right was much more effective in 2010 than the Left was in 2006."

Dean enjoyed a better relationship with the Obama administration after Rahm's departure and had met with the chief of staff, Bill Daley, a number of times in the White House. Daley wanted to know how the administration could "bring progressives back into the fold," Dean said.

"Treat them honestly," Dean told him. "Have a serious dialogue that isn't cooked ahead of time."

But the administration seemed more interested in catering to the elusive Independent voter than in fighting for its progressive base. After three years of constant disappointments, Democratic activists had finally acknowledged in Minneapolis that they could often not rely on Democratic politicians, Obama included, to advance a progressive political agenda. Chris Bowers, an early Dean supporter who was now director of activism for the liberal blog Daily Kos, wrote a thoughtful manifesto on this subject after returning from Minneapolis:

> A majority of legislators and candidates believe their electoral chances suffer more if they oppose conservative policy goals than if they oppose progressive ones. That was even the case in 2009–2010, when Democrats held massive majorities in Congress. As long [as] the majority of candidates and members of Congress continue to believe that veering to the left hurts them electorally, progressives will continue to see their public policy goals go largely unachieved even when Democrats are governing . . .
>
> We have to start winning elections in ways so that the majority of political observers believe the defeated candidate lost because s/he opposed one or more progressive legislative priorities. Just defeating someone who opposes progressive legislation with someone who supports it is not enough. A wide array of pundits, candidates and political professionals must believe that opposition to progressive policies was the primary reason an elected official was removed from office. That is the only way we are going to start convincing people that opposing progressive legislation is truly [a] bad idea for someone's political career. As such, it's

also the only way we're going to start getting progressive legislation passed on a regular basis.

Whether there would be an Obama movement in 2012—and whether Democratic and progressive activists would embrace it—remained an unsettled question heading into the campaign. "The Obama movement has to be revived and expanded so that electing Obama is part of the goal of the movement, but it's not the goal of the movement," Dean said. "The real goal of the movement is to change America and get it ready for this new generation of extraordinarily diverse Americans to lead." Giving Obama another term in the White House would not be considered a victory in and of itself, as it was in 2008. To flourish beyond Obama's reelection, the movement would have to figure out how to reinvent the Democratic Party, and American politics, once again.

The unease among Democrats at Netroots Nation and across the country barely registered in the Obama White House following the 2010 election.

Immediately following the Democrats' electoral shellacking, a wide array of pundits urged Obama to "pull a Clinton," in the words of *Politico*: move to the center (as if he weren't already there), find common ground with the GOP, and adopt the "triangulation" strategy employed by Bill Clinton after the Democratic setback in the 1994 midterms. "Is 'triangulation' just another word for the politics of the possible?" asked *The New York Times*. "Can Obama do a Clinton?" seconded *The Economist*. And so on. In the span of two years, the Clinton presidency went from being Obama's floor to being his ceiling.

Obama had already packed his White House with insiders from the Clinton administration and began year three with prominent Clinton alums as his chief of staff (Bill Daley), top economic adviser (Gene Sperling), and budget director (Jack Lew). Although Rahm Emanuel left to run for mayor of Chicago a month before the election, the administration still reflected his Clintonian ethos, in some ways more than ever.

The president's first legislative deal after the election, agreeing to extend all of Bush's controversial tax cuts, included major concessions to the GOP in a highly Clintonesque compromise. And there was the Big Dog himself, at the White House press podium in December 2010, defending the agreement while Obama was under fire from his own party, a predicament Clinton was no stranger to. Shortly thereafter, Obama decided that reducing the deficit would become the signature postelection priority of his administration. The Clinton era had returned, minus the peace and prosperity (and Monica's blue dress).

At the hopeful beginning of his presidency, Obama devoured biographies of Lincoln (*Team of Rivals* by Doris Kearns Goodwin, *Lincoln: The Biography of a Writer* by Fred Kaplan) and FDR (*The Defining Moment* by Jonathan Alter, *FDR* by Jean Edward Smith), two unquestionably great presidents who put their unique stamp on history. By the end of a productive yet turbulent two years in office, Obama's reading list was replaced with biographies of Clinton and Reagan, presidents who stumbled in their early days and suffered bad losses in their first midterm elections yet eventually regained their footing—though in markedly different ways. Clinton, for much of his presidency, shaded the difference between liberalism and conservatism in favor of a "third way," while Reagan stuck to an unabashedly conservative ideology on foreign and domestic policy.

On the campaign trail in 2008, Obama argued that Reagan had "changed the trajectory of America . . . in a way that Bill Clinton did not." Yet although his candidacy resembled a political movement, like Reagan's, it quickly became clear that Obama had no intention of governing as a movement president.

According to Marshall Ganz, Obama moved from being a "transformational" leader during the campaign to a "transactional" politician as president. Some of that, of course, was to be expected; candidates need to inspire, while presidents have to govern. Governing, by nature, is often transactional. Nonetheless, transformational leaders find a way to get beyond transactional politics, Ganz argued, pointing to Reagan as a prime example. "Reagan shows exactly how to govern, which is aligning yourself with a movement outside Washington that is capable of mobilizing pressure on forces inside Washington so that you can change the rules of the game," he said. That was also the model Obama invoked during the campaign but had chosen not to employ as president. He played by the conventional Washington rules instead of trying to change them. "Our basic attitude was, we've gotta get some things done, in some cases quickly . . . and in order to do that, [we] basically worked with the process as opposed to transformed the process, and there's no doubt that that frustrated folks," Obama told Jon Stewart shortly before the 2010 election.

"He shifted from a politics of advocacy to a politics of compromise," Ganz said. Once inside the White House, Obama viewed his own grassroots network "like a tiger you can't control." The attitude toward his supporters, Ganz argued, changed from "Yes We Can" to "Yes I Can."

As a presidential candidate, Obama had disparaged the bite-size politics of the Clinton era and maintained that he'd rather be a consequential president in one term than a mushy centrist for eight years. When Rahm urged him not to pursue health-care reform in 2009, Obama responded, "I wasn't sent here to do school uniforms."

Yet here's the rub: compromise, for Obama, appeared to be even more of a core value than it was for Clinton; he believed instinctively, from his days as a community organizer onward, in getting what he could out of a deal, even if it's less than he wanted, and moving on. What Obama considered the purism of the left bothered him as much as the ideological extremity of the right, and as president he often lumped both poles together, even as the center continued to drift to the right.

The *Washington Post* blogger Adam Serwer persuasively argued that "what in the past the [Obama] administration has referred to as 'pragmatism' is merely triangulating by another name." The difference is rhetorical, not substantive. "Obama makes it clear that he agrees with liberals on substance, before arguing that the political situation necessitates some kind of compromise," Serwer wrote. Obama professes not to like the compromise he's agreeing to—abandoning the public option on health care, loading up the stimulus with tax cuts, extending the Bush tax cuts for the wealthiest Americans, dramatically cutting spending to reduce the deficit—but he compromises all the same. "You can't always get what you want" might as well have described Obama's governing philosophy.

Despite saying that he wanted to be like Reagan, not Clinton, Obama had yet to make a sustained case for his own corresponding vision for the country, as Reagan successfully did. Reagan attacked liberalism throughout his presidency: big government was the problem, and lower taxes and fewer regulations were the solution. No matter the deals he eventually struck, whether they be with the Democratic leader Tip O'Neill or Soviet Russia, capitalism was the hero and government the villain. Reaganism became an ideology, and the GOP is still following that script today. One can scarcely say the same about Obamaism—whatever that may be.

"Just where Mr. Obama actually lives on the ideological continuum," wrote Matt Bai of *The New York Times*, "is the most vexing question of his presidency." Obama has been quite clear about his allergy to ideological thinking. "I don't think in ideological terms," he told *The Nation* in 2006. "I never have." But the president's relentless attachment to "pragmatism," which had become an ideology unto itself, allowed the GOP's dominant narrative about the economic crisis—that big government, once again, was to blame—to go unchallenged, especially when Obama sided with Republicans on issues like deficit reduction and freezes on discretionary spending and federal pay. "In the absence of an alternative narrative the Republican story is the only one the public hears," Robert Reich noted on his blog. Hence the rise of the Tea Party and the potency of anti-government right-wing populism in the 2010 election.

Obama's supporters didn't expect him to govern as an ideological leftist. But a president without clear principles leaves his base dispirited and the public confused about where he stands on the biggest issues of the day. Obama won a number of legislative battles, but he forfeited the war of ideas.

After Obama's election, it was easy to forget just how much Clinton had shifted the structure of the Democratic Party away from its populist roots and toward Wall Street and major corporate interests. Once in office, Obama presided over not one but two Democratic Parties, noted the former Bush administration speechwriter Michael Gerson.

"One consists of European-style social democrats, represented by leaders such as Nancy Pelosi," Gerson wrote in *The Washington Post*. "The other Democratic Party is socially liberal and pro-business . . . The ideological distance between social Democrats and pro-business Democrats is wider than any ideological gap on the Republican side." After flirting with both groups, by year three of his presidency Obama was firmly in the neoliberal camp. He could have mobilized his grassroots political supporters in opposition to the corporate Democrats, but once inside the White House he chose the path of least resistance and sided with the Clintonites over the insurgent elements of the Obama coalition.

To run his reelection campaign, Obama turned to his deputy chief of staff in the White House, Jim Messina (not to be confused with the Loggins and Messina of soft rock fame), who had worked as a top lieutenant for Rahm and as a longtime aide to Max Baucus. Messina's MO in the White House keenly illustrated how the Obama administration operated in Washington—insistent on demanding total control, hostile to any public pressure from Democratic activists on dissident Democrats or administration allies, committed to working the system inside Washington rather than changing it.

Unlike David Plouffe, who became a revered figure among

Obama supporters, Messina began the reelection campaign with a significant amount of baggage. As a former chief of staff to Baucus and enforcer to Emanuel, Messina had clashed with progressive activists and grassroots Obama supporters both inside and outside Washington over political strategy and on issues like health-care reform and gay rights, alienating parts of the very constituencies that worked so hard for Obama in 2008 and that the campaign needed to reinspire and reactivate in 2012. "He is not of the Obama movement," said one top Democratic strategist in Washington. "There is not a bone in his body that speaks to or comprehends the idea of a movement and that grassroots energy. To me, that's bothersome."

Under Messina, Obama 2012 more closely resembled the electoral strategy of Clinton in 1996—cautious, calculating, top-down in structure, devoted to small-bore issues that blurred the differences between the parties (remember V-chips, teen curfews, and school uniforms?)—than Obama 2008, a grassroots effort on a scale modern politics had never seen. In 1996, only 49 percent of the electorate bothered to vote, the lowest turnout in a presidential election since Adams versus Jackson in 1824. It was widely assumed that "remote-control TV politics" had triumphed over civic participation.

If the 2008 campaign was fresh, exciting, and inspirational, the 2012 campaign would likely be a long, tough, dirty slog, premised less on hope than on fear of the Republican alternative. Plouffe predicted a "street fight for the presidency." A new kind of politics had given way to by any means necessary. Messina reflected the prevailing center of gravity inside Obama's inner circle and reelection campaign. Going into 2012, Democratic activists faced a very different question than they did in 2008: What becomes of a political movement after it loses its leader?

Democrats at the local level most acutely felt the pain after the 2010 election.

Texas didn't go blue. Neither did most states. One-party rule returned to Indiana, while fractious divided government gripped North Carolina and Colorado. With a few exceptions, the electoral map once again resembled a giant blob of red. Republicans controlled the governor's mansion and both legislative chambers in twenty-one states, including pivotal swing states like Florida, Michigan, Ohio, Pennsylvania, and Wisconsin.

The unlikely success stories of the Democratic fifty-state strategy suffered a particularly cruel fate. Fourteen Democratic members of the congressional class of 2006 and twenty-one members of the class of 2008 went down, as Republicans posted big gains in the industrial Midwest, Northeast, and South. Only twelve Democratic representatives from 2006 and a mere six from 2008 managed to hang on. Following the election, at least two dozen Democratic state legislators in Alabama, Georgia, Louisiana, Mississippi, and Texas switched parties.

Under the guise of deficit reduction, a new crop of Republican governors immediately went after their number one political opponents—Democratic-aligned labor unions—and introduced a harsh austerity agenda of cut, cut, cut. In Congress, House Republicans backed Representative Paul Ryan's radical plan to privatize Medicare and gut the social safety net. Republicans were intent on fulfilling the vow of the antitax crusader Grover Norquist to "shrink government to the size where we can drown it in a bathtub."

The public, however, had other ideas and quickly began to experience a severe case of buyer's remorse. New Republican governors like Scott Walker in Wisconsin, John Kasich in Ohio, and Rick Scott in Florida soon became among the most loathed state leaders in the nation. The unpopularity of the Ryan budget plan helped Democrats unexpectedly win a special election in upstate New York's heavily Republican Twenty-sixth Congressional District. The DCCC chairman, Steve Israel, noted that ninety-seven seats held by Republican House members were more moderate in complexion (although redistricting in 2012 could change that). Suddenly Democrats had a chance to reclaim the House just one cycle after suffering their worst loss since World War II.

The Tea Party movement, though still powerful, showed signs of running out of steam. It was older, whiter, wealthier, more male dominated, and more conservative than the country as a whole. That hadn't mattered in 2010, when the anti-incumbent public soured on the ruling Democrats, but it would become a liability in future elections. If the Tea Party didn't expand its base in 2012, it would have a hard time keeping up with Obama's rainbow coalition. The open-source, bottom-up, technological shift in American politics ultimately favored the Democrats.

Yet Democrats would only win in 2012 by resurrecting the feisty, decentralized, activist party that prevailed in 2006 and 2008. That party was nowhere to be seen in 2010 and was similarly MIA heading into 2012. The divide between Democratic activists at the local level and the national party in Washington, which Dean tried to bridge, had only intensified during the great recession.

Three years into the economic crisis, with the unemployment rate still at perilously high levels, Democratic activists wanted a bold jobs plan from Washington. But the Obama administration stubbornly fixated on reducing the deficit and cutting spending for much of 2011, which brought only more pain for struggling Americans. "It's like they're living on a different freakin' planet," the Democratic activist Pam Williamson from Western North Carolina said of the White House.

To help elect Democratic candidates in 2012, Williamson and the local Democratic Party in Watauga County, North Carolina, planned to "hammer the hell out of Republicans" for wanting to cut or privatize Medicare and Social Security, she said, the same rallying cry Democrats had successfully used in New York's Twenty-sixth Congressional District and hoped to replicate across the country. "Republicans want to give seniors coupons," Williamson said. "That's what we've been saying, to great effect. As Democrats, we're not gonna let it happen."

But, for a time, Williamson wasn't sure if Obama would defend these core Democratic achievements, in the White House and on the campaign trail, or side with Republicans to restructure them as part of a grand bargain to cut the deficit. "If President Obama wants to go out there and commit political suicide by saying he's going to cut Social Security and Medicare, we're going to have to get as far away from him as possible," she said in July 2011.

It was only after economic growth slowed to a crawl in August and John Boehner rejected Obama's $4 trillion deficit offer, which the *New York Times* columnist David Brooks described as "an astonishing concession" by the White House and "the deal of the century" for Republicans, that the president bucked the austerity class and introduced the jobs plan Democrats had been demanding. Obama campaigned energetically across the country in support of the idea, rallying supporters around the new initiative. If Republicans in Congress blocked the bill, Obama made it clear that he had no qualms about running against the "do-nothing Congress," like Harry Truman had successfully done in 1948.

"Fingers crossed that the administration finally woke up, and I am happy the president is out on the road in real America rocking his jobs plan," said Williamson. "The president is now doing what he should have been doing for the past three years. I hope it's not too late for his reelection prospects."

Still, the country's grim economic news threatened to overshadow whatever Obama did. It had certainly taken a toll on his party's political fortunes. Obama admitted he would now be the "underdog" in 2012. The polling reinforced his unenviable position. When Gallup asked voters in September 2011 if they were more enthusiastic about voting in 2012 than they were in 2008, Republicans held a twenty-seven-point advantage over Democrats.

Democratic activists like Williamson faced an uphill climb in 2012. After sweeping elections in 2006 and 2008, Democrats lost nearly everything in Watauga County in 2010, including their state representative and state senator, all three county commissioners, all but one candidate for school board, and a marquee race for Congress. "We went down because of national reasons," she said, "and there wasn't a damn thing we could do about it." The best local organizing couldn't save the party. Watauga's election returns mirrored the results statewide, as the GOP took over the state legislature for the first time since Reconstruction. Republicans quickly began plotting how to eliminate even more Democrats through redistricting in 2012.

North Carolina's Democratic governor, Bev Perdue, vetoed fifteen bills in the first legislative session, a state record. That included the far-right state budget, which the legislature successfully overrode in the wee hours of the morning. Perdue predicted it could lead to thirty thousand layoffs of state and local employees (the GOP put the number at eighteen thousand), with education—always a top priority in the state—hit the hardest. "We are about to see the largest public layoff in North Carolina and maybe in American history," Perdue said afterward. The *Charlotte Observer* columnist Rob Christensen likened the clashes in the legislature to the "Equal Rights Amendment battle in the 1970s and the civil rights fights of the 1960s." Perdue called it "a battle for the heart and soul of North Carolina."

The same kinds of fights played out across the country. In Indiana, Republicans picked up a Senate seat and two House seats and took control of both houses of the state legislature in 2010, assembling their largest majority in twenty-five years. The Republican governor, Mitch Daniels, and the GOP legislature responded by cutting off funding for Planned Parenthood, closing public schools, and firing state workers. Thirty-nine house Democrats boycotted the legislative session in early 2011 and fled to Illinois for nearly six weeks to prevent Republicans from enacting the budget cuts. They won a few concessions upon return—such as blocking a bill that would have prevented state employees from paying union dues—but were unable to halt much of the GOP's right-wing agenda. "We've seen drastic cuts to education, to social services, to public employees," said Patrick Bauer, the house Democratic leader, after the legislative session.

Those red areas, such as Hamilton County, where the Obama campaign had done so much organizing in 2008, now seemed impenetrable. "The Tea Party movement is alive and well in Hamilton County, as it is throughout Indiana," said Chuck Lasker, a formerly Republican Obama supporter. Local politics had become so extreme that Lasker and his wife moved from Indiana to Hawaii, Obama's birthplace, "to get away from the radical craziness of the new GOP," he said.

The Democratic dream of turning Texas blue also seemed far off on the horizon. In 2010, the incumbent governor, Rick Perry, easily defeated the former Houston mayor Bill White, the strongest gubernatorial candidate Democrats had fielded in years. Republicans picked up twenty-two seats in the Texas House, dashing Democratic hopes of taking over the body anytime soon and ensuring that Republicans would control the all-important process of drawing new congressional districts in 2012. Tom DeLay's master plan for permanent Republican control of the state, which looked to be unraveling in 2008, had received a powerful shot in the arm.

Dallas County, where the local Democratic Party effectively organized in 2006 and 2008, remained a rare bright spot, with Democrats winning control of city government and reelecting many incumbents, but most of the state turned from red to redder. Democrats lost every race on the ballot in Waco's McLennan County, from Congress to county clerk. "Republicans were really excited to come out to vote," said the local Obama activist Kelly McDonald, "and the Democrats weren't." Longtime civil servants changed their party registration from Democrat to Republican just to save their jobs. A huge billboard along I-35 between Dallas and Waco denounced Obama as a "socialist by conduct."

The toxic political climate in Washington and in statehouses around the nation had depressed even some of Obama's most loyal volunteers from 2008. At the beginning of 2011, I received a heart-breaking note from Daniel Ayala, a refugee from Central America who'd registered nearly a thousand voters for the Obama campaign during the North Carolina primary in 2008. He wrote:

> I am disappointed with Obama as one of his strong former supporters; he has made my life difficult. Under his watch all the immigrants native of South and Central America have been sacrificed for his political gain. He has permitted—and increased—the destruction of the family and future of more than one million families from Latin America in his first two years. Most of these cases are violations of civil rights and human rights. Right now, he is passing more laws directed against 20 million undocumented families living in the US, and adding more personnel into the ICE force.
>
> The facts are that while he is destroying some families and other poor people are losing their jobs and homes, THE RICH ARE GETTING RICHER!!
>
> Also, going to school and getting an education is now prohibited for some children, other schools are re-segregating, affirmative action has been banned in some states and hate for people of color is rising. These kind of things should not be ignored and should be openly addressed by President Obama. I am not sure which side he is on.

After reading the letter, I recalled visiting Ayala's modest home in Durham after the campaign, looking at pictures of him standing next to the president, and being struck by how much that meant to him. Now that hope was gone and was unlikely to ever come back.

Heading into 2012, I had difficulty finding any consensus among the many Democratic and Obama activists I interviewed for this book. They seemed as divided as the electorate as a whole: some still supported the president as enthusiastically as they did in 2008; some said they would vote and volunteer for Obama in 2012 despite their disappointments; and others, like Ayala, were angry and dispirited.

Colorado was a more hopeful place for Democrats. In 2010, Republicans picked up two congressional seats and won back the Colorado House by one vote (Democrats held the senate), but they blew winnable races for U.S. Senate and governor by nominating extreme Tea Party–backed candidates. "Despite red wave, Colorado stayed a quirky shade of purple," *The Denver Post* reported. Nor was there a broader ideological shift to the right. Colorado voters rejected three tax-slashing ballot measures, an initiative to block the implementation of health-care reform, and an antichoice proposal to define a fetus as a "person."

Mike Maday, an Obama super-volunteer from Colorado Springs, sent me a note after the election explaining how his local organizing in 2010 could be a national model in 2012. He wrote:

> Our US Senate race may point the way to how things can work here and elsewhere in 2012 for progressive candidates and the President. Democratic candidate Michael Bennet kept the race close until Election Day. In most polls he was even with his opponent with registered voters but down a few points with likely voters, the enthusiasm gap. That's where the Democrats' field effort came in. In 2008 the Obama campaign made Colorado one of the top battlegrounds in the country, pouring hundreds of trained organizers into the state.
>
> Here in conservative El Paso County, "the Belly of the Beast," those organizers recruited 2,400 volunteers. I was involved from the start but by Election Day I'd walk through rooms of volunteers and recognize nary a face. It was great. In 2010 the Bennet campaign used a much smaller staff to

tap into that volunteer base. Many of these volunteers had never made political phone calls or knocked on doors prior to 2008.

In 2010 we did not have the numbers of volunteers we had in '08 but the group we had was ready to go. Some had become involved in the local Democratic Party or local campaigns over the last two years. Some had not been involved at all but when called upon they came out, phoned and knocked on doors in the end. According to the *Denver Post* direct voter contact made the difference in a Senate race where the margin was less than 1%. This is the legacy of Howard Dean's 50-state strategy and the amazing organizing efforts of the Obama campaign. If the President's re-election campaign can tap into these volunteers using the same organizing efforts as in 2008 it may again be the difference.

Even down in Waco, Kelly McDonald kept a glass-half-full mind-set and sensed the possibility of a backlash to Republican governance. Perry's $4 billion in cuts to public education, in a state that ranked near the bottom in high school graduation rates, had angered many Republicans and energized Democrats to become more active. "It will motivate people to vote in 2012 who didn't vote in 2010," she predicted.

Democratic activists had a mighty struggle ahead of them—beating back the Republican onslaught while pressing the Obama administration to fight for core Democratic priorities. The shift I noticed in Minneapolis now seemed apparent among a broader class of Democratic activists, who realized they couldn't rely on the national party or the Obama administration to solve their problems. It was time to stop waiting for a savior and to get down to work.

"Republicans didn't give up when Democrats had power," McDonald said, "so Democrats shouldn't give up now."

NOTES

All quotations and dialogue are from the author's interviews and reporting unless otherwise cited in the notes.

PROLOGUE

1 "They said this country": Remarks by Barack Obama, Des Moines, Jan. 3, 2008, www.nytimes.com/2008/01/03/us/politics/03obama-transcript .html.

1 "It's been a long": Remarks by Barack Obama, Chicago, *CNN.com*, Nov. 4, 2008, www.cnn.com/2008/POLITICS/11/04/obama.transcript/.

3 "mad as hell": Quoted from the film *Network*, directed by Sidney Lumet (MGM, 1977).

5 "He'll melt and melt": Quoted in Mark Z. Barabak and Faye Fiore, "Dean's Late-Night Battle Cry May Have Damaged Campaign," *Los Angeles Times*, Jan. 22, 2004.

5 "They said this day": Obama, Iowa caucus speech.

7 "permanent Republican majority": Quoted in Ethan Wallisan, "GOP Looks to Bush's Grass Roots for Help in '06," *Roll Call*, Nov. 29, 2004.

1 ★ INSURGENT VS. ESTABLISHMENT

12 "fifty people or so": Unpublished transcript of "True Believers: Life Inside the Dean Campaign," *CNN Presents*, CNN, March 7, 2004. Transcript courtesy of Kate Albright-Hanna.

12 "The last time": Quoted in Garance Franke-Ruta, "Shock of the Old," *American Prospect*, Nov. 1, 2003.

12 "unprecedented": Quoted in Jodi Wilogren, "Dean Readies Ad Blitz More Than Year Ahead of Election," *New York Times*, Aug. 26, 2003.

12 "a frickin' revolution": Quoted in Lisa DePaulo, "Joe Trippi's Wild Ride," *GQ*, March 2004.

13 "You see this flag?": Quoted in Joe Trippi, *The Revolution Will Not Be Televised* (New York: ReganBooks, 2004), 152.

13 "When are Democrats": Quoted in Tim Woodward, "Presidential Candidate Howard Dean Stumps in Boise," *Idaho Statesman*, Aug. 25, 2003.

13 "There's a bunch": "True Believers."

16 "What I want to know": Remarks by Howard Dean, Democratic National Committee Winter Meeting, Washington, D.C., Feb. 21, 2003, www.gwu.edu/~action/2004/dnc0203/dean022103spt.html.

17 "He just blew": Quoted in Michael Tomasky, "Left Unsaid," *American Prospect*, Feb. 26, 2003, www.prospect.org/cs/articles?article=left_unsaid.

18 "the Establishment": Quoted in Henry Fairlie, "Evolution of a Term," *New Yorker*, Oct. 19, 1968.

18 "I'm going to be dead last": Quoted in Robert Dreyfuss, "The Darkest Horse," *American Prospect*, July 14, 2002.

19 "preposterous": Quoted in Mark Singer, "Running on Instinct," *New Yorker*, Jan. 12, 2004.

21 "moderate Democrats": Quoted in David S. Broder, "For '04 Run, a Walk in Carter's Shoes," *Washington Post*, July 12, 2002.

22 "the Touch-Tone Rebellion": Walter Shapiro, "Politics 1-800-Pound Guerrillas," *Time*, April 6, 1992.

22 "For most of us": E. J. Dionne Jr., *Why Americans Hate Politics* (New York: Simon & Schuster, 1991), 10.

23 "Democrats are almost": Quoted in Dirk Van Susteren, ed., *Howard Dean:*

A Citizen's Guide to the Man Who Would Be President (South Royalton, Vt.: Steerforth, 2003), 6.

23 "fucking queer-loving": Quoted in ibid., 175.

24 "We cannot be successful": Quoted in Lisa Wangsness, "Vermont Governor Mulls Plans for 2004," *Concord Monitor*, Dec. 28, 2001.

24 "What a lot of people": Quoted in Walter Shapiro, *One-Car Caravan* (New York: PublicAffairs, 2003), 125.

26 "very good turnout": Quoted in Zephyr Teachout and Thomas Streeter, eds., *Mousepads, Shoe Leather, and Hope* (Boulder, Colo.: Paradigm, 2008), 48.

26 "It is time": Quoted in Trippi, *Revolution*, 99.

26 "Like Online Dating": Lisa Napoli, *New York Times*, March 13, 2003.

28 Such was the birth: For a comprehensive account of the birth of the netroots, see Jerome Armstrong and Markos Moulitsas, *Crashing the Gate* (White River Junction, Vt.: Chelsea Green, 2006).

29 "Everybody I gave": Quoted in Noam Scheiber, "Organization Man," *New Republic*, Nov. 17, 2003.

29 "There is no way": Joe Trippi, "The Perfect Storm," May 17, 2003, joetrippi .com/blog/?page_id=1378.

30 "politics of concentric circles": Quoted in Trippi, *Revolution*, 30.

30 "you could spread": Ibid., 30.

30 "concentric circles on steroids": Ibid., 94.

31 "the Democratic Party suicide bill": Quoted in Seth Gitell, "Making Sense of McCain-Feingold and Campaign-Finance Reform," *Atlantic*, July/Aug. 2003.

32 "You Have the Power": Remarks by Howard Dean, "The Great American Restoration," Burlington, Vt., June 23, 2003, www.4president.org/speeches/ howarddean2004announcement.htm.

32 "Our founders have implored": Ibid.

32 "End of Story": *Hotline*, July 1, 2003.

32 "shockwaves through": Unpublished transcript of "True Believers."

33 "This isn't Jimmy Carter": Paul Maslin, "Inside the Dean Campaign," *Atlantic*, April 8, 2004, www.theatlantic.com/doc/200404u/int2004-04-08.

33 "What activists like Dean": Quoted in Ari Berman, "Going Nowhere," *Nation*, March 21, 2005.

33 "fringe activists": Ibid.

34 "get with the [DLC] program": Ibid.

34 "The DLC has taken": Ibid.

34 "A Dean nomination": Quoted in Jonathan Alter, "The Left's Mr. Right?" *Newsweek*, Aug. 11, 2003.

34 "The Democratic Party is at risk": Quoted in "Lurch to the Left," *Daily Oklahoman*, Aug. 7, 2003.

35 *Slate* noted: Julia Turner, "Dean Is the New McCain . . . ," *Slate*, Aug. 7, 2003, slate.msn.com/id/2086718/.

35 "Mr. From fancies himself": Quoted in Berman, "Going Nowhere."

36 "few successful national campaigns": Joe Trippi, "Dean Team Strategy Memo," April 13, 2003, joetrippi.com/blog/?page_id=1380.

37 "In the past two": Dean for America, "Join Us," Aug. 4, 2003, www.gwu .edu/~action/2004/ads04/deanad080403.html.

37 "In Dean, some backers": Ken Herman, "In Dean, Some Backers See Hope for Texas' Ailing Democratic Party," *Austin American-Statesman*, Aug. 25, 2003.

38 "the new political bosses": Quoted in Joe Klein, *Politics Lost* (New York: Doubleday, 2006), 55.

41 "Organizing is not about": Quoted in Hanna Rosin, "People-Powered," *Washington Post*, Dec. 9, 2003.

42 "a connection between": Dean for America, "The House Meeting Program," www.hks.harvard.edu/organizing/tools/Files/dean_%20House%20Meet ingInformationPacket.pdf.

44 "secular tent revival": Rosin, "People-Powered."

44 "I am tired": Quoted in Jonathan Karl, "Clinton Praises Democratic Candidates in Iowa," CNN.com, Sept. 15, 2003, www.cnn.com/2003/ALLPOLITICS /09/14/elec04.prez.clinton.iowa/.

45 "Folks, go ahead": Ibid.

45 "It was hard": Paul Maslin, "The Front-Runner's Fall," *Atlantic*, May 2004.

45 "Bill particularly": Quoted in Katherine Q. Seelye, "Late-Arriving Candidate Got Push from Clintons," *New York Times*, Sept. 19, 2003.

45 "I need you": Howard Dean, *You Have the Power* (New York: Simon & Schuster, 2004), 113–14.

45 "vast right-wing conspiracy": Quoted in Joe Garofoli, "The Spinner," *San Francisco Chronicle*, Oct. 24, 2004.

46 "The Clark campaign": Joshua Green, "Playing Dirty," *Atlantic*, June 2004.

46 "dean of the 'Stop Dean' ": Howard Fineman, "The Dean Dilemma," *Newsweek*, Jan. 12, 2004.

46 "No Democrats": Ryan Lizza, "Outside In," *New Republic*, Nov. 24, 2003.

46 "I was a triangulator": Quoted in Matt Bai, "Dr. No and the Yes Men," *New York Times Magazine*, June 1, 2003.

47 "the New New Democrats": Ezra Klein, "The New New Gore, " *American Prospect*, March 19, 2006.

47 "I've decided I want": Katherine Q. Seelye, "Gore's Endorsement Was Won Over Time and Under the Radar," *New York Times*, Dec. 10, 2003.

47 "Howard Dean really is": "Gore Endorses Dean," CNN.com, Dec. 9, 2003, edition.cnn.hu/TRANSCRIPTS/0312/09/se.01.html.

48 "a pimple on the ass . . . you can ride that": Unpublished transcript of "True Believers."

49 "Congratulations to you": "Obama Questions Howard Dean on Iraq in 2003," YouTube, www.youtube.com/watch?v=jxwsdREgohY&feature=related.

49 "I am not opposed": Remarks by Barack Obama, Chicago, Oct. 2, 2002, www.danaroc.com/guests_barackobama_030209.html.

49 "I like Dean a lot": "Obama Questions Howard Dean."

50 "Petty jealousies": Maslin, "Front-Runner's Fall."

51 "It may have seemed": Maslin, "Inside the Dean Campaign."

51 "the capture of Saddam": Quoted in Tom Curry, "Dean Assails Bush on 'Unilateralism,'" MSNBC.com, Dec. 15, 2003, www.msnbc.msn.com/id /3718010/.

51 "We desperately needed": Maslin, "Front-Runner's Fall."

54 "dominated by special interests": Quoted in Jodi Wilgorn and Rachel L. Swarns, "Tape Shows Dean Maligning Iowa Caucuses," *New York Times*, Jan. 9, 2004.

55 "I kept telling everybody": Quoted in Ryan Lizza, "Mo' Better," *New Republic*, Feb. 2, 2004.

58 "I was about to say": Remarks by Howard Dean, Des Moines, Jan. 19, 2004, C-Span Video Library, www.c-spanvideo.org/program/180076-1.

60 "Cows in Iowa . . . screaming at voters there": George E. Condon Jr., "Voters Laughing at Dean as Support Fading in New Hampshire," Copley News Service, Jan. 21, 2004.

60 "In forty years": William Greider, "Dean's Rough Ride," *Nation*, Feb. 19, 2004.

61 "triumph": New Dem Dispatch, "A Vote for Hope over Anger," DLC.org, Jan. 28, 2004, www.dlc.org/ndol_ci.cfm?kaid=131&subid=192&contentid =252351.

2 ★ STORMING THE CASTLE

62 "We see the party": Quoted in Jim Morrill and Mark Johnson, "Easley's Pick No Shoo-In for Party Chairmanship," *Charlotte Observer*, Jan. 28, 2005.

62 "the man who energized": Transcript of 2004 Democratic National Convention Day Two, Boston, July 27, 2004, C-Span Video Library, www.c-spanvideo.org/program/182718-2.

62 "talked me down off": Howard Dean, *You Have the Power* (New York: Simon & Schuster, 2004), 25.

63 "We are going to": Remarks by Howard Dean, San Francisco, March 18, 2004, www.crocuta.net/Dean/Transcript_of_Dean_SF_Speech_18 March04.htm.

63 "DFA volunteers all over": Howard Dean, "The Dean Dozen," Blog for America, May 12, 2004, democracyforamerica.com/blog_posts/3902.

63 "With a record": Quoted in Ferman Mentrell, "Sparks Fly in U.S. Senate Race Here," *Chicago Defender*, May 20, 2004.

64 "Tonight we are all here": Remarks by Howard Dean, 2004 Democratic National Convention, Boston, July 27, 2004, www.c-spanvideo.org/program /182718-2.

65 "They were all talking": Quoted in Ari Berman, "The Prophet," *Nation*, Jan. 5, 2009.

67 "With the blue states in hand": "Dear Red States," About.com, political humor.about.com/library/jokes/bljokedearredstates.htm.

67 "God is going to": "California's Letter of Secession," About.com, political humor.about.com/library/jokes/bljokecaliforniasecession.htm.

67 "Fuck the South": www.fuckthesouth.com.

67 "Trying to recapture": Thomas F. Schaller, "A Route for 2004 That Doesn't Go Through Dixie," *Washington Post*, Nov. 16, 2003.

68 "Republican hegemony": Quoted in Eyal Press, "Is the Party Over?" *Nation*, June 2, 2008.

68 "party of the people": Thomas Frank, *What's the Matter with Kansas?* (New York: Henry Holt, 2005), 260.

69 "national-security Democrats": Quoted in Jeffrey Goldberg, "The Unbraiding," *New Yorker*, March 21, 2005.

69 "What leftist elites": Quoted in Ari Berman, "Going Nowhere," *Nation*, March 21, 2005.

69 "Democrats can't keep ignoring": Joe Trippi, "Only Grassroots Can Save the Democratic Party," *Wall Street Journal*, Nov. 30, 2004.

70 "I concluded it's faster": *Meet the Press*, NBC, Dec. 12, 2004, www.msnbc .msn.com/id/6702005/.

71 "cesspool": Sally Jenkins, "Return of the Angry Man," *Washington Post Magazine*, July 3, 2005.

71 "The number-one sport": Quoted in Ari Berman, "Where's the Plan, Democrats?" *Nation*, July 17, 2006.

71 "most controversial": Eric Alterman, "G.O.P. Chairman Lee Atwater: Playing Hardball," *New York Times*, April 30, 1989.

72 "Let me tell you": Remarks by Howard Dean, "The Future of the Democratic Party," Washington, D.C., Dec. 8, 2004, www.crocuta.net/Dean/ Dean_Speech_GWU_Dec8_2004.htm.

72 "80 percent of success": William Safire, "The Elision Fields," On Language, *New York Times Magazine*, Aug. 13, 1989.

72 "Chance favors": Quoted in Berman, "Prophet."

73 "the 447": Ryan Lizza, "The Outsiders," *New Republic*, Feb. 14, 2005.

74 "What's a Vermont Yankee": Remarks by Howard Dean at the Southern Caucus of the Democratic National Committee, Atlanta, Jan. 8, 2005, www.c-spanvideo.org/program/185087-1.

74 "If [Democrats] have": Quoted in "Dean Named Democratic Party Chief,"

CNN.com, Feb. 12, 2005, www.cnn.com/2005/ALLPOLITICS/02/12/dean
.dems/index.html.

74 "After 10 years": Quoted in Adam Nagourney and Anne E. Kornblut, "Dean Emerging as Likely Chief for Democrats," *New York Times*, Feb. 2, 2005.

74 "He will reinforce": Quoted in ibid.

74 "Making Dean their spokesman": "Scream 2," *New Republic*, Dec. 13, 2004.

75 "Dean is even less": Jonathan Chait, "A Suicidal Selection," *Los Angeles Times*, Feb. 4, 2005.

75 "Democrats are sure": David Brooks, "A Short History of Deanism," *New York Times*, Feb. 5, 2005.

77 "in Hindery's abandoned hotel": Lizza, "Outsiders."

77 "planning to endorse": Quoted in "DNC Chair: Her Life Is in Your Hands, Dude," *Hotline*, Dec. 22, 2004.

78 "There was a ton": Quoted in Howard Fineman, "Now Playing: 'Anybody but Dean Part 2,'" *Newsweek*, Jan. 31, 2005.

78 "does not reflect": Will Lester, "Ex-Clinton Aide Ickes Backs Dean for DNC," Associated Press, Jan. 29, 2005.

78 "Deanism isn't about turning": Paul Krugman, "The Fighting Moderates," *New York Times*, Feb. 15, 2005.

79 "The only knock": Quoted in "Florida Democrats Back Dean as Leader," *New York Times*, Jan. 18, 2005.

79 "a watershed event": Quoted in Matt Stoller, "Executive Committee of the ASDC Picks Donnie," MyDD.com, Jan. 30, 2005, mydd.com/2005/1/30/ executive-committee-of-the-asdc-picks-donnie#comment-32156.

80 "The thing that stuns": Quoted in Ryan Lizza, "Kiss the Ring," *GQ*, Jan. 2007.

81 "You are about to": Quoted in Todd S. Purdum, "From Ashes of '04 Effort, Dean Reinvents Himself," *New York Times*, Feb. 6, 2005.

81 "I think that Governor": Quoted in Nagourney and Kornblut, "Dean Emerging as Likely Chief for Democrats."

81 "The Democratic chairman has": Ibid.

81 "silent revolution": Jerome Armstrong, "The Silent Revolution Continues,"

MyDD.com, March 2, 2005, mydd.com/2005/3/2/the-silent-revolution-continues.

84 "While there are some": Quoted in Dan Kane, "Long Weighs in Against Easley's Pick to Lead Democrats," *News & Observer*, Jan. 3, 2005.

86 "fresh leadership": Quoted in Bob Geary, "The People Have Won," *Independent Weekly*, Feb. 23, 2005.

86 "I believe that our": Rob Christensen, "Democrats Pick Meek as Chief," *News & Observer*, Feb. 20, 2005.

86 "The people have won": Quoted in Geary, "The People Have Won."

86 "Insurgents don't realize": Rob Christensen, "N.C. Dems on Thin Ice," *News & Observer*, Feb. 27, 2005.

86 "Party activists now act": Jim Jenkins, "And the Meek Shall Inherit . . . ," *News & Observer*, Feb. 24, 2005.

87 "The Democrats' Mini-Deans": Terry M. Neal, *Washington Post*, Feb. 28, 2005.

3 ★ MIDTERMS

93 "Gas Price Crisis": North Carolina Democratic Party, news release, April 25, 2006, www.ncdp.org/node/1023.

95 "We're perceived as spineless": Mark Hufford, "Wordsmiths Needed," BlueNC.com, Aug. 1, 2006, www.bluenc.com/wordsmiths-needed.

95 Pew report: Pew Research Center for the People & the Press, "Beyond Red vs. Blue," May 10, 2005, people-press.org/report/242/beyond-red-vs-blue.

95 "You'll love your wife": Burma-Shave.org, burma-shave.org/jingles/1932/youll_love_your.

95 "The high price": Mack, "Western NC Democrats Branding," BlueNC.com, July 31, 2006, www.bluenc.com/western-nc-democrats-branding.

96 "Colored Girls": Matt Bai, *The Argument* (New York: Penguin, 2007), 167.

96 "moral values": Cornell Belcher, "Faith Voters in the Electorate—Key Findings," memo to Democratic National Committee, March 23, 2005.

98 "We sent fourteen thousand people": *Meet the Press*, NBC, Dec. 12, 2004, www.msnbc.msn.com/id/6702005/.

99 "Democratic presidents worked": Daniel Galvin, "Changing Course: Reversing the Organizational Trajectory of the Democratic Party from Bill Clinton to Barack Obama," *Forum* 6, no. 2 (2008).

99 "smelled *terrible*": Quoted in Nick Confessore, "The Plutocrat as Populist," *American Prospect*, July 1, 2001.

99 "We had a great": Quoted in Ari Berman, "The Prophet," *Nation*, Jan. 5, 2009.

99 "I hate the Republicans": Quoted in Jeff Jacoby, "Dean for DNC Chairman? Yeeaarrgghh!" *Boston Globe*, Feb. 3, 2005.

101 "I think Tom DeLay": Quoted in Andrea Mitchell, "Hold His Tongue? Not Howard Dean," MSNBC.com, June 6, 2005, www.msnbc.msn.com/id/8122027/.

101 "A lot of them": Ibid.

101 "a pretty monolithic party": Quoted in Carla Marinucci, "In S.F., Dean Calls GOP a 'White Christian Party,'" *San Francisco Chronicle*, June 7, 2005.

101 "He doesn't speak for me": Quoted in Mitchell, "Hold His Tongue?"

101 "It may get": *Meet the Press*, NBC, June 12, 2005, www.msnbc.msn.com/id/8130648/.

101 "I don't care": Quoted in James Warden, "Freudenthal Pushes Democrats to Think Independently," *Gillette News-Record*, Sept. 25, 2005.

102 "Forget Howard Dean's mouth": Chris Suellentrop, "Follow the Money," *Boston Globe*, June 26, 2005.

102 "Democrats Losing Race": Chris Cillizza, *Washington Post*, Nov. 12, 2005.

103 "a cross between": Quoted in Nina Easton, "Rahm Emanuel: Rejuvenating the Hopes of House Democrats," *Fortune*, Oct. 2, 2006.

104 "You don't get any": Quoted in Mike Dorning, "Emanuel Takes Office on High Note," *Chicago Tribune*, Jan. 8, 2003.

104 "Everybody is a fucking": Quoted in Ryan Lizza, "Kiss the Ring," *GQ*, Jan. 2007.

104 "I've met the kids": Quoted in Naftali Bendavid, *The Thumpin'* (New York: Doubleday, 2007), 87.

105 "Your field plan": Ibid., 85.

105 "There's frustration inside": Quoted in Ari Berman, "Where's the Plan, Democrats?" *Nation*, July 17, 2006.

106 "Democrats Are Fractured": Thomas B. Edsall, *Washington Post*, May 11, 2006.

106 "Dean and Party Leaders": Adam Nagourney, *New York Times*, May 11, 2006.

106 "Democrats Fear Rifts": Jeff Zeleny, *Chicago Tribune*, July 5, 2006.

106 "[Dean's] management of money": Quoted in Bendavid, *Thumpin'*, 166.

107 "I have my knee": Quoted in Bai, *Argument*, 175.

107 "As for Iraq policy": Quoted in Dan Balz, "Pelosi Hails Democrats' Diverse War Stances," *Washington Post*, Dec. 16, 2005.

107 "a culture of corruption": *Meet the Press*, NBC, May 22, 2005, www.msnbc .msn.com/id/7924139/.

108 "party subsidizers": Quoted in Ari Berman, "Big $$ for Progressive Politics," *Nation*, Oct. 16, 2006.

109 "I know how hard": Quoted in Berman, "Prophet."

110 "a vote of no": Thomas B. Edsall, "Democrats' Data Mining Stirs an Intraparty Battle," *Washington Post*, March 8, 2006.

110 "It's unclear": Ibid.

110 "He says it's": *The Situation Room*, CNN, May 11, 2006, transcripts.cnn .com/TRANSCRIPTS/0605/11/sitroom.01.html.

110 "Shame on you": Zack Exley, "Shame on You, Paul Begala," *Huffington Post*, May 16, 2006, www.huffingtonpost.com/zack-exley/shame-on-you -paul-begala_b_21116.html.

111 "I strongly believe": Paul Begala, "Bringing a Knife to a Gunfight," *Huffington Post*, May 19, 2006, www.huffingtonpost.com/paul-begala/bring ing-a-knife-to-a-gun_b_21275.html.

114 "I may not agree": Quoted in Bob Moser, *Blue Dixie* (New York: Times Books, 2008), 101.

115 "It's a sight": Quoted in Rob Christensen, "Spending Turns Red Areas Blue," *News & Observer*, Nov. 19, 2006.

116 "All over the mountain": Quoted in Gary D. Robertson, "Shuler's Win Aside, Democrats Surge in Western N.C.," Associated Press, Nov. 26, 2006.

116 "We're a poster child": Quoted in Berman, "Prophet."

117 "Schumer, Emanuel Engineer": Devlin Barrett and Christopher Wills, Associated Press, Nov. 9, 2006.

117 "the architect": Andrea Seabrook, "Rahm Emanuel, Architect for Democratic Rebound," *Weekend Edition Sunday*, National Public Radio, Nov. 19, 2006, www.npr.org/templates/story/story.php?storyId=6509653.

117 "There was a missed": Quoted in Adam Nagourney, "Flush of Victory Past, Democrats Revert to Finger-Pointing," *New York Times*, Nov. 16, 2006.

117 "In a word": Quoted in Scott Shepard, "Carville: Howard Dean Is 'Rumsfeldian,'" *Austin American-Statesman*, November 16, 2006.

118 "More resources": Quoted in Nagourney, "Flush of Victory Past, Democrats Revert to Finger-Pointing."

118 "Extra money": Josh Kraushaar, "The Carville Claims: A Closer Look," *Hotline On Call*, Nov. 17, 2006, hotlineoncall.nationaljournal.com/archives/2006/11/the_carville_cl.php.

118 "Asking Dean": Quoted in Nagourney, "Flush of Victory Past."

118 "I didn't support": Quoted in "The Odd Attack on Dean," *Nation*, Dec. 11, 2006.

119 of the twenty-one candidates: Paul Lukasiak, "How Rahm Emanuel Lost the House for Democrats," DownWithTyranny! Nov. 13, 2006, downwithtyranny.blogspot.com/2006/11/how-rahm-emanuel-lost-house-for.html.

119 Of the sixty-two candidates: James L., "Red to Blue: How Meaningful Is It?" Swing State Project, Sept. 13, 2008, www.swingstateproject.com/diary/3034/.

119 The top three candidates: Jonathan Singer, "Examining the DCCC v. Netroots Meme," MyDD.com, Nov. 9, 2006, mydd.com/2006/11/9/examining-the-dccc-v-netroots-meme.

119 Rahm supported primary challenges: Ibid.

119 "Thank you for": Remarks by Tim Walz, Executive Committee Meeting of Democratic National Committee, Washington, D.C., Dec. 2, 2006, www.c-spanvideo.org/program/195609-1.

120 "[I] decided to run": Remarks by Nancy Boyda, ibid.

120 "Howard Dean, vindicated": Joe Conason, "Howard Dean, Vindicated," *Salon*, Nov. 10, 2006, www.salon.com/opinion/conason/2006/11/10/dean_dems/.

120 subsequent study: Elaine C. Kamarck, "Assessing Howard Dean's Fifty State Strategy and the 2006 Midterm Elections," *Forum* 4, no. 3 (2006).

120 "You've got to do": Bendavid, *The Thumpin'*, 86.

120 "laying the groundwork": Thomas B. Edsall, "The Grudge," *New Republic*, Aug. 7, 2006.

4 ★ CLINTONISM VS. CHANGE

122 "We pioneered it": Quoted in Ari Berman, "The Dean Legacy," *Nation*, March 17, 2008.

124 "This is a much": Quoted in Marcus Kabel, "Obama Says Wal-Mart Is Part of Necessary Debate on Pay and Benefits," *USA Today*, Nov. 16, 2006.

124 "Folks on Wall Street": Quoted in Pallavi Gogoi, "Can Barack Wake Up Wal-Mart?" *BusinessWeek*, Nov. 16, 2006.

124 "undisputed brilliance": Anne E. Kornblut, "Clinton's PowerPointer," *Washington Post*, April 30, 2007.

125 "We have incredible image": Mark Penn, "'Launch Strategy' Ideas," *Atlantic*, Dec. 21, 2006, www.theatlantic.com/magazine/archive/2008/08/the-hillary -clinton-memos/6951/.

125 *The Way to Win*: Mark Halperin and John F. Harris, *The Way to Win* (New York: Random House, 2006).

125 "Gore easily defeated": Penn, "'Launch Strategy' Ideas."

125 "Obama is unelectable": Joshua Green, "The Front-Runner's Fall," *Atlantic*, Sept. 2008.

129 "Change won't come": Barack Obama, *Dreams from My Father* (New York: Three Rivers, 1995), 133.

132 "The first thing": Quoted in Sarah DiJulio and Andrea Wood, "Online Tactics & Success: An Examination of the Obama for America New Media Campaign," M+R Strategic Services, Aug. 2009.

132 "MyBeau": Stephen Moss and Sarah Phillips, "Is This Man the Future of Politics?" *Guardian*, Feb. 18, 2009.

133 "Every staff meeting": Quoted in Ellen McGirt, "The Kid Who Made Obama President," *Fast Company*, April 2009.

135 "It's pretty intense . . . through that lens": Buffy Wicks, "Camp Obama Introduction," San Francisco, Aug. 10, 2007, Blip.tv, blip.tv/file/364177.

136 "What's the main distinction": "Camp Obama New York," Aug. 18, 2007, YouTube, www.youtube.com/watch?v=WXtyEmhjDNY.

136 "We don't train volunteers": Quoted in Laura Flanders, "It's Not About Obama!" *Nation*, Oct. 1, 2007, www.thenation.com/blogs/state_of_change /238867.

136 "It becomes a contest": Quoted in Shaun Appleby, "Process vs. Policy: Organising," MyDD.com, Feb. 14, 2008, mydd.com/2008/2/14/process-vs-policy-organising.

137 "We want to register": Fannie Lou Hamer, "Testimony Before the Credentials Committee, Democratic National Committee," Aug. 22, 1964, amer icanradioworks.publicradio.org/features/sayitplain/flhamer.html.

138 "Talk about feeling history": Quoted in Scott Martelle, "Famed Organizer Sees History in the Making," *Los Angeles Times*, June 15, 2008.

138 "For those . . . new movement": "Marshall Ganz, PhD Sociology, Harvard Introduces the Camp Foundations," Camp Obama blog, Aug. 10, 2007, campobama.blogspot.com/2007/09/marshall-ganz-phd-sociology-harvard.html.

139 "How many of you": "Marshall Ganz Explains Development of Why You're Here Story of Self," Camp Obama blog, Aug. 11, 2007, campobama .blogspot.com/2007/09/10-movement-building-story-of-self-to.html.

140 "Let's face it": Barack Obama, Keynote Address at the 2004 Democratic National Convention, Boston, July 27, 2004, www.washingtonpost.com/ wp-dyn/articles/A19751-2004Jul27.html.

140 "What that talk": "Marshall Ganz Explains Development."

142 "Bill Clinton was intensely": Quoted in Shea Andersen, "Real Western," *Boise Weekly*, May 28, 2008.

142 "the international headquarters": Quoted in Timothy Egan, "Obama: The Shock of the Red," Opinionator blog, *New York Times*, Feb. 6, 2008, opinionator.blogs.nytimes.com/2008/02/06/obama-the-shock-of-the-red/.

142 "Mississippi of the mountains": Michael Ames, "Obama Prospects for Votes in the Red West," *Huffington Post*, Feb. 4, 2008, www.huffington post.com/michael-ames/obama-prospects-for-votes_b_84893.html.

142 "Usually, they": Quoted in Dan Popkey, "Obama Visit Grows from Grass Roots," *Idaho Statesman*, Feb. 1, 2008.

143 "I realize Idaho": Dave Ficks, "Obama Republicans," Obama for America Community Blogs, Feb. 17, 2007, my.barackobama.com/page/community/post/vision/C2Pg#extended.

143 "If people vote for": Quoted in Nathaniel Hoffman, "Obama's Idaho," *Boise Weekly*, April 4, 2007.

144 "makes Salt Lake City": Ames, "Obama Prospects for Votes in the Red West."

145 "Adam and Eve": Popkey, "Obama Visit Grows from Grass Roots."

145 "I heard about you": Quoted in ibid.

147 "We had to build": Quoted in Howard Hewitt, "Game Changer," *WM Online*, Nov. 26, 2008, www.wabash.edu/magazine/index.cfm?news_id=6483.

148 "If he pulls this off": Quoted in Christopher Cooper, Valerie Bauerlein, and Corey Dade, "In South, Democrats' Tactic May Change Political Game," *Wall Street Journal*, Jan. 23, 2008.

149 "I was one of": Quoted in Netroots Nation Sessions, "Organizing for Change: An Inside Look at Obama for America's Grassroots Strategy," Austin, Tex., July 19, 2008, www.netrootsnation.org/node/1014.

149 "I'm pretty impatient": Quoted in Hewitt, "Game Changer."

149 "Most of the presidents": Sam Graham-Felsen, "Video: Walking in South Carolina," Obama for America Community Blogs, July 13, 2007, my.barack obama.com/page/community/post/samgrahamfelsen/CtDL.

150 "I've never had": "Reflections on a House Meeting," Obama for America, YouTube, July 25, 2007, www.youtube.com/watch?v=Zuj3kMYA8ys&feature=player_embedded.

151 "eradicate the slander": Obama, 2004 Democratic National Convention.

151 "I don't come from": "South Carolina House Meeting," Obama for America, YouTube, July 25, 2007, www.youtube.com/watch?v=iF5jqtM-EkI&feature=player_embedded.

151 "No one really knew": Quoted in "Building Collective Capacity: New Forms of Political Organizing: A Conversation with Jeremy Bird," Berkman Center for Internet & Society at Harvard University, Boston, Dec. 10, 2008, cyber.law.harvard.edu/interactive/events/2008/12/internetandpolitics/bird.

151 "The Road to Change": Obama for America, "The Road to Change: South Carolina," my.barackobama.com/page/content/scroadtochange.

151 "Living the Campaign": Christi Parsons, "For Obama's S.C. Troops, It's a Campaign and a Lifestyle," *Chicago Tribune*, Jan. 5, 2008.

151 "B&B strategy": Krissah Williams, "A Shift Toward Obama Is Seen Among Blacks," *Washington Post*, Jan. 21, 2008.

151 "You go to the jailhouse": "Barack Obama: Barber Shop," Obama for America, YouTube, Aug. 24, 2007, www.youtube.com/watch?v=Ty5Uv_SXKF0 &feature=player_embedded.

152 "Every Democrat running": Quoted in Nedra Pickler, "Obama Faces Doubts Among S.C. Blacks," *USA Today*, July 27, 2007.

152 "Right now, we don't": Quoted in Bob Moser, "South Carolina: Inside the 'Black Primary,'" *Nation*, Jan. 7, 2008.

152 "You don't get": Ibid.

152 "Personally, I don't feel": Quoted in Katharine Q. Seelye, "Clinton-Obama Quandary for Many Black Women," *New York Times*, Oct. 14, 2007.

153 "Tomorrow is going to be": "Barack Obama and Oprah Winfrey Rally," Obama for America, YouTube, Dec. 8, 2007, www.youtube.com/watch?v= dnVE0rGofq0&feature=player_embedded.

153 "We know you've got": Quoted in Ben Smith, "Largest Phone Bank Ever," *Politico*, Dec. 9, 2007, www.politico.com/blogs/bensmith/1207/Largest_ phone_bank_ever.html.

154 "look like Facebook": Quoted in Brian Stelter, "The Facebooker Who Friended Obama," *New York Times*, July 7, 2008.

154 "Our supporters look like": Quoted in Roger Simon, "Jefferson Jackson a Warm-Up for Iowa," *Politico*, Nov. 17, 2007, www.politico.com/news/stories /1107/6815.html.

156 "The cynics who believed": Remarks by Barack Obama, Columbia, S.C., Jan. 26, 2008, www.cnn.com/2008/POLITICS/01/26/obama.transcript/ index.html.

156 "I'm really proud": Quoted in Hewitt, "Game Changer."

157 "Saturday's sunrise lines": Ames, "Obama Prospects for Votes in the Red West."

157 "I'm the grassroots guy": "T. J. Thomson and Kassie Cerami Speak at Obama Rally in Boise," YouTube, Feb. 2, 2008, www.youtube.com/watch?v=GrEfqAfuHNU.

158 "Man, what a beautiful": "Former Idaho Gov. Endorses Obama," Obama for America, YouTube, Feb. 2, 2008, www.youtube.com/watch?v=bgYbPjlYIrg.

158 "I'm older now": Quoted in Egan, "Obama: The Shock of the Red."

158 "just this side": Jill Kuraitis. "Obama in Boise: 'This Is Our Moment,'" *New West*, Feb. 2, 2008, www.newwest.net/city/article/obama_in_boise_this_is_our_moment/C108/L108/.

158 "Wow, look at this": "Barack Obama Comes to Boise, Idaho," YouTube, Feb. 2, 2008, www.youtube.com/watch?v=b6GuCv20vXQ&feature=related.

158 "They told me": Quoted in Scott Helman, "The Obama Show Comes to Boise," Political Intelligence blog, *Boston Globe*, Feb. 2, 2008, www.boston.com/news/politics/politicalintelligence/2008/02/boise_idaho_thi.html.

159 "Breaking! HRC Discovers Idaho": Red State Rebels, Jan. 27, 2008, redstaterebels.typepad.com/redstaterebelsnet/2008/01/breaking-hrc-di.html.

159 "If Bill Clinton had": Quoted in "Idaho Dems Miffed at Bill Clinton's Comments," Democratic Underground (via *Twin Falls Times-News*), May 8, 2008, www.democraticunderground.com/discuss/duboard.php?az=view_all&address=102x3301232.

160 "We hear Senator Obama": "Boise Mayor Bieter in Support of Obama at Idaho Caucus," YouTube, Feb. 5, 2008, www.youtube.com/watch?v=p5fwJEWLUv8&feature=related.

160 "If Mrs. Clinton won": Dave Eggers, "Losing to Idaho," *New York Times*, Feb. 17, 2008.

160 "People wonder": "Barack Obama in Indianapolis, IN," Obama for America, YouTube, April 30, 2008, www.youtube.com/watch?v=WyNzC9W2C8Q&feature=player_embedded.

162 "There's too much hair": Quoted in Philip A. Klinkner, *The Losing Parties* (New Haven, Conn.: Yale University Press, 1994), 106.

162 "We aren't going to": Quoted in Rick Perlstein, *Nixonland* (New York: Scribner, 2008), 514.

162 a priest and a warrior: Ron Brownstein, "Obama and Blue Collars: Do They Fit?" *Los Angeles Times*, March 25, 2007.

163 "They looked at '04": Quoted in Berman, "Dean Legacy."

164 "second-class delegates": Quoted in Ben Smith, "Second-Class Delegates," *Politico*, Feb. 18, 2008, www.politico.com/blogs/bensmith/0208/Second class_delegates.html.

164 "insult 40 states": Markos Moulitsas, "Clinton's 'Insult 40 States' Strategy," DailyKos.com, Feb. 14, 2008, www.dailykos.com/story/2008/2/14/113237 /023/979/456665.

165 "The Obama campaign seems": Quoted in Jonathan Tilove, "Obamania: Virtue or Vice?" *Trenton Times*, Feb. 17, 2008.

165 "The Holy Season": Ibid.

165 "Media Figures Call Obama": Ibid.

165 "Nothing will take": Cora Currier, "Debunking the Media's 'Obama Cult,'" *Nation*, Feb. 18, 2008, www.thenation.com/blogs/state_of_change /286613.

165 "You go into": Quoted in Mayhill Fowler, "Obama Exclusive (Audio): On V.P. and Foreign Policy, Courting the Working Class, and Hard-Pressed Pennsylvanians," *Huffington Post*, April 11, 2008, www.huffingtonpost .com/mayhill-fowler/obama-exclusive-audio-on_b_96333.html.

166 "beautiful losers": Quoted in Mark Schmitt, "Grading the Election Series," *American Prospect*, Nov. 10, 2008, www.prospect.org/cs/articles?arti cle=grading_the_election_theories.

166 "You can sit down": "Barack Obama in Greenville, NC," YouTube, April 17, 2008, www.youtube.com/watch?v=05HqrlQgxuk&feature=related.

167 "This lady right here": Quoted in Foon Rhee, "Easley Explains 'Pansy' Remark," *Boston Globe*, May 6, 2008.

167 "elitist, out of touch": Quoted in John M. Broder, "Democrats Wrangle over Words and Beliefs," *New York Times*, April 14, 2008.

167 "People are angry": "Barack Obama at ECU," YouTube, April 17, 2008, www .youtube.com/watch?v=JdoLp4rkdLI&feature=related.

167 "I met a gentleman": "Barack Obama Rally @ ECU 2," YouTube, April 17, 2008, www.youtube.com/watch?v=veLGl4y_znw&feature=related.

169 "Before the latest round": Transcript of Democratic presidential debate,

Los Angeles, Jan. 31, 2008, www.cnn.com/2008/POLITICS/01/31/dem
.debate.transcript/.

172 "Toast!": "Toast! Hill Blows Last Shot in Indy, NC Votes," *New York Post*,
May 8, 2008.

5 ★ NATIONALIZE THIS

173 "I might have something": "Speech to HQ Staff & Volunteers," Obama
for America, YouTube, June 7, 2008, www.youtube.com/watch?v=bnhm
ByYxEIo.

175 "I am proud": Quoted in Dana Goldstein and Ezra Klein, "It's His Party,"
American Prospect, Aug. 18, 2008.

177 "Respect. Empower. Include": Quoted in Christopher Hayes, "Community Organizers Discuss Obama's Role as an Activist," *Nation*, Sept. 1,
2008.

177 "Empowerment requires creating": Quoted in Christopher Hayes,
"Obama's Voter-Registration Drive," *Nation*, Sept. 1, 2008.

178 "the first truly national": Sam Stein, "Obama and Dean Team Up to Recast
the Political Map," *Huffington Post*, June 5, 2008, www.huffingtonpost
.com/2008/06/05/obama-and-dean-team-up-to_n_105419.html.

178 "There's not a liberal": Barack Obama, Keynote Address at the 2004
Democratic National Convention, Boston, July 27, 2004, www.washington
post.com/wp-dyn/articles/A19751-2004Jul27.html.

178 "If we can host": Quoted in George Merritt and Elizabeth Aguilera, " 'Our
Time' Proved Long Time Coming," *Denver Post*, Jan. 12, 2007.

179 "the gang of four": Stuart Steers, "The Gang of Four," *5280*, May 2005.

179 "I have long believed": Quoted in Karen E. Crummy, "Shift from South to
West," *Denver Post*, Jan. 12, 2007.

179 "If we're going to": Quoted in Adriel Bettelheim, "Democrats Look West
for Mile-High Gains," *CQ Weekly*, Jan. 12, 2007.

179 "If we win": Quoted in Nadine Elsibai and Jonathan D. Salant, "Democrats
Pick Denver for 2008 Convention," Bloomberg, Jan. 11, 2007, www.bloom
berg.com/apps/news?pid=20601103&sid=adRnTgTMh0Xw&refer=us.

180 "I can't tell you": Quoted in Paula Moore, "Wedgeworth Praised for Convention Effort," *Denver Business Journal*, Jan. 11, 2007.

180 "It'll be the best": Quoted in Stuart Steers and Daniel Chacon, "Democrats Tip Hat to Emerging West," *Rocky Mountain News*, Jan. 12, 2007.

181 "The real issue": Quoted in John Aguilar, "State Dems Wanted 'Change,'" *Rocky Mountain News*, March 7, 2005.

182 "You can smell Greeley": Eric Schlosser, *Fast Food Nation* (New York: HarperCollins, 2002), 149.

182 "a city of wide": Quoted in Rebecca Boyle, "A Place for the Weld County Democrats to Visit," *Greeley Tribune*, June 3, 2007.

183 "The Democrats' assembly": "Editorial: Independents Sure to Influence Campaign," *Denver Post*, May 22, 2006.

183 STOP GAY MARRIAGE: Quoted in Jim Rutenberg, "Bush Lends a Hand to G.O.P. Congresswoman in a Tight Race," *New York Times*, Nov. 5, 2006.

183 "It's good to be": Quoted in Michael Scherer, "W. Rocks the Vote," *Salon*, Nov. 5, 2006, www.salon.com/news/feature/2006/11/05/greeley/print.html.

184 "war against illegal immigration": Quoted in Marc Cooper, "Lockdown in Greeley," *Nation*, Feb. 26, 2007.

184 "stealth jihad": Acorcoran, "CAST: Taking a Stand Against the Spread of Shariah Law," Refugee Resettlement Watch, Aug. 10, 2009, refugeeresettlementwatch.wordpress.com/2009/08/10/cast-taking-a-stand-against-the-spread-of-shariah-law/.

185 "This has been our Katrina": Quoted in Cooper, "Lockdown in Greeley."

186 THE ROAD: Quoted in Tom Hamburger and Peter Wallsten, "Obama Works to Reclaim Latino Vote," *Los Angeles Times*, Feb. 2, 2008.

187 "Clearly, they've taken": Quoted in David Montero, "Obama Campaign to Open Five More Offices in Colorado," *Rocky Mountain News*, Jan. 26, 2008.

188 "We don't believe that": Quoted in Andrew Villegas, "Democratic Politicians Stump for Obama in Northern Colorado," *Greeley Tribune*, Oct. 9, 2008.

190 "whispering Republicans": Quoted in Emily Belz, "Republicans for Obama Has State Presence," *Indianapolis Star*, July 25, 2008.

190 "I'm Chuck Lasker": Chuck Lasker, "My Republicans for Obama Video Testimonial," Obama for America Community Blogs, July 29, 2008, my.barackobama.com/page/community/post/chucklasker/gGx9Xq.

191 "Your neighbors are probably": "Republicans for Obama in Indiana," Obama for America, YouTube, July 24, 2008, www.youtube.com/watch? v=--bYUTcsdV4&feature=channel_page.

191 "I'm a registered Republican": Ibid.

191 "hit home . . . hooked": Ibid.

192 "We're gonna be debating": "Barack Obama in Noblesville, IN," Obama for America, YouTube, May 3, 2008, www.youtube.com/watch?v=VKp -MOwcTd4.

193 "Hamilton County is an area": Quoted in Tania E. Lopez, "Democrats Open County Headquarters," *Indianapolis Star*, July 3, 2008.

193 "anti-politician, anti-government": Quoted in Thurston Clarke, *The Last Campaign* (New York: Henry Holt, 2008), 82.

193 "I loved the faces": Quoted in Jack Newfield, *RFK* (New York: Avalon, 2003), 261.

194 "You know, Bobby Kennedy": "Obama in Plainfield, IN: 'We Have to Come Together,'" Obama for America, YouTube, March 15, 2008, www.youtube .com/watch?v=6FsqDTVmlKk.

194 "solid GOP": Quoted in Nate Silver, "Briefings, Branding, and Bravado," Fivethirtyeight.com, June 8, 2008, www.fivethirtyeight.com/2008/06/brief ings-branding-and-bravado.html.

194 "We want [the GOP]": Quoted in Steven Gray, "Indiana, in Play, Keeps Obama Guessing," *Time*, Sept. 20, 2008, www.time.com/time/nation/ article/0,8599,1843103,00.html.

195 "campaign malpractice": Quoted in Brian Howey, "David Plouffe: How Obama Turned Indiana Blue," Howey Politics Indiana, Feb. 7, 2009, howeypolitics.com.

196 "There's really no model": Quoted in Anne Brewer, "Women for Change: Indiana State Director Emily Parcell," Obama for America Community Blogs, Aug. 6, 2008, my.barackobama.com/page/community/post/anne brewer/gG58VH.

196 "This is the most": Quoted in Jay Kenworthy, "Obama's Superficial Indi- ana Campaign Strikes Again," news release, Indiana Republican Party, Aug. 23, 2008, www.hoosierpoliticalreport.com/2008/08/release-obamas -superficial-ind.html.

197 "Having the national Democratic": Quoted in M. E. Sprengelmeyer, "Dems Reached Out to West," *Rocky Mountain News*, Nov. 4, 2008.

197 "The Colorado Model": Fred Barnes, *Weekly Standard*, July 7, 2008.

198 "Obama was losing ground": RBI Strategies, "MEMORANDUM, 2008 Post-election Analysis," March 25, 2009.

199 ElephantMan: Quoted in Timothy Noah, "Sarah Palin, Web Invention," *Slate*, Aug. 29, 2008, www.slate.com/id/2198949/#D.

199 "1) A energetic, young": Adam Brickley, "Why Sarah Palin?" Draft Sarah Palin for Vice President blog, Feb. 26, 2007, palinforvp.blogspot.com /2007/02/why-sarah-palin.html.

199 "WE DID IT": Adam Brickley, Draft Sarah Palin for Vice President blog, Aug. 29, 2008, palinforvp.blogspot.com/2008/08/we-did-it.html.

200 "U.S.A.! U.S.A.! U.S.A.!": "Colorado Springs Greets Sarah Palin," You-Tube, Sept. 6, 2008, www.youtube.com/watch?v=NJnpi2DwkdU.

200 "It is so great": "Sarah Palin, Speech in Colorado Springs," YouTube, September 6, 2008, www.youtube.com/watch?v=czx83Jk8yQ4.

200 "I don't consider it": Quoted in Tim Hoover, "Two Arrested at Dems' Gathering," *Denver Post*, May 18, 2008.

201 "The Great Liberal Invasion": Ralph Routon, "Dems: The Pleasure Is Ours," *Colorado Springs Independent*, May 15, 2008.

201 "El Paso County is": Quoted in Anthony Lane, "Democratic Dreamers," *Colorado Springs Independent*, May 22, 2008, www.csindy.com/colorado/democratic-dreamers/Content?oid=1143279.

201 "We're slowly turning it": Quoted in Cara Degette, "Live from the Colorado Democratic Convention—Day 2," *Colorado Independent*, May 17, 2008, coloradoindependent.com/4300/live-from-the-colorado-democratic-party-convention-day-two-2.

201 "the hate state": Quoted in Karen Abbott, "Colorado Reputation Took Hit When State Gave Its Support to Amendment 2," *Rocky Mountain News*, Nov. 30, 1999.

202 SIEGE THIS CITY: Jeff Sharlet, "Soldiers of Christ," *Harper's*, May 2005.

202 "The mega suburban churches": Quoted in Jeff Brady, "Colorado Springs a Mecca for Evangelical Christians," National Public Radio, Jan. 17, 2005, www.npr.org/templates/story/story.php?storyId=4287106.

202 "prayer shield": Ibid.

202 "If we weren't doing this": Quoted in Alix Spiegel, "77: Pray. Act One. Exodus," *This American Life*, Chicago Public Radio, Sept. 26, 1997, www .thisamericanlife.org/radio-archives/episode/77/Pray.

203 "Our public works department": Quoted in Jeff Brady, "July 4 Becomes Silent Night in Cash-Strapped Places," National Public Radio, July 2, 2009, www.npr.org/templates/transcript/transcript.php?storyId= 106208007.

207 "We have the best": "Joe Biden: Colorado Springs, Colorado," Obama for America, YouTube, Oct. 22, 2008, www.youtube.com/watch?v=xKQHM Ri3FhA.

207 "It is good": Quoted in Jenn Prosser, "Michelle Draws Big Crowd in Colorado Springs," Obama for America Community Blogs, Oct. 31, 2008, my .barackobama.com/page/community/post/jennprosser/gGgkZz.

208 "I have to win": Quoted in Karen E. Crummy, "McCain in Colorado: 'I Have to Win Here,'" *Denver Post*, July 30, 2008.

208 "Registering to vote": Quoted in Cara Degette, "Balink, GOP-Backed Student Voter Disenfranchisement Rages Anew," *Colorado Independent*, Oct. 16, 2008, coloradoindependent.com/11555/balink-gop-backed-student-voter-disenfranchisement-rages-anew.

208 "At best": Quoted in Leslie Jorgensen, "El Paso County Democrats Blast Balink," *Colorado Statesman*, Oct. 17, 2008.

209 "serious": Eric Gorski, "Focus on the Family Faces 'Serious' Shortfall," *Denver Post*, Aug. 11, 2009.

209 "The only advice": Quoted in Timothy Egan, "My Own Private Focus Group," Opinionator blog, *New York Times*, Oct. 8, 2008, opinionator .blogs.nytimes.com/2008/10/08/my-own-private-focus-group/.

209 "To be focused on": Ibid.

210 "breathtaking to even": Dan Slater, "Um . . . Wow," DemNotes, Oct. 26, 2008, demnotes.com/?p=396.

211 "The road to": Quoted in R. Scott Rappold, "Obama Asks for Help Crossing the Finish Line," *Colorado Springs Gazette*, Oct. 27, 2008.

211 "Goodness gracious": Ibid.

211 "That's what I'm talking": Quoted in Amanda Scott, "Barack Rallies 100,000

in Denver, CO," Obama for America Community Blogs, Oct. 26, 2008, my.barackobama.com/page/community/post/amandascott/gGgD2c.

211 "It is pretty": "Barack Obama in Fort Collins, Colorado @ CSU," YouTube, Oct. 26, 2008, www.youtube.com/watch?v=yT_ZjSqvVlo.

211 "This country and the dream": "Barack Obama at Ft. Collins Part 3," *9News.com*, Oct. 26, 2008, www.9news.com/video/default.aspx?bcrefid= 905872286#/Barack%20Obama%20Fort%20Collins%20Pt.%203 /49077893001.

213 "The Elkhart Project": Mike Brunker, "Why Elkhart?" *MSNBC.com*, April 7, 2009, elkhartprojectblog.msnbc.msn.com/_news/2009/04/07/2648590- why-elkhart.

213 "Elkhart is a real": Quoted in Ari Berman, "Hoosiers for Obama," *Nation*, Nov. 1, 2008, www.thenation.com/blogs/state_of_change/379204/hoosiers _for_obama.

214 "There were already": Quoted in "Video: Obama Barn Being Painted," *Elkhart Truth*, Sept. 3, 2008, www.etruth.com/Know/News/Story.aspx?id =460689.

214 IT'S NOT OUR BARN: Quoted in Sarah Rice, "Obama Barn Hurting Broth- er's Elkhart County Business," *WSBT.com*, Sept. 12, 2008, www.wsbt.com /news/local/28301909.html.

215 "When George Bush": "Sen. Barack Obama in Elkhart Indiana Part 2," YouTube, Aug. 6, 2008, www.youtube.com/watch?v=QBPNH3pvlxo&fea ture=related.

215 "We need help . . . here in Elkhart": "Sen. Barack Obama in Elkhart Indi- ana Part 4," YouTube, Aug. 6, 2008, www.youtube.com/watch?v=aVy3RYgy6 -8&feature=related.

216 "Now, more than ever": "Remarks of Senator Barack Obama, (Indianapo- lis, IN)," Obama for America (News & Speeches), Oct. 23, 2008, www .barackobama.com/2008/10/23/remarks_of_senator_barack_obam_146 .php.

217 "I see some sheet": "Barack Obama: Fairness in Our Economy," Obama for America, YouTube, Oct. 23, 2008, www.youtube.com/watch?v=Epibc ZmTks4.

217 "The Mac is back . . . counting on you": Quoted in Jim Shella, "McCain

Themes," *WISHTV.com*, Nov. 3, 2008, blogs.wishtv.com/2008/11/03/mccain-themes/.

217 "This is where the work": Quoted in Mark Halperin, "Pool Report of Obama at the Indiana UAW," *Time*, Nov. 4, 2008, thepage.time.com/pool-report-of-obama-at-the-indiana-uaw/.

218 "I think we can win": Quoted in Ari Berman, "Indiana Gets First Say," *Nation*, Nov. 4, 2008, www.thenation.com/blogs/state_of_change/380081/indiana_gets_first_say.

219 "weak, morally sick wretches": Quoted in "Media Downplay Bigotry of Jesse Helms," press release, Fairness and Accuracy in Reporting, Aug. 31, 2001, www.fair.org/index.php?page=1871.

219 "Dixie": Ibid.

219 "the last prominent": David S. Broder, "Jesse Helms, White Racist," *Washington Post*, Aug. 29, 2001.

219 "Where did Jesse Helms": Quoted in Chris Kromm, "What Would John Hope Franklin Say About the Legislature's Decision to Honor Jesse Helms?" *Carrboro Citizen*, July 2, 2009.

220 "When we started": "Barack Obama @ Vance/Aycock Dinner, Asheville, NC," YouTube, Oct. 4, 2008, www.youtube.com/watch?v=X3kawfKSqTo&feature=PlayList&p=9AAE6794B2A98204&playnext=1&playnext_from=PL&index=69.

220 "write off": Thomas F. Schaller, "The South Will Fall Again," *New York Times*, July 1, 2008.

221 "Thirty days out": Obama, Vance-Aycock Dinner.

221 "I have to say": Quoted in Steven Lee Myers and Jennifer Steinhauer, "Obama Calls Attacks on Him 'Out of Touch,'" *New York Times*, Oct. 6, 2008.

221 "Barack is Hawaiian": Quoted in Ryan Teague Beckwith, "Mike Easley, Stand-Up Comedian," *News Observer*, Oct. 5, 2008, projects.newsobserver.com/under_the_dome/mike_easley_stand_up_comedian.

221 "had nothing to do": Bob Moser, "Obamalina," *Nation*, Nov. 10, 2008.

221 "North Carolina just can't": "Obama 'Mills' Ad on McCain," YouTube, Oct. 8, 2008, www.youtube.com/watch?v=CwW_RYRo4iM.

224 "coalition of the ascendant": Ronald Brownstein, "Obama Buoyed by Coalition of the Ascendant," *National Journal*, Nov. 8, 2008.

226 "retirement home": "Governor Dean in Crawford, TX," YouTube, July 17, 2008, www.youtube.com/watch?v=Tg6-3eDlpt0.

226 "I'm not supposed to": "NN08 : Howard Dean July 17, 2008 Rally Netroots Nation (1/2)," YouTube, July 17, 2008, www.youtube.com/watch?v=baY5ZT _ck4g&feature=related.

226 "This is an opportunity": "NN08 : Howard Dean July 17, 2008 Rally Netroots Nation (2/2)," YouTube, July 17, 2008, www.youtube.com/watch?v= XgDNhEtyiG4&feature=related.

227 "I only get asked": "Howard Dean in Tucson," YouTube, Nov. 3, 2008, www.youtube.com/watch?v=wCtIOCSMiEY&feature=related.

6 ★ BLOWBACK

228 "You've got to be": Will Rogers, Wikiquote, en.wikiquote.org/wiki/Will_ Rogers.

228 "on all foes": Quoted in Ari Berman, "The Prophet," *Nation*, Jan. 5, 2009.

229 "I belong to no": Will Rogers Quotes, Politics/Government, CMGWorldwide, www.cmgworldwide.com/historic/rogers/quotes2.htm.

230 "personhood": Mark Barna, "AMENDMENT 48: 'Personhood' Issue Crushed," *Colorado Springs Gazette*, Nov. 4, 2008.

230 "baby blue": Quoted in Mary Beth Schneider, "True Blue? Shift to the Left Could Keep Indiana on Electoral Battleground," *Indianapolis Star*, Nov. 9, 2008.

231 "The idea that you're": Quoted in Berman, "Prophet."

231 "AWOL from Alaska": Ibid.

232 "We're gonna bring": Quoted in Jennifer Marisco, "Steele's 50 State Strategy," FrumForum, Feb. 2, 2009, www.frumforum.com/steeles-50 -state-strategy.

232 "Everybody laughed when Howard": John Feehery, "What's Next for the GOP?" *Politico*, Oct. 25, 2008, www.politico.com/news/stories/1008/14918 _Page2.html.

232 "Republicans have come down": Patrick Ruffini, "State and County Parties Need a Network Not a Website," The Next Right, Dec. 24, 2008, www

.thenextright.com/patrick-ruffini/state-and-county-parties-need-a-net work-not-a-website.

234 "We were facing": David Plouffe, *The Audacity to Win* (New York: Penguin, 2009), 372.

236 "Having steered": Quoted in Dave Rochelson, "Obama Announces Kaine as New DNC Chair," Change.gov, Jan. 8, 2009, change.gov/newsroom/ entry/obama_announces_kaine_as_new_dnc_chair/.

236 "I've got huge shoes": Ibid.

236 "I might have been": Quoted in Berman, "Prophet."

237 "A year in which": Adam Nagourney, "Dean Seeks Some Respect (and Credit) for Obama's Victory," *New York Times*, Nov. 12, 2008.

237 "the revitalization": James Carville, *40 More Years: How the Democrats Will Rule the Next Generation* (New York: Simon & Schuster, 2009), x.

237 "You know the expression": Quoted in Ari Berman, "The Dean Legacy," *Nation*, March 17, 2008.

238 "The fifty-state strategy": Quoted in Ari Berman, "Dean Steps Down, Kaine Steps Up," *Nation*, Jan. 21, 2009, www.thenation.com/blogs/state_ of_change/400282/dean_steps_down_kaine_steps_up.

238 "moderate in temperament": Quoted in Shaila Dewan and Anne E. Kornblut, "In Key House Races, Democrats Run to the Right," *New York Times*, Oct. 30, 2006.

238 "The Democratic Party helps": Quoted in Emily Belz, "Blue Dog Comeback?" *World Magazine*, Jan. 31, 2009.

239 "consistent with two": Quoted in Gordon Smith, "Heath Shuler Says Yes to Cleaner Energy Future," Scrutiny Hooligans, June 27, 2009, scrutinyhooli gans.us/2009/06/27/heath-shuler-says-yes-to-cleaner-energy-future/.

239 "No Democrat has done": Glenn Thrush, "Pelosi's List: Who's on Her Bad Side?" *Politico*, March 2, 2009, www.politico.com/news/stories/0309/19481 .html.

240 "Why don't you personally": My account of the Shuler meeting is based in part on Wally Hughes's blog post, "With Democrats Like This, Who Needs Republicans," BlueNC, Aug. 27, 2009, www.bluenc.com/democrats -who-needs-republicans.

243 "perfect rebound relationship": Gordon Smith, "Our Rebound Relationship

with Heath Shuler," Scrutiny Hooligans, March 2, 2009, scrutinyhooligans
.us/2009/03/02/our-rebound-relationship-with-heath-shuler/.

246 "It's not like I": *HouseQuake*, directed by Karen Elizabeth Price (2009),
www.housequakethefilm.com/Home.html.

246 "to be the candidate": Quoted in "Dems Battle over Confederate Flag,"
CNN.com, Nov. 2, 2003, www.cnn.com/2003/ALLPOLITICS/11/01/elec04
.prez.dean.confederate.flag/.

248 "the president's top choice": Peter Baker and Robert Pear, "Kansas Governor Seen as Top Choice in Health Post," *New York Times*, Feb. 18, 2009.

248 "Undersecretary for Go Fuck": Ryan Lizza, "The Gatekeeper," *New Yorker*,
March 2, 2009.

248 "the most practical": Quoted in Philip Rucker, "Dean Challenges Obama
to Deliver Reform," *Washington Post*, Aug. 20, 2009.

249 "a debate raged": Jonathan Cohn, "Stayin' Alive," *New Republic*, April 1,
2009.

249 "K Street's favorite Democrat": Ari Berman, "K Street's Favorite Democrat," *Nation*, March 19, 2007.

250 "We are here": Quoted in Jeffrey Young, "Unions Demand Public Plan in
Healthcare Bill," *Hill*, June 26, 2009.

250 "The Baucus bill": Quoted in Nikki Schwab, "Howard Dean Blasts Baucus
Healthcare Bill," Washington Whispers blog, *USNews*, Sept. 16, 2009,
www.usnews.com/blogs/washington-whispers/2009/09/16/howard-dean
-blasts-baucus-healthcare-bill.html.

250 "This is a bill": *Countdown*, MSNBC, Sept. 28, 2009, www.msnbc.msn
.com/id/33072145/ns/msnbc_tv-countdown_with_keith_olbermann/.

250 "revolt": Quoted in Sam Stein, "Dean: Dems 'in Deep Trouble' on Health
Care, the Only Options Are a Bad Bill or 2010 Losses," *Huffington Post*,
Nov. 23, 2009, www.huffingtonpost.com/2009/11/23/dean-dems-in-deep
-trouble_n_367666.html.

250 "New Campaign Highlights": Brian Beutler, Talking Points Memo,
Sept. 18, 2009, tpmdc.talkingpointsmemo.com/2009/09/new-campaign-
highlights-growing-rift-between-grassroots-liberals-and-the-democratic-
party.php.

250 "If we don't have": Quoted in Sarah Scott, "Without Public Option, Health Care Bill Is 'Worthless,' Dean Says," *Yale Daily News*, Nov. 30, 2009, www .yaledailynews.com/crosscampus/2009/11/30/without-public-option -health-care-bill-worthless-d/.

251 "This is essentially": Bob Kinzel, "Dean on Health Care: 'Kill the Senate Bill,'" Vermont Public Radio, Dec. 15, 2009, vpr.net/news_detail/86681/.

252 "I don't know what": "Briefing by White House Press Secretary Robert Gibbs," White House Press Briefing, Dec. 16, 2009, www.whitehouse.gov/ the-press-office/briefing-white-house-press-secretary-robert-gibbs -121609.

252 "They don't seem to be": Quoted in Jane Hamsher, "White House 'Irritated' with Howard Dean, Not Joe Lieberman," Firedoglake, Dec. 16, 2009, fdlaction.firedoglake.com/2009/12/16/white-house-irritated-with-howard -dean-not-joe-lieberman/.

252 "Has Howard Dean lost": Ruth Marcus, "Has Howard Dean Lost His Mind?" *Washington Post*, Dec. 16, 2009, voices.washingtonpost.com/ postpartisan/2009/12/has_howard_dean_lost_his_mind.html.

252 "I'll call you": "Clarification: Howard Dean Will Still Support Obama 'Vigorously' (VIDEO)," *Huffington Post*, Dec. 17, 2009, www.huffington post.com/2009/12/17/howard-dean-i-wont-suppor_n_395599.html.

252 "insane": Quoted in Garance Franke-Ruta, "Axelrod: 'Insane' for Democrats to Oppose Health-Reform Bill," *Washington Post*, Dec. 17, 2009, voices.washingtonpost.com/44/2009/12/axelrod-insane-for-democrats-t .html.

252 "he just wasn't familiar": *Meet the Press*, NBC, Dec. 20, 2009, www.msnbc .msn.com/id/34490422/ns/meet_the_press/.

252 "Here's the major problem": Ibid.

253 poll by the Progressive Change Campaign Committee: act.boldprogres sives.org/cms/sign/natpollresults121809/.

253 "skinny bill": Quoted in Sheryl Gay Stolberg, Jeff Zeleny, and Carl Hulse, "Health Vote Caps a Journey Back from the Brink," *New York Times*, March 20, 2010.

254 "We deserve a vote!": Quoted in Nicole Norfleet, "Thousands Rally to

Support Health-Care Reform in Downtown Washington," *Washington Post*, March 10, 2010.

254 "Tonight, at a time": Quoted in Jesse Lee, "This Is What Change Looks Like," The White House Blog, March 22, 2010, www.whitehouse.gov/blog /2010/03/22/what-change-looks.

254 "a huge win for": MSNBC interview with David Shuster, March 22, 2010.

255 "My sense is": Quoted in Plouffe, *Audacity to Win*, 294.

255 "What we are going": Quoted in Jeff Zeleny, "Obama Describes Team as Experienced yet Fresh," *New York Times*, Nov. 26, 2008.

EPILOGUE: THE NEXT FRONTIER

257 "The first rule": *The Democratic Promise: Saul Alinsky and His Legacy*, directed and produced by Bob Hercules and Bruce Orenstein (Chicago Video Project, 2000).

257 "If one voice can": Quoted in Raleigh-Elizabeth Smith, "Obama's Fired Up and Ready to Go," Veracifier, Sept. 27, 2007, www.veracifier.com/post /2913/obamas-fired-up-and-ready-to-go.

258 One national poll: "The 2010 Comprehensive Daily Kos/Research 2000 Poll of Self-Identified Republicans," *Daily Kos*, Feb. 2, 2010, www.dailykos .com/storyonly/2010/2/2/832988/-The-2010-Comprehensive-Daily-Kos -Research-2000-Poll-of-Self-Identified-Republicans.

260 "sliver": Quoted in Philip Elliott, "White House Appears Ready to Drop 'Public Option,'" Associated Press, Aug. 16, 2009.

260 "small part": Quoted in Greg Sargent, "Talking Points for Obama's Political Operation Describe Public Option as 'Small Part' of Reform," The Plum Line blog, Whorunsgov.com, Oct. 1, 2009, theplumline.whorunsgov .com/health-care/talking-points-for-obamas-political-operation-describe -public-option-as-small-part-of-reform/.

260 "take back America": Quoted in Kenneth P. Vogel, "Conservatives Grab for Tea Party Cash," *Politico*, Dec. 15, 2009, www.politico.com/news /stories/1209/30595.html.

262 Belcher found that 20 percent: Cornell Belcher, "A Stronger National Party: The Arc of the Democratic Party from 2004–2008," memo to Chairman Howard Dean/Democratic National Committee, Jan. 6, 2009, futuremajority.com/node/4323.

263 "first Independent president": John Heilemann, "The New Politics: Barack Obama, Party of One," *New York*, Jan. 11, 2009.

264 "bittersweet moment": Quoted in Chris Bowers, "Death of the Fifty-State Strategy, Follow-Up," Open Left, Nov. 10, 2008, www.openleft.com/show Diary.do?diaryId=9863.

265 Galvin argued in his book: Daniel J. Galvin, *Presidential Party Building* (Princeton, N.J.: Princeton University Press, 2010).

266 "50-state strategy on steroids": Marc Ambinder, "The Organizing DNC: The Future of Obama's Campaign," *Atlantic*, Jan. 5, 2009, marcambinder .theatlantic.com/archives/2009/01/the_organizing_dnc.php.

266 "coalition of the ascendant": Ronald Brownstein, "Obama Buoyed by Co- alition of the Ascendant," *National Journal*, Nov. 8, 2008.

267 "We Have the Hope": Peter Dreier and Marshall Ganz, *Washington Post*, Aug. 30, 2009.

267 "I will ask for": "Barack Obama: Call to Service in Colorado Springs, CO," YouTube, July 2, 2008, www.youtube.com/watch?v=Df2p6867_pw.

269 "Obama's health bill is": Robert Reich, "The Final Health Care Vote and What It Really Means," March 21, 2010, robertreich.org/post/463440906/ the-final-health-care-vote-and-what-it-really-means.

269 "We can change politics": "Gov. Kaine at 2009 NC JJ Dinner," YouTube, May 2, 2009, www.youtube.com/watch?v=Pg7NOYkyFPU.

270 "fucking retarded": Quoted in Peter Wallsten, "Chief of Staff Draws Fire from Left as Obama Falters," *Wall Street Journal*, Jan. 26, 2010.

272 "The untold numbers who": Quoted in Jesse Lee, "This Is What Change Looks Like," The White House Blog, March 22, 2010, www.whitehouse .gov/blog/2010/03/22/what-change-looks.

273 "The politics are probably": Molly Ivins, "Texas: Texas on Everything," in *These* Texas: *United States*, ed. John Leonard (New York: Thunder's Mouth Press/Nation Books, 2003), 423.

273 "intrepid delegation": "DNC Chairman Tim Kaine Speaks at the Party's Fall Meeting in Austin, Texas," YouTube, Sept. 11, 2009, www.youtube .com/watch?v=j4SoaKoxovA.

275 "Quitmire": Quoted in Natalie Gott, "Texas Senator Who Broke Boycott Is Treated like a Turncoat," Associated Press, Sept. 20, 2003.

275 "I want to thank": Quoted in Ralph Blumenthal, "Return of Texas Democrats Sparks Celebration," *New York Times*, Sept. 16, 2003.

276 "Even when there were": R. Kirk McPike, "How We Won: Dallas County Turns Blue," Burnt Orange Report, Nov. 15, 2006, www.burntorangere port.com/diary/2434/.

278 "As goes Harris County": Quoted in Rick Jervis, "Hurricanes May Help Steer Texas Politics," *USA Today*, Oct. 27, 2008.

278 "Hispanic Obama": Eric Celeste, "Is Rafael Anchia the Hispanic Obama?" *D Magazine*, May 2009.

278 "El Gobernador": Paul Burka, "El Gobernador," *Texas Monthly*, Feb. 2008.

281 "We've got a great union": Quoted in Kelley Shannon, "Perry Fires Up Anti-tax Crowd," Associated Press, April 15, 2009.

281 "Governor Goodhair": Ivins, "Texas: Texas on Everything," 427.

281 "Christian nation": Quoted in Russell Shorto, "How Christian Were the Founders?" *New York Times Magazine*, February 11, 2010.

286 "Geeky Mexican": twitter.com/onboleman.

286 "Mom, Dad": baylordemocrats.org/2009/09/10/recap-of-09-09-09/mock upbudems/.

AFTERWORD

287 "the spurned progressive Obama": Remarks by Michelle Malkin, Right-Online, Minneapolis, June 18, 2011.

288 "There has been a lot": Remarks by Howard Dean, Netroots Nation, Minneapolis, June 16, 2011.

288 "complete destruction": Remarks by Russ Feingold, Netroots Nation, Minneapolis, June 16, 2011.

288 "I fear the Democratic Party": Ibid.

289 "The president isn't our": Remarks by Joan McCarter, Netroots Nation, Minneapolis, June 17, 2011.

289 "the largest gap": Jeffrey M. Jones, "Record Midterm Enthusiasm as Voters Head to Polls," *Gallup*, Nov. 2, 2010, www.gallup.com/poll/144152/record -midterm-enthusiasm-voters-head-polls.aspx.

289 "The election results themselves": John B. Judis, "A Lost Generation," *New Republic*, Nov. 3, 2010, www.tnr.com/article/politics/78890/a-lost-genera tion.

289 "and the exits tell us": Michael Tomasky, "Turnout: Explains A Lot," *Guardian*, Nov. 3, 2010, www.guardian.co.uk/commentisfree/michaelto masky/2010/nov/03/us-midterm-elections-2010-turnout-says-a-lot.

290 "angrily reined in": Jackie Calmes, "Less Drama in White House After Staff Changes," *New York Times*, March 3, 2011.

291 "It's gotta be new": Remarks by Jeremy Bird, Netroots Nation, Minneapolis, June 17, 2011.

292 "build the biggest grassroots": "Obama 2012 Strategy Briefing," YouTube, www.youtube.com/watch?v=PH0fiMGvW2k&feature=player_embedded.

292 "grassrootsy": Micah L. Sifry, "Grassroots vs. Grassrootsy: How to Parse Technology's Role in Politics," *techPresident*, July 18, 2011, techpresident .com/blog-entry/grassroots-vs-grassrootsy-how-parse-technologys-role-politics.

292 "We Do Big Things": Quoted in Mike Allen, "Barack Obama 2012 Starts at Grassroots," *Politico*, Feb. 1, 2011, www.politico.com/news/stories/0211 /48584.html.

293 "Income Defense Industry": Jeffrey A. Winters, *Oligarchy* (New York: Cambridge University Press, 2011), 217.

293 "If you're losing": Remarks by Darcy Burner, Netroots Nation, Minneapolis, June 16, 2011.

294 "meta-brand": Remarks by Van Jones, Netroots Nation, Minneapolis, June 18, 2011.

294 "There is no president": Ibid.

295 "President Obama and Speaker Pelosi": Dick Armey, "Dick Armey on the

Tea Party Movement: The New Majority?" *Washington Post*, Feb. 8, 2010, www.washingtonpost.com/wp-dyn/content/discussion/2010/02/05/DI2010 020503095.html.

295 "the first time the party": *Political Capital*, Bloomberg TV, Nov. 5, 2010, findarticles.com/p/news-articles/analyst-wire/mi_8077/is_20101105/rnc-chairman-michael-steele-talks/ai_n56240662/.

295 "Netroots protests dragged": Mindy Finn and Patrick Ruffini, "How Republicans Won the Internet," *Washington Post*, Jan. 24, 2010.

298 "A majority of legislators": Chris Bowers, "Think Big: Choosing the Fights That Build Progressive Power," *Daily Kos*, June 19, 2011, www.dailykos .com/story/2011/06/19/984056/-Think-Big:-Choosing-the-fights-that -build-progressive-power?via=blog_508369.

299 "pull a Clinton": John F. Harris, "Can Barack Obama Pull a Bill Clinton?" *Politico*, Nov. 4, 2010, www.politico.com/news/stories/1110/44686.html.

299 "Is 'triangulation' just another": Matt Bai, "Is 'Triangulation' Just Another Word for the Politics of the Possible?" *New York Times*, Dec. 16, 2010.

299 "Can Obama do a Clinton?": Lexington, "Can Obama Do a Clinton?" *Economist*, Nov. 8, 2010.

300 "changed the trajectory": Quoted in Ari Berman, "Obama: Triangulation 2.0?" *Nation*, Feb. 7, 2010.

301 "Our basic attitude": *The Daily Show with Jon Stewart*, Comedy Central, Oct. 27, 2010, www.thedailyshow.com/watch/wed-october-27-2010/barack -obama-pt-1.

301 "I wasn't sent here": Quoted in Jonathan Alter, *The Promise* (New York: Simon & Schuster, 2010), 399.

301 "what in the past": Quoted in Berman, "Obama."

302 "Just where Mr. Obama": Matt Bai, "Debt-Busting Issue May Force Obama Off Fence," *New York Times*, Nov. 30, 2010.

302 "I don't think in": Quoted in David Sirota, "Mr. Obama Goes to Washington," *Nation*, June 26, 2006.

302 "In the absence of": Quoted in Berman, "Obama."

303 "One consists of European-style": Michael Gerson, "The Two Faces of the Democratic Party," *Washington Post*, May 19, 2011.

304 "He is not of": Quoted in Ari Berman, "Jim Messina, Obama's Enforcer," *Nation*, April 18, 2011.

304 "remote-control TV politics": Gene Randall, "Fix Unclear for Low Voter Turnout," CNN.com, Nov. 13, 1996, www-cgi.cnn.com/ALLPOLITICS /1996/news/9611/13/randall/.

304 "street fight for the presidency": Quoted in Doyle McManus, "Team Obama's Victory Plan," *Los Angeles Times*, July 7, 2011.

305 "shrink government": Quoted in "Grover Norquist," Sourcewatch.com, April 3, 2011, www.sourcewatch.org/index.php?title=Grover_Norquist.

307 "the deal of the": David Brooks, "The Mother of All No-Brainers," *New York Times*, July 4, 2011.

307 "underdog": Quoted in Russell Goldman, "President Obama Calls Himself 'Underdog' in 2012 Race for White House," ABC News, October 3, 2011.

308 "Equal Rights Amendment battle": Rob Christensen, "Lawmakers Move N.C. to the Right," *Charlotte Observer*, June 19, 2011.

308 "a battle for the heart": Ibid.

308 "We've seen drastic cuts": Quoted in Michael Powell and Monica Davey, "The Indiana Exception? Yes, but . . ." *New York Times*, June 23, 2011.

310 "Despite red wave": Karen E. Crummy and Elizabeth Miller, "Despite Red Wave, Colorado Stayed a Quirky Shade of Purple," *Denver Post*, Nov. 4, 2010.

ACKNOWLEDGMENTS

Writing a book is never easy, especially your first one! I'd like to thank the two hundred–plus people who agreed to be interviewed for this project and shared their time and insights. I enjoyed every single one. I'd particularly like to thank Howard Dean, who always made time in his busy schedule to answer the many questions I had. Our interview sessions were a highlight of this project for me. Many thanks as well to Kristina Powell, Emily Lamia, Tom McMahon, and Karen Finney for their ready help.

I'm forever grateful to Jonathan Galassi at Farrar, Straus and Giroux for taking a chance on my proposal; Eric Chinski for masterfully steering the manuscript from beginning to end; Eugenie Cha for her help on so many fronts; and Steve Weil and the rest of the FSG team for getting the word out. I hope this is the first of many terrific collaborations. Many thanks as well to David Rogers and the team at Picador for their work on this excellent paperback edition.

I couldn't have done this book without the support and encouragement of my agent, Nick Ellison, along with Chelsea Lindman, Meredith Haggery, and Sarah Dickman at the Nicholas Ellison Agency. Nick and I first discussed doing a book together in 2004 (I turned his idea down), so it feels great to have finally made it happen. And because of Nick I spent a wonderful October on the beautiful grounds of Ledig House in upstate New York. I'd like to thank D. W. Gibson and the staff at Art Omi for arranging such a fantastic residency.

I visited many fascinating places over the course of my reporting and would like to thank the generous hosts who put me up along the way: Zephyr Teachout and Hugh and Andrea Marcos in North Carolina; Dennis Lee and Julie Fox in Indiana; Michael and Jane Cuddehe and David Sirota in Colorado; Tommy McCutchon and Scott and Ginger Young in Texas; Fatin Abbas in Boston; and Dan Schwerin in Washington.

I've been so fortunate over the past seven years to enjoy the support and friendship of so many colleagues at *The Nation* and the Nation Institute. I'm particularly grateful to Katrina vanden Heuvel for giving me so many opportunities and being such a cherished mentor; Taya Kitman for always getting my back and providing a great place to work; Carl Bromley for planting the seed for this book in my head; and Eyal Press for offering invaluable advice and comradeship from the very beginning of this project. I can't wait to read his new book.

This book benefited greatly from the input and comments of Eyal, Sam Graham-Felsen, Joe Conason, and Chris Hayes, as well as the ace transcription skills of Lucas Mann, the thorough fact-checking and notes of Alana Levinson, and the additional research help of Dan Chandler, Jess Cambell, and Marissa Colon-Margolies.

I've been blessed with such a wonderful group of family and friends. I'm especially indebted to my parents, Warren and Harriet, and my sister, Ali, for their unconditional love and boundless encouragement through every facet of my life. And to Meredith, the best friend, editor, and partner anyone could have.

Finally, this book is dedicated to John Alexander, a great friend and brilliant journalist whose life was far too brief. John's insatiable curiosity and restless dynamism will always inspire me to aim higher, shoot for more, and leave a powerful imprint.

INDEX

Myers, Peachy, 155
Myers, Richard, 26

Nagourney, Adam, 237
Nashville, 48, 220
Nation, The, 60, 134, 165, 221, 249, 251, 302
National Association for the Repeal of Abortion Laws (NARAL), 35
National Journal, 32, 224
National Journal's Hotline, 118
National Rifle Association (NRA), 35, 92, 112
NBC, 252
Nebraska, 36, 119, 246
Neel, Todd, 241
Netroots Nation, 287, 288–89, 293, 294, 299
Nevada, 133, 145, 177, 228, 295; 2008 primary, 155
New Deal, 137
New Democratic Coalition, 34
New Democrat Network, 71
New Hampshire, 12, 20, 36, 38–44, 133; 2004 primary, 36, 38–44, 51, 52, 60–61; 2008 primary, 154–55
New Jersey, 75, 160, 266
New Mexico, 37, 77, 96, 198, 275, 278
New Republic, The, 29, 46, 69, 74, 77, 120, 166, 249, 289
New Right, 219, 270
Newsweek, 12, 34, 46
New York City, 11, 19, 25, 79, 136, 178, 201
New York magazine, 263
New York Post, 172
New York State, 158, 160, 293, 305, 306
New York Times, The, 26, 52, 71, 75, 78, 106, 117, 152, 160, 165, 220, 237, 248, 290, 299, 302
New York Times Magazine, 231
9/11 attacks, 6; aftermath of, 6, 23
Nixon, Richard, 31, 166, 176, 261; 1968 presidential campaign, 31, 67, 97; "Southern strategy" of, 67

No Child Left Behind, 16
NORAD, 202
Norquist, Grover, 305
North American Free Trade Agreement (NAFTA), 104
North Carolina, 6, 7, 8, 68, 81–87, 96, 163, 164, 176, 177, 305–308; aftermath of 2008 election and, 239–45; canvasses, 88–95, 222–24; Helms-era, 90, 167, 218–19; McCain in, 224–25; Obama in, 166–71, 218–26, 230–31, 243; 2004 Democratic Party chair race, 81–87; 2006 congressional elections, 111–16; "Watauga Model," 99–95, 112, 220, 224
Northcross, Chris, 133
North Dakota, 2, 227, 246

Obama, Barack, 1, 5–9, 49, 123–24, 287, 288; announces presidential candidacy, 124; *The Audacity of Hope,* 126, 190; Bittergate, 165, 167; blogs and, 135, 150–51; cabinet of, 232–38, 255–56; call-and-response style, 158, 212; in Colorado, 178–89, 197–212, 229; as community organizer, 129–30, 139, 147–48; Congress and, 256, 265; cult of personality, 6, 165; Dean and, 2–3, 8–9, 49, 56, 63–64, 125–26, 130–32, 163–64, 175, 232–38; disillusionment with, 289–91, 300, 303, 307, 309–10, 312; DNC and, 175–76, 261–72, 291, 294; *Dreams from My Father,* 129; early days of presidential campaign, 132–53; end of primaries, 173; fifty-state strategy, 164, 175–227, 236, 238; first year as president, 257–72, 300–303; fund-raising, 133–34, 164, 206, 242, 291–92; in general election of 2008, 175–227; grassroots base of, 129–72, 175–227, 237, 267–72, 290, 292, 303, 304;